Corporate Criminal Liability in Environmental Jurisprudence

Environmental jurisprudence is a dynamic field that integrates insights from various disciplines, including basic sciences, earth science, economics, and law. At its core, this discipline emphasizes the importance of enforcing rights, as environmental pollution poses significant threats to individuals and society as a whole. The repercussions of pollution are not confined to the immediate vicinity; they can reverberate across vast regions and impact countless future generations. Addressing pollution as a wrong or crime demands a nuanced understanding of the law, making the study of environmental jurisprudence essential.

This book explores corporate polluter liability within the framework of environmental jurisprudence. While protective measures for the environment have been embedded in various statutes since the early 20th century, the notion of environmental jurisprudence has only recently come to the forefront of legal discourse. This field is crucial for safeguarding the natural and legal rights of individuals, communities, and the state. With a comprehensive approach that encompasses both national and international dimensions, this book critically engages with the foundational concepts of environmental jurisprudence, exposing the rampant environmental violations perpetrated by corporations and outlining how these entities can be held accountable within regulatory frameworks. Furthermore, it provides a thorough analysis of essential international instruments aimed at combatting corporate-induced environmental degradation, offering recommendations to elevate corporate criminal liability within the realm of environmental jurisprudence scholarship.

Highlighting the urgent need for accountability but also inspiring action toward a sustainable future, this book will interest legal scholars researching on criminal liability and environmental law.

Indrajit Dube is Professor of Corporate Law at the Indian Institute of Technology (Kharagpur) and Vice-Chancellor of the National Law University, Meghalaya.

Mia Mahmudur Rahim is Associate Professor of Law at the University of New England and Professor in Residence at the National Law University, Meghalaya.

Routledge Research in International Environmental Law

Environmental Liability and the Interplay between EU Law and International Law
Dr Emanuela Orlando

Implementing International Environmental Law and Policy
An Interactive Approach to Environmental Regulation
Joanna Miller Smallwood

Environmental Law and Governance in India
Sairam Bhat and Centre for Environmental Law, Education, Research, and Advocacy (CEERA)

Environmental Law and Policy in India
Sairam Bhat and Centre for Environmental Law, Education, Research, and Advocacy (CEERA)

Protection of the Environment under International Law during Occupation
International Humanitarian, Human Rights and Environmental Law
Waad Abualrob

State Accountability for Environmental Damage in International Armed Conflict
Aïda Tamer Chammas

Corporate Environmental Responsibility and Pollution Control Laws
The Case of Oil Spills in the Niger Delta
Millicent Ele

Corporate Criminal Liability in Environmental Jurisprudence
Indrajit Dube and Mia Mahmudur Rahim

www.routledge.com/Routledge-Research-in-International-Environmental-Law/book-series/INTENVLAW

Corporate Criminal Liability in Environmental Jurisprudence

Indrajit Dube and Mia Mahmudur Rahim

Routledge
Taylor & Francis Group
LONDON AND NEW YORK

First published 2026
by Routledge
4 Park Square, Milton Park, Abingdon, Oxon OX14 4RN

and by Routledge
605 Third Avenue, New York, NY 10158

Routledge is an imprint of the Taylor & Francis Group, an informa business

British Library Cataloguing-in-Publication Data
A catalogue record for this book is available from the British Library

ISBN: 978-1-032-24498-3 (hbk)
ISBN: 978-1-032-24499-0 (pbk)
ISBN: 978-1-003-27900-6 (ebk)

DOI: 10.4324/9781003279006

Typeset in Galliard
by Apex CoVantage, LLC

To the majestic mountains, mighty sun, and
tranquil seas, the unsung heroes of many tales.

Contents

1 Introduction

> 'Every part of the earth is sacred. . . . Every shining pine needle, every sandy shore, every mist in the dark woods, every clearing and humming insect is holy in the memory and experience of my people. The Sap which courses through the trees carries the memories of the red man. . . . We are part of the earth and it is part of us. The perfumed flowers are our sisters; the horse, the great eagle, these are our brothers. The rocky crests, the juices in the meadows, the body heat of the pony, and man – all belong to the same family.'[1]

This passage is from a letter written by the wise Indian Chief in Seattle to the Great White Chief in Washington. It reflects a commendable awareness of the environment and the deep gratitude of the people toward nature's contribution to human development. The wise ancient sages recognized that human existence depended on nature's blessings.[2] Therefore, they revered trees, rivers, seas, and the air with a spiritual significance and took offenses like tree-cutting and water contamination seriously. Ancient texts such as *Manu Smriti*, *Katyayana*, and *Brihaspati Samhita* prescribed severe punishments for harming the environment.[3]

As civilization grew, humans became increasingly materialistic.[4] The relentless pursuit of material wealth led to the development of scientific inventions and new technologies, allowing modern humans to realize their dreams

1 *Sachidanand Panda* v. *State of W.B.* (1987) 2 SCC 295. (Per Chinappa Reddy J.).
2 Oelschlaeger, M. (1991). *The idea of wilderness: From prehistory to the age of ecology*. Yale University Press; Hughes, J. D. (2014). *Environmental problems of the Greeks and Romans: Ecology in the ancient Mediterranean*. Johns Hopkins University Press.
3 Redman, C. L. (1999). *Human impact on ancient environments*. University of Arizona Press; Coates, P. (2013). *Nature: Western attitudes since ancient times*. John Wiley & Sons; Butzer, K. W. (2012). Collapse, environment, and society. *Proceedings of the National Academy of Sciences*, *109*(10), 3628–3635.
4 LeCain, T. J. (2015). Against the Anthropocene: A neo-materialist perspective. *International Journal for History, Culture and Modernity*, *3*(1), 1–20; Hayes, C. J. H. (1941). *A generation of materialism, 1871–1900* (Vol. 17). Harper; Eagleton, T. (2017). *Materialism*. Yale University Press.

DOI: 10.4324/9781003279006-1

through the exploitation of nature. Unfortunately, this came at the cost of disregarding the wisdom of ancient sages, who warned that harming the environment could ultimately endanger humanity itself. While industrialization is foundational to progress, rapid and uncontrolled industrialization poses significant environmental threats.[5] Meeting the escalating demands of civilized society disrupts and devastates the natural world.

The post-industrial Revolution in Europe ushered in a period of immense industrial expansion that spread throughout the continent. This led to extensive consumption of natural resources on a global scale and the accumulation of pollutants from industrial activities in the surrounding areas, often surpassing the environment's sustainable capacity. World War II and industrial disasters further exacerbated pollution and environmental degradation worldwide.[6]

Efforts to understand the reasons behind environmental degradation have revealed that industrial exploitation of natural resources is a major contributor to environmental pollution. Some large corporations, such as Bayer, General Electric, Westinghouse, Ford, Saudi Aramco, Chevron, Coca-Cola, Cargill, and Adama, have been found liable for the production and emission of various carcinogenic pollutants through manufacturing and processing industrial commodities like plastic, chemicals, and numerous natural resource extraction processes.[7] They are notorious not only for polluting the environment but also for using organized syndicates to manage their environmental crimes illegally.[8] Green criminologists would categorize these as crimes against humanity committed by powerful institutions, including governments and transnational corporations (TNCs).[9]

Finding ways to help businesses continue their production without causing harm to natural resources is, therefore, a key topic in environmental

5 Ahmad, F., Ahmed, W., Khan, A., & Gupta, P. (2022). Environmental sustainability: Challenges and approaches. In *Natural resources conservation and advances for sustainability*; Porto, M. F. de S., & de Freitas, C. M. (1996). Major chemical accidents in industrializing countries: The socio-political amplification of risk. *Risk Analysis, 16*(1), 1–8; Pirages, D. C., & DeGeest, T. M. (2003). *Ecological security: An evolutionary perspective on globalization*. Rowman & Littlefield Publishers.

6 Adeola, F. O. (2012). *Industrial disasters, toxic waste, and community impact: Health effects and environmental justice struggles around the globe*. Lexington Books; Maximillian, J., Brusseau, M. L., Glenn, E. P., & Matthias, A. D. (2019). Pollution and environmental perturbations in the global system. In *Environmental and pollution science*. Elsevier.

7 Thorsberg, C. (2024, April 9). 80 percent of global CO_2 emissions come from just 57 companies, report shows. *Smithsonian*. www.smithsonianmag.com/smart-news/since-2016-80-percent-of-global-co2-emissions-come-from-just-57-companies-report-shows-180984118/; Maciejewska, A. (2008). Occupational exposure assessment to crystalline silica dust: Approach in Poland and worldwide. *International Journal of Occupational Medicine and Environmental Health, 21*(1); Huff, J., Jacobson, M. F., & Davis, D. L. (2008). The limits of two-year bioassay exposure regimens for identifying chemical carcinogens. *Environmental Health Perspectives, 116*(11).

8 Simon, D. R. (2017). Corporate environmental crimes and social inequality: New directions for environmental justice research. In *Green criminology*. Routledge.

9 Beirne, P., & South, N. (2013). *Issues in green criminology*. Routledge.

jurisprudence. This highlights the need for more effective environmental laws and a further discussion of corporate criminal liabilities for damaging natural resources. Environmental jurisprudence, although it has not been able to provide any absolute conclusion, has adequately raised numerous legal issues around corporate personhood and criminalizing environmental harm. This book examines these issues, presents different perspectives on corporate liabilities in managing the natural environment, and highlights approaches in environmental law for managing this liability.

1.1 Global Natural Environment

Defining 'environment' is a challenging task for legal researchers. The study of the environment encompasses various disciplines such as environmentology, natural science, ecology, pure sciences, oceanology, atmospheric sciences, life, living, and the cultural background of specific communities. The most suitable definition of the environment may stem from each of these disciplines to achieve their respective objectives. Therefore, the common understanding of the environment as surroundings, natural resources, atmosphere, and water bodies may not sufficiently support legal matters. In law, the concept of environment emphasizes rights, which revolve around the harmonious relationships between life, living beings, and the environment. Within legal terminology, these rights may stem from customary practices, long usage, easements, contracts, trade assignments, common law, statutory law, and, importantly, constitutional law. As a result, defining the environment in statutes has far-reaching consequences, as these rights can pertain to individuals, members of groups, society, or the entire country.

In their book, Stuart Bell and Donald McGillivray defined the environment as the 'surroundings,' which, in a relative sense, could encompass almost anything.[10] As such, it generally refers to the physical surroundings that are common to all of us, including air, space, water, land, plants, and wildlife. The authors emphasize the interdependence and interaction between the physical and biological elements of the environment and consider them to be the subject matter of environmental jurisprudence. They also stress that the meaning of the environment has not been developed based on a single and self-contained discipline; rather, it has developed by relying on other disciplines. Thus, this meaning may contain some incoherence, and the legal mechanisms available may not always be the best suited for addressing the issues of environmental protection, as the disciplines were not originally developed with environmental protection in mind.[11]

10 Bell, S., & McGillivray, D. (2000). *Environmental law*. Oxford University Press.
11 Ibid., p. 18.

The Stockholm Declaration[12] does not attempt to define the environment. It states that human beings are creators and shapers of the environment, which provides them with physical sustenance and opportunities for intellectual, moral, social, and spiritual growth.[13] It acknowledges that the environment has a significant impact on human life, and any unsustainable modification or harm could jeopardize the very existence of humankind. It highlights that environmental protection must be a central component of the development process and cannot be viewed in isolation to achieve sustainable development. This has established the foundation for the Rio Declaration, which underscores the sustainable interaction between biotic and abiotic components, as well as the equilibrium between environmental conservation and development.[14]

The definitions of environment in different legislations of various countries, although complementary, vary significantly in the process of implementing environmental rights. The *National Environmental Policy Act (NEPA)* of the United States defines the environment broadly, including the natural and physical environment and the relationship of people with that environment. The EU's environmental legislation often defines the environment as including air, water, soil, and biodiversity, emphasizing the interconnectedness of these elements. The *Environment Protection and Biodiversity Conservation Act 1999* of Australia defines the environment as including ecosystems and their constituent parts, including people and communities. The Brazilian Constitution recognizes the environment as a common good essential to a healthy quality of life, encompassing all natural resources and the ecological balance. The *National Environmental Management Act* of South Africa defines the environment as including the physical, biological, and social aspects of the surroundings, emphasizing sustainable development. The Environment (Protection) Act, 1986, belongs to a group of laws in India that defines 'environment' as comprising water, air, and land, including their inter-relationships with human beings, other living creatures, plants, microorganisms, and property. The comprehensive definition of 'environment' tailored by the Indian Parliament encompasses far more than just the constituent parts of the environment. It takes into account holistic interaction and balance of the physical and biological factors of nature and the role of microorganisms, which helps

12 The Stockholm Declaration emerged from the 1972 United Nations Conference on the Human Environment in Sweden. It consists of 26 principles that guide environmental policies, emphasizing sustainable development and the balance between economic growth and environmental protection. The conference also led to the establishment of the United Nations Environment Programme (UNEP) and influenced subsequent international environmental agreements and conferences, such as the Rio Declaration in 1992 and the Paris Agreement in 2015. For details, visit the www.un.org/en/conferences/environment/stockholm1972 (accessed August 13, 2024).

13 Declaration of the United National Conference on Human Environment, June 5–16, 1972, Stockholm.

14 The United Nations Conference on Environment and Development, June 3–14, 1992, Rio De Janeiro.

to maintain balance within internal and external ecology and all forms of life, which includes mankind as well as property. In practicing environmental law, Indian legislation seems to take into account all the components of the environment in such a manner that any issue arising from any of the disciplines that impact environmental rights is feasible to be legally regulated.[15] India has an advanced framework for the protection of natural resources, and the Indian judiciary has shown great interest in protected environmental resources, including nature, natural resources, ecology, and physical aspects of nature. In so doing, the purpose of the judiciary has not been to try and define what this so-called environment is, rather, and more importantly, to protect the environment by finding legal ways to protect it adequately judicially. The legal system has shown concern for balanced development and controlled development relating to the people, the environment, and the ecology of the nation.[16]

Environmental rights in the United States are primarily based on federal and state laws rather than a specific constitutional right. Individuals can file lawsuits under laws such as the *Clean Air Act (CAA) 1963* and *Clean Water Act 1972*, although access to justice may be limited by legal costs and procedural barriers. In India, the right to a healthy environment is recognized as part of the right to life under Article 21 of the Constitution. The *Environment Protection Act of 1986* of India provides a framework for environmental governance. However, aggrieved groups often rely on public interest litigation to enhance access to justice for environmental issues in this country. Brazilian laws encourage public participation in environmental decision-making, including the environmental impact assessment (EIA) process. Similarly, South Africa has established mechanisms for public involvement in environmental governance, including the right to access environmental information. In the EU, environmental rights are promoted through various directives and regulations that emphasize public participation and access to justice in environmental matters. The Aarhus Convention,[17] which the EU and its member

15 Ahmad, F. (2001). Origin and growth of environmental law in India. *Journal of the Indian Law Institute*, *43*(3); Harris, C., Schaeffer, S., Shenkman, E., & Kronk Warner, E. (2017). Environmental protection in Indian country: The fundamentals. *Environmental Law Reporter News & Analysis*, *47*.

16 Ramesh, J. (2015). *Green signals: Ecology, growth, and democracy in India*. Oxford University Press.

17 The Convention on Access to Information, Public Participation in Decision-Making and Access to Justice in Environmental Matters (Aarhus Convention) was adopted on June 25, 1998, in Aarhus, Denmark, and is part of the United Nations Economic Commission for Europe (UNECE) framework. It aims to promote transparency and accountability in environmental governance, empowering citizens to engage in environmental matters in the EU region. For more about this convention, see Hartley, N., & Wood, C. (2005). Public participation in environmental impact assessment – implementing the Aarhus Convention. *Environmental Impact Assessment Review*, *25*(4); Rodenhoff, V. (2002). The Aarhus Convention and its implications for the institutions of the European Community. *Review of European Community & International Environmental Law*, *11*.

states have ratified, ensures the public's right to access information, participate in decision-making, and seek justice in environmental matters. In China, recent legal reforms have started recognizing environmental rights, with the *Environmental Protection Law of 1989* emphasizing public participation and the right to sue for environmental harm.

1.2 Environmental Pollution

Our definition of 'environment' encompasses both the physical and biological components of nature which exist in a harmonious balance. It appears that nature has its own way of arranging and rearranging the components, but if this process is interrupted by outside forces, this is referred to as pollution. Such disturbances can happen due to several reasons, the most prominent of which is pollution by industries.

As per Halsbury's Laws of England, 'pollution' is defined as the man-made addition of substances or energy into the water body which is likely to cause danger to human health, harm to the living resources and the aquatic ecosystem, damage to the amenities or non-consumptive interference with the legitimate uses of water, respectively.[18] This definition pertains only to water pollution and does not cover other types of pollution. Even with regard to noise pollution, unwanted sound permeating in the air characterizes the term. Such sounds are void of pleasant or amicable quality, which is why they are deemed unwanted. Thus, noise is sound; however, when it becomes undesirable, it is referred to as a polluted sound.

Furthermore, the conception of pollution as evil helps society understand that mankind is a part of nature. Richard Mabey, in his Pollution Handbook, observes that the 'root cause of pollution probably lies in the sort of world we have chosen to build for ourselves and in our thoughtless worship of progress at any cost,'[19] illustrating that pollution is fundamentally a crisis of unchecked progress. Environmental pollution may also be described as the detrimental alteration of our surroundings, primarily caused by human activities. This pollution can occur due to changes in energy patterns, radiation levels, chemical and physical compositions, and the abundance of undesirable organisms. As such, environmental pollution encompasses various forms, such as air, water, and soil pollution/degradation, among others.[20]

Irrational damage to topsoil also pollutes the environment. Water and wind erode topsoil, affecting productivity.[21] Unchecked erosion leads to landslides in

18 Halsbury's Laws of England. (1973). *Environmental law* (4th ed., Vol. 38). Butterworths.
19 Mabey, R. (1974). *The pollution handbook*. Penguin Education.
20 See Chatterjee, B. (2002). *Environmental laws* (p. 2). Deep & Deep Publication.
21 Balasubramanian, A. (2017). *Soil erosion–causes and effects*. Centre for Advanced Studies in Earth Science, University of Mysore.

hilly areas.[22] Over-reliance on extensive and high-input farming systems leads to salinization, alkalization, as well as waterlogging. Preventing such degradation must be done to secure food availability and protect the environment for future generations. Forests are vital in sustaining ecological balance.[23] However, excessive human interference and random or unplanned tree-cutting add to the destruction of already fragile forest regions. The loss of vegetative cover leads to the destruction of water-improving sites, animal habitats, and even microbes.

Suspended particulate matter (SPM) is among the most prevalent types of air pollution.[24] The presence of sulfur dioxide (SO_2) pollution has been detected in the media-stratum region, and it is directly associated with industrialization and an increase in population numbers.[25] Oil refining, pulp and paper industries, chemicals, and iron and steel production, along with non-metallic mineral industries, are some of the strongest contributors to this pollution. Pollution comes from thermal power plants.[26] Urban traffic in kernel cities grows, and so do the levels of pollution.[27] The increase in private-owned two-stroke engine motorbikes, coupled with poorly maintained older vehicles, poor-quality roads, traffic jams, and no traffic control, are the primary causes of this problem.

Pollution impacts the quality of water.[28] Pollution of water is caused by organic pollutants from industries, runoff from land-based activities, and discharge of domestic sewage.[29] These affect water bodies such as lakes, rivers, and underground sources. Heavy metal contamination and the presence of

22 Govers, G., Poesen, J., & Goossens, D. (2004). Soil erosion – processes, damages, and countermeasures. In *Managing soil quality: Challenges in modern agriculture*. CABI Publishing.

23 Kimmins, J. P. (2004). Forest ecology. In *Fishes and forestry: Worldwide watershed interactions and management*.

24 Yadav, A. K., & Jamal, A. (2018). Suspended particulate matter and its management system surrounding opencast coal mines. *Environmental Quality Management*, *28*(2).

25 Li, R., Wang, X., Liu, Y., & Wang, S. (2019). The spatiotemporal variation and key factors of SO_2 in 336 cities across China. *Journal of Cleaner Production*, *210*, 712–723; Jion, M. M. M. F., et al. (2023). A critical review and prospect of NO_2 and SO_2 pollution over Asia: Hotspots, trends, and sources. *Science of the Total Environment*, *876*, 162851. https://doi.org/10.1016/j.scitotenv.2023.162851.

26 Vasistha, V. (2014). Effects of pollutants produced by thermal power plants on the environment: A review. *International Journal of Mechanical Engineering and Robotics Research*, *3*(2), 128–133.

27 Krzyżanowski, M., Apte, J. S., Bonjour, S. P., Brauer, M., Cohen, A. J., & Prüss-Ustun, A. (2014). Air pollution in the mega-cities. *Current Environmental Health Reports*, *1*, 185–191. https://doi.org/10.1007/s40572-014-0019-7

28 Igwe, P. U., Chukwudi, C. C., Ifenatuorah, F. C., Fagbeja, I. F., & Okeke, C. A. (2017). A review of environmental effects of surface water pollution. *International Journal of Advanced Engineering Research and Science*, *4*(12), 128–137. http://doi.org/10.22161/ijaers.4.12.21

29 Akhtar, N., Xu, H., Gao, Q., & Yuan, B. (2021). Various natural and anthropogenic factors responsible for water quality degradation: A review. *Water*, *13*(19); Xu, H., Gao, Q., & Yuan, B. (2022). Analysis and identification of pollution sources of comprehensive river water quality: Evidence from two river basins in China. *Ecological Indicators*, *135*.

bacteria also contribute to the water quality deterioration. The biochemical oxygen demand (BOD) values help define the state of pollution. A value of over 6 mg/liter is regarded as good.[30] Noise pollution is quantified in decibels, which are measured on a scale of 0–130, where 0 is the average least perceivable sound and 130 is deemed as the average level of pain.[31] Noise comes from cars and industrial equipment. The louder the noise, the greater the average pain level measured in decibels.[32]

Urban sprawling along with lacking infrastructure and poorly managed waste has resulted in uncontrolled pollution. Not only is it a health hazard, but it is an environmental one as well.[33] Hard waste in the municipal areas includes plastics, organic materials, cloth from residence etc. The presence of various kinds of industrial waste also contributes to the issue, most notably fly ash, phosphogypsum, and iron and steel slags.

Various industries, including chemical ones, dispose of their industrial waste into the sea.[34] Furthermore, coastal zones are subject to development-related environmental impacts such as uncontrolled and ill-planned coastal zone management, shipping and maritime activities, oil spills, sludge dumping, and petroleum and gas prospecting. The consequences of climate change and global warming manifest in increased sea levels (submersion of land), erosion, flooding, and increased cyclone activity and wave violence.[35]

1.3 Environmental Pollution by Business Corporations

The concept of ecological disorganization suggests that environmental damage is primarily caused by organizing the productive forces of the economy in line with capitalism.[36] The Treadmill of Production (ToP) theory argues that

30 Van Wyk, P., & Scarpa, J. (1999). Water quality requirements and management. In *Farming marine shrimp in recirculating freshwater systems* (pp. 45–60).

31 Mohamed, A. O. M., Paleologos, E. K., & Howari, F. M. (2021). Noise pollution and its impact on human health and the environment. In *Pollution assessment for sustainable practices in applied sciences and engineering* (pp. 367–396). Elsevier.

32 Murphy, E., & King, E. A. (2022). *Environmental noise pollution: Noise mapping, public health, and policy*. Elsevier.

33 Rahaman, M. A., Kalam, A., & Al-Mamun, M. (2023). Unplanned urbanization and health risks of Dhaka City in Bangladesh: Uncovering the associations between urban environment and public health. *Frontiers in Public Health, 11*; Aliyu, A. A., & Amadu, L. (2017). Urbanization, cities, and health: The challenges to Nigeria–A review. *Annals of African Medicine, 16*(4).

34 Hinrichsen, D. (2013). *Coastal waters of the world: Trends, threats, and strategies*. Island Press.

35 Zhang, K., Douglas, B. C., & Leatherman, S. P. (2004). Global warming and coastal erosion. *Climatic Change, 64*, 41–58; Griggs, G., & Reguero, B. G. (2021). Coastal adaptation to climate change and sea-level rise. *Water, 13*(16), 2205.

36 Lynch, M. J., Long, M. A., Stretesky, P. B., & Barrett, K. L. (2013). Is it a crime to produce ecological disorganization? Why green criminology and political economy matter in the analysis of global ecological harms. *British Journal of Criminology, 53*(6), 997–1016.

capitalism is responsible for ecological disorganization.[37] According to ToP, capitalism relies on continuous economic growth fueled by an expanding consumer population and increasing extraction of natural resources for sale in the market.[38] Business corporations, through their roles in natural resource utilization, have become the main drivers of capitalism. Their reckless use of natural resources, driven by their greed and ever-increasing capacities, has placed them at the top of the list of environmental polluters.

Environmental pollution by business corporations, known as corporate pollution, refers to the contamination of air, water, and land caused by the production and consumption of goods and services by business companies. This pollution significantly impacts the quality of the air we breathe, the water we drink, and the land we live on. Corporate pollution has been associated with respiratory diseases, cancer, and various health issues. Furthermore, it harms wildlife, ecosystems, and endangered species.

There are countless examples of companies damaging the environment through their operations. One of the most notable is the Exxon Valdez oil spill in 1989.[39] The Exxon Valdez tanker spilled millions of gallons of oil into the Prince William Sound in Alaska, causing significant damage to the environment and wildlife in the area, which took years to recover. The British Petroleum PLC's oil spill in the Gulf of Mexico in 2010 severely harmed not only marine life but also the local economy. The world would require half a century to recover from this loss.[40] Another example is the pollution caused by the textile industry.[41] Textile production pollutes through chemicals and dyes released into waterways.[42] The Aral Sea in Central Asia is a prime example

37 Maume, M. O., & Greife, M. J. (2023). Giving the green light: Corporate environmental crimes, the treadmill of production, and environmental justice. *Crime, Law and Social Change*, *79*(3), 281–301.

38 Gould, K. A., Pellow, D. N., & Schnaiberg, A. (2015). *Treadmill of production: Injustice and unsustainability in the global economy*. Routledge.

39 Morris, B. F., & Loughlin, T. R. (2013). Overview of the Exxon Valdez oil spill. In *Marine mammals and the Exxon Valdez* (pp. 1–22). Academic Press.

40 Schwartz, M. S. (2020). Beyond petroleum or bottom-line profits only? An ethical analysis of BP and the Gulf oil spill. *Business and Society Review*, *125*(1), 9–29; Riazi, M. R. (2021). Environmental, economic, and political impacts: Case of BP oil spill. In *Oil spill occurrence, simulation, and behavior* (pp. 145–162). CRC Press.

41 Ballachey, B. E., Bodkin, J. L., Esler, D., & Irons, D. B. (2014). Lessons from the 1989 Exxon Valdez oil spill: A biological perspective. In *Oil spill environmental forensics case studies* (pp. 59–88). CRC Press.

42 Islam, M. R., & Mostafa, M. G. (2018). Textile dyeing effluents and environment concerns – a review. *Journal of Environmental Science and Natural Resources*, *11*(1–2), 131–143; Islam, T., Mostafa, M. G., Hossain, S., & Alam, M. N. (2023). Impact of textile dyes on health and ecosystem: A review of structure, causes, and potential solutions. *Environmental Science and Pollution Research*, *30*(4), 9200–9216; Berradi, M., Hsissou, R., Khudhair, D., Assouag, M., Cherkaoui, O., El Bachiri, A., & El Harfi, A. (2019). Textile finishing dyes and their impact on aquatic environs. *Heliyon*, *5*(11), e02711.

of the devastating effects of textile pollution.[43] Of greater concern, the sea has shrunk by 90% due to water diversion for cotton production, leading to environmental and economic crises in the region exacerbated by pollution.[44] This dual problem of pollution and water depletion also faces corporate largesse in terms of addressing their environmental responsibilities. Companies like Nestlé and Coca-Cola have been accused of depleting water resources in areas where water is already scarce.[45] These companies have been criticized for their unsustainable use of water resources in countries like India and Pakistan, where access to clean water is a pressing issue.[46]

In the Niger Delta, there are approximately 900 wells, 1,000 flow stations, 1,500 km of trunk lines, and 45,000 km of oil and gas lines, primarily operated by Exxon Mobil, Chevron Texaco, Royal Dutch Shell, Agip, and Elf. These companies are responsible for an average of 2,921 oil spills per year. Most of these spills occur in the land, swamp, estuaries, or coastal waters of mangrove forests, the latter being one of the most productive ecosystems on the planet.[47] While it is possible to use the gas emitted from the earth drilled for oil, these corporations burn this gas, which blazes unceasingly for years. Each flaming pillar of gas is estimated to contain over 250 toxins. A Human Rights Watch report has pegged one flare as capable of emitting as many as 35 million tons of carbon dioxide and 12 tons of methane into the atmosphere yearly.[48] Although flaring has been banned since 1979, Agip has been able to manage the local authorities for its 200-foot-high flare burning since 1972.[49] Companies engaging in such behavior are not restricted to least-developed to developing economies; they tend to maximally exploit the natural environment wherever possible. The stretch of land along the Mississippi River from Baton Rouge to New Orleans, spanning 150 miles, has earned the nickname 'cancer alley' due to its concentration of over 150 petrochemical, chemical,

43 Rudenko, I., & Lamers, J. P. A. (2010). The Aral Sea: An ecological disaster. In J. P. A. Lamers (Ed.), *The Aral Sea Basin* (pp. 145–155). Springer.

44 White, K. D. (2014). Nature and economy in the Aral Sea basin. In P. Micklin (Ed.), *The Aral Sea: The devastation and partial rehabilitation of a Great Lake* (pp. 67–80). Springer; Gupta, A. (2020). Shrinking of Aral Sea: An environmental disaster in Central Asia. *International Journal of Humanities, Arts and Social Sciences, 6*(4), 172–180.

45 Walsh, H., & Dowding, T. J. (2012). Sustainability and the Coca-Cola company: The global water crisis and Coca-Cola's business case for water stewardship. *International Journal of Business Insights & Transformation, 4*, 1–12; O'Handley, M. (2019). *Green criminology and the corporate extraction of water in Canada* [Master's thesis, Saint Mary's University].

46 Jaffee, D. (2023). *Unbottled: The fight against plastic water and for water justice.* University of California Press; Sutherlin, L. (2024). *Procter & Gamble, Mondelēz, and Nestlé are among 10 leading consumer brands driving global deforestation.* CounterPunch.

47 Katz, R. S. (2012). Environmental pollution: Corporate crime and cancer mortality. *Contemporary Justice Review, 15*(1), 85–102.

48 Hondros, C. (2007). The fire: The price of oil in the Niger Delta. *The Virginia Quarterly Review, 83*(1), 25–39.

49 Katz, R. S. (2012). Environmental pollution: Corporate crime and cancer mortality. *Contemporary Justice Review, 15*(1), 85–102.

refining, and industrial plants, along with numerous hazardous waste sites. These facilities produce harmful pesticides, chemicals, plastics, gasoline, synthetic fibers, and more.[50]

Another example is Volkswagen, which was caught cheating on emissions tests in 2015.[51] The company had installed software in its diesel cars that manipulated the test results, allowing the vehicles to emit pollutants at levels higher than legally permitted. Mining companies adversely impact the environment due to their over-extraction of minerals and metals.[52] Mining can lead to deforestation, soil erosion, and water pollution. The use of cyanide in gold mining has been linked to environmental and health problems in areas where mining occurs. The meat industry further exacerbates the misuse of natural resources.[53] Producing meat and dairy requires large amounts of water, feed, and land. Meat processing companies have been criticized for having a detrimental impact on forests and increasing greenhouse gas (GHG) emissions and water pollution. Livestock companies are a significant contributor to methane emissions.[54] Palm oil companies, known for their misuse of natural resources, produce palm oil used in various products, from food to cosmetics, but its production is a major cause of deforestation in countries like Indonesia and Malaysia, resulting in habitat destruction and biodiversity loss.[55]

Corporate pollution has significant consequences for the environment and public health. The burning of fossil fuels by industries and transportation is a

50 Human Rights Watch. (2024). *'We're dying here': The fight for life in a Louisiana fossil fuel sacrifice zone*. Human Rights Watch; Blatt, H. (2011). *America's environmental report card: Are we making the grade?* MIT Press.

51 Lynch, L. J., Wicks, A. C., & Swenson, A. (2016). *The Volkswagen emissions scandal*. Darden Business Publishing Cases; Cavico, F. J., & Mujtaba, B. G. (2016). Volkswagen emissions scandal: A global case study of legal, ethical, and practical consequences and recommendations for sustainable management. *Global Journal of Research in Business & Management*, *4*(2), 1–18; Fitzgerald, A. J., & Spencer, D. (2020). Governmentality and environmental rights: Regulatory failure and the Volkswagen emissions fraud case. *Critical Criminology*, *28*(2), 157–174.

52 Dudka, S., & Adriano, D. C. (1997). Environmental impacts of metal ore mining and processing: A review. *Journal of Environmental Quality*, *26*(3), 590–602; Jacka, J. K. (2018). The anthropology of mining: The social and environmental impacts of resource extraction in the mineral age. *Annual Review of Anthropology*, *47*(1), 61–77.

53 Parker, C., Haines, F., & Boehm, L. (2018). The promise of ecological regulation: The case of intensive meat. *Jurimetrics*, *59*(1), 1–26.

54 Sejian, V., Bhatta, R., Gaughan, J. B., Dunshea, F. R., & Lacetera, N. (2016). Livestock as sources of greenhouse gases and its significance to climate change. *Greenhouse Gases*, *11*, 9–16.

55 Meijaard, E., Garcia-Ulloa, J., Sheil, D., Carlson, K. M., Wich, S. A., Juffe-Bignoli, D., & Brooks, T. M. (2020). The environmental impacts of palm oil in context. *Nature Plants*, *6*(12), 1418–1426; Azhar, B., Saadun, N., Puan, C. L., Kamarudin, N., Aziz, N., Nurhidayu, S., & Fischer, J. (2017). The global palm oil sector must change to save biodiversity and improve food security in the tropics. *Journal of Environmental Management*, *203*, 457–466; Teng, S., Khong, K. W., & Ha, N. C. (2020). Palm oil and its environmental impacts: A big data analytics study. *Journal of Cleaner Production*, *274*, 122901.

major contributor to air pollution.[56] The World Health Organization (WHO) estimates that air pollution is responsible for seven million deaths each year. Industrial release of GHGs has led to a warming of the planet, resulting in rising sea levels, extreme weather events, and the loss of biodiversity.[57] The effects of climate change are felt worldwide, from melting polar ice caps and glaciers to coral bleaching.[58] Industrial runoff can contaminate water sources, making them unsafe for human consumption.[59] Finally, the use of pesticides produced by large corporations in agriculture has been linked to water pollution and the decline of aquatic ecosystems.[60]

The economic and social costs of corporate pollution are significant. The loss of biodiversity has far-reaching economic and social impacts, affecting livelihoods through industries like tourism and fishing. Communities living near polluting industries are often disproportionately affected by the health impacts of pollution, leading to increased healthcare costs and lost productivity. The pollution burden is often felt most strongly by marginalized communities and low-income populations.

The future consequences of corporate pollution are alarming. As the global population grows, the demand for resources will only increase, putting further strain on the environment. Ironically, since the signing of the Paris Agreement in 2015, 58 of the top 100 carbon-producing companies have recorded an increase in their emission levels. This trend was particularly noticeable in Asia, where 13 out of 15 companies intensified their operations. Similar trends were observed in the Middle East (7 out of 10), Europe (13 out of 23),

56 Colvile, R. N., Hutchinson, E. J., Mindell, J. S., & Warren, R. F. (2001). The transport sector as a source of air pollution. *Atmospheric Environment*, *35*(9), 1537–1565; Inambao, M. S. P. F. (2018). Transportation, pollution and the environment. *International Journal of Applied Engineering Research*, *13*(4), 2734–2741.

57 Kumar, A., Nagar, S., & Anand, S. (2021). Climate change and existential threats. In *Global climate change* (pp. 155–174). Elsevier; Sivalingam, S., Harish, A., & Selva, M. R. (2024). Environmental and health effects of global warming. In *Health and environmental effects of ambient air pollution* (pp. 55–68). Elsevier.

58 Shivanna, K. R. (2022). Climate change and its impact on biodiversity and human welfare. *Proceedings of the Indian National Science Academy*, *88*(2), 105–115; Gahlawat, I. N., & Lakra, P. (2020). Global climate change and its effects. *Integrated Journal of Social Sciences*, *7*(1), 18–25.

59 World Health Organization. (2014). 7 million premature deaths annually linked to air pollution. *World Health Organization*. www.who.int/news/item/25-03-2014-7-million-premature-deaths-annually-linked-to-air-pollution.

60 Kumar, P., Kashyap, V. K., Bishnoi, S., Tandon, R., & Mathur, P. (2023). Impact of pesticides application on aquatic ecosystem and biodiversity: A review. *Biology Bulletin*, *50*(6), 799–812; Tudi, M., Daniel Ruan, H., Wang, L., Lyu, J., Sadler, R., Connell, D., Chu, C., & Phung, D. T. (2021). Agriculture development, pesticide application and its impact on the environment. *International Journal of Environmental Research and Public Health*, *18*(3), 1112; Kumar, A., Nagar, S., & Anand, S. (2021). Climate change and existential threats. In *Global climate change* (pp. 155–174). Elsevier.

South America (3 out of 5), Australia (3 out of 4), and Africa (3 out of 6). Notably, in North America, 16 out of 37 companies, constituting 43%, have experienced an increase in their emissions since 2016.[61] As such, addressing regulatory frameworks against corporate pollution is vital in environmental jurisprudence. Equally important is determining how to allocate public resources to help businesses minimize their pollution of the natural environment, which plays a key role in business strategies, economic progress, and sustainable development.

1.4 Regulating Environmental Pollution

Over the centuries, global environmental degradation has been a significant issue. Before 1500 CE, major extinction events like the Permian and Cretaceous periods led to the loss of up to 90% of species, and overhunting contributed to the decline of many large mammals. Additionally, there were cross-continental movements of microbes stemming from increased merchant navy and colonialist expeditions, leading to epidemics and long-term natural climate changes. Between 1500 and 1760, the ecological expansion and capitalist growth in Europe led to increasing resource shortages, land degradation, demographic shifts, and the ecological transformation of the Americas.[62] Between the years 1760 and 1945, the processes of capitalist industrialization, urbanization, the concentration of population centers, ecological expansion, and colonization resulted in the depletion of local resources, extensive urban air, soil, and water pollution, alterations in rural environments, deforestation, some instances of global species extinction, and contributed significantly to global warming. Following World War II, the global community began to confront issues such as global warming, marine resource depletion, shortages of water supply, deforestation, desertification, soil degradation, waste overflow, hazardous waste management, acid deposition, nuclear risks, and the deterioration of the global ecosystem, all exacerbated by Western economic growth and consumption patterns. Presently, socialist industrialization, industrialization within the Global South, emerging technological risks, and conflicts pose significant threats to our shared global environment.[63]

61 Thorsberg, C. (2024). 80 percent of global CO_2 emissions come from just 57 companies, report shows. *Environmental Sustainability Report, 15*, 72–84.

62 Owen, L. A., Pickering, K. T., & Pickering, K. T. (2006). *An introduction to global environmental issues*. Routledge.

63 De Vogli, R. (2013). *Progress or collapse: The crises of market greed*. Routledge; Penn, D. J. (2003). The evolutionary roots of our environmental problems: Toward a Darwinian ecology. *The Quarterly Review of Biology*, *78*(3), 275–301. https://doi.org/10.1086/378921

Manufacturing, processing, transportation, and consumption deplete natural resources and contribute to environmental stress by generating waste.[64] The productivity of the economic system depends on the supply and quality of natural resources. While water, soil, air, forests, and fisheries are productive assets, pollution – including 'greenhouse effects,'[65] 'global warming,'[66] and 'acid precipitation'[67] – are by-products of economic development, especially industrialization and urbanization.

Pollution is an 'external cost' (sometimes called a 'spillover cost' or a 'neighborhood cost').[68] Untreated or improperly treated waste turns into pollution, raising both private and social costs. Environmental degradation, which often becomes irreversible, inflicts damage costs on the economy, leading to output and human losses, decreased labor productivity due to ill health, and reduced crop output.

Pollution degrades the environment, depleting the earth's ozone layer and creating holes in it.[69] Industrial effluents and carbon monoxide emissions

64 Singh, R. L., & Singh, P. K. (2017). Global environmental problems. In *Principles and applications of environmental biotechnology for a sustainable future* (pp. 1–20). Springer; Bilen, K., Aydin, H., & Yilmaz, S. (2008). Energy production, consumption, and environmental pollution for sustainable development: A case study in Turkey. *Renewable and Sustainable Energy Reviews, 12*(6), 1836–1850. https://doi.org/10.1016/j.rser.2007.06.004

65 The greenhouse effect is a natural process that warms the Earth's surface by trapping some of the Sun's energy. Human activities, such as burning fossil fuels and deforestation, have increased greenhouse gases, leading to global warming and climate change, which cause rising sea levels, changing weather patterns, and increased extreme weather events. See Mitchell, J. F. B. (1989). The "greenhouse" effect and climate change. *Reviews of Geophysics, 27*(1), 115–130. https://doi.org/10.1029/RG027i001p00115

66 The average global temperatures have significantly increased since the mid-20th century, primarily due to human-induced emissions. This has led to extreme weather events such as an increased frequency and intensity of heatwaves, droughts, heavy rainfall, and hurricanes. The rise in world temperatures has also led to the rapid melting of glaciers and polar ice caps, contributing to rising sea levels, which result in coastal flooding and habitat loss. These climate changes have a significant impact on biodiversity, leading to habitat loss and increased extinction rates for various species. See Kerr, R. A. (2007). Global warming is changing the world. *Science, 316*(5822), 187–188. https://doi.org/10.1126/science.316.5822.187

67 Acid precipitation, also known as acid rain, refers to any form of precipitation (such as rain, snow, fog, or mist) that has a lower pH than normal, making it more acidic. This phenomenon is mainly caused by human activities that release pollutants into the atmosphere. Acid rain can significantly harm lakes, streams, and wetlands by increasing water acidity. Higher acidity levels can cause aluminum to leach from soil into water bodies, which is toxic to fish and other aquatic organisms. Many species are sensitive to changes in pH, and increased acidity can lead to decreased populations or even extinction in severe cases. Acid rain can also damage forests, especially at higher elevations. For more, see Haines, T. A. (1981). Acidic precipitation and its consequences for aquatic ecosystems: A review. *Transactions of the American Fisheries Society, 110*(6), 659–668.

68 Venkateswarlu, C. (2013). Role of the judiciary in environment protection in India. *Asian Journal of Research in Social Sciences and Humanities, 3*(10), 98–105.

69 Bais, A. F., Manua, C., Tzatzalos, K., & Avissar, R. (2018). Environmental effects of ozone depletion, UV radiation and interactions with climate change: UNEP Environmental Effects Assessment Panel, update 2017. *Photochemical & Photobiological Sciences, 17*(2), 253–285.

threaten the environment. Overfishing harms the fragile marine ecosystem. Numerous studies have demonstrated that air and water pollution severely impact human life, particularly in developing countries, leading to health issues and premature deaths.[70] Thus, controlling environmental pollution through meaningful regulation assumes greater significance in ensuring sustainable development.

Crimes against the environment are common. Like individuals and other organizations, including the government, business corporations can be held responsible for environmentally harmful actions with criminal intent. While the regulatory frameworks and the principles for holding an individual liable for damaging natural resources have been pretty much settled, it can be challenging to hold corporations criminally accountable for environmental crimes. Adopting the core of the theoretical framework of the ToP, the Treadmill of Crime theory suggests that business corporations are not often penalized severely for these crimes, as doing so may harm economic growth.[71] This theory predicts that the punishment for corporate polluters is designed in a way that avoids disrupting the processes necessary for economic growth. Corporate polluters often view fines as simply a cost of doing business and strongly oppose the idea of corporate criminal liability in environmental jurisprudence.[72]

Regulating environmental pollution, particularly corporate criminal liability for damaging the environment, is complex due to its close connection to various issues. Environmental pollution involves the misuse of resources for minimal or zero gain, lack of security for future generations, challenges in maintaining livelihoods, economic hurdles, disruptions in production activities, and more. This complexity makes it challenging to criminalize this pollution.[73] Garland used a funnel as a metaphor to describe this challenge.[74] He explained that at the wide mouth of the funnel, there are various environmental violations committed by criminals. Only a small fraction of these violations come to the attention of enforcement agents. Among the cases that are investigated, only a portion result in penalties from public organizations,

70 Manisalidis, I., Stavropoulou, E., Papadopoulos, G. A., & Koutouzis, M. (2020). Environmental and health impacts of air pollution: A review. *Frontiers in Public Health*, *8*, 14. https://doi.org/10.3389/fpubh.2020.00014; Lin, L., Yang, H., & Xu, X. (2022). Effects of water pollution on human health and disease heterogeneity: A review. *Frontiers in Environmental Science*, *10*, 834643. https://doi.org/10.3389/fenvs.2022.834643

71 Maume, O., & Greife, M. J. (2023). Giving the green light: Corporate environmental crimes, the treadmill of production, and environmental justice. *Crime, Law and Social Change*, *79*(3), 245–260. https://doi.org/10.1007/s10611-022-10039-y

72 Ibid.

73 Johnson, E. W., Schwartz, J., & Inlow, A. R. (2020). The criminalization of environmental harm: A study of the most serious environmental offenses prosecuted by the US federal government, 1985–2010. *Environmental Sociology*, *6*(3), 206–220. https://doi.org/10.1080/23251042.2020.1782691

74 Garland, D. (2001). *The culture of control: Crime and social order in contemporary society*. University of Chicago Press.

typically through administrative or civil routes.[75] Thus, only a small number of cases investigated by public organizations face criminal prosecution, and the majority of them do not result in punishment.[76]

While economic, social, and political strategies are crucial in governing environmental pollution, environmental jurisprudence focuses on using legal regulations to reduce pollution. 'Legal regulation' is about regulating a matter through laws, established customs, and administrative orders from legitimate authorities. International agreements, industry-supported guidelines, and agreements among stakeholders are also considered tools for legal regulation. When these tools are combined with traditional civil rights, constitutional guarantees, judicial opinions, and philosophical observations, they form 'environmental jurisprudence'[77] – a major source of regulating environmental pollution.[78] This book focuses solely on discussing this source and does not critically discuss non-legal sources for pollution regulation.

Although predominantly legal in character, environmental jurisprudence also deals with eco-centric principles for natural resource governance. It focuses on upholding environmental rights and explores how they are integrated into legal and political systems. This jurisprudence also considers the types and appropriateness of penalties for violating these environmental rights. For example, it questions the effectiveness of large fines and discusses the emergence of the 'enforcement undertaking' as an outcome of imposing hefty fines for environmental damage recovery. Likewise, the use of special executive liability to hold corporate managers and directors personally responsible for environmental damage is a heavily debated topic in this jurisprudence. The *Environmental Legislation Amendment Act 2022* of New South Wales, Australia, has expanded the use of this strategy. One impact of this is that government organizations responsible for environmental protection are more proactive, but this has also raised concerns about potential miscarriages of justice and increased costs for starting a business. The issuance of Clean Up and Preventive Notices by authorities like the Environment Protection Authority is now a subject of mixed debate in this jurisprudence. Organizations such as the Environmental Protection Agency (EPA) have the authority to place

75 Johnson, E. W., Schwartz, J., & Inlow, A. R. (2020). The criminalization of environmental harm: A study of the most serious environmental offenses prosecuted by the US federal government, 1985–2010. *Environmental Sociology*, *6*(3), 206–220. https://doi.org/10.1080/23251042.2020.1782691

76 Lynch, M. J., Stretesky, P. B., & Long, M. A. (2016). The weak probability of punishment for environmental offenses and deterrence of environmental offenders: A discussion based on USEPA criminal cases, 1983–2013. *Deviant Behavior*, *37*(10), 1144–1163. https://doi.org/10.1080/01639625.2016.1172742

77 Ito, M., & Montini, M. (2018). Nature's rights and earth jurisprudence: A new ecologically based paradigm for environmental law. In *The right to nature* (pp. 1–21). Routledge.

78 Madaoui, N. (2023). Evolving jurisprudence of environmental law: A doctrinal analysis. *Analytical and Comparative Jurisprudence*, *6*, 1–22. https://doi.org/10.1515/acj-2023-0001

restrictive or affirmative stipulations on land in order to enforce the terms of an Environmental Protection License. They can also review the compliance history of current directors of a corporation to decide whether it is a fit and proper person for performing environment-related operations.

Constitutional provisions and statutory laws are at the core of this jurisprudence. It is influenced by international treaties, such as the *Paris Agreement* on Climate Change, the *Convention on Biological Diversity* (CBD), and the *Aarhus Convention*, which emphasizes access to information, public participation, and justice in environmental matters. Courts play a crucial role in developing this jurisprudence as they interpret environmental laws and principles. Landmark cases often set precedents that shape environmental jurisprudence. For instance, the *Minors Oposa v. Factoran* case in the Philippines recognized the right of future generations to a healthy environment. Through expanding the scope of environmental rights, judicial activism in some jurisdictions has assisted in the progress of this jurisprudence.[79]

The objective of this jurisprudence is multifarious. It urges balancing economic development with environmental protection to ensure that resources are available for future generations. It encourages promoting preventive measures in response to uncertainty about environmental damage, transferring the burden of proof to those suggesting potentially harmful activities.[80] Elaborating on how to hold polluters financially responsible for the environmental damage they cause and provide incentives for cleaner practices are some of the underlying aims of the regulatory approaches. It also highlights the need for using deterrence, physical punishment, and harsh measures where suitable for curbing the culture of exploiting natural resources.[81]

The main goal of this jurisprudence is to advance environmental justice by fighting against environmental injustice. Environmental injustice can be caused in various ways, including the exploitation of natural resources near poor and minority communities. This is unfair because corporations do this intentionally, and these communities are disproportionately exposed to and harmed by the most serious environmental hazards.[82] These communities are often less organized and lack the ability to stand up against this injustice. To address this, an emerging area of environmental law recognizes the rights of

79 Cha, J. M. (2005). A critical examination of the environmental jurisprudence of the courts of India. *Albany Law Environmental Outlook*, *10*, 1–25.

80 Cameron, J., & Abouchar, J. (1991). The precautionary principle: A fundamental principle of law and policy for the protection of the global environment. *Boston College International and Comparative Law Review*, *14*, 1–27; M'Gonigle, R. M., Morrow, A. R., & Wilson, D. (1994). Taking uncertainty seriously: From permissive regulation to preventative design in environmental decision making. *Osgoode Hall Law Journal*, *32*, 43–84.

81 Dube, I. (2007). *Environmental jurisprudence: Polluter's liability*. LexisNexis Butterworths.

82 Greife, M., McCaffrey, C., & Pomeroy, S. (2017). Corporate environmental crime and environmental justice. *Criminal Justice Policy Review*, *28*(4), 331–351. https://doi.org/10.1177/0887403415589531

natural entities (such as rivers, forests, and ecosystems) to exist and thrive.[83] This concept has been legally acknowledged in some areas, allowing for legal action on behalf of nature. The discussion within this legal framework is currently focused on how to enhance the enforcement of environmental rights, ensure access to environmental justice, and balance the interests of all stakeholders in the natural environment.[84]

Environmental jurisprudence is an ever-changing field that plays a critical role in guiding how societies tackle environmental issues. It should consider recent developments in regulations that challenge traditional domestic and international policymaking processes. The growing use of regulations that prescribe specific behaviors has involved private interests and capabilities in this process. Additionally, the increasing use of market-driven policy tools has allowed global civil societies to incorporate their concerns into policy settings.[85] These changes have led to the privatization of regulatory governance at both domestic and global levels. In this context, environmental law must encompass a wide range of legal principles, frameworks, and judicial interpretations to safeguard the environment against corporate pollution. As global environmental issues become more urgent, the importance of robust environmental law will continue to increase.

1.5 Corporate Polluters in Environmental Jurisprudence

Corporate polluters are a key focus of environmental jurisprudence, with legal frameworks developing to hold them responsible for their environmental impact.[86] Through regulations, court decisions, and public interest litigation, environmental jurisprudence aims to ensure that corporations operate sustainably and responsibly. As environmental challenges increase, the role of environmental jurisprudence in regulating corporate criminal liability will become more and more crucial.[87]

83 McDonough, C. (2019). Will the river ever get a chance to speak: Standing up for the legal rights of nature. *Villanova Environmental Law Journal*, *31*, 1–23; Pain, N., & Pepper, R. (2021). Can personhood protect the environment? Affording legal rights to nature. *Fordham International Law Journal*, *45*, 1–35.

84 Sood, S. (2023). Environmental jurisprudence vis-a-vis the principle of sustainable development. *Indian Journal of Integrated Research in Law*, *3*, 1–25.

85 Cashore, B. (2017). Legitimacy and the privatization of environmental governance: How non-state market-driven (NSMD) governance systems gain rule-making authority. In *International environmental governance* (pp. 45–67). Routledge.

86 Laughran, H. S. (1972). The law and the corporate polluter: Flexibility and adaptation in the developing law of the environment. *Mercer Law Review*, *23*, 1–28; Humphreys, S. L. (1989). An enemy of the people: Prosecuting the corporate polluter as a common law criminal. *American University Law Review*, *39*, 1–25.

87 Spence, D. B. (2001). The shadow of the rational polluter: Rethinking the role of rational actor models in environmental law. *California Law Review*, *89*(1), 197–237. https://doi.org/10.2307/3481353

In general jurisprudence, the discussion for determining criminal liability is a vital component, as the consequences of being proved as a criminal are more significant than being proved responsible for civil liabilities. Criminal liability is hard to prove, and the available remedy for criminal liability is physical punishment, including other penalties. Arguing for corporate criminal liability and imposing physical punishments on business corporations is harder.

Acknowledging corporate criminal liability is a relatively modern development within the legal system, largely emerging in the 20th century due to the expansion of common law concepts.[88] The majority of theories regarding corporate criminal liability have been shaped through individual cases in the common law system. Corporate criminal responsibility is founded on the principle of *respondeat superior*, which posits that organizations are liable for the conduct of their representatives, provided that such conduct falls within the parameters of their designated authority and furthers the interests of the organization.[89] At the outset, there existed significant opposition to the application of criminal law to corporate entities, as the judiciary maintained the perspective that corporations did not possess the requisite *mens rea* (guilty mind) necessary for criminal convictions.[90] The arguments around 'reasonable care,' 'due care and skill,' 'scope of employment,' '*ultra viers* conduct,' and 'remote relationship' made it hard to relate criminal intent to an alleged corporate crime.[91] Nonetheless, the arguments based on the 'identification theory' and 'alter-ego' principle progressed toward including the *mens rea* with a corporate act.

There are arguments suggesting that a non-human defendant cannot be convicted of a criminal offense due to gross negligence without evidence proving the guilt of a specific human individual. As such, the legal status of business corporations as 'artificial persons' presents challenges in holding them criminally liable.[92] It is more difficult to determine the intent of an artificial person, and identifying appropriate forms of physical punishment for them is even more challenging. As such, the definition of criminal liability and how to deal with such liability is vital in environmental jurisprudence.

Legal regulation, a dominant regulatory source in environmental jurisprudence, plays a crucial role in managing corporate pollution.[93] It serves

88 Pitt, H. L., & Groskaufmanis, K. A. (1989). Minimizing corporate civil and criminal liability: A second look at corporate codes of conduct. *Georgetown Law Journal*, *78*, 261–280.

89 Vu, S. N. (2004). Corporate criminal liability: Patchwork verdicts and the problem of locating a guilty agent. *Columbia Law Review*, *104*(3), 893–931. https://doi.org/10.2307/4099488

90 Singh, V. K. (2010). Criminal liability of corporations – An environmental perspective. In *Environmental crimes: Corporate liability* (pp. Chapter 3). ISBN 978-81-314-2521-3. SSRN: https://ssrn.com/abstract=2972053

91 Ibid.

92 Laufer, W. S. (2006). *Corporate bodies and guilty minds: The failure of corporate criminal liability*. University of Chicago Press.

93 Zhao, J. (2017). Promoting more socially responsible corporations through a corporate law regulatory framework. *Legal Studies*, *37*(1), 103–130.

to safeguard the environment, minimize harm to wildlife and ecosystems, and enhance public health. Moreover, it fosters fair competition among corporations, ensuring that those operating in an environmentally responsible manner are not disadvantaged. Additionally, it can spur innovation as corporations endeavor to develop new technologies and processes to lessen their environmental impact. Conversely, the absence of regulation results in widespread pollution and environmental deterioration, with little recourse for those affected.

Despite the vital role of legal regulation in controlling corporate pollution, most countries do not have adequate environmental legislation.[94] Business corporations often manage to circumvent or completely ignore these regulations.[95] They may exploit legal loopholes or use weak enforcement to continue their harmful practices. Some countries have no laws or regulations to protect the environment, and their governments lack the resources to enforce these regulations effectively. Even in countries with strong environmental laws, local governments may lack the resources or political will to enforce them effectively. Another challenge in regulating corporate polluters is the absence of global laws. Many corporations operate across borders, making it difficult for individual countries to regulate their activities effectively.[96] While there are international environmental agreements, such as the Paris Agreement on Climate Change, these agreements are often non-binding and lack enforcement mechanisms.[97]

Implementing criminal liability for causing damage to the environment is more complex than implementing this liability for intentionally causing harm to a person. A person can ask for judicial redress against a criminal act; in

94 Fadil, A. (1985). Citizen suits against polluters: Picking up the pace. *Harvard Environmental Law Review*, *9*, 57–97.

95 Wagner, W. E. (2003). Commons ignorance: The failure of environmental law to produce needed information on health and the environment. *Duke Law Journal*, *53*, 1619–1744; Frynas, J. G. (2005). The false developmental promise of corporate social responsibility: Evidence from multinational oil companies. *International Affairs*, *81*(3), 581–598; Cashore, B. (2017). Legitimacy and the privatization of environmental governance: How non-state market-driven (NSMD) governance systems gain rule-making authority. In *International environmental governance* (pp. 115–143). Routledge; Lyon, T. P., & Maxwell, J. W. (2011). Greenwash: Corporate environmental disclosure under threat of audit. *Journal of Economics & Management Strategy*, *20*(1), 3–41.

96 Stiglitz, J. E. (2007). Regulating multinational corporations: Towards principles of cross-border legal framework in a globalized world balancing rights with responsibilities. *American University International Law Review*, *23*, 451–496; Detomasi, D. A. (2007). The multinational corporation and global governance: Modelling global public policy networks. *Journal of Business Ethics*, *71*, 321–334.

97 Kellenberg, D., & Levinson, A. (2014). Waste of effort? International environmental agreements. *Journal of the Association of Environmental and Resource Economists*, *1*(1/2), 135–169; Brunnée, J. (2004). Of sense and sensibility: Reflections on international liability regimes as tools for environmental protection. *International & Comparative Law Quarterly*, *53*(2), 351–370.

most countries, laws governing criminal offenses against a person are pretty much well-defined. This is not the case for the laws that deal with a criminal act committed against the environment. Natural personhood of the environment, the nature of environmental properties, and their associated rights are still contentious matters in environmental governance. Acknowledging that the environment or a part of it as a legal person may bar the government from using environmental issues for political aims. Like business corporations, the environment as a legal person can be more active in restoring its rights through its agents.[98] The idea and its application are still evolving; some countries like Ecuador, Bolivia, and India have taken bold steps to establish environmental personhood, bringing this subject to the limelight of environmental jurisprudence.[99]

Environmental jurisprudence progressed the implementation of corporate criminal liability for damaging natural resources. This progress has been based on five theories: (a) the theory of identification, (b) strict liability, (c) vicarious liability, (d) aggregation theory, and (d) the doctrine of corporate culture model. The theory of identification suggests that a corporation can be held accountable for various offenses through an individual closely linked to the corporation, who acts on its behalf. Under strict liability theory, a corporation can be criminally responsible without the need to prove intent, focusing instead on the actions taken.[100] Vicarious liability holds a corporation responsible for the actions of its employees while they are working for the company, based on the principle of *respondeat superior*, which concerns the relationship between a superior and a subordinate or an employer and an employee. The relationship is further supported by the adage *qui facit per alium facit per se*, meaning that actions taken through another person are considered the same as if done by the individual. According to the aggregation theory, errors from multiple individuals can be attributed to corporations, making them liable. Essentially, this doctrine asserts that all actions and mental states (*mens rea*) of relevant individuals within the corporate setting are considered the actions of the corporation as a whole. The doctrine of corporate culture is influenced by the presumption that corporate acts and policies are not just a result of individual choices but they often reflect the actions and policies of the company itself. Corporate culture is defined as the prevailing attitudes, policies, rules, conduct, or practices within the company in general or within the specific area

98 Stone, C. D. (2017). Should trees have standing? – Toward legal rights for natural objects. In *Environmental rights* (pp. 23–44). Routledge; Akhtar-Khavari, A., & Telesetsky, A. (2022). From protection to restoration: A challenge for environmental governance. In *Research handbook on fundamental concepts of environmental law* (pp. 207–223).

99 Clark, C., Emmanouil, S., & Page, J. (2019). Can you hear the rivers sing? Legal personhood, ontology, and the nitty-gritty of governance. *Ecology Law Quarterly*, *45*(4), 787–831.

100 Satria, H. (2018). Environmental pollution: Assessing the criminal liability of corporations. *Hasanuddin Law Review*, *4*(2), 203–218.

where relevant activities occur. At the core of this doctrine is the explicit and implicit corporate policy that influences the operations of the legal entity.[101]

Along with absorbing the core of these theories, this jurisprudence describes the principles and liabilities necessary to protect the environment and narrates the procedures for bringing action against environmental damages and pollution. However, these may change through changes in legal descriptions and prescriptions and changes in governments' aims and capacities. Nonetheless, implementation of the tenets of this jurisprudence through laws is a usual practice in environmental governance. In any case, more robust laws are required to address the complexities of regulating corporate polluters. Governments should implement stringent laws that are difficult to circumvent to ensure effective enforcement.[102] Along with sufficient environmental laws, environmental jurisprudence needs to explore extralegal approaches such as robust monitoring and reporting systems, and multifaceted collaboration, to assist global business corporations in minimizing their negative impact on the natural environment.[103]

1.6 Scheme of the Book

The core of Chapter 2 is a critical analysis of the criminal liability of a polluter in environmental jurisprudence. In the absence of any overarching definition of environmental jurisprudence, this chapter critically assesses the key principles of this jurisprudence. Taking this jurisprudence as a nexus of liberal approaches for governing environmental concerns, it elaborates the interface of other perspectives like deep ecology, Marxism, and the notion of the Anthropocene into this jurisprudence. This chapter also illustrates the concept of criminal liability, the elements necessary for establishing this liability, the development of this liability scholarship, and how this liability has been incorporated into environmental jurisprudence, mainly through environment-related laws.

Corporations are under increasing scrutiny for their environmental performance. In recent years, there have been significant environmental and judicial attitudes toward corporate environmental wrongdoing and accountability. This is not surprising considering that the threat of pollution and other forms of environmental damage, both internationally and domestically, primarily originates from the manufacturing, mining, and agricultural

101 Ibid.

102 Doerr, B. H. (1984). Prosecuting corporate polluters: The sparing use of criminal sanctions. *University of Detroit Journal of Urban Law*, *62*, 85–124.

103 Gunningham, N. (2009). The new collaborative environmental governance: The localization of regulation. *Journal of Law and Society*, *36*(1), 145–166; Orts, E. W. (2019). Reflexive environmental law. *Environmental Law Review*, 27–49; Karkkainen, B. C. (2002). Adaptive ecosystem management and regulatory penalty defaults: Toward a bounded pragmatism. *Minnesota Law Review*, *87*, 943–1035.

sectors, which are largely controlled by corporations. As such, a critical analysis of the definitional construct of the criminal liability of corporate polluters is vital, and this is the purpose of Chapter 3. This chapter discusses the theoretical justification of this corporate liability and how this liability is being treated under environmental protection frameworks. To explicate the judicial observations of criminal liability of corporate polluters, this chapter ponders upon judicial observations of some significant environmental disasters caused by corporations. Thus, Chapter 3 highlights how the judiciaries in different countries contribute to creating and bringing eventual changes to jurisprudential principles for regulating corporate criminal acts against the environment.

Chapter 4 is about the international frameworks for regulating corporate polluters. The dissemination of global norms of corporate environmental liability is best conceptualized as a dynamic process where international intergovernmental organizations and strong economies play vital roles, often in conjunction with global corporations and non-governmental organizations. The role of these actors and norms around global political and economic governance reflects the growing complexity of regulating global actors like TNCs. Against this backdrop, Chapter 4 examines the norms for settling the global framework for regulating corporate polluters, assessing the roles of the institutions that contribute to this settlement and highlighting the tenets of the private ordering system in global environmental regulation frameworks. The end of this chapter presents a critical view of the position of TNCs within this system.

Countries are different from each other in many respects. Socio-economic conditions, cultural backgrounds, and the philosophical basis of some countries' judicial administration and justice delivery systems are different and contesting. Nonetheless, most countries have systems for protecting their environment and laws against polluters. Chapter 5 examines the dominant principles of some of these countries' environmental jurisprudence. It explains how far the differences at the jurisprudential principle level impact the gaps among these countries' regulatory frameworks against corporate polluters. For this examination and explanation, this chapter elaborates on the regulation of corporate polluters in some countries, including but not limited to the United Kingdom (UK), the United States, Australia, Canada, Finland, Germany, Japan, China, and India. This chapter ultimately explains why some domestic frameworks better prevent corporate pollution than others.

Chapter 6 is about sentencing corporate polluters. Sentencing corporate polluters can be problematic in environmental jurisprudence. There are several reasons behind this. This is so mainly because corporations are economically and politically powerful and considered instrumental to economic development. Many jurisdictions consider pollution by corporations as 'unprovoked aggression' and commit to pursuing other goals and 'necessities' such as economic advantage. However, it is strongly believed that economic development at the cost of degrading the environment is unsustainable. Additionally, it assaults the individual and strips them of their social, cultural, and economic advantages. This viewpoint situates corporate environmental damage within a broader framework of harm, abuse of power, and severe injustice. From this vantage point, this chapter explores the moral and ethical foundations that allow contemporary law to endorse corporate exploitation of the environment. It also examines the nexus of different regulatory approaches for sentencing corporate polluters and critically assesses the development of this sentencing scholarship in environmental jurisprudence.

Chapter 7 concludes the book.

References

Abraham, C. M. (1991). The Indian judiciary and the development of environmental law. *South Asia Research, 11*(1), 61–69.

Adeola, F. O. (2012). *Industrial disasters, toxic waste, and community impact: Health effects and environmental justice struggles around the globe*. Lexington Books.

Ahmad, F. (2001). Origin and growth of environmental law in India. *Journal of the Indian Law Institute, 43*(3), 358–387.

Ahmad, F., Saeed, Q., Shah, S. M. U., Gondal, M. A., & Mumtaz, S. (2022). Environmental sustainability: Challenges and approaches. In *Natural resources conservation and advances for sustainability* (pp. 243–270). Elsevier.

Akhtar, N., Ishak, M. I. S., Bhawani, S. A., & Umar, K. (2021). Various natural and anthropogenic factors responsible for water quality degradation: A review. *Water, 13*(19), 2660.

Akhtar-Khavari, A., & Telesetsky, A. (2022). From protection to restoration: A challenge for environmental governance. In *Research handbook on fundamental concepts of environmental law* (pp. 45–70). Edward Elgar Publishing.

Aliyu, A. A., & Amadu, L. (2017). Urbanization, cities, and health: The challenges to Nigeria – a review. *Annals of African Medicine, 16*(4), 149–158.

Azhar, B., Saadun, N., Prideaux, M., & Lindenmayer, D. B. (2017). The global palm oil sector must change to save biodiversity and improve food security in the tropics. *Journal of Environmental Management, 203*, 457–466.

Bais, A. F., Lucas, R. M., Bornman, J. F., Williamson, C. E., Sulzberger, B., Austin, A. T., Wilson, S. R., Andrady, A. L., Bernhard, G., McKenzie, R. L., Aucamp, P. J., Madronich, S., Neale, R. E., Yazar, S., Young, A. R., De Gruijl, F. R., Norval, M., Takizawa, Y., Barnes, P. W., . . . Heikkilä, A. M. (2018). Environmental effects of ozone depletion, UV radiation and interactions with climate change: UNEP environmental effects assessment panel, update 2017. *Photochemical & Photobiological Sciences, 17*(2), 127–179.

Balasubramanian, A. (2017). *Soil erosion – causes and effects*. Centre for Advanced Studies in Earth Science, University of Mysore.

Ballachey, B. E., Bodkin, J. L., Esler, D., & Rice, S. D. (2014). *Lessons from the 1989 Exxon Valdez oil spill: A biological perspective* (pp. 181–198). CRC Press.

Beirne, P., & South, N. (2013). *Issues in green criminology*. Routledge.

Berradi, M., Hsissou, R., Khudhair, M., Assouag, M., Cherkaoui, O., El Bachiri, A., & El Harfi, A. (2019). Textile finishing dyes and their impact on aquatic environs. *Heliyon, 5*(11).

Bilen, K., Ozyurt, O., Bakırcı, K., Karslı, S., Erdogan, S., Yılmaz, M., & Comaklı, O. (2008). Energy production, consumption, and environmental pollution for

sustainable development: A case study in Turkey. *Renewable and Sustainable Energy Reviews*, *12*(6), 1529–1561.
Blatt, H. (2011). *America's environmental report card: Are we making the grade?* MIT Press.
BrunnÉee, J. (2004). Of sense and sensibility: Reflections on international liability regimes as tools for environmental protection. *International & Comparative Law Quarterly*, *53*(2), 351–368.
Butzer, K. W. (2012). Collapse, environment, and society. *Proceedings of the National Academy of Sciences*, *109*(10), 3632–3639.
Cameron, J., & Abouchar, J. (1991). The precautionary principle: A fundamental principle of law and policy for the protection of the global environment. *BC International & Comparative Law Review*, *14*, 1.
Cashore, B. (2017). Legitimacy and the privatization of environmental governance: How non-state market-driven (NSMD) governance systems gain rule-making authority. In *International environmental governance* (pp. 339–361). Routledge.
Cavico, F. J., & Mujtaba, B. G. (2016). Volkswagen emissions scandal: A global case study of legal, ethical, and practical consequences and recommendations for sustainable management. *Global Journal of Research in Business & Management*, *4*(2).
Cha, J. M. (2005). A critical examination of the environmental jurisprudence of the courts of India. *Albany Law Environmental Outlook*, *10*, 197.
Clark, C., Emmanouil, N., Page, J., & Pelizzon, A. (2019). Can you hear the rivers sing? Legal personhood, ontology, and the nitty-gritty of governance. *Ecology Law Quarterly*, *45*(4), 787–844.
Coates, P. (2013). *Nature: Western attitudes since ancient times*. John Wiley & Sons.
Colvile, R. N., Hutchinson, E. J., Mindell, J. S., & Warren, R. F. (2001). The transport sector as a source of air pollution. *Atmospheric Environment*, *35*(9), 1537–1565.
de Souza Porto, M. F., & de Freitas, C. M. (1996). Major chemical accidents in industrializing countries: The socio-political amplification of risk. *Risk Analysis*, *16*(1), 19–29.
Detomasi, D. A. (2007). The multinational corporation and global governance: Modelling global public policy networks. *Journal of Business Ethics*, *71*, 321–334.
De Vogli, R. (2013). *Progress or collapse: The crises of market greed*. Routledge.
Doerr, B. H. (1984). Prosecuting corporate polluters: The sparing use of criminal sanctions. *University of Detroit Journal of Urban Law*, *62*, 659–659.
Dube, I. (2007). Environmental jurisprudence-polluter's liability. In *Environmental jurisprudence: Polluter's liability*. LexisNexis Butterworths.
Dudka, S., & Adriano, D. C. (1997). Environmental impacts of metal ore mining and processing: A review. *Journal of Environmental Quality*, *26*(3), 590–602.
Eagleton, T. (2017). *Materialism*. Yale University Press.
Fadil, A. (1985). Citizen suits against polluters: Picking up the pace. *Harvard Environmental Law Review*, *9*, 23–23.
Fitzgerald, A. J., & Spencer, D. (2020). Governmentality and environmental rights: Regulatory failure and the Volkswagen emissions fraud case. *Critical Criminology*, *28*, 43–63.
Frynas, J. G. (2005). The false developmental promise of corporate social responsibility: Evidence from multinational oil companies. *International Affairs*, *81*(3), 581–598.
Gahlawat, I. N., & Lakra, P. (2020). Global climate change and its effects. *Integrated Journal of Social Sciences*, *7*(1), 14–23.
Garland, D. (2001). *The culture of control: Crime and social order in contemporary society*. University of Chicago Press.
Gould, K. A., Pellow, D. N., & Schnaiberg, A. (2015). *Treadmill of production: Injustice and unsustainability in the global economy*. Routledge.

Govers, G., Poesen, J., & Goossens, D. (2004). Soil erosion-processes, damages and countermeasures. In *Managing soil quality: Challenges in modern agriculture* (pp. 199–217). CABI Publishing.

Greife, M., Stretesky, P. B., Shelley, T. O., & Pogrebin, M. (2017). Corporate environmental crime and environmental justice. *Criminal Justice Policy Review*, *28*(4), 327–346.

Griggs, G., & Reguero, B. G. (2021). Coastal adaptation to climate change and sea-level rise. *Water*, *13*(16), 2151.

Gunningham, N. (2009). The new collaborative environmental governance: The localization of regulation. *Journal of Law and Society*, *36*(1), 145–166.

Gupta, A. (2020). Shrinking of Aral Sea: An environmental disaster in Central Asia. *International Journal of Humanities, Arts and Social Sciences*, *6*(4), 162.

Haines, T. A. (1981). Acidic precipitation and its consequences for aquatic ecosystems: A review. *Transactions of the American Fisheries Society*, *110*(6), 669–707.

Halsbury's Laws of England. (1977). *Environmental law* (4th ed., Vol. 38). LexisNexis Butterworths.

Harris, C., Schaeffer, S., Shenkman, E., & Kronk Warner, E. (2017). Environmental protection in Indian country: The fundamentals. *Environmental Law Reporter News & Analysis*, *47*, 10905.

Hartley, N., & Wood, C. (2005). Public participation in environmental impact assessment – Implementing the Aarhus Convention. *Environmental Impact Assessment Review*, *25*(4), 319–340.

Hayes, C. J. H. (1941). *A generation of materialism, 1871–1900* (Vol. 17). Harper.

Hinrichsen, D. (2013). *Coastal waters of the world: Trends, threats, and strategies*. Island Press.

Hondros, C. (2007). The fire: The price of oil in the Niger Delta. *The Virginia Quarterly Review*, *83*(1), 28.

Huff, J., Jacobson, M. F., & Davis, D. L. (2008). The limits of two-year bioassay exposure regimens for identifying chemical carcinogens. *Environmental Health Perspectives*, *116*(11), 1439–1442.

Hughes, J. D. (2014). *Environmental problems of the Greeks and Romans: Ecology in the ancient Mediterranean*. JHU Press.

Human Rights Watch. (2024). *We're dying here: The fight for life in a Louisiana fossil fuel sacrifice zone*. Human Rights Watch.

Humphreys, S. L. (1989). An enemy of the people: Prosecuting the corporate polluter as a common law criminal. *American University Law Review*, *39*, 311.

Igwe, P. U., Chukwudi, C. C., Ifenatuorah, F. C., Fagbeja, I. F., & Okeke, C. A. (2017). A review of environmental effects of surface water pollution. *International Journal of Advanced Engineering Research and Science*, *4*(12), 237340.

Inambao, M. S. P. F. (2018). Transportation, pollution and the environment. *International Journal of Applied Engineering Research*, *13*, 3187–3199.

Islam, M. R., & Mostafa, M. G. (2018). Textile dyeing effluents and environment concerns: A review. *Journal of Environmental Science and Natural Resources*, *11*(1–2), 131–144.

Islam, T., Repon, M. R., Islam, T., Sarwar, Z., & Rahman, M. M. (2023). Impact of textile dyes on health and ecosystem: A review of structure, causes, and potential solutions. *Environmental Science and Pollution Research*, *30*(4), 9207–9242.

Ito, M., & Montini, M. (2018). Nature's rights and Earth jurisprudence–A new ecologically based paradigm for environmental law. In *The right to nature* (pp. 221–233). Routledge.

Jacka, J. K. (2018). The anthropology of mining: The social and environmental impacts of resource extraction in the mineral age. *Annual Review of Anthropology*, *47*(1), 61–77.

Jaffee, D. (2023). *Unbottled: The fight against plastic water and for water justice.* University of California Press.
Jion, M. M. M. F., Jannat, J. N., Mia, M. Y., Ali, M. A., Islam, M. S., Ibrahim, S. M., Pal, S. C., Islam, A., Sarker, A., Malafaia, G., & Bilal, M. A. (2023). A critical review and prospect of NO_2 and SO_2 pollution over Asia: Hotspots, trends, and sources. *Science of the Total Environment, 876*, 162851.
Johnson, E. W., Schwartz, J., & Inlow, A. R. (2020). The criminalization of environmental harm: A study of the most serious environmental offenses prosecuted by the U.S. federal government, 1985–2010. *Environmental Sociology, 6*(3), 307–321.
Karkkainen, B. C. (2002). Adaptive ecosystem management and regulatory penalty defaults: Toward a bounded pragmatism. *Minnesota Law Review, 87*, 943.
Katz, R. S. (2012). Environmental pollution: Corporate crime and cancer mortality. *Contemporary Justice Review, 15*(1), 97–125.
Kellenberg, D., & Levinson, A. (2014). Waste of effort? International environmental agreements. *Journal of the Association of Environmental and Resource Economists, 1*(1/2), 135–169.
Kerr, R. A. (2007). Global warming is changing the world. *Science, 316*(5822), 188–190.
Kimmins, J. P. (2004). Forest ecology. In *Fishes and forestry: Worldwide watershed interactions and management* (pp. 17–43). Blackwell Publishing.
Krzyzanowski, M., Apte, J. S., Bonjour, S. P., Brauer, M., Cohen, A. J., & Prüss-Ustun, A. (2014). Air pollution in the mega-cities. *Current Environmental Health Reports, 1*, 185–191.
Kumar, A., Nagar, S., & Anand, S. (2021). Climate change and existential threats. In *Global climate change* (pp. 1–31). Elsevier.
Kumar, P., Kumar, R., Thakur, K., Mahajan, D., Brar, B., Sharma, D., Kumar, S., & Sharma, A. K. (2023). Impact of pesticide application on aquatic ecosystem and biodiversity: A review. *Biology Bulletin, 50*(6), 1362–1375.
Laufer, W. S. (2006). *Corporate bodies and guilty minds: The failure of corporate criminal liability.* University of Chicago Press.
Laughran, H. S. (1972). The law and the corporate polluter: Flexibility and adaptation in the developing law of the environment. *Mercer Law Review, 23*, 571.
LeCain, T. J. (2015). Against the Anthropocene: A neo-materialist perspective. *International Journal for History, Culture and Modernity, 3*(1), 1–28.
Li, R., Fu, H., Cui, L., Li, J., Wu, Y., Meng, Y., Wang, Y., & Chen, J. (2019). The spatiotemporal variation and key factors of SO_2 in 336 cities across China. *Journal of Cleaner Production, 210*, 602–611.
Lin, L., Yang, H., & Xu, X. (2022). Effects of water pollution on human health and disease heterogeneity: A review. *Frontiers in Environmental Science, 10*, 880246.
Loodin, N. (2020). Aral Sea: An environmental disaster in twentieth-century Central Asia. *Modeling Earth Systems and Environment, 6*(4), 2495–2503.
Lynch, L. J., Coleman, A. R., & Cutro, C. (2016). *The Volkswagen emissions scandal.* Darden Business Publishing Cases.
Lynch, M. J., Barrett, K. L., Stretesky, P. B., & Long, M. A. (2016). The weak probability of punishment for environmental offenses and deterrence of environmental offenders: A discussion based on USEPA criminal cases, 1983–2013. *Deviant Behavior, 37*(10), 1095–1109.
Lynch, M. J., Long, M. A., Barrett, K. L., & Stretesky, P. B. (2013). Is it a crime to produce ecological disorganization? Why green criminology and political economy matter in the analysis of global ecological harms. *British Journal of Criminology, 53*(6), 997–1016.
Lyon, T. P., & Maxwell, J. W. (2011). Greenwash: Corporate environmental disclosure under threat of audit. *Journal of Economics & Management Strategy, 20*(1), 3–41.

Mabey, R. (1974). *The pollution handbook*. Penguin Education.
Maciejewska, A. (2008). Occupational exposure assessment to crystalline silica dust: Approach in Poland and worldwide. *International Journal of Occupational Medicine and Environmental Health*, *21*(1), 1.
Madaoui, N. (2023). Evolving jurisprudence of environmental law: A doctrinal analysis. *Analytical and Comparative Jurisprudence*, *6*, 386–396.
Manisalidis, I., Stavropoulou, E., Stavropoulos, A., & Bezirtzoglou, E. (2020). Environmental and health impacts of air pollution: A review. *Frontiers in Public Health*, *8*, 14.
Maume, M. O., & Greife, M. J. (2023). Giving the green light: Corporate environmental crimes, the treadmill of production, and environmental justice. *Crime, Law and Social Change*, *79*(3), 241–261.
Maximillian, J., Brusseau, M. L., Glenn, E. P., & Matthias, A. D. (2019). Pollution and environmental perturbations in the global system. In *Environmental and pollution science* (pp. 457–476). Elsevier.
McDonough, C. (2019). Will the river ever get a chance to speak: Standing up for the legal rights of nature. *Villanova Environmental Law Journal*, *31*, 143.
Meijaard, E., Brooks, T. M., Carlson, K. M., Slade, E. M., Garcia-Ulloa, J., Gaveau, D. L. A., Lee, J. S. H., Santika, T., Juffe-Bignoli, D., Struebig, M. J., Wich, S. A., Ancrenaz, M., Koh, L. P., Zamira, N., Abrams, J. F., Prins, H. H. T., Sendashonga, C. N., Murdiyarso, D., Furumo, P. R., . . . Sheil, D. (2020). The environmental impacts of palm oil in context. *Nature Plants*, *6*(12), 1418–1426.
M'Gonigle, R. M., Jamieson, T. L., McAllister, M. K., & Peterman, R. M. (1994). Taking uncertainty seriously: From permissive regulation to preventative design in environmental decision-making. *Osgoode Hall Law Journal*, *32*, 99.
Mitchell, J. F. B. (1989). The "greenhouse" effect and climate change. *Reviews of Geophysics*, *27*(1), 115–139.
Mittal, A. (2021). Role of judiciary in protecting and preserving the environment. *International Journal of Law Management & Humanities*, *4*(3), 4001.
Mohamed, A.-M. O., Paleologos, E. K., & Howari, F. M. (2021). Noise pollution and its impact on human health and the environment. In *Pollution assessment for sustainable practices in applied sciences and engineering* (pp. 975–1026). Elsevier.
Morris, B. F., & Loughlin, T. R. (2013). Overview of the Exxon Valdez Oil Spill. In T. R. Loughlin (Ed.), *Marine mammals and the Exxon Valdez* (pp. 1–22). Academic Press.
Murphy, E., & King, E. A. (2022). *Environmental noise pollution: Noise mapping, public health, and policy*. Elsevier.
Oelschlaeger, M. (1991). *The idea of wilderness: From prehistory to the age of ecology*. Yale University Press.
O'Handley, M. (2019). *Green criminology and the corporate extraction of water in Canada* [Master's thesis, Saint Mary's University].
Orts, E. W. (2019). Reflexive environmental law. *Environmental Law*, 347–460.
Owen, L. A., Pickering, K. T., & Pickering, K. T. (2006). *An introduction to global environmental issues*. Routledge.
Pain, N., & Pepper, R. (2021). Can personhood protect the environment? Affording legal rights to nature. *Fordham International Law Journal*, *45*, 315–339.
Parker, C., Haines, F., & Boehm, L. (2018). The promise of ecological regulation: The case of intensive meat. *Jurimetrics*, *59*, 15–32.
Penn, D. J. (2003). The evolutionary roots of our environmental problems: Toward a Darwinian ecology. *The Quarterly Review of Biology*, *78*(3), 275–301.
Pirages, D. C., & DeGeest, T. M. (2003). *Ecological security: An evolutionary perspective on globalization*. Rowman & Littlefield Publishers.

Pitt, H. L., & Groskaufmanis, K. A. (1989). Minimizing corporate civil and criminal liability: A second look at corporate codes of conduct. *Georgetown Law Journal*, *78*, 1559.

Rahaman, M. A., Kalam, A., & Md Al-Mamun, M. (2023). Unplanned urbanization and health risks of Dhaka City in Bangladesh: Uncovering the associations between urban environment and public health. *Frontiers in Public Health*, *11*, 1269362.

Ramesh, J. (2015). *Green signals: Ecology, growth, and democracy in India*. Oxford University Press.

Redman, C. L. (1999). *Human impact on ancient environments*. University of Arizona Press.

Riazi, M. R. (2021). Environmental, economic, and political impacts: Case of Bp oil spill. In *Oil spill occurrence, simulation, and behavior* (pp. 135–162). CRC Press.

Rodenhoff, V. (2002). The Aarhus Convention and its implications for the institutions of the European Community. *Review of European, Comparative & International Environmental Law*, *11*, 343–358.

Rudenko, I., & Lamers, J. P. A. (2010). The Aral Sea: An ecological disaster. In *The handbook of environmental chemistry: Water resources in the former Soviet Union*. Springer.

Satria, H. (2018). Environmental pollution: Assessing the criminal liability of corporations. *Hasanuddin Law Review*, *4*(2), 194–203.

Schwartz, M. S. (2020). Beyond petroleum or bottom line profits only? An ethical analysis of Bp and the Gulf Oil Spill. *Business and Society Review*, *125*(1), 71–88.

Sejian, V., Bhatta, R., Malik, P. K., Madiajagan, B., Saif Al-Hosni, Y. A., Sullivan, M., & Gaughan, J. B. (2016). Livestock as sources of greenhouse gases and its significance to climate change. *Greenhouse Gases*, *11*, 243–259.

Shivanna, K. R. (2022). Climate change and its impact on biodiversity and human welfare. *Proceedings of the Indian National Science Academy*, *88*(2), 160–171.

Simon, D. R. (2017). Corporate environmental crimes and social inequality: New directions for environmental justice research. In *Green criminology* (pp. 171–184). Routledge.

Singh, R. L., & Singh, P. K. (2017). Global environmental problems. In *Principles and applications of environmental biotechnology for a sustainable future* (pp. 13–41). Springer.

Singh, V. K. (2010). Criminal liability of corporations – An environmental perspective. In *Environmental crimes: Corporate liability* (Chapter 3). ISBN 978–81-314-2521-3. https://ssrn.com/abstract=2972053

Sivalingam, S., Harish, A., & Selva, M. R. (2024). Environmental and health effects of global warming. In *Health and environmental effects of ambient air pollution* (pp. 109–129). Elsevier.

Sood, S. (2023). Environmental jurisprudence vis-à-vis the principle of sustainable development. *Part 2 Indian Journal of Integrated Research in Law*, *3*, 1.

Spence, D. B. (2001). The shadow of the rational polluter: Rethinking the role of rational actor models in environmental law. *California Law Review*, *89*, 917–944.

Stiglitz, J. E. (2007). Regulating multinational corporations: Towards principles of cross-border legal framework in a globalized world balancing rights with responsibilities. *American University International Law Review*, *23*, 451–488.

Stone, C. D. (2017). Should trees have standing? – Toward legal rights for natural objects. In *Environmental rights* (pp. 283–334). Routledge.

Sutherlin, L. (2024, April 9). *Procter & Gamble, Mondelēz, and Nestlé are among 10 of the leading consumer brands driving global deforestation*. CounterPunch.

Teng, S., Khong, K. W., & Ha, N. C. (2020). Palm oil and its environmental impacts: A big data analytics study. *Journal of Cleaner Production*, *274*, 122901.

Thorsberg, C. (2024, April 9). 80 percent of global CO_2 emissions come from just 57 companies, report shows. *Smithsonian Magazine.* www.smithsonianmag.com/smart-news/since-2016-80-percent-of-global-co2-emissions-come-from-just-57-companies-report-shows-180984118/

Tudi, M., Ruan, H. D., Wang, L., Lyu, J., Sadler, R., Connell, D., Chu, C., & Phung, D. T. (2021). Agriculture development, pesticide application and its impact on the environment. *International Journal of Environmental Research and Public Health, 18*(3), 1112. MDPI. https://doi.org/10.3390/ijerph18031112

Van Wyk, P., & Scarpa, J. (1999). Water quality requirements and management. In *Farming marine shrimp in recirculating freshwater systems* (pp. 141–161). Florida Department of Agriculture and Consumer Services.

Vasistha, V. (2014). Effects of pollutants produced by thermal power plant on environment: A review. *International Journal of Mechanical Engineering and Robotics Research, 3*(2), 202.

Venkateswarlu, C. (2013). Role of the judiciary in environment protection in India. *Asian Journal of Research in Social Sciences and Humanities, 3*(10), 260–274.

Vu, S. N. (2004). Corporate criminal liability: Patchwork verdicts and the problem of locating a guilty agent. *Columbia Law Review, 104*, 459.

Wagner, W. E. (2003). Commons ignorance: The failure of environmental law to produce needed information on health and the environment. *Duke Law Journal, 53*, 1619.

Walsh, H., & Dowding, T. J. (2012). Sustainability and the Coca-Cola Company: The global water crisis and Coca-Cola's business case for water stewardship. *International Journal of Business Insights & Transformation, 4.*

White, K. D. (2014). Nature and economy in the Aral Sea basin. In *The Aral Sea: The devastation and partial rehabilitation of a Great Lake* (pp. 301–335). Springer.

World Health Organization. (2014). "7 million premature deaths annually linked to air pollution." *Geneva.* www.who.int/news/item/25-03-2014-7-million-premature-deaths-annually-linked-to-air-pollution

Xu, H., Gao, Q., & Yuan, B. (2022). Analysis and identification of pollution sources of comprehensive river water quality: Evidence from two river basins in China. *Ecological Indicators, 135*, 108561. https://doi.org/10.1016/j.ecolind.2021.108561

Yadav, A. K., & Jamal, A. (2018). Suspended particulate matter and its management system surrounding opencast coal mines. *Environmental Quality Management, 28*(2), 123–128. https://doi.org/10.1002/tqem.21585

Zhang, K., Douglas, B. C., & Leatherman, S. P. (2004). Global warming and coastal erosion. *Climatic Change, 64*, 41–58. https://doi.org/10.1023/B:CLIM.0000024690.32682.48

Zhao, J. (2017). Promoting more socially responsible corporations through a corporate law regulatory framework. *Legal Studies, 37*(1), 103–136. https://doi.org/10.1111/lest.12145

2 Criminal Liability in Environmental Jurisprudence

2.1 Introduction

Environmental jurisprudence is a legal system that helps develop eco-centric principles for natural resource governance. It focuses on environmental rights and how they can be integrated into legal and political systems. Since there is no universal definition of environmental jurisprudence, we will assess its fundamental principles in this chapter. We will also explore how other perspectives, such as deep ecology, Marxism, and the notion of the Anthropocene, intersect with this legal system. This will help us understand how liberal approaches can be used to govern environmental concerns.

This chapter further explores the idea of 'criminal liability' as well as how it is understood as a part of environmental law. Within the broad scope of the law, the consideration of criminal liability is important because the implications of being guilty of committing a crime are more damaging than being liable for civil obligations. Criminal liability is very difficult to prove, and the remedy available is a sentence that may result in some form of physical retaliation or other forms of punishment. Understanding criminal liability in relation to environmental damage is far more complex, though, than understanding liability for the infliction of harm on a person. An individual can claim a legal right for something done against them, which, in many countries, laws dealing with crimes against a natural person are, in most cases, well formulated. This does not happen to Laws that deal with the environment. The personhood of the environment, the nature of environmental property, and the rights and issues related to them are still debated in the context of environmental governance. Thus, then, the calculation of liability and how to address it remain one of the key issues in environmental law, which is, in fact, criminal liability.

Environmental laws outline the duties and liabilities required to safeguard the environment and provide guidance on how to take legal action against environmental damages and pollution. These legal requirements may change as governments' goals and capabilities evolve. However, recognizing the environment or a portion of it as a legal entity may deter the government from using environmental issues for political purposes. Like business corporations, the environment, as a legal entity, can be accorded a more active role

DOI: 10.4324/9781003279006-2

in restoring its rights through its representatives. Nevertheless, this concept and its implementation are still developing. Some countries, such as Ecuador, Bolivia, and India, have taken bold steps to establish environmental personhood, bringing this subject to the forefront of environmental jurisprudence. This chapter also focuses on this development in environmental jurisprudence.

This chapter starts by introducing the concept of criminal liability and the elements required to establish it. It explores the development of this liability scholarship. It then examines how this concept has been integrated into environmental jurisprudence. Finally, it provides an account of environmental jurisprudence.

2.2 The Concept of Legal Liability

Legal liability refers to the legal responsibility or obligation that a party has for their action or inaction. It can be civil or criminal in nature. In civil cases, a defendant may be held liable for damages or other remedies, while in criminal cases, liability can result in criminal charges and penalties. The concept of legal liability means that individuals or entities may be held legally accountable for the consequences of their actions.[1]

Legal liabilities for causing harm or damages can be categorized into four principal types: primary liability, secondary liability, vicarious liability, and enterprise liability. Primary liability pertains to the direct responsibility or fault of a party in causing harm or damage. It constitutes the initial and foremost accountability for the repercussions of one's actions or omissions. Within the realm of tort law, primary liability emerges when an individual or entity engages in intentional misconduct or neglects to exercise a reasonable standard of care, thereby resulting in harm to another party. This encompasses actions such as intentionally striking another individual or failing to exhibit the level of care expected of a reasonable person. Determining primary liability is contingent upon the specific circumstances and applicable laws.

According to English law, a parent company may be held liable for any harm caused if it breaches its duty of care toward those affected by the actions of its foreign affiliate. However, establishing this duty of care can pose challenges, particularly due to the complicated role of the foreign affiliate in the

1 There are different types of civil remedies that can be pursued in legal cases. One type is monetary compensation, where the defendant pays a specific amount of money to the plaintiff to compensate for injury or damage. This can include expenses such as medical bills or estimated pain and inconvenience. Another type of civil remedy is an injunction, which is a court order that either requires or prevents a certain action. Injunctions can effectively prevent future damage to the plaintiff's reputation, but they do not compensate for any loss already suffered. Equitable remedies, such as specific performance, injunction, and restitution, may also be available in certain cases. The ultimate goal of civil remedies is to restore the injured party to their original position. For more about the meaning of legal liability, see the Legal Information Institute of the Cornell Law School (www.law.cornell.edu/wex/liability).

events that precede the claim. The plaintiff may present arguments in two distinct manners: first, by asserting that the parent company is responsible for the hazardous activities conducted by its subsidiaries, and second, by emphasizing the parent company's overarching obligation to maintain effective control over its subsidiaries. The imposition of liability on the parent company is possible when the likelihood of harm is foreseeable and when the plaintiff is in close proximity to the parent company.[2] In order to effectively hold a parent company liable for damages incurred due to actions taken by its foreign affiliates, the plaintiffs must establish, at a minimum, the following elements: (a) the parent company possessed full knowledge of the health and environmental risks associated with the activities, processes, or technologies employed by its foreign affiliates; (b) the parent company was significantly engaged in the routine operations of the foreign affiliates; (c) the parent company failed to exercise reasonable diligence in light of the circumstances; and (d) the failures of the parent company were a direct cause of the injury or damage, irrespective of whether they were the sole cause.[3] The question of whether a parent company can be deemed accountable for the actions of its affiliates as the primary wrongdoer represents a substantial policy concern. Will an increase in foreign direct liability claims against multinational parent companies compel them to assume greater responsibility for their foreign subsidiaries' corporate social responsibility standards, as articulated in their corporate social responsibility (CSR) reports? Alternatively, will they determine that a 'hands-off' approach is the most effective means of mitigating legal risks? Following the Bhopal gas tragedy, it was suggested that parent companies could diminish their legal obligations by granting as much autonomy as possible to their foreign affiliates concerning operational matters.[4]

Secondary liability refers to the legal responsibility or fault of a party for harm or damage caused by the actions of another party. Unlike primary liability, secondary liability arises when the party held accountable did not directly cause harm or damage, but they are held responsible due to their relationship or association with the primary wrongdoer. This can include situations where a person or entity aids, encourages, or enables the primary wrongdoer's actions, or fails to prevent them despite having the ability to do so. Secondary liability is often determined based on the principles of vicarious liability, contributory negligence, or aiding and abetting, depending on the jurisdiction and applicable laws.

Vicarious liability refers to the legal responsibility or fault of one party for the unlawful or reckless actions of a third party. It allows individuals who have

2 Zerk, J. A. (2006). *Multinationals and corporate social responsibility: Limitations and opportunities in international law* (Vol. 48, pp. 217–226). Cambridge University Press.

3 Ibid., p. 222.

4 Seward III, A. C. (1987). After Bhopal: Implications for parent company liability. *International Lawyer*, *21*, 706.

been harmed to pursue a claim against those who were in control of the person who caused the harm. Vicarious liability is generally classified as a tort, defined as an act or omission that leads to the harm or injury of another individual. In simpler terms, it means that someone can be held accountable for the actions of another person if they have control or authority over that person.

Vicarious liability is a common issue for companies, often arising from their employers' roles. There are valid reasons why companies should be held accountable for the actions of their employees while they are on the job. One such reason is that the employer has control over how their employees perform their work and, therefore, should be responsible for any negative consequences arising from their employees' negligence. Another reason is that the employee acts within the scope of their employer's business, creating a causal relationship between the employer and any harm caused by the employee while on the job. Additionally, the 'deep pocket'[5] argument suggests that the employer should bear the financial responsibility for any harm caused by their employee. While some argue for a more flexible approach to vicarious liability, English courts limit its application to narrowly defined agency situations. In contrast, United States courts have recognized the principle that parent corporations may bear liability for the actions of their foreign subsidiaries, a notion that is supported by several cases adjudicated under the Alien Tort Claims Act.[6]

Enterprise liability is the legal doctrine that holds separate businesses liable for shared practices or actions that cause harm or damage. In the case where a plaintiff suffers damages as a result of an industry's common practice, all the firms within that industry may be held liable at once under the doctrine of enterprise liability. This doctrine, along with others, lies under tort law which concerns civil suits arising from acts that cause injuries to others. The reason behind enterprise liability is that an enterprise should assume the risks and costs of harm or damage that may result from their policies or practices.

Courts generally do not ignore the legal distinction between a parent company and its subsidiary. This is typically done in situations involving fraudulent activity, where the corporate structure has been abused by its owners to evade liability or to undermine the legal rights of a third party.[7]

5 A 'deep pocket' argument refers to a legal strategy where a plaintiff sues a defendant not necessarily because they believe the defendant is solely responsible for the harm, but rather because the defendant has significant financial resources. The purpose of this strategy is to target the defendant's deep pockets in hopes of securing a larger financial settlement or judgment. The argument suggests that the defendant should be held accountable based on their ability to pay rather than solely on their level of fault. This tactic is commonly employed in cases involving personal injury, product liability, or medical malpractice, where the plaintiff's attorney seeks to maximize compensation for their client.

6 Zerk, J. A. (2006). *Multinationals and corporate social responsibility: Limitations and opportunities in international law* (Vol. 48, p. 226). Cambridge University Press.

7 *Jones v Lipman* [1962] 1 AII ER 442; *Gilford Motor Co v Horne* [1933] Ch 935.

In rare cases, a court may disregard the legal distinction between a parent company and its subsidiary, typically in fraud cases.[8] Although a subsidiary may be liable for negligence, it may not have enough funds to provide full compensation, especially in mass disasters, leaving the victims under-compensated and the parent company largely immune from legal action.[9] In exceptional circumstances, courts have been persuaded to disregard the legal separation between a parent company and its subsidiary. This is commonly seen in cases of fraudulent activity, where the corporate structure has been misused by its proprietors to avoid responsibility or to infringe upon the legal rights of a third party.

2.3 Criminal Liability

In primitive societies, there was no concept of criminal liability. As society evolved, certain actions that were harmful to both the preservation of society and individuals began to be considered unacceptable. Society then prescribed certain behavior patterns for its members, and deviation from these standards was deemed 'wrong.' However, at that time, society did not provide a means of redress for the wrongs committed, leaving it up to individuals to act to rectify the situation. This led to the development of the concepts of 'blood feud' and *deodand*.

The notion of *deodand* was based on the Roman law rules of *naxal surrender*. As stated by Holdsworth, 'the owner of a thing through which harm has been done is guilty unless he will surrender.'[10] In English law, it signified 'the idea that guilt attaches to the thing by which wrong has been done.'[11]

> [A]n object termed *deodand* had to be handed over to the king to be dealt with under his directions for the appearing of god's wrath. Here, there is a combination of at least three forces: a fear of angry divinity, a primitive physical reaction to pain, and somewhat more advanced but childishly ignorant attribution even to an inanimate object, both of life and of a conscious intention to hurt.[12]

8 *Adams v Cape Industries* [1990] Ch 433, 544; Hansmann, H., & Kraakman, R. (1990). Toward unlimited shareholder liability for corporate torts. *Yale Law Journal, 100*, 1879; Fettet, B. (1995). Limited liability – a principle for the 21st century? *Current Legal Problems, 48*(Part 2), 125–159; Halpern, P., Trebilcock, M., & Turnbull, S. (1980). An economic analysis of limited liability in corporation law. *University of Toronto Law Journal, 30*, 117; Baxi, U. (1999). *Mass torts, multinational enterprise liability and private international law*. Hague Academy of International Law.

9 Baxi, U. (1999). *Mass torts, multinational enterprise liability and private international law*. Hague Academy of International Law.

10 Holdsworth, W. (1936/1966). *History of English law* (Vol. II, 4th ed., p. 52). Sweet & Maxwell.

11 Ibid., p. 46.

12 Turner, J. W. C. (1964). *Russell on crime* (Vol. 1, 4th ed., p. 18). Stevens & Sons.

Deodand, thus, assumed the character of compensation as the money received from it being sold was distributed by the king to the poor relatives of the deceased.[13] In the Anglo-Saxon period, it was called 'barne' – the slayer – handed over to the family of the man killed so that they might seek vengeance upon it.[14] As stated earlier, the other concept prevalent in those times was a blood feud. It was a private redressal for wrongs committed, and the injured person or his kinsmen were given the right to inflict the same wrong on the offender. Holdsworth stated that the idea of the blood feud existed in the Anglo-Saxon codes in several forms.[15] '[T]he law of Alfred represents the condition under which the feud may be prosecuted. One of the laws of Edmund regulates how the Witan shall appease the feud. The law of Cnut shows that the feud was still prosecuted.'[16] In time, society realized the barbarity ingrained in the blood feud concept and specified the occasions when it could be resorted to. The latter part of the Anglo-Saxon period witnessed the prohibition of self-defense as a plea for the feud. Penalties were imposed on persons if they engaged in blood feuds without seeking justice.[17] To replace the feud, therefore, payment of monetary compensation emerged. It took three forms, namely *bot*, *wer*, and *wite.*

The *bot* was a monetary compensation given to the injured person. *Wer* was a payment made to the relatives or kin of the slain, the amount of which varied according to the victim's rank and status. It should be emphasized that the dispute will be pursued if the injured individual declines to accept the compensation (*bot*) or if the relatives of the deceased opt not to accept the *wer* for their deceased relative.[18]

On the other hand, *wite* was a sort of tariff to be paid to the king for the infringement of the king's peace. This *wite* was a good source of revenue for the royals. In the legal texts, we discern the nascent idea that wrongdoing is not merely the concern of the aggrieved party – this concept precedes the evolution of criminal law. A wrongdoing was perceived as a violation of the *grith*, *faith*, or *mund* of the king, a community, and an individual tasked with maintaining order. This payment of monetary compensation to the victim or his family bore evidence that it was a period of strict or absolute liability, wherein much concern was shown for the injured but not for the accused, and the circumstances which led to the commission of the crime. This element is *sine qua non* for criminal liability in modern times. In exceptional cases, however,

13 Turner, J. W. C. (1966). *Kenny's outlines of criminal law* (9th ed., p. 8). Cambridge University Press.
14 Ibid., p. 7.
15 Holdsworth, W. (1966). *History of English law* (Vol. II, 4th ed., pp. 43–44). Sweet & Maxwell. (Original work published 1936).
16 Ibid.
17 Ibid., pp. 44–45.
18 Ibid., p. 74.

wite was insufficient to preserve the king's peace; on the contrary, corporal punishment was awarded for felony offenses against property or neglect of the royal duty and libel against the king. These sorts of offenses *were* known as *botless* offenses.

Significant developments occurred in the centuries following the Norman Conquest. First, during this period, *wite* evolved from being a fixed payment to a system of discretionary fines. After the 13th century, serious offenses classified as felonies were no longer allowed to be redressed through compensation, but through severe punishments. This century

> [h]owever saw the beginnings of the modern distinction between crime and tort; the old compensatory payments (*wer* and *bot*) disappeared and were replaced by damages where an individual's claim was heard. In such cases, there came to be recognition of the need for some test whereby a reasonable limit could be set to a man's legal responsibility for the ever-extending claim of consequence which could be traced to any act he committed. On the criminal side also, there was a need for some limitations of the rule of strict liability to suffer the extreme penalty for harm resulting from misadventure, as from a remote act by the person accused.[19]

Kenny states that the development of criminal liability could be associated with three outstanding features. First, an individual was deemed strictly accountable for any detrimental outcomes that could be directly attributed to his actions or conduct; second, the consequential principle, that a man was not liable when he had done nothing active, even though his omission to act may have been the cause of the harm; and third, the great severity of the penal system when the sanction of compensatory payment was replaced by afflictive punishment.[20]

2.3.1 Mental Element in Criminal Liability

The period following the Norman Conquest laid emphasis on the ethical element of wrongdoing. It was felt that the intent with which an act was committed was significant for the imposition of liability. As observed by St. Augustine, *ream linguam non facit nisi mens rea*.[21] It was a phrase destined to gain widespread acceptance and become the most recognized maxim in English criminal law. In words ultimately used by Coke to express it, *et actus non facit reum nisi men sit rea*. It signified the clear distinction between the active conduct

19 Turner, J. W. C. (1964). *Russel on crime* (Vol. 1, 4th ed., p. 20). Steven & Sons.
20 Ibid., p. 10.
21 Ibid., p. 13.

of an individual (*actus*) and his mental process (*mens*). Thus, in the later part of the development of Criminal law, mental blameworthiness, foresight, and circumstances became important for the imposition of criminal liability. At the same time, it should be noted that only culpability of mind was not sufficient for imposition of liability; it was essential that some wrongful act should accompany the culpable mind. In short, the *actus* of a person is *prima facie* evidence of *mens rea*. The maxim, *actus non facit reum nisi mens sit rea*, became the canon for the imposition of criminal liability. The problem, however, arose when criminal law sought to impose liability upon corporations[22] because a corporation has a mere fictitious personality, with no mind or body of its own. Initially, in the later part of the 16th and 17th centuries, the court denied imposing any liability on corporations, though gradually, a change was witnessed.

'Traditional Criminal Liability' hereby means imposition of liability on the basis of the maxim *actus non facit reum nisi mens sit rea*. The Latin maxim loosely translates to 'an act does not make a person guilty of a crime unless their mind is also guilty.' The legal definition of *mens rea* refers to the mental state or guilty mind of a defendant who is accused of committing a crime. It is a Latin term that translates to 'guilty mind.' In criminal law, both *mens rea* and *actus reus* (the guilty act) must be proven in order to establish criminal liability. *Mens rea* pertains to the defendant's mental state at the time the offense was perpetrated. It encompasses a range of mental states, including intention, knowledge, recklessness, and criminal negligence. The specific degree of *mens rea* mandated for a given offense may differ based on the jurisdiction and the nature of the crime. *Actus reus* is a legal term that denotes the physical actions or conduct of a defendant that are deemed criminal in nature. It is a crucial element in establishing criminal liability and means 'guilty act' in Latin. The term encompasses voluntary bodily movement that harms another person or damages property. It can also include the omission or failure to act, which is considered an act of criminal negligence. However, there are exceptions to actus reus, such as involuntary actions performed during a spasm or while asleep or unconscious.

As both *mens rea* and *actus reus* are vital in establishing criminal liability, until recently, the judicial systems held that since corporations are artificial legal entities, they lack the necessary *mens rea* (intent) to be convicted of a crime.[23] Nonetheless, the common law judicial system began holding corporations accountable for their involvement in criminal activities in the 20th century. It applied the principle of sweeping expansion to extend criminal

22 Legal person, Fictitious person, Company, etc.

23 Singh, V. K. (2010). Criminal liability of corporations – An environmental perspective. In *Environmental crimes: Corporate liability* (Chapter 3). ISBN 978–81-314-2521-3. SSRN: https://ssrn.com/abstract=2972053.

liability to corporate bodies, basing the idea of corporate criminal liability on the theory of ***respondeat superior***.[24] According to this legal principle, corporations are responsible for the wrongful actions of their agents and must pay for any damages caused to affected parties.

2.3.2 Emergence of Strict Criminal Liability

Strict liability reigns over a type of legal responsibility; in this case, an individual or corporation is held liable for their actions or products, with no regard to fault or intent. Simply put, a party is held responsible for damages even when there was no negligence on their part. The defendant shall be answerable for the result of their acts or products whether or not they took precautions or safety measures.

The application of strict liability principles is common in mitigating disputes with defective products. If a product is found to be defective and a consumer gets hurt, then the manufacturer or seller can be held strictly liable for all injuries that are caused if the product is sold, no matter what care was taken in its design or production. Maintaining a strict liability policy is also pertinent for blasting or storing dangerous materials or keeping wild animals. If damage results from these activities, a person or entity engaging in these activities can be subject to strict liability for all damages that are likely to result. The burden of proof with regard to strict liability is generally less demanding than in negligence claims. The plaintiff should mainly prove that some harm has occurred and that some action or product of the defendant was responsible for it. Responsibility as such is enormous, especially in liability cases. Some defenses are granted to the defendants, for example, misuse of a product in a way that cannot be anticipated or having a warning concerning this product or activity.

Strict Liability Offenses are criminal acts, and therefore, these offenses are prohibited and punishable by law, regardless of the person's mental intent when committing the act. This means a person can be held responsible for the offense, even if they did not intend to commit it. The concept has evolved to address situations where an act may be committed without the actor having the intention or knowledge (***mens rea***) to commit it. It contributes to legal certainty by establishing clear parameters for criminal

24 *Respondeat superior* is a legal doctrine that holds employers or principals accountable for the actions of their employees or agents. This principle is relevant in tort cases, making employers or principals liable for any wrongful acts committed by their employees or agents while acting within the scope of their employment. It is acknowledged in both common law and civil law jurisdictions. The doctrine has its origins in ancient Rome and has been expanded to include not only human agents but also animals and family members in some cases. For details, visit Merriam-Webster. (2023, October 11). *Respondeat superior*. www.merriam-webster.com/legal/respondeat%20superior.

liability, particularly in cases where intent or fault may be difficult to prove. Applying strict liability in certain criminal offenses, especially those related to public safety and regulatory compliance, emphasizes preventing harm and maintaining societal standards. This principle encourages individuals and corporations to prioritize adherence to regulations, thereby contributing to the overall welfare of the community. Applying strict liability can introduce complexity and nuances in criminal jurisprudence, especially when determining the scope of liability in evolving regulatory environments or in cases with mitigating circumstances. Courts are, therefore, required to carefully interpret statutes to determine the extent of liability and balance the need for public protection with the rights of individuals or entities facing strict liability charges.

2.4 Corporate Criminal Liability

2.4.1 Defining a Corporation/Company

A corporation is a group of individuals who come together to advance their shared interests and have a designated entity to act on their behalf.[25] According to Gray, a corporation is an 'organic body of men' to which the state entrusts the power to safeguard its interests. This power is set in motion by the will of specific individuals, determined according to the corporation's structure.[26] Salmond explains that a corporation is a legal construct that treats a group of people as a single entity.[27]

The notion of a corporation possessing a juristic personality was initially acknowledged by Roman law. Sir Henry Maine posited that a semblance of corporate responsibility constituted the fundamental aspect of the primitive legal system. Nevertheless, English common law did not embrace the doctrine until the 15th century. Before this, the law acknowledged institutions such as chapters, monasteries, boroughs, municipalities, guilds, and universities, which possessed a type of juristic personality. These institutions were established

25 Nigam, R. C. (1964). *Law of crimes in India* (Vol. 1, pp. 220–221). Asian Publishing House.

26 Ibid.

27 John Salmond, a legal scholar, contributed significantly to the field of jurisprudence. He believed that law is a social phenomenon and should be studied as such. Law is a body of rules created by the state to maintain social order and regulate human conduct. Salmond emphasized the importance of understanding the social and historical context of laws. He explored the relationship between law and morality, stating that while closely related, they are not the same thing. Salmond's ideas continue to be studied and debated by legal scholars today. For more about Salmond's ideas on jurisprudence, see Fitzgerald, P. J. (1992). *Salmond on jurisprudence*. Sweet & Maxwell.

either by Royal Charter[28] or through a prescription receipt.[29] In the 15th century, common law ultimately recognized that a corporation possesses a distinct juristic personality, separate from that of its members.[30] This differentiation implies that a corporation can enter into contracts, own property, initiate or defend legal actions, and engage in legal activities independently. The concept of the 'corporate veil'[31] protects the personal assets of owners or shareholders from being held responsible for the company's debts or legal obligations, which can be lifted in cases of fraud or misconduct. A separate legal entity offers limited liability for shareholders, perpetual succession, and the ability to raise capital by issuing shares.

Recognizing corporate personality led to legal accountability for corporations, but imposing penal sanctions raised difficulties. The issue of corporate criminal liability has been a topic of debate for many years. Some critics argue that it goes against the basic principles of criminal law and weakens the criminal justice system. One of the primary arguments against corporate criminal liability is that corporations are not individuals and, therefore, cannot have intent, which is a crucial element of criminal liability. Critics also claim that prosecuting corporations for criminal activity may lead to cover-ups of illegal practices and harm innocent parties. Another criticism is that it may harm businesses and result in overcriminalization. Finally, some argue that it is better to prosecute the individuals responsible for illegal actions within an organization, but this may not be possible in larger organizations.[32]

28 Royal charters are formal grants created by a monarch under royal prerogative and are usually in the form of letters patent. These charters have been used since the 13th century to establish and incorporate various bodies and organizations. The process of creating a royal charter involves the privy council, which grants the charter and is not required to put it before parliament. The charter acts as a governance document, providing regulation and forming a new corporate body. Some well-known organizations established by royal charter include the BBC, the Bank of England, the British Red Cross, and the British Council.

29 Gower. (1992). *Principles of modern company law* (p. 232). Sweet & Maxwell.

30 Ibid.

31 The 'corporate veil' is a legal concept that distinguishes a company from its owners or shareholders. This concept helps to encourage investment, entrepreneurship, and risk-taking while shielding shareholders from liability. It is important to note, however, that this concept is not absolute. In certain exceptional circumstances, the courts may 'pierce the corporate veil' and hold shareholders personally responsible for the company's actions. This typically occurs when there is evidence of fraud, improper conduct, or an abuse of the corporate structure to avoid legal obligations.

32 Khanna, V. S. (1996). Corporate criminal liability: What purpose does it serve? *Harvard Law Review*, *109*(7), 1477, 1479–1480. For more about these critiques, see "Corporate Criminal Responsibility – Critique of Corporate Criminal Liability" on JRank Law. (2023, October 13). https://law.jrank.org/pages/745/Corporate-Criminal-Responsibility-Critique-corporate-criminal-liability.html.

2.4.2 Criminal Liability of a Corporation

Corporate criminal liability raises concerns about treating corporations as entities under criminal law.[33] Whether a corporation can have the moral culpability required by criminal law is debatable.[34] Moreover, some people question the purpose of imposing criminal liability on corporations when civil penalties can be imposed instead. As such, it is worth considering whether corporate criminal responsibility is advantageous over holding individual corporate officers criminally liable.

Over time, several theories have been proposed to ensure the liability of corporations. While an individual's mental state when committing a crime determines their moral responsibility, it cannot be applied to a corporation, a legal entity without a mind or soul of its own. Three primary theories justify corporations' liability for criminal acts.[35] The first theory explains the imposition of criminal liability under the doctrine of agency and vicarious liability. Gower has opined that the circumstances which bind the natural person to

33 There are numerous literatures on corporate criminal liability. Some of them are as follows. Orland, L. (1980). Reflections on corporate crime: Law in search of theory and scholarship. *American Criminal Law Review, 17*, 501; Stone, C. (1980). The place of enterprise liability in the control of corporate conduct. *Yale Law Journal, 90*, 1; Coffee Jr., J. C. (1981). No soul to damn: No body to kick: An unscandalized inquiry into the problem of corporate punishment. *Michigan Law Review, 79*, 386; Fisse, B. (1983). Reconstructing corporate criminal law: Deterrence, retribution, fault, and sanctions. *Southern California Law Review, 56*, 1141; Stessens, G. (1994). Corporate criminal liability: A comparative perspective. *International and Comparative Law Quarterly*, 493–520; Goodpaster, K. (1983). The concept of corporate responsibility. *Journal of Business Ethics, 2*, 1; Byam, J. T. (1982). The economic inefficiency of corporate criminal liability. *Journal of Criminal Law & Criminology, 73*, 582; Leigh, L. H. (1982). The criminal liability of corporations and other groups: A comparative view. *Michigan Law Review, 80*, 1508; Arlen, J. (1994). The potentially perverse effects of corporate criminal liability. *Journal of Legal Studies, 23*, 833; Simpson, S. (2002). *Corporate crime, law, and social control.* Cambridge University Press; Beale, S. S., & Safwat, A. G. (2005). What developments in Western Europe tell us about American critiques of corporate criminal liability. *Buffalo Criminal Law Review, 8*, 89; Gauropa, N. (2000). Corporate criminal law and organizational incentives: A managerial perspective. *Managerial and Decision Economics, 21*, 243; Weissmann, A. (2007). A new approach to corporate criminal liability. *American Criminal Law Review, 44*, 1319; International Congress of Comparative Law. (2010). *General report on corporate criminal liability.*

34 Some of the works that argue for this liability include French, P. (1984). *Collective and corporate responsibility.* Columbia University Press; Braithwaite, B. F., & Braithwaite, J. (1993). *Corporations, crime, and accountability.* Cambridge University Press; Pettit, P. (2007). Responsibility incorporated. *Ethics, 117*, 171; Rich, S. (2016). Corporate criminals and punishment theory. *Canadian Journal of Law & Jurisprudence, 29*, 97; Thomas, W. R. (2019). Making sense of corporate criminals: A tentative taxonomy. *Georgetown Journal of Law and Public Policy, 17*, 775. For critiques against corporate criminal liability, see, for example, Khanna, V. S. (1996). Corporate criminal liability: What purpose does it serve? *Harvard Law Review, 109*(7), 1477; Fischel, D. R., & Sykes, A. O. (1996). Corporate crime. *Journal of Legal Studies, 25*, 319; Alschuler, A. W. (2009). Two ways to think about the punishment of corporations. *American Criminal Law Review, 46*(4), 1359.

35 Kadish, S. H. (1979). Developments in the law: Corporate crime: Regulating corporate behaviour through criminal sanctions. *Harvard Law Review, 92*(6), 1227–1375, 1241. https://doi.org/10.2307/1340445

the acts of his agents would also bind the corporation.[36] This theory advocates that the principal is responsible (*respondeat superior*)[37] for the acts of his agents. Also, a corporation is liable when an agent commits a crime for the corporation's benefit.[38] On the doctrine of *respondeat superior*, a corporation is vicariously liable for the criminal acts of its employees. Even in instances where subordinate employees engage in unlawful activities without the awareness of senior management and in violation of explicit corporate policies or directives, the corporation remains liable. This liability is established for the actions of an employee (a) who has perpetrated a crime, (b) while operating within the bounds of his authority, and (c) to benefit the corporation.

The second theory suggests that a corporation can be identified with its policymaking officials. Hence, they can be held morally responsible for their acts and intent.[39] Viscount Haldane has described this theory as the organic theory. In the well-known case of *Lannards Carrying Company Ltd v. Asiatic Petroleum Company Ltd.*,[40] it has been contended:

> [A] company is an abstraction. It has no mind of its own any more than it has a body of its own; its directing will consequently be sought in the person of somebody who for some purposes may be called an agent, but who is the directing mind and will of the corporation, the very ego and center of the personality of the corporation . . . the board of directors is the brain of the corporation, which is the body and the company can do acts only through them.[41]

36 Ibid.

37 Himmelhoch, S. D. (1992). Environmental crimes: Recent efforts to develop a role for traditional criminal law in the environmental protection effort. *Environmental Law*, *22*, 1469, 1482.

38 Glanville, W. (1978). *Textbook of criminal law*. Steven & Sons.

39 Kadish, S. H. (1979). Developments in the law: Corporate crime: Regulating corporate behavior through criminal sanctions. *Harvard Law Review*, *92*(6), 1227–1375. https://doi.org/10.2307/1340445

40 In 1915, a case was heard in the House of Lords that established a crucial principle regarding the responsibilities of a company and its directors. The case involved *Lannards Carrying Company Ltd*, a shipping company, and *Asiatic Petroleum Company Ltd*, an oil company, which had entered into a contract for the transportation of oil. Unfortunately, a fire broke out during transportation, causing significant damage. Lannards went to court and argued that Asiatic Petroleum is liable for the damages as the damage was caused due to this company's agent's negligence. However, the House of Lords ruled in favor of Asiatic Petroleum, stating that a company cannot be held liable for the actions of its agents unless it can be proven that the agents were acting within the scope of their authority. The court determined that the contract was not within the ordinary course of the company's business, and the actions leading to the fire were unauthorized by the directors. This case has had significant implications for corporate liability in the UK, and the decision given in this case has been cited in many subsequent cases. This case decision emphasizes the importance of companies having robust systems to ensure that their agents act within the boundaries of their authority and that the company itself is not responsible for unauthorized actions.

41 [1915] A.C. 705 H.L., at pp. 713–714.

Thus, the policymaking body for the board of directors is the alter ego of the corporation whose will and intention can be compared with the mental setting of a natural person.

Lord Reid, in *Tesco Supermarkets Ltd* v. *Nattrass,*[42] furthered this theory. He forwarded the general principle as follows:

> Normally the board of directors, the managing director, and perhaps other superior officers of the company carry out the functions of management and speak and act as the company. Their subordinates do not. They carry orders from above, and it can make no difference that they are given some discretion. The board of directors may delegate some part of their functions of management to their delegates, for difficulties in holding that they have thereby put such a delegate in their place so that within the scope of the delegation, he can act as a company. It may not always be easy to draw the line, but there are cases in which it must be drawn.[43]

Lord Reid made it clear that the liability of a company for its directors or policymakers is equivalent to the personal liability of a human being.[44] However, determining the actions and intentions constituting the *mens rea* and *actus reus* of a crime becomes more complex when the offender is a legal entity rather than an individual.[45] Nonetheless, a corporation can still be held liable if its agents or employees commit illegal acts while acting on behalf of the corporation, to benefit it.[46] Managerial *mens rea* requires proving that a high-ranking agent within the organization committed, directed, or tolerated the criminal conduct.[47] Strategic *mens rea* considers the collective knowledge of all employees as a whole and attributes it to the corporation.[48] As such, a

42 *Tesco Supermarkets Ltd. v. Nattrass* was a landmark case in UK company law, establishing the principle that a company can only act through its directors. In this case, Tesco was accused of violating the Restrictive Trade Practices Act 1956 by fixing prices of margarine with its competitors. The court held that the company could not be held liable as a separate entity and that only the directors who authorized the illegal activity could be held responsible. This case has significant implications for corporate liability and has been cited in numerous subsequent cases.

43 [1972] A.C. 170, at p. 173.

44 Gower, L. (1992). *The principles of modern company law*. Sweet and Maxwell.

45 Wilkinson, M. (2003). Corporate criminal liability – the move towards recognising genuine corporate fault. *Canterbury Law Review, 9*, 142.

46 *N.Y. Cent. & Hudson River R.R. Co. v. United States*, 212 U.S. 481, 491–495 (1909); see also *United States v. Photogrammetric Data Services*, 259 F.3d 229, 242 (4th Cir. 2001) (holding that a corporation can act only through the conduct of its agents); *United States v. One Parcel of Land*, 965 F.2d 311, 316 (7th Cir. 1992) (citing *Zero v. United States*, 459 U.S. 991 (1982)).

47 Fisse, B. (1982). Reconstructing corporate criminal law: Deterrence, retribution, fault, and sanctions. *Southern California Law Review, 56*, 1141, 1186.

48 *United States v. T.I.M.E. D.C., Inc.*, 381 F. Supp. 730, 738–739 (W.D. Va. 1974).

corporation could be held liable for a particular state of mind if a single individual within the organization possesses that.[49]

The third theory proposes that the criminal liability of a corporation is based on its internal process. It is not dependent upon the intent of any particular person or criminal act of his single agent 'but an overall reasonableness of corporate practices and procedures designed to avert injurious regulatory offenses.'[50] Thus, in modern times, the corporation can be held liable like a natural person, except in two cases.[51] In the first place, where from its very nature, the corporation cannot commit such offenses, for example, perjury, bigamy, or rape. But under the vicarious liability principle, or the fast theory, discussed earlier, the company can be liable for wrongful acts of its own or its servants or agents.[52] The counterargument forwarded by some jurists is that the company will be liable in limited cases for the acts committed by its servants or agents, and it is liable only in those cases where the servants and agents act within the scope of authorities delegated to them. The second exception operates where no effective order can be made against the corporation, namely, offenses where death sentence or imprisonment is the punishment prescribed by the law.[53]

This theoretical development has been reflected in the gradual acceptance of corporate criminal liability by the world's legal systems. The U.S. Supreme Court extended the scope of the U.S. criminal justice system to include corporations in 1909.[54] The court expanded legal liability to include offenses of active behavior, in addition to offenses of omission. This meant that the court of first instance could now deal with matters related to offenses with criminal intent, and it gradually shifted from a basis of vicarious liability to direct liability in judicial proceedings.[55] This has resulted in the merging of vicarious and strict liabilities, allowing corporations to be held accountable for crimes they attempted to prevent. Since 1987, corporations have been liable for legal penalties. To align with the development of international laws on corporate liability, Italy established a generic model of corporate quasi-criminal liability in 2001. The model aimed to administer corporate liabilities with criminal intent through the courts.[56] During the 1990s, France amended its legal provisions

49 *First Equity Corp. of Fla. v. Standard & Poor's Corp.*, 690 F. Supp. 256, 260 (S.D.N.Y. 1988). For comment, see Foerschler, A. (1990). Corporate criminal intent: Toward a better understanding of corporate misconduct. *California Law Review*, *78*, 1287.

50 Supra note 20, at p. 1243.

51 Cross, R., & Jones, P. A. (1964). *An introduction to criminal law* (5th ed., p. 99). Butterworth.

52 Braithwaite, J. (2013). *Corporate crime in the pharmaceutical industry* (Routledge Revivals, p. 6). Routledge.

53 *I.C.R. Honbage Ltd.* (1944) K.B. 551.

54 *New York Central & Hudson River Railroad v. United States*, 212 U.S. 481.

55 Lederman, E. (1985). Criminal law, perpetrator and corporation: Rethinking a complex triangle. *Journal of Criminal Law & Criminology*, *76*, 285, 288–289.

56 Ibid.

to allow for the criminal prosecution of business corporations.[57] Article 121–2 of the French Criminal Code holds corporations accountable for offenses committed by their agents or employees while acting on their behalf. It provides various penalties that apply to all legal entities, including corporations. The Council of Europe has recommended that European countries incorporate corporate criminal liability into their regulatory frameworks. This echoes the need to legally hold corporations accountable for criminal actions, rather than solely focusing on individual responsibility in the criminal justice system.[58]

While most European countries adhere to the prescriptions given by the European Union (EU), some European countries include 'open' or holistic models of corporate liabilities for severe economic and organized crimes. Greece, The Czech Republic, and the Slovak Republic have come out of their long-standing objections to corporate liability; they have now adopted corporate liability principles with computational models. Japan, Korea, and Hong Kong have adopted the general corporate liability principles in their corporate laws. China adopted this liability in its regulation for dealing with economic crimes only. Canada modified its common law approach by amending its Criminal Code 2003, thereby shifting the criminal prosecution of a corporate crime away from the 'directing mind' principle to a corporation's senior officials.[59] In New Zealand, a corporation's directing mind and will are determined by interpreting the relevant norm, considering language, content, and policy.[60] Australia uses a comprehensive model for identifying corporate criminal liability.[61] Under federal law, proving that a human stakeholder committed an offense is permissible but unnecessary. The prosecution may rely on corporate culture provisions for evidence of attitudes, policies, rules, and behavior patterns or practices.

Corporations are not just fictional entities but very real and powerful actors that can cause significant harm to individuals and society. They are indeed real because they exist as organizations composed of individuals working toward common goals. They have a tangible impact on society, the economy, and the environment. They employ people, produce goods and services, and interact with various stakeholders. Recognizing corporations as 'real' is essential for understanding their influence and holding them accountable for their actions. While distinct from individual persons, corporations are recognized as legal entities with rights and responsibilities. Large corporations possess significant

57 Jorg, N., & Field, S. A. (1991). Corporate liability and manslaughter: Should we be going Dutch? *Criminal Law Review* (March), 156–171.

58 Engelhart, M. (2014). Corporate criminal liability from a comparative perspective. In Dominik Brodowski et al. (Eds.), *Regulating corporate criminal liability* (pp. 53, 54–57). Springer International Publishing.

59 *Canadian Dredge and Dock Co. v. R.*, [1985] 1 SCR 662, paras. 29, 32 (Estey J.).

60 *Meridian Global Funds Asia Ltd. v. Securities Commission*, [1995] 2 AC 500, at p. 507 (per Hoffman LJ).

61 Sections 12.2 & 12.3, *Criminal Code Act 1995* (Cth).

wealth and resources that rival those of nation-states. Regarding financial power, some multinational corporations are on par with the largest economies in the world. These corporations, such as Apple and Starbucks, have a global reach and influence that allows them to compete with states for power and influence in international politics. Additionally, corporations have resources beyond just financial assets. They possess tangible assets such as infrastructure and technological resources, as well as intellectual property and natural resources.[62] The power dynamics in international politics are no longer solely dictated by states, as corporations play a crucial role in shaping global power relations. Even the mineral companies can have a significant impact on national policy framing. One example is the mining industry in Chile, which has been influenced by global demand for minerals, mainly those needed for the green economy. Chile has significant lithium reserves, a crucial mineral for renewable energy technologies. The country has implemented the National Mining Policy 2050, which aims to develop a safe, inclusive, and sustainable mining sector while promoting the valorization of mining by society and strengthening state-owned companies.[63] These policies are driven by the demand for green transition minerals and the need to recover greater profits and promote localized processing for the green economy.[64] In this way, global mineral companies shape national policy framing by influencing the focus and objectives of mining policies. In recent years, the trend of seeking corporate liability for human rights violations and environmental damages has been growing.[65] This trend is particularly noticeable in cases involving TNCs and corporate crimes. The UK has taken steps to address this issue by enacting, for example, the Bribery Act 2010, which imposes liability on corporations if they fail to prevent bribery by their employees or associated persons. Similarly, France has introduced the Sapin II Law, which establishes corporate criminal liability for corruption offenses such as bribery and money laundering. Germany has implemented the Administrative Offenses Act, which enables authorities to impose fines on corporations for various offenses, including bribery, tax evasion, and money laundering. The Netherlands has implemented the Dutch Corporate Governance Code; the core aim of this Code is to promote responsible corporate behavior and hold corporations accountable for their actions.

62 Gaspar, V., Harris, J., & Tieman, A. F. (2018). *The wealth of nations: Governments can better manage what they own and owe*. International Monetary Fund. Retrieved October 13, 2023, from www.imf.org/en/Blogs/Articles/2018/10/10/blog-FM-the-wealth-of-nations-govts-can-better-manage-what-they-own-owe

63 National Mining Policy. Retrieved October 13, 2023, from www.iea.org/policies/16047-national-mining-policy

64 For a report on this matter. Retrieved October 13, 2023, from www.csis.org/analysis/specter-haunting-latin-american-mining-not-so-fast

65 Zerk, J. (2014). *Corporate liability for gross human rights abuses: Towards a fairer and more effective system of domestic law remedies*. OHCHR. Retrieved 2019 May, from http://www.ohchr.org/Documents/Issues/Business/DomesticLawRemedies/StudyDomesticeLawRemedies.pdf

Not all corporations may be held criminally liable. Corporations that possess a certain level of internal self-referential complexity can be subjected to the mandates of criminal law. However, not all corporations have the same level of internal complexity.[66] Some corporations may lack the necessary internal organization, structure, and culture to commit a crime knowingly or recklessly. These corporations may be considered corporate offenders with 'diminished capacity' or 'immaturity' and not subject to 'real' punishment. Instead, they may be subject to remedial measures such as education, training, and compliance programs. Therefore, a sound corporate criminal regulation system must differentiate between corporations with criminal capacity (i.e., those who may be considered guilty at trial) and those with diminished capacity. This distinction is crucial to ensure that corporate criminal liability is fair, just, and effective in deterring corporate wrongdoing while avoiding punishing corporations incapable of forming the requisite *mens rea* for a crime.

Understanding the concept of organizational blameworthiness is crucial for comprehending corporations' liability in criminal cases and the potential consequences of being held criminally responsible. Organizational blameworthiness holds corporations responsible for their actions and considers them entities with distinct and identifiable personalities independent of specific individuals. This means that the corporation can be held criminally responsible in its own right, and the actions of individuals are considered in light of the corporation itself.[67] The critical thing to note is that the corporation possesses all the knowledge that is divided between many individuals, and this knowledge is used to make decisions. Thus, the corporation is responsible for any wrongdoing that occurs within the organization. This responsibility is a form of general or plenary liability based on a holistic view of corporate behavior, where the collective actions of its employees form a corporation's behavior.[68]

The concept of corporate fault refers to the collective responsibility of a corporation for any crimes it commits. The idea is that, rather than focusing on the blameworthiness of individual employees, we should hold the corporation as a whole accountable for its actions.[69] This approach is based on the assumption that companies with sufficient organizational complexity develop an intentionality and reason for acting that exists separately from the intentions and motivations of any individual employee.[70] In this

66 Diez, C. G.-J. (2011). Corporate criminal liability in the twenty-first century: Are all corporations equally capable of wrongdoing? *Stetson Law Review*, *41*, 41.

67 Fisse, B. (1991). The attribution of criminal liability to corporations: A statutory model. *Sydney Law Review*, *13*, 277, 279–280.

68 Colvin, E. (1995). Corporate personality and criminal liability. *Criminal Law Forum*, *6*, 1, 24.

69 Sullivan, G. (1995). Expressing corporate guilt. *Oxford Journal of Legal Studies*, *15*, 281, 284.

70 Ibid., p. 284.

approach, criminal liability is assigned to the corporation as the wrongdoer.[71] Supporters of corporate blameworthiness argue that this approach is more efficient and satisfactory than the Natrass approach and vicarious liability. The Natrass approach holds individual employees criminally liable for the actions of the corporation. This approach has been criticized for being inefficient and unsatisfactory, as it can be challenging to prove that an individual employee had the necessary knowledge and intent to commit a crime on behalf of the corporation. On the contrary, vicarious liability aims to hold the employer responsible for the actions of its employees. Nonetheless, this approach has also been criticized for failing to hold companies accountable for their actions. In summary, the corporate fault doctrine is regarded as a mechanism to ensure that corporations are held accountable for their actions and to deter instances of corporate misconduct. By assigning criminal liability to the corporation itself, we can avoid the difficulties and inefficiencies of the Natrass approach and vicarious liability and focus on holding the corporation responsible for its actions.[72]

2.5 Environmental Jurisprudence

Jurisprudence is the study of the philosophy and principles of law. It is a vast field with no universal definition.[73] Environmental jurisprudence is a subset of this field. Twining considers jurisprudence and legal theory interchangeably, with legal philosophy being its most theoretical component.[74]

The study of jurisprudence dates back to the Romans, who referred to it as 'knowledge of law' or 'skill in law.' Roman jurists such as Ulpian and Paulus delineated jurisprudence as the understanding of divine and human matters, an inquiry into what constitutes justice and injustice, with the law emerging from established principles rather than being derived from them. These definitions were vague, but they laid the foundation for a legal science independent of particular societal institutions.[75]

The word jurisprudence was commonly used in England during the early formative period of the common law. However, it had little significance beyond being a study of or skill in law. It was only in the early 19th century that Bentham and his disciple Austin began to give it technical significance

71 Buell, S. W. (2006). The blaming function of entity criminal liability. *Indiana Law Journal*, *81*, 473, 477–478.

72 Wells, C. (1996). The corporate manslaughter proposals: Pragmatism, paradox, and peninsularity. *Criminal Law Review*, *545*, 574.

73 Twining, W. (2009). *General jurisprudence: Understanding law from a global perspective* (p. 8). Cambridge University Press.

74 Ibid., p. 8.

75 Mahajan, V. D. (1987). *Jurisprudence and legal theory* (p. 3). Eastern Book Company.

among English lawyers.[76] Bentham differentiated between the examination of law as it exists and as it should exist. Austin concentrated on expository jurisprudence, with his work primarily consisting of a formal analysis of the structure of English law.[77] The analytical exposition that Bentham pioneered and Austin developed dominated English legal thought until modern times. To them, the word 'jurisprudence' almost exclusively means analyzing the formal structure of law and its concepts. However, in the last century, there has been a shift in the meaning of jurisprudence. Today, it is envisioned in a broader and more sweeping sense than what Austin understood. Julius Stone characterizes jurisprudence as 'the lawyer's extraversion.' It constitutes the analysis of the principles, ideals, and methodologies of law in light of contemporary knowledge acquired from disciplines beyond the legal field. Salmond differentiates between the generic and specific applications of the term jurisprudence. Generic jurisprudence encompasses the entire corpus of legal doctrines, whereas specific jurisprudence pertains to a particular subset of those doctrines.[78] Indeed, the ideas around jurisprudence can be packed into three groups: general jurisprudence, analytical jurisprudence, and normative jurisprudence.

The distinction between general and particular jurisprudence within English law diverges from the prevalent interpretations found in continental Europe. In his publication, 'What is Legal Theory?', Mark van Hoecke elucidates the historical development of general jurisprudence as perceived within civil law traditions. General jurisprudence pertains to the examination of concrete

76 Jeremy Bentham, an English jurist and philosopher, is considered to be the greatest historical figure in British legal positivism. In his book, *An Introduction to the Principles of Morals and Legislation*, Bentham laid the foundation for a theory of law as the expressed will of a sovereign. He further developed this theory in detail in a sequel called. *Of Laws in General.* However, over time, John Austin's work titled, *The Province of Jurisprudence Determined*, which was written by one of Bentham's disciples, gained more influence and became the most significant treatise on legal positivism. Bentham defined law in chapter one of *Of Laws* in a stipulated manner, stating what he believed should be the accepted meaning of 'law.' This definition circumvents many of the shortcomings that affected Austin's subsequent endeavors and preempts numerous refinements introduced by contemporary legal positivists. According to Austin, positive law consists of directives issued by a political sovereign, enforced through sanctions against those who contravene them. This concept of law encompasses three fundamental elements: (a) political sovereign, (b) command, and (c) sanction. Austin argued that a society devoid of a political sovereign lacks law in the stringent interpretation of positive law; instead, it possesses what he referred to as 'laws improperly so-called' or positive morality. Austin perceived the political sovereign as an indispensable component of an autonomous political society. In the absence of a sovereign, there exists no independent political society, and conversely, where there is no political society, a sovereign does not exist. For more about their understanding of jurisprudence, see Twining, W. (2009). *General jurisprudence: Understanding law from a global perspective* (pp. 33, 35, 45). Cambridge University Press.

77 Mahajan, V. D. (1987). *Jurisprudence and legal theory* (p. 3). Eastern Book Company.

78 Ibid, p. 3.

legal systems at a relatively elevated level of abstraction. It is conceived as a mid-level theory that bridges abstract legal philosophy and legal dogma. Notably, the designation 'general' in this context signifies a level of abstraction rather than a geographical scope.[79] Conversely, the English analytical tradition employs the term 'general' to specifically denote an extension in spatial dimensions. For instance, Jeremy Bentham differentiated between universal and local jurisprudence. During the 19th century, general jurisprudence encompassed the study of two or more legal systems, predominantly focusing on those classified as advanced or civilized. Universal jurisprudence, in this era, was akin to global jurisprudence but often limited to the laws governing sovereign nation-states. With the rise of globalization, the term 'general jurisprudence' has evolved to embody a more expansive and adaptable definition. It now pertains to the theoretical exploration of two or more legal traditions, cultures, or orders, ranging from micro-comparative analyses to universal considerations. Nevertheless, it is imperative to recognize that global jurisprudence may be rendered inconsequential if it merely entails viewing law exclusively or primarily from a global standpoint.[80]

Analytical jurisprudence is often associated with linguistic analysis or clarifying abstract concepts, but this view is too limited. While some analytical jurists in the Anglo-American tradition, such as Austin, Holland, Hohfeld, Kocourek, and Salmond, focused on elucidating abstract concepts, this was not their only interest. For example, Hart included several other topics within analytical jurisprudence, including examining the form and structure of legal systems, issues of legal reasoning, and the definition of law.[81] Hart also emphasized the importance of critically analyzing the assumptions and presuppositions of legal discourse as a key task of legal philosophy.[82] This broader perspective allows for contemporary jurists such as Raz, McCormick,[83] and even Dworkin, who have incorporated some of the conceptual analysis techniques developed by analytical philosophers like Hart, but have also moved on to address substantive issues. As the field of law becomes more globally diverse, jurisprudence must expand its scope to account for non-Western legal traditions, a more comprehensive range of legal phenomena, and different levels of normative

79 Twining, W. (2009). *General jurisprudence: Understanding law from a global perspective* (p. 19). Cambridge University Press.
80 Ibid., p. 20.
81 Hart, H. L. A. (1967). *The concept of law*. Oxford University Press; Hart, H. L. A. (1983). *Essays on Bentham: Jurisprudence and political theory*. Oxford University Press.
82 Hart, H. L. A. (1987). *Law, liberty, and morality* (pp. 35, 40). Stanford University Press.
83 McCormick's legal interpretivism defines jurisprudence as a complex system of social practices that require interpretation. He emphasizes the role of judges in making legal judgments based on both legal principles and moral values, considering the intentions of lawmakers and the broader social context. Overall, McCormick's jurisprudence highlights the importance of interpretation and the dynamic nature of the law.

and legal relationships and orders. It also needs a more empirical orientation at the core of legal scholarship.[84]

Normative jurisprudence addresses the interplay between law, politics, and morality. It encompasses overarching inquiries concerning values and law, including debates regarding the nature of law as a fundamental political obligation and the concept of civil disobedience. This discipline engages with questions pertaining to the existence, scope, and status of natural, moral, and non-legal rights, as well as the relationship between needs, rights, interests, and entitlements. Furthermore, it incorporates theories related to justice, constitutionalism, and democracy, along with standards designed to guide and evaluate legal institutions, regulations, practices, and decisions. Presently, normative jurisprudence represents a significant area of focus within Anglo-American jurisprudence, with scholars such as Bentham, Dworkin,[85] Finnis,[86] Rawls,[87] and Raz,[88] and modern critical theory contributing to the discussion. The classification of normative theories of reasoning and rationality, as well as inquiries regarding skepticism and relativism pertaining to them under normative or analytical jurisprudence, is primarily a matter of convenience.[89]

Environmental jurisprudence is a subfield of environmental law that delves into the philosophical, ethical, and legal principles that serve as a foundation for environmental protection. The core objective of this jurisprudence is to develop legal frameworks that prioritize sustainable development and the preservation

84 Twining, W. (2009). *General jurisprudence: Understanding law from a global perspective* (p. 37). Cambridge University Press.

85 Dworkin's normative jurisprudence evaluates moral principles in the legal system. He advocated for a 'moral reading' of the U.S. Constitution, stressing the importance of analyzing legal texts in light of moral principles like justice and fairness. His work critiqued legal positivism, which denies the necessary connection between law and morality. For more, see Caplan, R. L. (1977). Professor Dworkin's jurisprudence. *American Journal of Jurisprudence*, *22*, 118. *Philosophy of Law*. Retrieved October 10, 2023, from https://iep.utm.edu/law-phil/

86 Finnis believes in human freedom and the common good within the legal system. He emphasizes making choices that align with basic goods, asserting that freedom involves exercising it. Citizens can consider justice when deciding to obey a law. Legal obligation is constant with no offense or sanction worse than another. For more about Finnis's concept of jurisprudence, see Nye, H. (2020). Finnis's divided view of law: Problems for adjudicative theory. *Jurisprudence*, *11*(4), 503–529.

87 Rawls's jurisprudence centers on 'Justice as Fairness,' promoting equality and fairness for all members of society. He proposed two principles of justice: equal basic rights and liberties and fair equality of opportunities, with a guaranteed minimum for all. These principles represent a fair and impartial point of view in his theory of justice.

88 Raz's jurisprudence is based on legal positivism, which sees law as a social construct without necessary ties to morality or natural law. The legitimacy of law depends on its coherence and guidance to individuals. Raz emphasizes the role of discretion and judges in interpreting and applying law, focusing on its practicality and effectiveness.

89 Twining, W. (2009). *General jurisprudence: Understanding law from a global perspective* (p. 122). Cambridge University Press.

of the natural environment.[90] It recognizes the relationship between humans and the natural world, and it acknowledges that the environment is not just a collection of resources to be exploited. Rather, the natural environment is a complex and interconnected system that sustains all life forms. Environmental jurisprudence is about facilitating legal frameworks that honor the intrinsic value of nature and promote the long-term health and well-being of all living beings.[91]

The philosophies and principles in environmental jurisprudence have progressed over the decades. Likewise, there have been significant changes in environmental law, reflecting the increased awareness of environmental issues and the changing political and social landscape. At first, the change was on regulating pollution and managing resources. However, as environmental jurisprudence gained momentum, environmental law expanded to cover a wider range of concerns, including biodiversity conservation, climate change, and sustainable development.[92] Environmental law now regulates and protects the natural world, including impact assessment, pollution control, and resource management.[93] The philosophical base of environmental jurisprudence, particularly the principle of sustainable development, has assisted environmental law.[94] With this principle, environmental law is more attuned to balance economic, social, and environmental considerations during decision-making.[95] It recognizes that human activities have environmental consequences, and managing these impacts is critical to ensuring the long-term sustainability of human societies.[96]

Recognizing the interdependence between human and natural systems is considered one of the most significant developments in environmental jurisprudence. This recognition has led to the creation of legal frameworks that promote ecosystem-based management and acknowledge the intrinsic value

90 Huffman, J. L. (2022). Judge Stephen Williams's environmental jurisprudence. *NYU Journal of Law & Liberty*, *16*, 67.

91 Westbrook, D. A. (1993). Liberal environmental jurisprudence. *UC Davis Law Review*, *27*, 619.

92 Zainuddin, F., & Syafi'i, I. (2023). Environmental jurisprudence; Environmental preservation efforts in Islam. *Nusantara: Journal of Law Studies*, *2*(1), 23–30.

93 Bell, S., McGillivray, D., & Pedersen, O. (2013). *Environmental law*. Oxford University Press.

94 Sustainable development balances human development goals with natural systems' ability to provide resources without harming the environment. It aims to meet human needs while promoting economic development, environmental protection, and social well-being. The Brundtland Report in 1987 defined sustainable development as meeting the present generation's needs without compromising future generations' ability to meet their needs. In 2015, the United Nations General Assembly adopted the Sustainable Development Goals (2015–2030) to achieve sustainable development globally. However, some criticize the concept as unsustainable, and part of the problem is that 'development' is not consistently defined. For details, see Baker, S. (2015). *Sustainable development*. Routledge; Holmberg, J., & Sandbrook, R. (2019). Sustainable development: What is to be done? In *Policies for a small planet* (pp. 19–38). Routledge; Rogers, P. P., Jalal, K. F., & Boyd, J. A. (2012). *An introduction to sustainable development*. Routledge.

95 Lazarus, R. J. (2023). *The making of environmental law*. University of Chicago Press.

96 Bell, S., McGillivray, D., & Pedersen, O. (2013). *Environmental law*. Oxford University Press.

of nature.[97] Additionally, legal frameworks have been developed to address the underlying causes of environmental degradation, such as unsustainable consumption and production patterns.[98]

Environmental jurisprudence is built upon three key elements: (a) environmental ethics, (b) scientific knowledge, and (c) legal frameworks. Environmental ethics provides the philosophical basis for environmental law, highlighting the inherent value of nature and the significance of protecting the environment.[99] Scientific knowledge is necessary for comprehending the intricate ecological systems that support environmental protection,[100] while legal frameworks offer the necessary legal instruments to accomplish environmental objectives.[101] At its conceptual core, environmental jurisprudence thus converges the principles of 'deep ecology,' 'Marxism,' and the 'Anthropocene.'

Deep ecology[102] is an environmental philosophy that believes in the inherent value of all living beings, regardless of their usefulness to humans. It

97 Trachtman, J. P. (2018). WTO trade and environment jurisprudence: Avoiding environmental catastrophe. *Harvard International Law Journal, 58*(2), 1–38, 273.

98 Ibid., p. 273.

99 Environmental ethics emerged as a significant subfield of philosophy during the 1970s. This discipline represents a branch of applied philosophy that underpins environmental values and addresses pressing issues related to societal attitudes, actions, and policies aimed at the protection and preservation of biodiversity and ecological systems. Environmental ethics can be categorized into three primary types: libertarian extension, ecological extension, and conservation ethics. The concept of libertarian extension is predicated on the belief that individuals possess the right to exploit nature for their personal objectives. Together, these types of ethics explore the philosophical questions concerning human interactions with the natural environment. For more about this ethics, see Palmer, C., McShane, K., & Sandler, R. (2014). Environmental ethics. *Annual Review of Environment and Resources, 39*(1), 419–442; DesJardins, J. R. (2013). *Environmental ethics: An introduction to environmental philosophy*. Cengage Learning; Attfield, R. (2014). *Environmental ethics: An overview for the twenty-first century* (2nd ed.). Polity.

100 Young, O. R., Berkhout, F., Gallopin, G. C., Janssen, M. A., Ostrom, E., & Van der Leeuw, S. (2006). The globalization of socio-ecological systems: An agenda for scientific research. *Global Environmental Change, 16*(3), 304–316; Carpenter, S. R., Mooney, H. A., Agard, J., Capistrano, D., DeFries, R. S., Díaz, S., Dietz, T., Duraiappah, A. K., Oteng-Yeboah, A., & Pereira, H. M. (2009). Science for managing ecosystem services: Beyond the Millennium Ecosystem Assessment. *Proceedings of the National Academy of Sciences, 106*(5), 1305–1312.

101 Gouldson, A., & Murphy, J. (2013). *Regulatory realities: The implementation and impact of industrial environmental regulation*. Routledge.

102 The concepts of 'ecological justice' and 'deep ecology' share the same underlying meaning. While the term 'ecological justice' is often associated with a 1998 publication by Nicolas Low and Brendan Gleeson, its origins can be traced back to Aldo Leopold's 1948 work, *A Sand County Almanac*. In this text, Leopold argued for expanding our moral community to include the natural world, laying the foundation for the ecological justice movement. Norwegian philosopher Arne Naess further developed this concept in his 1973 essay, referring to it as 'deep ecology.' Some of his works on deep ecology are as follows: Sessions, G. (2014). Deep ecology, new conservation, and the Anthropocene worldview. *The Trumpeter, 30*(2), 106–114; Naess, A., & Haukeland, P. I. (2008). *Life's philosophy: Reason and feeling in a deeper world*. University of Georgia Press; Naess, A. (1979). Self-realization in mixed communities of humans, bears, sheep, and wolves. *Inquiry, 22*(1–4), 231–241.

emphasizes the interdependence of all living things and advocates for a more holistic approach to environmental issues.[103] Deep ecologists promote sustainable living practices and call for reevaluating societal values to prioritize the well-being of the entire ecosystem over individual or human-centered interests. However, some critics argue that deep ecology's principles may conflict with practical environmental conservation efforts and that its emphasis on non-anthropocentric values could hinder human progress. Moreover, some scholars have raised concerns about the potential for deep ecology to neglect social justice issues in favor of a purely ecological focus. Despite these criticisms, the principles of deep ecology represent a significant shift in environmental thinking, advocating for a more profound and inclusive approach to understanding humanity's place within the natural world. Incorporating deep ecology principles into environmental jurisprudence signifies a rising acknowledgment of the interdependence of all life forms and ecosystems in legal decision-making procedures. As environmental law progresses, the effects of deep ecology principles may help adopt a more equitable and sustainable approach to tackling intricate environmental challenges within the legal system.

The principles of the Anthropocene are well-received in environmental jurisprudence.[104] Anthropocene refers to a proposed geological epoch in which human activities have had a significant impact on the Earth's geology and ecosystems.[105] The principles of the Anthropocene reflect the recognition of humans as a dominant force shaping the planet's environment and the need for sustainable and responsible stewardship of Earth's resources. Recognizing the need for resilience and adaptation in the face of environmental changes, the principles of the Anthropocene stress the importance of mitigating and addressing the impacts of human activities. They underscore the ethical responsibility of individuals, organizations, and governments to act in ways that minimize harm to the planet and its inhabitants and call for policy and governance frameworks that prioritize environmental protection, conservation, and sustainable development.[106]

The principles of the Anthropocene reflect a paradigm shift in how humans perceive their relationship with the Earth and the urgent need for sustainable, ethical, and responsible actions to address the challenges posed by

103 Sessions, G. (1987). The deep ecology movement: A review. *Environmental Review*, *11*(2), 105–125. George Sessions further developed the principles of deep ecology. For details, see Naess, A., & Sessions, G. (1986). The basic principles of deep ecology. *The Trumpeter*, *3*(4); Sessions, G. (2014). Deep ecology, new conservation, and the Anthropocene worldview. *The Trumpeter*, *30*(2), 106–114.

104 Malhi, Y. (2017). The concept of the Anthropocene. *Annual Review of Environment and Resources*, *42*(1), 77–104.

105 Schmidt, M., Soentgen, J., & Zapf, H. (2022). Anthropocene – perspectives from the environmental humanities. *Journal of the Geographical Society of Berlin*, *153*(3), 178–187.

106 Angus, I. (2016). *Facing the anthropocene: Fossil capitalism and the crisis of the earth system*. NYU Press.

human-induced environmental changes.[107] This shift has led to the development of a specific set of norms, institutions, and procedural mechanisms dedicated to environmental protection, acknowledging the unique character of environmental law and governance in the Anthropocene era. For many, the Paris Agreement is an example that exemplifies this shift. The conventional state-centric approach to international environmental law (IEL) and governance has evolved into unconventional, multi-tiered, and informal governance frameworks that incorporate both state and non-state participants, including Indigenous peoples.[108] The main actors in environmental governance have shifted from a state-centric focus to a framework involving other actors, where the principles of integration, proportionality, and cooperation take a prominent role.[109]

Recent developments in environmental jurisprudence underscore the urgency of addressing environmental challenges and adapting legal frameworks to reflect the principles and unique character of the Anthropocene.[110] Environmental jurisprudence has evolved to manage natural resources benevolently and guarantee fundamental rights in reaction to environmental degradation and climate change.[111] This jurisprudence is further directed at building a unitary, global, holistic understanding of the notion of 'environment,' considering its inherently fuzzy nature and the interactions between natural resources.[112] It is now better positioned to raise a profound reflection on the necessity to transform humankind's relationship with nature, emphasizing a system-wide transformation to achieve well-being for all within the Earth's capacity to support life.[113] Policies like the European Green Deal and the 8th Environment Action Programme signify steps in the right direction but highlight the necessity for profound transformations in established mindsets and paradigms, such as consumerism, to move toward a more sustainable future.[114]

107 Cassotta, S. (2019). The development of environmental law within a changing environmental governance context: Towards a new paradigm shift in the Anthropocene era. *Yearbook of International Environmental Law*, *30*(1), 54–67.

108 Ibid., pp. 54–67.

109 Ibid., pp. 54–67.

110 Fukurai, H. (2020). President's farewell message: The Anthropocene, earth jurisprudence, and the rights of nature. *Asian Journal of Law and Society*, *7*(3), 613–622; Kotzé, L. J. (2014). Human rights and the environment in the Anthropocene. *The Anthropocene Review*, *1*(3), 252–275.

111 Cassotta, S. (2019). The development of environmental law within a changing environmental governance context: towards a new paradigm shift in the Anthropocene era. *Yearbook of International Environmental Law*, *30*(1), 54–67.

112 Ibid., pp. 54–67.

113 Ibid.

114 Strand, R., Kovacic, Z., Funtowicz, S., Benini, L., & Jesus, A. (2022). Exiting the anthropocene? Exploring fundamental change in our relationship with nature. *European Environment Agency, Briefing*, *24*, 2022.

Marxism, as a socio-political and economic theory, has influenced various aspects of law, society, and politics.[115] In the context of environmental jurisprudence, Marxism offers a critical lens through which to analyze the relationship between society, the economy, and the environment.[116] Its perspectives contribute to the development of environmental policies that prioritize the well-being of communities and ecosystems over corporate interests. This can influence the formulation of laws related to pollution control, land use, and natural resource management. Within the legal realm, Marxist analysis informs litigation and advocacy efforts to hold corporations and governments accountable for environmental harm. It underscores the need for legal remedies that address systemic issues contributing to ecological crises. Marxist ideas have implications for IEL and governance, particularly concerning global resource distribution, climate justice, and the rights of developing nations in the face of environmental exploitation by more powerful states.

The application of Marxist thought in environmental law can be politically contentious, leading to debates about the role of the state, property rights, and the balance between economic development and environmental protection. Implementing Marxist principles in environmental jurisprudence may challenge reconciling ideological goals with practical legal frameworks and governance structures. Nonetheless, Marxism offers a thought-provoking framework for understanding and addressing environmental issues within the field of jurisprudence. By critiquing the impact of capitalism on the environment and emphasizing social justice, Marxism contributes to evolving conversations about the intersection of law, society, and ecology.[117]

Environmental jurisprudence is significant for several reasons. First and foremost, it provides a legal framework for addressing environmental issues and promoting sustainable development. This legal framework enables governments, businesses, and citizens to work together to protect the environment and ensure the long-term viability of human societies. Public participation is, therefore, a crucial component of environmental jurisprudence. Environmental jurisprudence acknowledges that protecting the environment is a shared responsibility, and the public plays a significant role in decision-making.[118] By participating in environmental decision-making, citizens can voice their opinions and ensure that the needs and values of their communities are reflected in environmental policies. Second, environmental jurisprudence has the potential to drive social change. By recognizing the intrinsic value of nature and promoting sustainable development, environmental jurisprudence

115 Burns, E., & Marx, K. (1939). *What is Marxism?* (pp. 377–388) V. Gollancz; Boucher, G. (2014). *Understanding Marxism*. Routledge.

116 Burdon, P. D. (2014). *Earth jurisprudence: Private property and the environment*. Routledge.

117 Sagoff, M. (1985). Can environmentalists be liberals – Jurisprudential foundations of environmentalism. *Environmental Law*, *16*, 775.

118 Sun, Z., Behrens, P., Tukker, A., Bruckner, M., & Scherer, L. (2022). Shared and environmentally just responsibility for global biodiversity loss. *Ecological Economics*, *194*, 107339.

can help to shift societal values and norms toward a more environmentally sustainable future. This can lead to changes in consumption patterns, production practices, and social norms that support environmental protection and sustainable development.

Environmental jurisprudence is not just a theoretical concept – it is being implemented worldwide. One example is the United Nations Framework Convention on Climate Change (UNFCCC),[119] which provides a legal framework for addressing climate change globally. The UNFCCC recognizes the importance of reducing GHG emissions and promoting sustainable development and provides a framework for countries to work together to achieve these goals. Another example of environmental jurisprudence in action is the development of ecosystem-based management frameworks.[120] These frameworks recognize the interdependence of human and natural systems and seek to manage natural resources in a way that promotes sustainable development and the protection of the environment. This approach has been successful in some contexts, including marine conservation and forest management.[121]

Despite the progress that has been made in environmental jurisprudence, there are still many challenges that need to be addressed. One of the biggest challenges is the lack of political will to implement environmental laws and regulations.[122] Many governments are reluctant to act on environmental issues. Against this backdrop, the UNFCCC is an international environmental treaty established to combat 'dangerous human interference with the climate system.' Its main objective is to stabilize GHG concentrations in the atmosphere. The treaty was signed by 154 states during the United Nations Conference on Environment and Development (UNCED), also known as the Earth Summit, held in Rio de Janeiro from June 3 to June 14, 1992.

119 United Nations Framework Convention on Climate Change (UNFCCC). (1992). *The UNFCCC treaty*. Rio de Janeiro: United Nations Conference on Environment and Development (UNCED). The Kyoto Protocol and Paris Agreement are among subsequent agreements under the UNFCCC. Retrieved 2022, from UNFCCC.org

120 Delacámara, G., O'Higgins, T. G., Lago, M., & Langhans, S. (2020). Ecosystem-based management: Moving from concept to practice. In *Ecosystem-based management, ecosystem services and aquatic biodiversity: Theory, tools and applications* (pp. 39–60). Springer International Publishing; Tallis, H., Levin, P. S., Ruckelshaus, M., Lester, S. E., McLeod, K. L., Fluharty, D. L., & Halpern, B. S. (2010). The many faces of ecosystem-based management: Making the process work today in real places. *Marine Policy*, *34*(2), 340–348.

121 Curtin, R., & Prellezo, R. (2010). Understanding marine ecosystem-based management: A literature review. *Marine Policy*, *34*(5), 821–830; Chaves, R. B., Durigan, G., Brancalion, P. H., & Aronson, J. (2015). On the need for legal frameworks for assessing restoration project success: New perspectives from São Paulo state (Brazil). *Restoration Ecology*, *23*(6), 754–759.

122 Howes, M., Wortley, L., Potts, R., Dedekorkut-Howes, A., Serrao-Neumann, S., Davidson, J., Smith, T., & Nunn, P. (2017). Environmental sustainability: A case of policy implementation failure? *Sustainability*, *9*(2), 165; Gunningham, N., & Sinclair, D. (2017). *Leaders and laggards: Next-generation environmental regulation*. Routledge.

Originally, the treaty's secretariat was located in Geneva, but in 1996, it was relocated to Bonn. On March 21, 1994, it came into force, mandating regular scientific research, meetings, negotiations, and policy agreements to enable states to manage ecosystems toward adapting to climate change, ensure food production is not threatened, and enable sustainable economic development. The Kyoto Protocol, which was signed in 1997 and was valid from 2005 to 2020, was the first implementation of measures under the UNFCCC. The Paris Agreement, which entered into force in 2016, replaced the Kyoto Protocol. As of 2022, the UNFCCC has 198 parties. The Conference of the Parties (COP), its supreme decision-making body, meets annually to assess progress in dealing with climate change. Even so, difficulties have arisen, either because of competing priorities or pressure from industry groups[123] or because of the lack of enforcement mechanisms for environmental laws.[124] Even when environmental laws and regulations are in place, there is often a lack of resources and political will to enforce them effectively. This can lead to environmental laws not being effectively implemented, leading to unchecked environmental degradation. However, as the world becomes more aware of the impact of human activities on the environment, there is a growing demand for effective legal frameworks that promote environmental protection and sustainability.[125]

Environmental jurisprudence is a critical component of environmental law, providing the philosophical, ethical, and legal foundations for environmental protection and sustainable development.[126] As the impact of human activities on the environment becomes more evident, there will be continue to emerge a growing demand for legal frameworks that promote environmental protection and sustainability. While there are still challenges to be addressed, environmental jurisprudence has the potential to drive social change and promote a more sustainable future for all.

123 Egberase, O. C. (2016). *The politics of environmental regulations and implementation in Nigeria*. Delta State University; Sousa, R., Veiga, M., Van Zyl, D., Telmer, K., Spiegel, S., & Selder, J. (2011). Policies and regulations for Brazil's artisanal gold mining sector: Analysis and recommendations. *Journal of Cleaner Production, 19*(6–7), 742–750; Blackman, A., Li, Z., & Liu, A. A. (2018). Efficacy of command-and-control and market-based environmental regulation in developing countries. *Annual Review of Resource Economics, 10*(1), 381–404.

124 Ijaiya, H., & Joseph, O. (2014). Rethinking environmental law enforcement in Nigeria. *Beijing Law Review, 5*, 306; Kingston, S., Alblas, E., Callaghan, M., & Foulon, J. (2021). Magnetic law: Designing environmental enforcement laws to encourage us to go further. *Regulation & Governance, 15*, S143–S162; Zhao, Y. (2015). Innovative measures to improve environmental law enforcement in China. *China-EU Law Journal, 4*, 155–172.

125 Chaves, R. B., Durigan, G., Brancalion, P. H., & Aronson, J. (2015). On the need for legal frameworks for assessing restoration project success: New perspectives from São Paulo state (Brazil). *Restoration Ecology, 23*(6), 754–759.

126 Dana, D. A. (2019). The new "contractarian" paradigm in environmental regulation. In *Environmental law* (pp. 139–163). Routledge.

2.6 Conclusion

Environmental law is a complex and interdisciplinary field that regulates the interactions between humans and the environment. It covers many subjects, including pollution control, natural resource management, and biodiversity conservation. Its primary goal is to ensure that human and corporate functions are not harmful to the environment and that natural resources are used sustainably.

Criminal liability in environmental law refers to the legal responsibility individuals or corporations face when violating environmental laws. Environmental crimes can be multifarious, from illegal dumping of hazardous waste to deforestation, and they can have significant and lasting impacts on the environment. Criminal liability is crucial in enforcing environmental laws and holding individuals and corporations accountable for their actions.

Over the years, criminal liability in environmental law has undergone significant changes. Environmental crimes were considered minor offenses in the past, and the penalties were not severe. However, as the gravity of environmental issues became more apparent, lawmakers realized the need for stricter laws and penalties to address them effectively. In 1972, the United States' Clean Water Act became the first significant step toward environmental criminal liability.[127] This law made it a crime to discharge pollutants into navigable waters without a permit. The passage of this law signaled a change in how environmental crimes were perceived, and it paved the way for the introduction of stricter environmental laws. Significant environmental laws were passed in the United States in the following years, such as the Resource Conservation and Recovery Act of 1976 and the Comprehensive Environmental Response, Compensation, and Liability Act (CERCLA) of 1980.[128] These laws established criminal liability for individuals and corporations committing various environmental offenses, including illegal disposal of hazardous waste and oil spills.

Several high-profile environmental law violations have resulted in criminal liability over the years. One of the most significant cases is the 2010 Deepwater

127 Clean Water Act (CWA). The CWA establishes the fundamental framework for regulating discharges of pollutants into U.S. waters and controlling quality standards for surface waters.

128 Comprehensive Environmental Response, Compensation, and Liability Act (CERCLA or Superfund). The CERCLA program, managed by the EPA, addresses hazardous waste cleanup, emergency pollutant releases, and accident spill responses across the United States. Reauthorized by the Superfund Amendments and Reauthorization Act (SARA) in 1986, CERCLA received expanded provisions for site-specific requirements, enforcement authorities, and technical guidelines. Additionally, SARA Title III established the Emergency Planning and Community Right-to-Know Act (EPCRA).

Horizon oil spill.[129] The oil spill was one of the worst environmental catastrophes in the history of the United States, and BP, the company responsible for the spill, faced criminal charges for its actions. BP pleaded guilty to 11 counts of manslaughter and other criminal charges and paid over $20 billion in fines and penalties.[130] Another case worth mentioning is the Volkswagen emissions scandal, which was exposed in 2015. Volkswagen has been heavily fined for installing software in its diesel cars that manipulated emissions tests. The company was later charged with multiple criminal offenses, including conspiracy to defraud the United States and the violation of the CAA. Volkswagen ultimately pleaded guilty to three felony charges and paid over USD four billion in fines and penalties.[131]

Enforcing criminal liability in environmental jurisprudence can be challenging due to the complexity of environmental crimes and the difficulty in proving them. The penalties for committing environmental crimes can be severe. Moreover, corporations and individuals usually have significant resources that make it challenging for enforcement agencies to hold them accountable. One of the biggest challenges is the global nature of many environmental crimes. Environmental issues are frequently global, so enforcement agencies may have to collaborate across borders to investigate and prosecute environmental crimes. This process can be time-consuming and complex, requiring significant resources and cooperation between countries. The judiciary plays an essential role in enforcing criminal liability in environmental jurisprudence. They interpret environmental laws and determine whether individuals and corporations have violated them. If found guilty of environmental crimes, judges impose penalties on them. Moreover, the judiciary can also shape environmental law by setting precedents through their decisions. They can influence the

129 The Deepwater Horizon oil spill, also known as the BP oil spill, occurred on 20 April 2010 off the coast of the United States in the Gulf of Mexico. The disaster took place on the BP-operated Macondo Prospect and is considered to be the largest marine oil spill in the history of the petroleum industry. The spill was estimated to be 8%–31% larger in volume than the previous largest spill, the Ixtoc I oil spill, which also occurred in the Gulf of Mexico. The total discharge of the oil spill was estimated to be 4.9 MMbbl (210,000,000 U.S. gal; 780,000 m^3) by the United States federal government. After several unsuccessful attempts to contain the flow, the well was finally sealed on September 19, 2010. However, reports in early 2012 indicated that the well site was still leaking.

130 Issacharoff, S., & Rave, D. T. (2013). The BP Oil Spill Settlement and the paradox of public litigation. *Louisiana Law Review*, *74*, 397; Gyo Lee, Y., Garza-Gomez, X., & Lee, R. M. (2018). Ultimate costs of the disaster: Seven years after the Deepwater Horizon oil spill. *Journal of Corporate Accounting & Finance*, *29*(1), 69–79.

131 Gyo Lee, Y., Garza-Gomez, X., & Lee, R. M. (2018). Ultimate costs of the disaster: Seven years after the Deepwater Horizon oil spill. *Journal of Corporate Accounting & Finance*, *29*(1), 69–79; Reitze Jr., A. W. (2016). The Volkswagen air pollution emissions litigation. *Environmental Law Reporter News & Analysis*, *46*, 10564.

development of environmental law and ensure that it aligns with the principles of environmental jurisprudence.

As our understanding of environmental problems deepens, criminal liability is expected to be more significant in addressing such issues. The direction of criminal liability in environmental jurisprudence will be influenced by various factors, including the growing awareness of environmental issues, technological advancements, and increased global cooperation. Ultimately, criminal liability will remain crucial in ensuring that human activities do not harm the environment and that natural resources are used sustainably.

References

Angus, I. (2016). *Facing the anthropocene: Fossil capitalism and the crisis of the earth system*. NYU Press.

Attfield, R. (2014). *Environmental ethics: An overview for the twenty-first century* (2nd ed.). Polity.

Bell, S., McGillivray, D., & Pedersen, O. (2013). *Environmental law*. Oxford University Press.

Blackman, A., Li, Z., & Liu, A. A. (2018). Efficacy of command-and-control and market-based environmental regulation in developing countries. *Annual Review of Resource Economics, 10*(1), 381–404.

Boucher, G. (2014). *Understanding Marxism*. Routledge.

Braithwaite, J. (2013). *Corporate crime in the pharmaceutical industry (Routledge Revivals)*. Routledge.

Buell, S. W. (2006). The blaming function of entity criminal liability. *Indiana Law Journal, 81*, 473.

Burdon, P. D. (2014). *Earth jurisprudence: Private property and the environment*. Routledge.

Burns, E., & Marx, K. (1939). *What is Marxism?* V. Gollancz.

Carpenter, S. R., Mooney, H. A., Agard, J., Capistrano, D., DeFries, R. S., Díaz, S., Dietz, T., Duraiappah, A. K., Oteng-Yeboah, A., & Pereira, H. M. (2009). Science for managing ecosystem services: Beyond the Millennium Ecosystem Assessment. *Proceedings of the National Academy of Sciences, 106*(5), 1305–1312.

Cassotta, S. (2019). The development of environmental law within a changing environmental governance context: Towards a new paradigm shift in the Anthropocene era. *Yearbook of International Environmental Law, 30*(1), 54–67.

Chaves, R. B., Durigan, G., Brancalion, P. H., & Aronson, J. (2015). On the need of legal frameworks for assessing restoration projects success: New perspectives from São Paulo state (Brazil). *Restoration Ecology, 23*(6), 754–759.

Colvin, E. (1995). Corporate personality and criminal liability. *Criminal Law Forum, 6*, 1.

Curtin, R., & Prellezo, R. (2010). Understanding marine ecosystem-based management: A literature review. *Marine Policy, 34*(5), 821–830.

Dana, D. A. (2019). The new "contractarian" paradigm in environmental regulation. In *Environmental law* (pp. 139–163). Routledge.

Delacámara, G., O'Higgins, T. G., Lago, M., & Langhans, S. (2020). Ecosystem-based management: Moving from concept to practice. In *Ecosystem-based management, ecosystem services and aquatic biodiversity: Theory, tools and applications* (pp. 39–60). Springer International Publishing.

DesJardins, J. R. (2013). *Environmental ethics: An introduction to environmental philosophy*. Cengage Learning.

Diez, C. G.-J. (2011). Corporate criminal liability in the twenty-first century: Are all corporations equally capable of wrongdoing. *Stetson Law Review*, *41*, 41.
Egberase, O. C. (2016). *The politics of environmental regulations and implementation in Nigeria*. Delta State University.
Fisse, B. (1982). Reconstructing corporate criminal law: Deterrence, retribution, fault, and sanctions. *Southern California Law Review*, *56*, 1141.
Fisse, B. (1991). The attribution of criminal liability to corporations: A statutory model. *Sydney Law Review*, *13*, 277.
Foerschler, A. (1990). Corporate criminal intent: Toward a better understanding of corporate misconduct. *California Law Review*, *78*, 1287.
Fukurai, H. (2020). President's farewell message: The Anthropocene, earth jurisprudence, and the rights of nature. *Asian Journal of Law and Society*, *7*(3), 613–622.
Gouldson, A., & Murphy, J. (2013). *Regulatory realities: The implementation and impact of industrial environmental regulation*. Routledge.
Gower, L. (1992). *The principles of modern company law*. Sweet and Maxwell.
Gunningham, N., & Sinclair, D. (2017). *Leaders and laggards: Next-generation environmental regulation*. Routledge.
Gyo Lee, Y., Garza-Gomez, X., & Lee, R. M. (2018). Ultimate costs of the disaster: Seven years after the Deepwater Horizon oil spill. *Journal of Corporate Accounting & Finance*, *29*(1), 69–79.
Himmelhoch, S. D. (1992). Environmental crimes: Recent efforts to develop a role for traditional criminal law in the environmental protection effort. *Environmental Law*, *22*, 1469.
Holmberg, J., & Sandbrook, R. (2019). Sustainable development: What is to be done? In *Policies for a small planet* (pp. 19–38). Routledge.
Howes, M., Wortley, L., Potts, R., Dedekorkut-Howes, A., Serrao-Neumann, S., Davidson, J., Smith, T., & Nunn, P. (2017). Environmental sustainability: A case of policy implementation failure? *Sustainability*, *9*(2), 165.
Ijaiya, H., & Joseph, O. (2014). Rethinking environmental law enforcement in Nigeria. *Beijing Law Review*, *5*, 306.
Issacharoff, S., & Rave, D. T. (2013). The BP oil spill settlement and the paradox of public litigation. *Louisiana Law Review*, *74*, 397.
Jorg, N., & Field, S. A. (1991, March). Corporate liability and manslaughter: Should we be going Dutch? *Criminal Law Review*, 156–171.
Kadish, S. H. (1979). Developments in the law–corporate crime: Regulating corporate behaviour through criminal sanctions. *Harvard Law Review*, *92*, 1227.
Kingston, S., Alblas, E., Callaghan, M., & Foulon, J. (2021). Magnetic law: Designing environmental enforcement laws to encourage us to go further. *Regulation & Governance*, *15*, S143–S162.
Kotzé, L. J. (2014). Human rights and the environment in the Anthropocene. *The Anthropocene Review*, *1*(3), 252–275.
Lazarus, R. J. (2023). *The making of environmental law*. University of Chicago Press.
Lederman, E. (1985). Criminal law, perpetrator and corporation: Rethinking a complex triangle. *Journal of Criminal Law & Criminology*, *76*, 285.
Malhi, Y. (2017). The concept of the Anthropocene. *Annual Review of Environment and Resources*, *42*(1), 77–104.
Naess, A. (1979). Self-realization in mixed communities of humans, bears, sheep, and wolves. *Inquiry*, *22*(1–4), 231–241.
Naess, A., & Haukeland, P. I. (2008). *Life's philosophy: Reason and feeling in a deeper world*. University of Georgia Press.
Naess, A., & Sessions, G. (1986). The basic principles of deep ecology. *The Trumpeter*, *3*(4).

Palmer, C., McShane, K., & Sandler, R. (2014). Environmental ethics. *Annual Review of Environment and Resources, 39*(1), 419–442.
Reitze Jr., A. W. (2016). The Volkswagen air pollution emissions litigation. *Environmental Law Reporter News & Analysis, 46*, 10564.
Rogers, P. P., Jalal, K. F., & Boyd, J. A. (2012). *An introduction to sustainable development.* Routledge.
Sagoff, M. (1985). Can environmentalists be liberals-jurisprudential foundations of environmentalism. *Environmental Law, 16*, 775.
Schmidt, M., Soentgen, J., & Zapf, H. (2022). Anthropocene–perspectives from the environmental humanities. *Journal of the Geographical Society of Berlin, 153*(3), 178–187.
Sessions, G. (1987). The deep ecology movement: A review. *Environmental Review, 11*(2), 105–125.
Sessions, G. (2014). Deep ecology, new conservation, and the Anthropocene worldview. *The Trumpeter, 30*(2), 106–114.
Sousa, R., Veiga, M., Van Zyl, D., Telmer, K., Spiegel, S., & Selder, J. (2011). Policies and regulations for Brazil's artisanal gold mining sector: Analysis and recommendations. *Journal of Cleaner Production, 19*(6–7), 742–750.
Strand, R., Kovacic, Z., Funtowicz, S., Benini, L., & Jesus, A. (2022). Exiting the Anthropocene? Exploring fundamental change in our relationship with nature. *European Environment Agency, Briefing, 24*, 2022.
Sullivan, G. (1995). Expressing corporate guilt. *Oxford Journal of Legal Studies, 15*, 281.
Sun, Z., Behrens, P., Tukker, A., Bruckner, M., & Scherer, L. (2022). Shared and environmentally just responsibility for global biodiversity loss. *Ecological Economics, 194*, 107339.
Tallis, H., Levin, P. S., Ruckelshaus, M., Lester, S. E., McLeod, K. L., Fluharty, D. L., & Halpern, B. S. (2010). The many faces of ecosystem-based management: Making the process work today in real places. *Marine Policy, 34*(2), 340–348.
Trachtman, J. P. (2018). WTO trade and environment jurisprudence: Avoiding environmental catastrophe. *Harvard International Law Journal, 58*(2), 1–38.
Twining, W. (2009). *General jurisprudence: Understanding law from a global perspective.* Cambridge University Press.
Wilkinson, M. (2003). Corporate criminal liability – the move towards recognizing genuine corporate fault. *Canterbury Law Review, 9*, 142.
Young, O. R., Berkhout, F., Gallopin, G. C., Janssen, M. A., Ostrom, E., & Van der Leeuw, S. (2006). The globalization of socio-ecological systems: An agenda for scientific research. *Global Environmental Change, 16*(3), 304–316.
Zerk, J. A. (2006). *Multinationals and corporate social responsibility: Limitations and opportunities in international law* (Vol. 48). Cambridge University Press.
Zhao, Y. (2015). Innovative measures to improve environmental law enforcement in China. *China-EU Law Journal, 4*, 155–172.

3 Criminal Liability of Corporate Polluters

3.1 Introduction

Corporations are facing increasing scrutiny for their impact on the environment. In recent years, there has been a significant shift in attitudes toward holding corporations accountable for environmental harm. This is not surprising, as corporations in industries such as manufacturing, mining, and agriculture pose a significant threat of pollution and environmental damage, both domestically and internationally. Therefore, it is crucial to understand the scope of the harm caused by corporations and the legal frameworks in place to regulate criminal liability. This chapter will examine significant environmental disasters caused by corporations and the legal frameworks in some jurisdictions that hold polluting corporations criminally liable.

3.2 Corporate Criminal Liabilities for Environmental Damages

The theory of corporate personality, known as the fiction or nominalist view, suggests that a corporation is a legal construct representing a group of individuals.[1] The corporation can only operate through its human representatives and may be held criminally liable if it can be associated with a human individual who acts as its directing mind and will. This approach is known as the identification or alter ego model of corporate criminal liability. In contrast to the fiction or nominalist theory, the reality theory recognizes corporations as legal entities that can be held accountable for their employees' actions. It gives rise to holistic and aggregative models of liability, which recognize that corporations can commit crimes through established internal decision-making processes. Aggregative approaches view the corporation as the main offender by combining individual stakeholders' actions and mindsets, and as such, they

1 For more on the theoretical construction of corporate criminal liability, see the judgment by Denning LJ in *H.L. Bolton (Engineering) Co. Ltd. v. T.J. Graham & Sons Ltd.* [1957] 1 QB 159, 172.

DOI: 10.4324/9781003279006-3

offer a compromise between vicarious liability and holistic perspectives. Also, it highlights the need to establish the element of fault when holding a corporation accountable for criminal acts.[2] The principle of corporate fault ensures that the concept of organizational blameworthiness and corporate culture is considered in determining corporate criminal liability. In essence, this principle ensures that corporations are held accountable for their actions and the culture they promote within the organization.

Corporations, as legal entities, enjoy rights similar to those of human beings but cannot be morally responsible. Their legal personality and limited liability play a significant role in their potential to restrict or avoid liability for environmental harm. Corporations' legal personality grants them certain rights but does not consider their impact on the environment. Limited liability, however, allows corporations to evade accountability for their actions. These aspects of corporate structure present challenges when holding companies liable for their environmental damage.

At the international level, corporations have a somewhat ambiguous status under the law. They are primarily objects, rather than subjects, of the international legal system. While corporations may benefit from certain aspects of international law, such as bilateral investment treaties, they often rely on states to advocate. Unfortunately, this also means that corporations are shielded from liability, as general principles of IEL have not explicitly addressed enterprises. The polluter pays principle, for instance, has not been directly applied to corporations. Against this backdrop, environmental crime, including illegal exploitation of natural fauna and flora, pollution, garbage dumping, and trash trading, has become a significant concern worldwide. In recent years, the number of environment-related offenses has significantly increased. For example, in India, the number of cases classified as environment-related offenses climbed by 78.1% in 2020 alone. These crimes against the environment have devastating consequences for ecosystems, biodiversity, and human welfare.

Environmental problems can broadly be categorized into three groups – climatic changes, waste disposal, and resource depletion. While traditional criminal law may not effectively control most of these problems, as they arise from millions of small actions that are difficult to prevent, it can be applicable in cases where individuals or organizations engage in actions that cause significant environmental damage. Such actions can be like traditional criminal behavior, and therefore, it is important to examine the use of traditional criminal

2 Woolf, T. (1997). The Criminal Code Act 1995 (Cth) – Towards a realistic vision of corporate criminal liability. *Criminal Law Journal*, 257–272, at 258; *Tesco Supermarkets v. Nattrass* [1972] A.C. 153; *Universal Telecasters (Qld) Ltd. v. Guthrie* (1978) 32 F.L.R. 361; *Collins v. State Rail Authority of New South Wales* [1986] 5 N.S.W.L.R. 209; *Nordik Industries Ltd. v. Regional Controller of Inland Revenue* [1976] 1 N.Z.L.R. 194; *Canadian Dredge & Dock Co. Ltd. v. The Queen* (1985) 19 CCC (3d) 1; *Canadian Dredge & Dock Co. Ltd. v. The Queen* (1985) 19 CCC (3d) 1.

law in such cases.[3] The major climatic issues, including global warming,[4] acid rain,[5] and depletion of the ozone layer,[6] are the result of individual actions. While each individual action may not significantly harm the environment, the cumulative effect of these actions is a real problem. This makes it difficult to apply traditional criminal law as it is unlikely that any individual act would be considered a crime. Traditional criminal law can be divided into five categories: crimes against the administration of justice (e.g., obstruction of justice or destruction of evidence), racketeering and conspiracy offenses, vice crimes (such as prostitution and gambling), crimes against individuals (like murder, assault, and rape), and crimes against property (such as theft, arson, or criminal mischief). However, many of these categories do not apply to the actions that lead to climatic change.

Assault crimes[7] are theoretically applicable to actions leading to climate change, since some pollutants that lead to climatic change, such as nitrogen oxide and sulfur dioxide, harm human health. However, most assault crimes require a 'serious physical injury' or at least a 'reckless' state of mind. In most jurisdictions, a person acts recklessly if they are 'aware of and consciously disre-

3 Himmelhoch, S. D. (1992). Environmental crimes: Recent efforts to develop a role for traditional criminal law in the environmental protection effort. *Environmental Law*, *22*, 1469, at 1471.

4 Global warming refers to the gradual increase in the Earth's surface temperature observed since the pre-industrial period (1850–1900). This phenomenon is primarily caused by human activities, such as the burning of fossil fuels, which releases greenhouse gases that trap heat in the atmosphere, leading to global warming and climate change. Notably, the current warming rate is faster than at any previous recorded point. For further details, see Houghton, J. (2005). Global warming reports on progress. *Physics*, *68*(6), 1340–1403, at 1343; Haldar, I. (2011). *Global warming: The causes and consequences*. Readworthy.

5 Acid rain occurs when sulfur dioxide (SO_2) and nitrogen oxides (NO_x) are released into the atmosphere, carried by wind, and react with water, oxygen, and other chemicals to create sulfuric and nitric acids. A warmer atmosphere may increase acid rain's severity, as higher temperatures accelerate the reactions that produce acidic compounds. For more information, see the United States Environmental Protection Agency. (2023). *What is acid rain?* Retrieved April 4, 2024 from www.epa.gov/acidrain/what-acid-rain

6 As a result of the emission of certain ozone-depleting compounds such as chlorine or bromine, the ozone layer that exists in the upper atmosphere is thinning over time. Industrial pollutants are chemically detrimental to ozone and break ozone molecules as soon as they come in contact with them. The rate of destruction caused by ozone supersedes the rate of natural production, as 100,000 ozone molecules can be destroyed by a single chlorine atom during its stay within the stratosphere. For additional information, see Britannica. *Ozone depletion*. Retrieved September 28, from www.britannica.com/science/ozone-depletion

7 'Assault crimes' involve intentional acts causing another person to reasonably fear imminent harm or offensive contact. Assault, considered an intentional tort, often accompanies battery and includes the defendant's action, intent to cause apprehension, and the victim's reasonable apprehension. Physical injury is unnecessary; the victim must genuinely believe harm or offensive contact is imminent. Assault may be a misdemeanor or felony depending on jurisdiction and severity. Aggravated assault includes assault under aggravating circumstances. For more information, visit Cornell Law School's Legal Information Institute (2023). *Assault*. Retrieved October 11, from www.law.cornell.edu/wex/assault

gard a substantial and unjustifiable risk' that a result will occur. The individual harm of commuting without a carpool, for instance, cannot be considered a 'substantial and unjustifiable risk.' Similarly, property crimes[8] do not apply to the actions causing climate change. Crimes such as robbery, burglary, theft, and destruction of property involve either violence or acquisition of possession. The overly consumptive lifestyles causing climate change involve neither of these elements.[9]

Resource depletion is a major environmental issue that affects virtually every resource known to humanity. It includes the depletion of soil, water (including surface, ground, and marine water), as well as different species of plants and animals. The decrease in the number of species threatens the stability of the Earth's ecosystem. Natural resources are primarily depleted due to society's demands exceeding nature's regenerative capacity. These excessive demands result from the unprecedented size of the human population and the wasteful manner in which developed countries use resources. Therefore, the effects of human-caused resource depletion, such as climatic changes and non-toxic waste disposal, are unlikely to be corrected through criminal prosecutions, as the individual acts leading to resource depletion are generally not significant enough to warrant individual criminal prosecutions.[10]

The legal concept of *actus non facit reum nisi mens sit rea* became obsolete with the onset of the Industrial Revolution. This meant that individuals could be held criminally liable for offenses committed without the intention to cause harm. The scope of offenses also expanded from physical harm to social, economic, and political harm. It was challenging to attribute these complex offenses to any one individual, leading the legal community to quantify liability based on the impact on society, the gravity of the act, the impression on people's minds, and the actual harm caused. This gave rise to statutory strict criminal liability, which involves doctrines such as the identification doctrine, organizational blameworthiness, and collective knowledge doctrine. These doctrines regulate corporate criminal liability for environmental damage and overexploitation of environmental resources.

The identification doctrine establishes a method for attributing corporate criminal liability. Corporations can be held legally responsible for crimes if an individual, serving as the company's 'directing mind and will,' engages in

8 Property crime includes offenses against private property, such as burglary, theft, arson, and vandalism, often motivated by financial gain or property acquisition. Property crimes are divided into those involving property destruction (e.g., arson, vandalism) and those involving property theft (e.g., robbery, embezzlement).

9 Himmelhoch, S. D. (1992). Environmental crimes: Recent efforts to develop a role for traditional criminal law in the environmental protection effort. *Environmental Law*, *22*, 1469, at 1477.

10 Ibid., p. 1483.

unlawful actions.[11] This aspect of jurisprudence reflects concerns regarding the challenge of adequately addressing misconduct by corporations and other 'non-natural persons,' emphasizing the need for a more robust framework intersecting environment, pollution, ethics, and corporate governance.[12]

Initially, the doctrine necessitated proving a 'directing mind and will,' in that, the corporation had a specific mental state to attribute liability.[13] According to the Corporate Manslaughter and Corporate Homicide Act 2007 in the UK, senior management is held responsible for any gross breach of their duty of care rather than identifying an individual who failed to fulfill their duty under common law. This is because senior management plays a significant role in the management and decision-making of the entire or part of the company's operations.

One of the challenges of attributing the core of this doctrine to regulation is determining the directing mind and will of medium- to large-sized corporations. In modern decentralized organizations, senior officers are often removed from the relevant conduct, with considerable authority vested within middle managers.[14] As a result, the relevant person is sometimes defined more broadly. To deal with this issue, Australia uses a form of attribution based on the conduct of a 'high managerial agent' who is defined as 'an employee, agent, or officer of the body corporate with duties of such responsibility that their conduct may fairly be assumed to represent the body corporate's policy.'[15] The Canadian criminal code has included 'senior officers' in the list of individuals who can be considered 'directing minds and wills.'[16] A New Zealand court has established a test to clarify the directing mind and will of a company.[17] The Economic Crime and Corporate Transparency Act 2023 of the UK broadens the scope of this doctrine to include a broader range of economic crimes, making it easier to prosecute the directing mind and will of a corporation.[18] The reform redefines 'senior management' as individuals significantly involved in

11 *Moore v. Brisler* [1944] 2 All ER 515; Hunt, R. (2024). *Expansion of corporate criminal liability*. Clyde & Co. Retrieved March 28, from www.clydeco.com/en/insights/2024/01/expansion-of-corporate-criminal-liability

12 Lewis, P. (2024). *Corporate criminal liability*. Law Commission of the United Kingdom. Retrieved March 28, from Corporate Criminal Liability.

13 O'Neil, B., Giles, E., McEvoy, S., Edwards, A., & Benson, J. (2023). *Reform of the UK identification doctrine: Significant expansion of corporate criminal liability for economic crimes*. Allen & Overy. Retrieved March 28, from www.allenovery.com/en-gb/global/blogs/investigations-insight/reform-of-the-identification-principle-significant-expansion-to-corporate-criminal-liability-for-economic-crimes

14 Clough, J. (2009). A glaring omission: Corporate liability for negligent manslaughter. *Monash University Faculty of Law Legal Studies Research Paper* (2007/41), *29*, at 32–33.

15 *Criminal Code 1995* (Cth) s 12.3(6).

16 *An Act to amend the Criminal Code (Criminal Liability of Organizations)* SC 2003, c 21.

17 *Meulens Hair Stylists v. Commissioner for Inland Revenue* [1963] NZLR 797.

18 Harle, K., Saleh, Z., & Partridge-Smith, S. (2024). Corporate crime: Changes to corporate liability. *Dentons*. Retrieved March 28, from www.dentons.com/en/insights/articles/2024/march/4/corporate-crime-changes-to-corporate-liability

managing or organizing substantial parts of the company's activities.[19] This amendment applies to UK businesses and non-UK entities operating within its jurisdiction, highlighting its global reach.[20]

These reforms signify a shift toward a more inclusive and practical approach to corporate criminal liability, particularly in addressing complex economic crimes.[21] The modifications in laws based on the modified principles of the 'identification doctrine' provide prosecutors and possibly private entities more leverage in holding companies accountable for misconduct by senior managers within their scope of authority.[22] This reform equips enforcement agencies with an additional tool for accountability[23] and extends these reforms to all criminal offenses, potentially increasing corporate responsibility for a broader range of misconduct.[24]

The exploration into the identification doctrine and its subsequent evolution through the *Economic Crime and Corporate Transparency Act 2023* underscores a paradigm shift in addressing corporate criminal liability. By expanding the scope of liability and redefining the parameters of senior management's responsibilities, the legal framework now more closely mirrors the complexities of modern corporate structures and the multifaceted nature of economic crimes. These reforms not only increase the capacity for holding corporations accountable but also reflect a deeper understanding of the intricacies involved in corporate decision-making processes and the necessity for a robust compliance and governance framework.

19 O'Neil, B., Giles, E., McEvoy, S., Edwards, A., & Benson, J. (2023). *Reform of the UK identification doctrine – significant expansion of corporate criminal liability for economic crimes.* Allen & Overy. Retrieved March 28, from www.allenovery.com/en-gb/global/blogs/investigations-insight/reform-of-the-identification-principle-significant-expansion-to-corporate-criminal-liability-for-economic-crimes

20 Ibid.

21 Colvin, E. (1995). Corporate personality and criminal liability. *Criminal Law Forum*, *6*, 1, at 13.

22 O'Neil, B., Giles, E., McEvoy, S., Edwards, A., & Benson, J. (2023). *Reform of the UK identification doctrine: Significant expansion of corporate criminal liability for economic crimes.* Allen & Overy. Retrieved March 28, from www.allenovery.com/en-gb/global/blogs/investigations-insight/reform-of-the-identification-principle-significant-expansion-to-corporate-criminal-liability-for-economic-crimes; Rundle, D. (2023). *How will changes to corporate criminal liability impact the banking sector.* BCLP. Retrieved March 28, from www.bclplaw.com/en-US/events-insights-news/how-will-changes-to-corporate-criminal-liability-impact-the-banking-sector.html

23 O'Neil, B., Giles, E., McEvoy, S., Edwards, A., & Benson, J. (2023). *Reform of the UK identification doctrine: Significant expansion of corporate criminal liability for economic crimes.* Allen & Overy. Retrieved March 28, from www.allenovery.com/en-gb/global/blogs/investigations-insight/reform-of-the-identification-principle-significant-expansion-to-corporate-criminal-liability-for-economic-crimes

24 Harle, K., Saleh, Z., & Partridge-Smith, S. (2024). Corporate crime: Changes to corporate liability. *Dentons.* Retrieved March 28, from www.dentons.com/en/insights/articles/2024/march/4/corporate-crime-changes-to-corporate-liability

The organizational blameworthiness doctrine in corporate criminal liability embodies a critical approach in attributing blame to corporations, intertwining psychological, social, and legal elements.[25] This doctrine not only plays a significant role in the social practice of blaming institutions but also carries a substantial communicative impact, reinforced by the legal process's clarity and authority.[26] The core of this doctrine is the principle of entity criminal liability. This principle advocates for a selective approach, focusing on cases according to entity blameworthiness. This approach emphasizes enhancing the examination of the agent's *mens rea*, imposing fault only if the agent acted primarily to benefit the firm.[27]

Application of this doctrine in any regulatory framework is challenging. The Australian Law Reform Commission proposes a simplified method combining aspects of the current attribution methodology, focusing on conduct and fault from 'associates' and incorporating a due diligence defense. This includes attributing conduct and fault for actions done 'for or on behalf of' the corporation and allowing corporations to defend by providing reasonable steps to prevent the conduct.[28] Regulatory and law enforcement authorities have developed model compliance, self-reporting, and amnesty programs influenced by organizational sentencing guidelines. Industry and peer organizations share best practices for compliance training and ethics awareness.[29]

Through exploring the organizational blameworthiness doctrine in corporate criminal liability, it becomes evident that this area of law intricately weaves together psychological, legal, and social threads to create a comprehensive approach to holding corporations accountable for their actions. The discussion highlighted the significance of tailoring entity criminal liability, the critical role of effective compliance programs, and the necessity for reforms that simplify and enhance the current legal frameworks. These elements underscore the complexity of attributing criminal liability to corporate entities and showcase the potential influence of legal principles on corporate behavior and governance.

The collective knowledge doctrine holds that a corporation incurs liability for the knowledge and conduct of its employees, irrespective of whether they were meant to act on behalf of the corporation or not. Hence, this means that the corporation possesses the collective knowledge of all employees and fails

25 Titus, V., & Mbaraonye, I. (2023). Blame: Stakeholder judgments that impact organizations and entrepreneurs. In *Oxford research encyclopedia of business and management*.

26 Buell, S. W. (2006). The blaming function of entity criminal liability. *Indiana Law Journal*, *81*, 473.

27 Ibid.

28 Commission, A. L. R. (2019). *Corporate attribution – Principled simplicity*. Australian Government. Retrieved March 28, from www.alrc.gov.au/news/corporate-attribution-principled-simplicity/

29 Desio, P. (2024). *An overview of the organizational guidelines*. U.S. Sentencing Commission.

to act after being made aware of such knowledge.[30] The aggregation principle is used when the *actus reus* and *mens rea* of multiple employees are combined to satisfy all the elements of a crime, rather than just one person's actions or intent. In this case, the conduct and mental states of those within the corporation are viewed as a whole and attributed to the corporation.[31]

The collective knowledge doctrine serves as a powerful tool in promoting corporate accountability.[32] It recognizes that a corporation should not be shielded from liability simply because an employee acted outside the boundaries of their official duties. Instead, this doctrine recognizes that a corporation should bear the consequences of its employees' actions, regardless of whether those actions were authorized or not. It allows prosecutors to pierce the corporate veil and hold the entire organization accountable for the actions of its employees, rather than solely focusing on individual wrongdoers.[33] This comprehensive approach ensures that justice is served and that corporate entities cannot escape liability by simply scapegoating a few individuals.[34] Furthermore, the collective knowledge doctrine creates a more just and equitable society. By imposing liability on corporations for the actions of their employees, this doctrine sends a clear message that unethical behavior will not be tolerated.[35] It encourages corporations to implement robust compliance programs and ethical standards, as they are aware that they can be held responsible for any misconduct that occurs within their ranks.[36] This, in turn, fosters a culture of integrity and accountability within organizations, benefiting not only the employees but also the wider society.[37]

The final section of this chapter explores the underlying concepts that different countries have used to establish their frameworks for regulating corporate crime with natural resources. While this section will not delve into

30 Gobert, J. (1994). Corporate criminality: Four models of fault. *Legal Studies, 14*(3), 393–410.

31 Weinstein, M. J., & Ball, P. B. (1994). Criminal law's greatest mystery thriller: Corporate guilt through collective knowledge. *New England Law Review, 29*, 65.

32 Ragozino, A. (1994). Replacing the collective knowledge doctrine with a better theory for establishing corporate mens rea: The duty stratification approach. *Southwestern University Law Review, 24*, 423.

33 Colvin, E. (1995). Corporate personality and criminal liability. *Criminal Law Forum, 6*, 1.

34 Baer, M. H. (2008). Insuring corporate crime. *Indiana Law Journal, 83*, 1035.

35 Moohr, G. S. (2007). Of bad apples and bad trees: Considering fault-based liability for the complicit corporation. *American Criminal Law Review, 44*, 1343.

36 It is to be noted that the collective knowledge doctrine is not universally accepted. For example, commonwealth countries like Australia and the UK have not adopted this doctrine in their regulatory frameworks. In *Commonwealth Bank of Australia v Kojic* (2016) FCAFC 186, the court determined there was no general doctrine in Australia allowing the attribution of an aggregate knowledge of various agents to a corporation. In *R v HM Coroner for East Kent ex parte Spooner* (1989) 88 Cr App R 10, a UK court stated, 'A case against a personal defendant cannot be fortified by evidence against another defendant. The case against a corporation can only be made by evidence properly addressed to showing guilt on the part of the corporation as such.'

37 Diamantis, M. E. (2015). Corporate criminal minds. *Notre Dame Law Review, 91*, 2049.

the actual regulations surrounding corporate criminal liability, it will highlight the basis for such regulation. Chapter 5 will provide a detailed discussion of corporate criminal regulation frameworks across various countries. The subsequent sections of this chapter will summarize some of the most significant and recent cases of environmental pollution caused by corporations. This discussion serves not only to provide an understanding of the nature and extent of corporate criminal liability for damage to natural resources but also to provide insight into the foundations that countries should establish for their corporate criminal liability regulations.

3.2.1 Bhopal Gas Disaster

The Bhopal gas leak incident is regarded as one of the worst industrial calamities.[38] The incident occurred at Bhopal in Madhya Pradesh, India, on December 2–3, 1984.[39] There was a company named Union Carbide India Ltd. (UCIL), an undertaking of the American industrial giant Union Carbide Corporation (UCC), that was set up to manufacture pesticides and innovate solutions for agriculture in infertile areas, including Bhopal.[40] At the time, Bhopal was a bustling city of one million people and was considered an ideal industrial destination due to its cheap labor and connectivity with other parts of India.[41] The horror of the disaster witnessed the release of over 40 tons[42] of methyl isocyanate (MIC) gas overnight, 'the most toxic chemical in industrial use,' from the UCIL plant, which was the main catalyst for the incident.[43] Residents of Bhopal, including children, faced toxic gas exposure, leading to a large number of fatalities and an even larger number saddled with a lifetime of various respiratory diseases, including 'coughing, vomiting, severe eye irritation and a feeling of suffocation.'[44] The world witnessed the untimely death of thousands of 'poor' people, estimated between 2,000 and 15,000, and perpetual injury

38 Mandavilli, A. (2018). The world's worst industrial disaster is still unfolding. *The Atlantic, 10*; Khan, F. I., & Abbasi, S. (1999). The world's worst industrial accident of the 1990s: What happened and what might have been – A quantitative study. *Process Safety Progress, 18*(3), 135–145; Bloch, K. (2016). *Rethinking Bhopal: A definitive guide to investigating, preventing, and learning from industrial disasters*. Elsevier.

39 Basha, O., Alajmy, J., & Newaz, T. (2020). *Bhopal gas tragedy: A safety case study* (Report No. CHEN 455). Texas A&M University at Qatar; Morehouse, W. (1994). Unfinished business: Bhopal ten years after. *The Ecologist, 24*(5), 164–169.

40 Fortun, K. (2009). *Advocacy after Bhopal: Environmentalism, disaster, new global orders* (p. xv). University of Chicago Press.

41 Ibid., p. xvii.

42 Gupta, R. C., & Varma, D. R. (2020). Methyl isocyanate: The Bhopal gas. In *Handbook of toxicology of chemical warfare agents* (pp. 389–402). Elsevier.

43 Varma, D. R., & Mulay, S. (2009). Methyl isocyanate: The Bhopal gas. In *Handbook of toxicology of chemical warfare agents* (pp. 293–312). Elsevier.

44 Kumar, D. (2021). Legal aspects of the Bhopal gas tragedy. *Legal Service India*. Retrieved April 4, from www.legalservicesindia.com/article/373/Legal-Aspects-of-the-Bhopal-Gas-Tragedy.html

to millions of people.[45] This incident has significant legal implications in environmental law, tort law, corporate law, and constitutional law.[46]

Following the incident, various actions were initiated in India and abroad, including in the United States. About 150 suits claiming compensation were filed in the United States in 1984, just four days after the incident.[47] On the other hand, numerous actions, including 6,500 suits, over 650,000 administrative personal injury claims, and 7,100 administrative death claims, were brought forth in India.[48]

Most suits in the United States were dismissed by the Federal District Court in New York on the grounds of *forum non conveniens.*[49] As a result, these suits were pursued in Indian courts as 'convenient forums.'[50] The legal actions in India commenced in 1986.[51] This led to the court-approved settlement between the parties wherein UCC agreed to pay $465 million (some data indicates this as $470 million), and the UCC paid the amount accordingly. However, the Indian Government postponed the distribution of the paid amount until the Supreme Court resolved all cases.[52]

The initiation of innumerable monetary claims by the victims led the Indian Government to pass the Bhopal Gas Leak Disaster (Processing of Claims) Act (the Bhopal Act) in 1985.[53] The act empowers the government to manage all applications regarding the Bhopal incident 'speedily, effectively, equitably and to the best advantage of the claimants.'[54] It confers on the government an

> exclusive right to represent and act in place of (whether within or outside of India) every person who has made or is entitled to claim for all purposes connected with such claim in the same manner and to the same effect as such person.[55]

45 Ibid

46 Subramanya, T., & Bhattacharya, S. (2020). The evolution of tort law and related developments in India after the Bhopal gas leak: An assessment. *CMR University Journal for Contemporary Legal Affairs*, *2*, 31; Anderson, M. (2001). Transnational corporations and environmental damage: Is tort law the answer. *Washburn Law Journal*, *41*, 399; Parisaboina, S. (2021). A critical analysis of absolute liability and its role in environment law. *International Journal of Law Management & Humanities*, *4*(3), 405.

47 Covell, T. (1991). The Bhopal disaster litigation: It's not over yet. *North Carolina Journal of International Law and Commercial Regulation*, *16*, 279.

48 Ibid.

49 In *Re Union Carbide Corp. Gas Plant Disaster*, 634 F. Supp. 842 (S.D.N.Y. 1986).

50 Kumar, D. (2021). Legal aspects of the Bhopal gas tragedy. *Legal Service India*. Retrieved April 4, from www.legalservicesindia.com/article/373/Legal-Aspects-of-the-Bhopal-Gas-Tragedy.html

51 Covell, T. (1991). The Bhopal disaster litigation: It's not over yet. *North Carolina Journal of International Law and Commercial Regulation*, *16*, 279.

52 Ibid.

53 Ibid.

54 Bhopal Gas Leak Disaster (Processing of Claims) Act (1985). Preamble.

55 Ibid.

The word 'claim' has a broader connotation, excluding criminal claims.[56] The applicants are entitled under this act to make legal representation in a limited way[57] and to engage pleaders.[58] The act further empowered the government to appoint a Commissioner in appropriate cases to aid the government in implementing the act's provisions[59] and to make a scheme or framework for the smooth distribution of settlement money among the entitled people.[60] Consequently, the government prepared a scheme empowering a Deputy Commissioner to manage and distribute settlement money, allowing the person(s) aggrieved by the Deputy Commissioner's decision to appeal to such Commissioner as may be appointed under the act but not specifically providing for judicial review.[61]

Shortly after the passing of the act, its constitutionality was challenged in the Supreme Court of India.[62] The main argument was that the act curtailed access to justice for potential claimants by depriving them of the right to fight for justice.[63] The Court ruling maintained its constitutionality, opining that the act contained a special procedure that could not be seen as a denial of access to justice.[64]

As to enacting authority, the Court recognized the government's sovereign power to act as *parens patriae* to uphold people's interest and to rescue it from being violated at the hands of a multinational company.[65] In applying the doctrine of *parens patriae*, the Court deviated from the traditional scope of the doctrine regarding the existence of peoples' absolute disability; rather, the exceptional situation of the Bhopal incident brought in such disability in the narrow sense.[66] The Court rebutted the petitioner's reliance on conflict of interest theory, as the government held shares in UCIL, by stating that the act did not put any bar to file suits against the government in the future.[67] Moreover, considering the extraordinary nature of the Bhopal tragedy, the Court waived the non-adherence of natural justice principles in the act.[68] However, the Court held the act as subject to judicial review.[69]

56 Ibid., p. 2(b).
57 Ibid., p. 3(1).
58 Ibid., p. 4.
59 Ibid., p. 6.
60 Ibid., p. 9(2).
61 Covell, T. (1991). The Bhopal disaster litigation: It's not over yet. *North Carolina Journal of International Law and Commercial Regulation, 16*, 279.
62 *Sanu v Union of India [1989]* Writ Petition No. 258.
63 Ibid.
64 Ibid.
65 Ibid.
66 Ibid.
67 Ibid.
68 Ibid.
69 Ibid.

Besides the suits claiming compensation, the Bhopal incident opened the scope of criminal cases starting in December 1984. In one criminal case, UCC President Warren Anderson and two senior UCIL officials in India were arrested by the police and charged with several offenses punishable under the Indian Penal Code, including 'criminal conspiracy, culpable homicide not amounting to murder, causing a death by negligence, mischief in the killing of livestock, making the atmosphere noxious to health, and negligent conduct in respect to poisonous substances.'[70] They were enlarged on bail, and Warren Anderson fled India for good.[71] In the same case, the magistrate issued a warrant for the arrest of Mr. Anderson and some others, but the process could not be executed, and consequently, Mr. Anderson was adjudged an 'absconding offender.'[72] In this way, the criminal cases could not be taken forward beyond the pre-proceeding stage.[73]

As mentioned earlier, the Bhopal Act was objected to as it restrained the civil claims from individuals; the act viewed such claims as a proliferation and subsequently removed more than 6,500 claims by granting the Government of India the status of primary litigant.[74] Thereafter, in 1985, the Government of India instituted a civil suit against the UCC in the Bhopal Court.[75] The government brought *de novo* arguments in terms of introducing absolute and multinational liability.[76] The former is due to UCC's engagement in 'ultra-hazardous activities,' and hence the general principle of act-cause is not relevant here.[77] These arguments brought forth the liability of the multinational UCC via its subsidiary UCIL whenever the exactness of responsibility for any injury cannot be reached.[78] The UCC argued that an unidentified saboteur employee mixed water with the MIC tank, causing a toxic reaction that caused this disastrous incident.[79] The Indian Government denied the involvement of any saboteur whatsoever and attributed the responsibility to a loosened 'safety standard and poor plant maintenance.'[80]

70 Covell, T. (1991). The Bhopal disaster litigation: It's not over yet. *North Carolina Journal of International Law and Commercial Regulation, 16*, 279; Mohan, M. R. (2019). *Criminal negligence and directors' liability under Indian Penal Code: The case of Bhopal gas tragedy.* Indian Institute of Management; Singh, P. (2021). Corporate criminal liability and the environment. *Indian Journal of Law and Legal Research, 3*, 1.

71 Covell, T. (1991). The Bhopal disaster litigation: It's not over yet. *North Carolina Journal of International Law and Commercial Regulation, 16*, 279.

72 Ibid.

73 Ibid.

74 Ibid.

75 *Union of India v Union Carbide Corp. [1986]* D. Bhopal No.1 113.

76 Ibid.

77 Ibid.

78 Ibid.

79 In *Re Union Carbide Corp. Gas Plant Disaster [1986]* S.D.N.Y. 634 F. Supp. 842.

80 Ibid.

The origin for the government's 'multinational enterprise liability theory' is the M. C. Mehta case,[81] wherein the Court held:

> [It is] necessary to construct a new principle of liability to deal with an unusual situation which ha[d] arisen . . . on account of hazardous or inherently dangerous industries which are concomitant to an industrial economy. . . . [T]he measures of compensation . . . must be correlated to the magnitude and capacity of the enterprise because such compensation must have a deterrent effect. The larger and more prosperous the enterprise, greater must be the amount of compensation payable.[82]

The Court accepted the government's argument and made the UCC responsible for UCIL's ultra-hazardous activities by lifting the corporate veil between a holding company and its subsidiary.[83] As a result, the Court ordered UCC to pay $270 million as interim relief to be paid within two months.[84] Feeling aggrieved by the order, UCC appealed to the Madhya Pradesh High Court, which upheld the lower court's order, reducing the relief to $190 million. The court saw that order as an application of the common law of torts.[85] The Court also recognized that the Bhopal incident attracted the absolute liability principle established in the Mehta case, which is more aggravated than the strict liability principle established in the Rylands case.[86] The Court set out the following essential elements as requirements for absolute liability:

> (1) [I]f the action proceeded to trial the plaintiff would obtain judgment for substantial damages; and (2) the payer is (a) insured in respect of plaintiff's claims, (b) a public authority, or (c) a person whose means and resources are such as to enable him to make the interim payment.

The reason for reducing the compensation amount, as explained by the Court, was the reasonable proportionality in light of the estimation of sufferers. The court categorized the sufferers and awarded compensation in the following scheme:

> (a) $12,100 for death, (b) $12,100 for total disability (c) $6,050 for permanent partial disability, and (d) $3,025 for temporary partial disability.[87]

81 *Metha v Union of India* [1987] AIR 1086 (S.C.).
82 Ibid.
83 *Union of India v Union Carbide Corp.* [1986] D. Bhopal No.1 113.
84 Ibid.
85 *Union Carbide Corp. v Union of India* [1988] No. 26/88 (Madhya Pradesh H.C.) 99–100.
86 *Rylands v Fletcher* [1868] UKHL 1.
87 *Union Carbide Corp. v Union of India* [1988] No. 26/88 (Madhya Pradesh H.C.) 99–100.

Dissatisfied with the Madhya Pradesh High Court's decision, both the UCC and the government preferred an application for leave to appeal to the Supreme Court, which it was granted.[88] In the appeal, the government opposed the High Court's reduction of the amount. At the same time, the UCC reaffirmed its initial appeal-averment, that is, the involvement of the saboteur employee and the non-existence of UCC's responsibility.[89]

The negotiation between UCC and the Indian government over the amount of settlement reveals that the claims and counterclaims started from $615 million from the government and $350 million from UCC and finally stood at $500 million and $420 million, respectively.[90] These talks were the basis for ordering a 'sudden' settlement by the Supreme Court to the amount of $470 million.[91] Thus, UCC was obligated to pay the amount by March 31, 1989, as a final settlement of 'all claims, rights, and liabilities related to and arising out of the Bhopal Gas disaster.' This settlement vacated all pending civil proceedings as deemed concluded and quashed all pending criminal proceedings.[92]

The order was regarded by the Court itself as 'just, equitable . . . reasonable' and complying with judicious, natural, and restorative principles.[93] However, the order faced severe criticism and resulted in numerous constitutional review applications being filed.[94] The prime reason was that the order was much lesser (15%) to make good all the losses and injuries.[95] The amount was alleged to be inadequate for various costs, including medication, rehabilitation, and restoration.[96] The order, although termed as the settlement of the government-UCC clash, was in no way considered as the true settlement between the real victims-UCC clashes.[97] Even so, the order ousted every past, present, and future challenge and granted absolute immunity to UCC and all its persons and is echoed in the following words:

> This settlement shall finally dispose of all past, present and future claims, causes of action and civil and criminal proceedings (of any nature whatsoever, wherever pending) by all Indian citizens and all public and private

88 *Union Carbide Corp. v Union of India* [1988] Appeal No. 13080 (SC) 11.
89 Ibid.
90 Ibid.
91 Desai, B. (1993). The Bhopal gas leak disaster litigation: An overview. *Asian Yearbook of International Law, 3*(1993), 163–179, 173.
92 *Union Carbide Corp. v Union of India* [1988] Appeal No. 13080 (SC) 11.
93 Desai, B. (1993). The Bhopal gas leak disaster litigation: An overview. *Asian Yearbook of International Law, 3*(1993), 163–179, 173.
94 Ibid., p. 177.
95 Kumar, D. (2021). Legal aspects of the Bhopal gas tragedy. *Legal Service India*. Retrieved April 4, from www.legalservicesindia.com/article/373/Legal-Aspects-of-the-Bhopal-Gas-Tragedy.html
96 Chouhan, T. R. (1994). *Bhopal: The inside story* (pp. 71–72). The Other India Press.
97 Kumar, D. (2021). Legal aspects of the Bhopal gas tragedy. *Legal Service India*. Retrieved April 4, from www.legalservicesindia.com/article/373/Legal-Aspects-of-the-Bhopal-Gas-Tragedy.html

> entities with respect to all past, present and future deaths, personal injuries health effects compensation, losses, damages and civil and criminal complaints of any nature whatsoever against UCC, Union Carbide India Limited, Union Carbide Eastern, and all of their subsidiaries and affiliates as well as each of their present and former directors, officers, employees, agents representatives, attorneys, advocates and solicitors arising out of, relating to or concerned with the Bhopal gas leak disaster, including past, present and future claims, causes of action and proceedings against each other.[98]

Keeping aside the quantum of compensation, it is important to scrutinize some other settlement features in light of the standard practice.[99] These features cited may differ as to agreements. However, they cover all bases wisely: (a) velocity, (b) ignorance of excess transaction expenditures, (c) settlement of all disputes, (d) equitable assessment of the victims' claims, (e) reasonable and just compensation, and (f) instruction control (punitive impact).[100] The settlement lacked speed as four years elapsed to settle down the quantum of compensation through many hurdles.[101] The costs generally involved in legal action, ranging from court fees to lawyers' remunerations, were about zero for victims because the government was the litigant incurring costs on behalf of the injured people.[102] Although the settlement claimed it as all-embracing in terms of resolving all claims and debarring any further action on the cause of the Bhopal disaster, various other cases were subsequently filed in the courts of India and the United States.[103] Intending to ensure fairness in ascertaining the claims of the injured people and in distributing the compensation amount, the actions of the government, ranging from constituting more than 50 judicial forums to establishing a supervisory working group, were, although praiseworthy, apprehended to be an overall failure mainly because of the anomalous record-maintaining of victims and reckless corruption involved generally in the distribution of public funds.[104]

There were mixed reactions among the victims regarding the adequacy of the amount to be distributed proportionately to the extent of injury, loss of life, and grievous hurt.[105] The effects of a compensatory settlement are restorative and sometimes punitive. Still, the present settlement had no punitive

98 *Union Carbide Corp. v Union of India* [1988] Appeal No. 13080 (SC) 11.

99 Covell, T. (1991). Bhopal disaster litigation: It's not over yet. *North Carolina Journal of International Law and Commercial Regulation, 16*, 279.

100 Magraw, D. B. (1985). The Bhopal disaster: Structuring a solution. *University of Colorado Law Review, 57*, 835, 845.

101 Covell, T. (1991). Bhopal disaster litigation: It's not over yet. *North Carolina Journal of International Law and Commercial Regulation, 16*, 279.

102 Ibid.

103 Ibid.

104 Ibid.

105 Ibid.

effect as the quantum of compensation was much less than half of the profits made by the UCC globally in just two years (1988–1989).[106]

The lack of legal provisions requiring compliance with safety procedures intended to prevent industrial disasters is the biggest gap that can continue to impact lives and property.[107] The Bhopal disaster holds a unique position mainly due to the day-light-like negligence, not counting the accident itself, on the part of UCC that led to unprecedented injuries in the industrial arena.[108] Such negligence can be considered both civil and criminal, giving rise to damages and sentences to be inflicted on every person responsible for carrying out the business of the corporation. UCC, in effect, cannot be allowed to raise the 'corporate veil' plea.[109] Rather, there should be set examples of bringing the corporate criminals or industrial culprits to book and imposing personal liability for their negligent acts to remove the long-standing difficulty in convicting corporate executives who have tainted their hands by simply using the pen ink negligently.[110] Additionally, there must be an independent watchdog organization set up to ensure triple-protective measures, that is, by the companies, respective trade unions, and the inspectors from the Labour Ministry. Above all, there shall be a judicial forum to review the actions of these bodies; such a forum may be the very Labour Court itself or a separate tribunal such as the 'Industrial Disaster Prevention Tribunal.'

An important development in the aftermath of the Bhopal judgment is that the glooms over victims and pressure groups, with quashing criminal cases filed against the UCC personnel, were erased by the Supreme Court's decision on the retrial of criminal cases.[111] The decision was seen as a prospect for prosecuting the personnel for their corporate misconduct and grave crimes, that is, overlooking safety defects for passing building designs.[112] The successful completion of these retrials would likely expose all the ins and outs of the disaster that are, as corporate tendency suggests, claimed as 'trade secrets'

106 Ibid.
107 Ibid.
108 Chouhan, T. R. (1994). *Bhopal: The inside story* (p. 71). The Other India Press.
109 Ibid., p. 71; Baxi, U. (2017). Writing about impunity and environment: The "silver jubilee" of the Bhopal catastrophe. In *Globalization and common responsibilities of states* (pp. 473–494). Routledge.
110 Chouhan, T. R. (1994). *Bhopal: The inside story* (p. 72). The Other India Press.
111 Ibid., p. 71; Dhavan, R. (1985). For whom – and for what – reflections on the legal aftermath of Bhopal. *Texas International Law Journal, 20*, 295; Patel, N. A., & Petlakh, K. (2014). Gandhi's nightmare: Bhopal and the need for a mindful jurisprudence. *Harvard Journal on Racial & Ethnic Justice, 30*, 151.
112 Chouhan, T. R. (1994). *Bhopal: The inside story* (p. 72). The Other India Press; Cassels, J. (1991). The uncertain promise of law: Lessons from Bhopal. *Osgoode Hall Law Journal, 29*, 1.

inappropriately.[113] Another development of the Bhopal resolution is that it started with individuals filing claims and got interpleaded by the government to reach an 'out-of-court' settlement approved by the Court.[114] This opened the horizon of extra-judicial settlement through negotiations or commercial arbitration in industrial dispute cases.

3.2.2 Gulf Oil Spill

The Gulf Oil Spill, also known as the Deepwater Horizon oil spill, is considered the largest offshore oil spill in U.S. history.[115] This environmental disaster showcased the devastating consequences of corporate negligence and the extensive legal repercussions that followed.[116]

The Gulf Oil Spill began on April 20, 2010, when an explosion occurred on the Deepwater Horizon drilling rig, killing 11 workers and causing a massive blowout, severely affecting the marine ecosystem and coastal areas in six states.[117] The oil company BP, along with its drilling partners, struggled to contain the runaway well until it was finally capped on July 12 and permanently sealed in mid-September.[118] Over the course of three months, the Macondo well released more than three million barrels of oil into the Gulf of Mexico. The spill resulted in widespread environmental damage, including the deaths of thousands of seabirds, turtles, and dolphins, as well as extensive damage to the coastal economy and public health.[119]

113 Chouhan, T. R. (1994). *Bhopal: The inside story* (p. 73). The Other India Press; Ramanathan, U. (2019). The Bhopal case: Retrospect and prospect. In *Research handbook on law, environment and the Global South* (pp. 138–145). Edward Elgar Publishing.

114 Chouhan, T. R. (1994). *Bhopal: The inside story* (pp. 71–72). The Other India Press; Fortun, K. (2000). Remembering Bhopal, re-figuring liability. *Interventions, 2*(2), 187–198.

115 Kwok, R. K., Engel, L. S., Miller, A. K., Blair, A., Curry, M. D., Jackson, W. B., Stewart, P. A., Stenzel, M. R., Birnbaum, L. S., & Sandler, D. P. (2017). The Gulf study: A prospective study of persons involved in the Deepwater Horizon oil spill response and clean-up. *Environmental Health Perspectives, 125*(4), 570–578.

116 Thornton, J. C. (2023). *An analysis of the Oil Pollution Act of 1990: Regulatory calibration in anticipation of 21st-century environmental disasters.* University of South Florida; Gilles, M. (2011). Public-private approaches to mass tort victim compensation: Some thoughts on the Gulf Coast Claims Facility. *DePaul Law Review, 61*, 419.

117 Beyer, J., Trannum, H. C., Bakke, T., Hodson, P. V., & Collier, T. K. (2016). Environmental effects of the Deepwater Horizon oil spill: A review. *Marine Pollution Bulletin, 110*(1), 28–51.

118 Incardona, J. P., & Scholz, N. L. (2018). Case study: The 2010 Deepwater Horizon oil spill and its environmental developmental impacts. *Development and Environment*, 235–283.

119 Shultz, J. M., Walsh, L., Garfin, D. R., Wilson, F. E., & Neria, Y. (2015). The 2010 Deepwater Horizon oil spill: The trauma signature of an ecological disaster. *The Journal of Behavioral Health Services & Research, 42*, 58–76; Incardona, J. P., & Scholz, N. L. (2018). Case study: The 2010 Deepwater Horizon oil spill and its environmental developmental impacts. *Development and Environment*, 235–283.

The Gulf Oil Spill led to numerous civil and criminal investigations involving various federal agencies, such as the National Commission on the BP Deepwater Horizon Oil Spill and Offshore Drilling, the Department of Justice (DOJ), and the EPA. Additionally, independent agencies like the U.S. Chemical Safety and Hazard Investigation Board also investigated the causes of the spill. The legal proceedings against BP and its partners, including Transocean and Halliburton, spanned nearly six years and consisted of three trials, over 500 days of depositions, and 100 expert reports.[120]

In 2012, BP faced legal action on the basis of 14 charges or counts of criminal actions, which included but were not limited to manslaughter, congressional obstruction, and violations of the Cleanup Procedures of the 1972 Water Act and the 1918 Migratory Bird Treaty Act. This resulted in a payment of 4.5 billion dollars, which sets the record for the largest penalty in the history of the United States. Later on, in 2015, together with the Justice Department and the Gulf Coast states, they reached a settlement for more than 20 billion dollars in civil settlement financially through BP. In the agreement was included a penalty of 5.5 billion dollars under the Clean Water Act, 8.1 billion dollars in damages for natural resources, and 5.9 billion for payments to local authorities and states. BP also incurred costs from the spill, approximately 15 billion dollars for cleanup expenses and 20 billion for economic damages to businesses and individuals.[121]

The Gulf Oil Spill had a profound impact on the environment, affecting everything from wetlands and beaches to deep ocean ecosystems. The spill smothered coral reefs, disrupted the reproductive cycles of commercial and recreational fish species, and led to the deaths of numerous marine animals.[122] Moreover, the spill highlighted the risks associated with offshore drilling and the need for stricter safety regulations and oversight to prevent future environmental disasters. Unfortunately, despite the severity of the spill, Congress did not pass any new environmental protection laws in its aftermath, leaving the industry largely unchanged.[123] Nevertheless, the settlements in the Gulf Oil Spill set precedents for future corporate wrongdoing, with companies like

120 Cruden, J. C., O'Rourke, S., & Himmelhoch, S. D. (2016). The Deepwater Horizon oil spill litigation: Proof of concept for the manual for complex litigation and the 2015 amendments to the federal rules of civil procedure. *Michigan Journal of Environmental & Administrative Law*, *6*, 65.

121 Uhlmann, D. (2020, April 6). BP paid a steep price for the Gulf oil spill, but for the US a decade later, it's business as usual. *The Conversation*. https://theconversation.com/bp-paid-a-steep-price-for-the-gulf-oil-spill-but-for-the-us-a-decade-later-its-business-as-usual-136905

122 Beyer, J., Trannum, H. C., Bakke, T., Hodson, P. V., & Collier, T. K. (2016). Environmental effects of the Deepwater Horizon oil spill: A review. *Marine Pollution Bulletin*, *110*(1), 28–51.

123 Schoenbaum, T. J. (2012). Liability for damages in oil spill accidents: Evaluating the USA and international law regimes in the light of Deepwater Horizon. *Journal of Environmental Law*, *24*(3), 395–416.

Volkswagen, Bank of America, and JPMorgan Chase facing billions of dollars in fines for various misconducts in subsequent years.

The settlements reached in the Gulf Oil Spill case were a significant deterrent for corporations engaging in high-risk activities, as they demonstrated the immense legal exposure and financial consequences that can result from negligence and misconduct. In the wake of the spill, companies in the oil and gas industry have become more committed to well containment efforts and are more aware of the risks associated with their operations.[124] The magnitude of the legal consequences in the Gulf Oil Spill case has undoubtedly impacted corporate decision-making and risk management strategies.[125] It underscored the need for greater corporate accountability and responsibility, as well as the importance of robust government regulation and oversight of high-risk industries.[126]

While the Gulf Oil Spill settlements held BP and its partners accountable for their actions, the disaster also exposed the shortcomings of the U.S. government's regulatory oversight. The Minerals Management Service, responsible for monitoring offshore drilling safety, was criticized for not adequately supervising safety procedures on the rig and failing to scrutinize BP's actions. The National Commission's final report on the spill recommended a series of changes, including raising the liability cap for oil spills, establishing a new government safety agency to oversee the offshore oil industry, and increasing safety regulations similar to those in Norway and the UK. However, many of these recommendations have yet to be implemented, and Congressional approval is needed for some of them. Ten years after the Gulf Oil Spill, the legal landscape governing offshore drilling remains largely unchanged.[127] The United States continues to subcontract drilling safety and spill response to the very industries that undertake drilling operations. In addition, the country has not lessened its dependence on fossil fuels to increase the use of clean energy. After ten years, it is still an open question when the world's leading economies, including the United States, will begin to take real steps to assume responsibility for the disaster and implement concrete steps to mitigate further ecological disasters.

124 Weber, J. M., & Crew Jr., R. E. (2000). Deterrence theory and marine oil spills: Do coast guard civil penalties deter pollution? *Journal of Environmental Management*, *58*(3), 161–168.

125 Kanso, A. M., Nelson, R. A., & Kitchen, P. J. (2020). BP and the Deepwater Horizon oil spill: A case study of how company management employed public relations to restore a damaged brand. *Journal of Marketing Communications*, *26*(7), 703–731.

126 Windsor, C., & McNicholas, P. (2012). *The BP Gulf oil spill: Public and corporate governance failures.*

127 Gyo Lee, Y., Garza-Gomez, X., & Lee, R. M. (2018). Ultimate costs of the disaster: Seven years after the Deepwater Horizon oil spill. *Journal of Corporate Accounting & Finance*, *29*(1), 69–79.

The Gulf Oil Spill had far-reaching legal consequences, highlighting the importance of corporate criminal liability and corporations' role as environmental polluters.[128] While the settlements served as a deterrent for future misconduct, the lack of significant regulatory changes and the continued dependence on fossil fuels underscore the need for greater corporate accountability and action to protect the environment and prevent future disasters.[129]

3.2.3 The Love Canal Disaster

The Love Canal disaster is a grim reminder of the catastrophic effects of environmental pollution and the devastating impact it can have on human life.[130] The Love Canal disaster was one of the worst environmental disasters in the history of the United States.[131] It was a man-made tragedy that resulted in the loss of innocent lives, caused widespread illnesses, and devastated an entire community.[132]

The disaster occurred in the late 1970s in Niagara Falls, New York. The Love Canal area was originally a landfill site for Hooker Chemical Company.[133] In the 1940s, the company covered the landfill with soil and sold the land to the Niagara Falls School Board for one dollar. The school board then built an elementary school and a residential neighborhood on the landfill. The toxic waste was buried underneath the school and the neighborhood. In the 1950s and 1960s, residents of the Love Canal area began to notice strange odors and substances oozing out of the ground.[134] There were reports of chemical burns and other health problems. However, it was not until the 1970s that the full extent of the disaster was revealed.[135] The waste dumped by Hooker Chemical Company contained over 80 different toxic chemicals, including dioxin, benzene, and PCBs. The toxic chemicals dumped into the canal seeped into the ground, contaminating the soil and groundwater. This resulted in the wide-

128 Steinzor, R. (2016). How criminal law can help save the environment. *Environmental Law*, 209–239.

129 Issacharoff, S., & Rave, D. T. (2013). The BP oil spill settlement and the paradox of public litigation. *Louisiana Law Review*, *74*, 397; Dybing, S. S. (2016). Environmental harm: Social causes and shifting legislative dynamics. In *Eco-global crimes* (pp. 273–294). Routledge.

130 Davies, K. (2023). *The rise of the US environmental health movement*. Rowman & Littlefield.

131 Beck, E. C. (1979, September 22). *The Love Canal tragedy*. U.S. Environmental Protection Agency. Retrieved April 4, 2016, from www.epa.gov/archive/epa/aboutepa/love-canal-tragedy.html

132 Phillips, A. S., Hung, Y.-T., & Bosela, P. A. (2007). Love Canal tragedy. *Journal of Performance of Constructed Facilities*, *21*(4), 313–319.

133 Kleiman, J. (2024). *Love Canal: A brief history*. Geneseo. Retrieved April 5, from www.geneseo.edu/history/love_canal_history

134 Ibid.

135 Ibid.

spread contamination of the environment, including the air, water, and soil.[136] The toxic chemicals cause a host of health problems, including birth defects, cancer, and other illnesses. The disaster displaced thousands of people who had to abandon their homes and businesses.[137] It also resulted in widespread illnesses, birth defects, and other health problems.[138]

The Love Canal disaster highlighted the role of corporations as polluters. The Hooker Chemical Company was responsible for dumping toxic waste into the Love Canal, which resulted in the disaster. The company was aware of the dangerous chemicals it was dumping but chose to ignore them to pursue profits. Furthermore, the company had failed to properly dispose of the toxic waste, which resulted in its seepage into the ground and the contamination of the environment. The Love Canal disaster is a stark reminder of the need for corporations to act responsibly and prioritize the health and safety of the environment and the people who live in it.[139] The residents of the Love Canal area, who had suffered the devastating effects of the disaster, filed lawsuits against the company. The lawsuits alleged that the company was responsible for the disaster and that it had failed to properly dispose of the toxic waste. The lawsuits resulted in a settlement of $129 million, which was used to compensate the victims.[140]

The Love Canal disaster was not just an accident; it was a result of corporate criminality.[141] The Hooker Chemical Company was aware of the dangers of the chemicals it was dumping into the Love Canal. The company had also failed to properly dispose of the toxic waste, which resulted in its seepage into the ground and the contamination of the environment. The Love Canal disaster was not just a result of the company's negligence but a result of its deliberate actions to maximize profits at the expense of the environment and the people who lived in it.[142]

The Love Canal disaster also highlighted the importance of environmental regulations as an institutional mechanism. The disaster resulted from the

136 Herdman, R. C., Haughie, G. E., Campbell, L. E., Axelrod, D., Vianna, N., Hennessy, W., Sachs, J., Hoffman, C., Cuddy, M., Hennessy, W., Whalen, R. P., & Grushky, A. (1978). *Love Canal – Public health time bomb*. State of New York. www.health.ny.gov/environmental/investigations/love_canal/lctimbmb.htm

137 Ibid.

138 Ibid.

139 Worthley, J. A., & Torkelson, R. (1981). Managing the toxic waste problem: Lessons from the Love Canal. *Administration & Society*, *13*(2), 145–160.

140 Albanese, J. S. (1984). Love Canal six years later: The legal legacy. *Federal Probation*, *48*, 53.

141 Spurgeon, W. A., & Fagan, T. P. (2010). Criminal liability for life-endangering corporate conduct. *Journal of Criminal Law & Criminology*, *100*, xxxi.

142 DiMento, J. F., & Badiee, A. (2017). Historical pollution and criminal liability in the United States. In *Historical pollution: Comparative legal responses to environmental crimes* (pp. 197–223).

government's failure to regulate corporations' dumping of toxic waste.[143] It led to the enactment of the CERCLA, which provides a framework for cleaning hazardous waste sites and enforcing environmental regulations.[144]

3.2.4 Three Mile Island Disaster

On March 28, 1979, the Three Mile Island disaster unfolded in Pennsylvania, the United States.[145] A cooling malfunction in the second reactor of the nuclear power plant led to a partial meltdown of the reactor core, resulting in the release of radioactive gas into the atmosphere.[146] This catastrophic event is considered one of the worst nuclear accidents in the history of the United States.[147] The incident raised concerns about the safety of nuclear power plants and highlighted the dark side of corporate culture, which contributed significantly to the disaster.[148]

The Three Mile Island disaster prompted an intense investigation by the Nuclear Regulatory Commission (NRC) and other government agencies. The investigations revealed several factors that contributed to the accident, including the corporate culture of the plant's operator, Metropolitan Edison.[149] The company's management had a history of cutting corners and disregarding safety regulations for cost reduction. This resulted in inadequate training of plant operators, insufficient maintenance of equipment, and an overall lack of emphasis on safety.[150] Furthermore, the company's hierarchical structure and communication barriers prevented open dialogue between employees and management, creating an environment where safety concerns were often silenced or ignored. This toxic corporate culture ultimately set the stage for the disaster, as employees were unable or unwilling to raise concerns about the

143 Newman, R. S. (2016). *Love Canal: A toxic history from colonial times to the present.* Oxford University Press.

144 Mah, A. (2020). Toxic legacies and environmental justice. In *Environmental justice* (pp. 121–131). Routledge; Worthley, J. A., & Torkelson, R. (1981). Managing the toxic waste problem: Lessons from the Love Canal. *Administration & Society, 13*(2), 145–160.

145 Widoff, M. P. (1981). The accident at Three Mile Island. *Western New England Law Review, 4*, 223.

146 Smith, J. S., & Fisher, J. H. (1981). Three Mile Island: The silent disaster. *JAMA, 245*(16), 1656–1659.

147 Walker, J. S. (2004). *Three Mile Island: A nuclear crisis in historical perspective* (Vol. 41). University of California Press; Staats, E. B. (1980). *Three Mile Island: The most studied nuclear accident in history* (Comptroller General of the United States report to Congress, Report Number EMD-80-109). https://doi.org/10.2172/6941962

148 Hopkins, A. (2001). Was Three Mile Island a "normal accident"? *Journal of Contingencies and Crisis Management, 9*(2), 65–72; Etzkowitz, H. (1984). Corporate induced disaster: Three Mile Island and the delegitimation of nuclear power. *Humanity & Society, 8*(3), 228–252.

149 Etzkowitz, H. (1984). Corporate induced disaster: Three Mile Island and the delegitimation of nuclear power. *Humanity & Society, 8*(3), 228–252.

150 Ibid.

faulty equipment and poor safety practices that led to the cooling malfunction and subsequent reactor meltdown.[151] Another contributing factor to the disaster was the lack of regulatory oversight by the NRC. This government agency was responsible for ensuring the safety of nuclear power plants. Still, it was plagued by bureaucratic inefficiencies and a cozy relationship with the industry it was supposed to regulate. This lack of effective oversight contributed to the lax safety culture at Three Mile Island and other nuclear plants nationwide.

The Three Mile Island disaster resulted in releasing radioactive gases into the atmosphere, exposing nearby residents to elevated radiation levels.[152] While the immediate health impacts of this exposure were limited to a small increase in cancer risk, the long-term environmental consequences were more significant.[153] The release of radioactive materials contaminated soil, water, and vegetation around the plant, increasing background radiation levels in the area.[154] The cleanup process took over a decade, cost billions of dollars, and involved removing and disposing of contaminated materials. Despite these efforts, the lingering effects of the accident can still be detected in the form of elevated radiation levels in the environment. Additionally, the disaster sparked widespread fear of nuclear power and contributed to a decline in the construction of new nuclear power plants in the United States. As a result, the country became more reliant on fossil fuels, which have their own set of negative environmental impacts, such as air pollution and GHG emissions.

The Three Mile Island disaster offers several valuable lessons for corporations and regulators.[155] One of the most important takeaways from the incident is the crucial role of corporate culture in promoting safety and environmental responsibility.[156] Companies must foster a culture that values transparency, open communication, and a commitment to safety and sustainability. This includes investing in employee training, maintaining equipment, and prioritizing safety over profits. Another lesson from the disaster is the importance of robust regulatory oversight. Government agencies must be adequately funded, staffed, and empowered to hold corporations accountable for their actions. This requires a proactive approach to regulation and a willingness to challenge the status quo and demand higher standards from the industry. Finally, the Three Mile Island disaster highlights the need for greater public awareness

151 Ibid.

152 Rogovin, M. (1980). *Three Mile Island: A report to the commissioners and to the public* (Vol. 1250). Nuclear Regulatory Commission, Special Inquiry Group.

153 Davidson, L. M., Baum, A., & Gisriel, M. M. (2020). Toxic exposure and chronic stress at Three Mile Island. In *Advances in environmental psychology* (Vol. 6, pp. 35–46). Routledge.

154 Rogovin, M. (1980). *Three Mile Island: A report to the commissioners and to the public* (Vol. 1250). Nuclear Regulatory Commission, Special Inquiry Group.

155 Wells, C., Morgan, D., & Quick, O. (1999). Disasters: A challenge for the law. *Washburn Law Journal, 39*, 496.

156 Sturgis, S. (2010). *Investigation: Revelations about Three Mile Island disaster raise doubts over nuclear plant safety: A special facing south investigation by Sue Sturgis.* Sage Publications.

and engagement in issues related to corporate environmental responsibility. By staying informed and holding corporations accountable for their actions, consumers and shareholders can play a vital role in driving positive change and creating a responsible corporate culture.

Creating a responsible corporate culture requires a multifaceted approach that addresses both internal and external factors. Some strategies for fostering a culture of responsibility include (a) leadership commitment, (b) employee engagement, (c) transparency and accountability, (d) collaboration with stakeholders, and (e) continuous improvement.[157]

Corporate accountability and transparency are essential components of a responsible corporate culture. By being open and honest about their environmental performance, companies can build trust with stakeholders, demonstrate their commitment to sustainability, and drive improvements in their operations.[158] Some ways that corporations can promote accountability and transparency include (a) regularly reporting on environmental performance, using standardized metrics and frameworks to ensure consistency and comparability, (b) engaging with stakeholders to gather feedback and address concerns, demonstrating a genuine commitment to continuous improvement, (c) participating in third-party audits and certifications to validate their sustainability claims and provide external performance assurance, and (d) collaborating with industry peers, regulators, and NGOs to share best practices and drive collective action on sustainability issues.[159]

The Three Mile Island disaster is a stark reminder of the dark side of corporate culture and the devastating consequences of prioritizing profits over people and the environment.[160] As we move forward, we must learn from this and other incidents and work together to create a corporate culture that values responsibility, transparency, and sustainability. By holding corporations accountable for their actions, fostering a culture of continuous improvement, and promoting collaboration between stakeholders, we can help drive progress toward a more sustainable future. The lessons from Three Mile Island must not be forgotten but rather serve as a catalyst for positive change and a reminder of the critical role that corporations play in protecting our planet and its inhabitants.[161]

157 Waddock, S., & Rasche, A. (2012). *Building the responsible enterprise: Where vision and values add value.* Stanford University Press.

158 Linnenluecke, M. K., & Griffiths, A. (2010). Corporate sustainability and organizational culture. *Journal of World Business, 45*(4), 357–366.

159 Ganescu, C., & Gangone, A. (2017). A model of socially responsible organizational culture. *Studia Universitatis "Vasile Goldis" Arad–Economics Series, 27*(2), 45–59.

160 Malmsheimer, L. M. (1986). Three Mile Island: Fact, frame, and fiction. *American Quarterly, 38*(1), 35–52.

161 Sandman, P. M. (2004). Three Mile Island – 25 years later. *Safety at Work*, 7–11; Osif, B. A., Baratta, A. J., & Conkling, T. W. (2004). *TMI 25 years later: The Three Mile Island nuclear power plant accident and its impact.* Penn State Press.

3.2.5 Ballast Water Induced Pollution

Ballast water has long been an issue of concern for global biodiversity levels.[162] Ballast water carries bacteria,[163] diatoms and fish,[164] harmful algae,[165] parasites,[166] and virus-like particles.[167] If not managed effectively, through this water, non-Indigenous species can move around the world and alter the composition of ecological communities.[168]

The threat of invasion by nonnative species through ballast water has been ever-increasing, since it was first recognized by scientists in 1903 in

162 Geller, J., Carlton, J., & Powers, D. (1993). Interspecific and intrapopulation variation in mitochondrial ribosomal DNA sequences of *Mytilus* spp. (Bivalvia: Mollusca). *Molecular Marine Biology and Biotechnology, 2*(1), 44–50; Mimura, H., Katakura, R., & Ishida, H. (2005). Changes of microbial populations in a ship's ballast water and sediments on a voyage from Japan to Qatar. *Marine Pollution Bulletin, 50*(7), 751–757; Pimentel, D., Lach, L., Zuniga, R., & Morrison, D. (2000). Environmental and economic costs of non-indigenous species in the United States. *BioScience, 50*(1), 53–65. Pimentel, D., Lach, L., Zuniga, R., & Morrison, D. (2000). Environmental and economic costs of nonindigenous species in the United States. *BioScience, 50*(1), 53–65; Sala, O. E., Chapin, F. S., Armesto, J. J., Berlow, E., Bloomfield, J., Dirzo, R., Huber-Sanwald, E., Huenneke, L. F., Jackson, R. B., & Kinzig, A. (2000). Global biodiversity scenarios for the year 2100. *Science, 287*(5459), 1770–1774.

163 McCarthy, S. A., & Khambaty, F. M. (1994). International dissemination of epidemic Vibrio cholerae by cargo ship ballast and other nonpotable waters. *Applied and Environmental Microbiology, 60*(7), 2597–2601; Ruiz, G. M., Rawlings, T. K., Dobbs, F. C., Drake, L. A., Mullady, T., Huq, A., & Colwell, R. R. (2000). Global spread of microorganisms by ships. *Nature, 408*(6808), 49–50.

164 Geller, J., Carlton, J., & Powers, D. (1993). Interspecific and intrapopulation variation in mitochondrial ribosomal DNA sequences of *Mytilus* spp. (Bivalvia: Mollusca). *Molecular Marine Biology and Biotechnology, 2*(1), 44–50.

165 McCarthy, S. A., & Khambaty, F. M. (1994). International dissemination of epidemic *Vibrio cholerae* by cargo ship ballast and other nonpotable waters. *Applied and Environmental Microbiology, 60*(7), 2597–2601.

166 McCollin, T., Shanks, A. M., & Dunn, J. (2007). The efficiency of regional ballast water exchange: Changes in phytoplankton abundance and diversity. *Harmful Algae, 6*(4), 531–546.

167 Carlton, J. T., Thompson, J. K., Schemel, L. E., & Nichols, F. H. (1990). Remarkable invasion of San Francisco Bay (California, USA), by the Asian clam Potamocorbula amurensis. I. Introduction and dispersal. *Marine Ecology Progress Series, 66*, 81–94; Ruiz, G. M., Rawlings, T. K., Dobbs, F. C., Drake, L. A., Mullady, T., Huq, A., & Colwell, R. R. (2000). Global spread of microorganisms by ships. *Nature, 408*(6808), 49–50; Ruiz, G. M., Rawlings, T. K., Dobbs, F. C., Drake, L. A., Mullady, T., Huq, A., & Colwell, R. R. (2000). Global spread of microorganisms by ships. *Nature, 408*(6808), 49–50.

168 Briski, E., Bailey, S. A., Casas-Monroy, O., DiBacco, C., Kaczmarska, I., Levings, C., MacGillivary, M. L., McKindsey, C. W., Nasmith, L. E., & Parenteau, M. (2012). Relationship between propagule pressure and colonization pressure in invasion ecology: A test with ships' ballast. *Proceedings of the Royal Society of London B: Biological Sciences*, rspb20112671., David, M., Gollasch, S., & Pavliha, M. (2013). Global ballast water management and the "same location" concept: A clear term or a clear issue? *Ecological Applications, 23*(2), 331–338; Ranjan, R. (2008). Special issue: Economics of invasive species management. *Journal of Environmental Management, 89*(4), 271–349.

the North Sea.[169] However, it was not treated as a serious problem until the 1970s. In the late 1980s, the issue gained significant attention in the face of ballast water-related problems in Canada and Australia.[170] At this time, these countries provided scientific evidence of invasion by nonnative species and brought this issue to the attention of the International Maritime Organization (IMO). Different entities, such as local government, environmentalist groups, UN bodies, research bodies, universities, and other stakeholders, have been warning of the negative aspects of ballast water and have been working on developing a solution, which is commonly known as 'ballast water management.' The United Nations (UN) has declared ballast water as one of the four greatest threats to the world's oceans and seas.[171] But, other than open ocean ballast water exchange, no other viable methods of ballast water management have been developed so far. There are two generic technologies, solid–liquid separation and disinfection, to treat ballast water in the ports. As a mechanical process, however, solid–liquid separation does not entirely kill harmful organisms. While the disinfection process can completely destroy potentially harmful organisms, it generates a large amount of relevant chemicals.[172]

Shipping and shipping corporations are at the focal point in ballast water management. Shipping is considered the main mechanism for the movement of nonnative species from one place to another.[173] The current global regulatory framework for international shipping involves the facilitation of states and the global shipping industry to operate the transportation of goods sustainably. However, none of the instruments within this framework incorporate accountability standards for large shipping corporations for vessel performance in ballast water management.

Regulating ballast water is difficult, as the volume of this water loaded and discharged by vessels is extremely high. The Australian Marine Environment Protection Association (AUSMEPA) estimates the amount to be ten billion

169 International Maritime Organization (IMO). (2015a). *Ballast water management.* Retrieved February 9, 2023, from http://www.imo.org/OurWork/Environment/BallastWaterManagement/Pages/Default.aspx

170 Ibid.

171 David, M., Gollasch, S., & Pavliha, M. (2013). Global ballast water management and the "same location" concept: a clear term or a clear issue? *Ecological Applications, 23*(2), 331–338, 331; International Maritime Organization (IMO). (2016). *GoBallast partnerships: Home.* Retrieved February 9, 2023, from http://globallast.imo.org/index.asp

172 Pérez, W., Ñahui, M., Ellis, D., & Forbes, G. A. (2014). Wide phenotypic diversity for resistance to *Phytophthora infestans* found in potato landraces from Peru. *Plant Disease, 98*(11), 1530–1533.

173 Fofonoff, P. W., Ruiz, G. M., Steves, B., & Carlton, J. T. (2003). In ships or on ships? Mechanisms of transfer and invasion for nonnative species to the coasts of North America. In *Invasive species: Vectors and management strategies* (pp. 152–182); Hewitt, C. L., Gollasch, S., & Minchin, D. (2009). The vessel as a vector: Biofouling, ballast water, and sediments. In *Biological invasions in marine ecosystems* (pp. 117–131). Springer.

tons per year globally.[174] The IMO has also calculated that the yearly international and domestic ballast water amounts to 6–10 billion tons per year.[175] Properly managing such a large amount of water is critical for preventing unwanted aquatic species' movement via carriage in the vessels. However, there is no binding international instrument for regulating ballast water and incidents involving ballast water movement other than limited regional legislation. The IMO is the global authoritative institution for the development of rules and guidelines for maritime shipping, including those regarding ballast water. The IMO has previously attempted to introduce a new regulatory instrument, but due to the lack of ratification by its member states, the instrument is not yet in effect.

Aside from the proposed instrument, which has been developed by the IMO, two existing conventions already adopted by the UN are significant for the regulation of ballast water and the transfer of marine species. The UN introduced these conventions, targeting biodiversity and the transfer of marine species around the world: the United Nations Convention on the Law of the Sea in 1982 and the CBD in 1992.[176] In 1991, the Marine Environmental Protection Committee (MPEC) of the IMO issued voluntary International Guidelines for Preventing the Introduction of Unwanted Aquatic Organisms and Pathogens for Ships' Ballast Water and Sediment Discharges.[177] This resolution was drafted by Canada and subsequently modified after additional information was sourced from Australia. In November 1993, at a diplomatic conference, the IMO adopted the modified guidelines as International Guidelines for Preventing the Introduction of Unwanted Aquatic Organisms and Pathogens for Ships' Ballast Water and Sediment Discharges[178] and requested member countries to use the guidelines. However, it was found that only a few countries followed the guidelines provided, and subsequently, in 1994, the MPEC formed a 'ballast water working group' to formulate new regulations. The working group developed draft regulations and a comprehensive guideline; it was adopted in 1997 as Guidelines for the Control and Management of Ships' Ballast Water to Minimize the Transfer of Harmful

174 Australian Marine Environment Protection Association (AUSMEPA). (2015). *Ballast water: The issue*. Retrieved February 10, 2023, from http://www.ausmepa.org.au/pests/default.asp?pageid=33&nav=19

175 International Maritime Organization (IMO). (2015b). *GoBallast partnerships: The problem*. Retrieved February 8, 2023, from http://globallast.imo.org/index.asp?page=problem.htm.

176 Adopted in the United Nations Conference on Environment and Development. (1992). *Agenda 21*. 31 I.L.M. 818.

177 For details, see MPEC Resolution 50(31) in 1991. For a thorough discussion on this matter, see Buck, E. H. (2010). *Ballast water management to combat invasive species*. Congressional Research Service Reports, 25. https://digitalcommons.unl.edu/crsdocs/25

178 International Maritime Organization. (1993). *IMO Assembly Resolution A774 (18), Guidelines for preventing the introduction of unwanted organisms and pathogens from ships' ballast water and sediments discharges*, November 4, 1993.

Organisms and Pathogens.[179] Later, in February 2004, the IMO, in its London conference on 'ballast water management for ships,' adopted the final draft of a convention on ballast water, namely, *The International Convention for the Control and Management of Ships' Ballast Water and Sediments.*[180] This proposed international convention must be ratified by a minimum of 30 member states, representing at least 35% of the world's gross registered tonnage. As of October 2014, 43 countries have ratified the convention.[181] But the tonnage they represent is only 32.54%.[182] This convention, therefore, is still not in effect.

The proposed IMO convention on ballast water management focuses on countries' responsibilities, with little emphasis on the roles of global shipping corporations. Moreover, some provisions have been criticized for their lack of clarity. For instance, it exempts vessels that load and offload ballast water at the same location from implementing the ballast water management plan.[183] However, it does not clearly define the term 'same location.' In a large sea or large areas with multiple ports, the term 'same location' can cover a significant area, including regions with different environmental characteristics. The movement of ballast water in the 'same location' under the terms of the instrument could, therefore, allow for the disadvantageous transfer of marine species. Furthermore, the proposed convention does not specify how the invasion of nonnative species will be prevented by ships labeled with NOBOB (No Ballast on Board).

Under the proposed convention, each vessel must carry a ballast water record book to record intake and discharge-related information.[184] The record book must be readily available for inspection, and the records are to be saved for at least two years following the final entry in the book. This record book is the main source of data that the 'ballast water reporting form' requires, and this is expected by many countries, including Australia, Canada, and the United States. Though there is a provision for inspection under this convention, there are real concerns about the data provided in the ballast water reporting forms.

179 International Maritime Organization. (1997). *IMO Resolution A. 868(20), Guidelines for the control and management of ships' ballast water to minimize the transfer of harmful organisms and pathogens*, November 27, 1997.

180 International Maritime Organization. (2004). *International convention for the control and management of ship's ballast water and sediments* (IMO Doc. BMW/CONF/36, February 16, 2004).

181 Hamworthy. (2016). *Hamworthy: Ballast water management*. Hamworthy. Retrieved February 9, 2024, from http://www.hamworthy.com/ballast_water_management

182 Ibid.

183 David, M., Gollasch, S., & Pavliha, M. (2013). Global ballast water management and the "same location" concept: A clear term or a clear issue? *Ecological Applications*, *23*(2), 331–338.

184 Annex, Regulation B2 of *Guidelines for the control and management of ships' ballast water to minimize the transfer of harmful organisms and pathogens.*

The information is self-reported,[185] and this raises questions regarding its validity and reliability. Miller et al. (2011), in their research on ballast water management in the United States, found that several vessels arrived in a port with little explanation for the amount of ballast water they discharged into the sea within the port area.[186] They also found a disparity between the frequency of vessels' arrival and the amount of ballast water discharged; ports with a high volume of shipping transport do not necessarily hold a greater volume of water due to ballast discharge. Therefore, it has been identified that there is scope for vessels to provide inaccurate data on ballast water or even to manipulate the data. Verifying this kind of information is difficult, if not impossible, as the volume of global port traffic is significant. This also raises questions about the effectiveness of existing inspection regimes. In a study of ballast water management in California, Brown (2012) proposed that only 25% of vessels arriving in port are boarded by inspectors who check logs, salinity levels, and ballast water management plans and reporting.[187]

Ballast water management (BWM) is mainly couched regarding shareholder value maximization or a strong profit incentive. Mostly, it is considered a regulatory tick box that needs to be achieved through minimal and, at times, obscure reporting. Corporations are careful not to 'over-disclose' information as this may provide ammunition for recourse in the future, either by regulatory threat or through consumers 'walking with their feet.' Many corporations simply do not disclose any information at all. With China Shipping Container Lines, mention of 'stakeholders' in relation to ballast water management generally concerns unknown and unknowable future generations reducing any ability to measure the impact of present actions on the environment. Other corporations discuss the importance of BWM for the environment, but few details are provided as to the scale of investment in such activities. As found in other studies of external corporate social responsibility disclosure, this may be because disclosure is used more as a legitimating strategy[188] in response to a low level of perceived external pressure. Thus, the power of the entity that demands an account may well be determined by the extent to which shareholder (profit maximization) concerns are privileged over those of wider (and more dispersed) stakeholders. Consequently, disclosure practice (and thus the

185 Miller, A. W., Minton, M. S., & Ruiz, G. M. (2011). Geographic limitations and regional differences in ships' ballast water management to reduce marine invasions in the contiguous United States. *BioScience, 61*(11), 880–887, 882.

186 Ibid., p. 882.

187 Brown, C. (2012). *Patterns of management, compliance and geography of ballast water in California*. California State Lands Commission. http://www.slc.ca.gov/About/Prevention_First/2012/California-BallastMgmt.pdf

188 See, for example, O'Donovan, G. (2002). Environmental disclosures in the annual report: Extending the applicability and predictive power of legitimacy theory. *Accounting, Auditing & Accountability Journal, 15*(3), 344–371; Tilling, M. V., & Tilt, C. A. (2010). The edge of legitimacy: Voluntary social and environmental reporting in Rothmans' 1956–1999 annual reports. *Accounting, Auditing & Accountability Journal, 23*(1), 55–81.

discharge of accountability) is much more definable for 'narrow' shareholder concerns. Furthermore, regulation is also more easily created and enforced because of these definable constraints. With wider stakeholders, the 'concreteness' of the accountability relationship allows for opportunities for the arbitrage of information. Reporting in annual reports is primarily directed at shareholders (and mandatorily required in many jurisdictions). However, the information provided to 'other stakeholders' does not have the same precision and rigor because accountability relationships are less well articulated. For this reason, regulation also becomes more difficult, but we argue, all the more important. Especially, to ensure that accountability is strengthened and 'voiceless' stakeholders who do not necessarily have the ability but the right to demand an account are heard.

3.2.6 Wildlife Crime

With the expansion of economic globalization, corporations have emerged as major contributors to the global economy and have operations in several countries.[189] While corporations have helped in job creation and economic growth, their activities can also pose significant harm to the environment and wildlife. Corporations are often responsible for pollution, habitat destruction, and the illegal trade of wildlife and their products.[190] As a result, it has become necessary to closely scrutinize corporate actions and hold them responsible for wildlife crime.

Wildlife crime by corporations is a complex issue that requires a deep understanding of various factors, including legal, economic, and social dimensions. This crime can take many forms, from direct actions such as illegal logging, poaching, and the illegal trade of wildlife and their products to indirect activities like pollution, habitat destruction, and the financing of illegal activities. The severity of these crimes can range from minor violations to large-scale operations that threaten entire ecosystems and species. Corporations engage in wildlife crime for several reasons, including competitive advantage, profit, and a lack of awareness or concern for environmental regulations. In some instances, corporations may be directly involved in illegal activities, while in others, they may simply turn a blind eye to their suppliers, contractors, or subsidiaries' actions.

Several global companies have been implicated in contributing to deforestation, which often involves illegal logging practices. Cargill, a U.S.-based

189 Porwal, S., & Mittal, J. K. (2020). The impact of transnational corporations on global environment: A critical study. *International Journal of Management (IJM)*, *11*(8).

190 Narreddy, V., & Shashidhar, E. S. (2024). Wildlife crime: Causes, consequences and countermeasures: A review. *International Journal of Science and Research Archive*, *11*(1), 1773–1786; Kurland, J., Pires, S. F., McFann, S. C., & Moreto, W. D. (2017). Wildlife crime: A conceptual integration, literature review, and methodological critique. *Crime Science*, *6*, 1–15.

firm, is among the most prominent names, with its activities leading to significant deforestation.[191] Another such company is Nestlé, the Swiss multinational food and beverage conglomerate, which has faced accusations of driving deforestation through its sourcing of conflict palm oil.[192] Other companies implicated in deforestation and linked human rights abuses include Archer-Daniels Midland, Bunge, Indofood, JBS, Tyson Foods, Felda Global Ventures, and Glencore PLC. These companies, involved in palm oil, paper/pulp, rubber, timber, and cattle production, have been associated with illegal land clearing and labor violations, including sourcing from areas with illegal deforestation and slave labor practices.[193] While some of these companies have faced fines and sanctions, others have been involved in corruption scandals. Notably, Tyson Foods announced plans to assess deforestation risks and develop a Forests Protection Policy in 2020, while FGV is facing a potential import ban in the United States due to labor abuse concerns.[194] Despite these measures, the overall industry efforts to eliminate deforestation have been limited.[195]

Corporations' environmental damages can have severe and far-reaching consequences on wildlife, ecosystems, and human populations.[196] These damages can lead to the loss of biodiversity, habitat degradation, and the disruption of ecosystem services that are vital to the health and well-being of all living creatures.[197] When corporations engage in illegal activities such as poaching, illegal logging, and the illegal trade of wildlife and their products, they contribute to the decline of animal populations and the extinction of species.[198] This loss of biodiversity can have cascading effects on ecosystems, as it can disrupt food chains, alter habitats, and impact ecological processes. Habitat destruction is another severe consequence of environmental damage caused by corporations. Activities such as deforestation, mining, and infrastructure development can lead to the fragmentation and loss of critical habitats for wildlife, causing the

191 Lai, O. (2023). 13 major companies responsible for deforestation. *Earth.Org*. Retrieved April 7, 2023, from https://earth.org/major-companies-responsible-for-deforestation/#

192 Deforestation-Risk Companies. (2023). *Deforestation free funds*. Retrieved April 7, 2023, from https://deforestationfreefunds.org/companies

193 Ibid.

194 Ibid.

195 Tompkins, L. (2022, January 20). Hundreds of companies promised to help save forests. Did they? *The New York Times*. www.nytimes.com/2021/12/02/climate/companies-net-zero-deforestation.html

196 Thakur, R. S. (2010). *Transnational corporations and environmental damages*. SSRN 1955445.

197 Senanayake, M., Harymawan, I., Dorfleitner, G., Lee, S., Rhee, J. H., & Ok, Y. S. (2024). Toward more nature-positive outcomes: A review of corporate disclosure and decision making on biodiversity. *Sustainability*, *16*(18), 8110.

198 Wyatt, T., van Uhm, D., & Nurse, A. (2020). Differentiating criminal networks in the illegal wildlife trade: Organized, corporate and disorganized crime. *Trends in Organized Crime*, *23*, 350–366.

displacement of species, reduced breeding opportunities, and increased vulnerability to predation and disease.

Litigation is an essential tool in holding corporations accountable for their actions and seeking compensation for the damages caused by wildlife crime. Environmental litigation for wildlife crime involves several crucial elements, including the identification of responsible parties, the collection of evidence, and the pursuit of legal remedies.[199] The first step in such litigation is to identify the responsible parties, which requires investigating the involvement of a corporation, its subsidiaries, and its supply chain. In some cases, it may also be necessary to establish the personal liability of corporate officers or employees who have played a role in the illegal activities. The collection of evidence is another critical aspect of environmental litigation for wildlife crime, which may involve gathering documentation, conducting interviews, and analyzing data to build a strong case against the responsible parties. In some cases, experts such as environmental scientists, wildlife biologists, and forensic specialists may need to be consulted to provide expert testimony and analysis.

Most countries have their laws to address corporate liability in wildlife crime, with the aim of conserving biodiversity, promoting sustainable business practices, and ensuring the fair and equitable sharing of benefits arising from the utilization of genetic resources.[200] Strengthening laws and regulations is one of the most effective strategies to combat wildlife crime by corporations. This can be achieved by updating existing laws to better address the issue of corporate liability in wildlife crime, increasing penalties for offenders, and implementing new regulatory measures to prevent illegal activities. Moreover, international cooperation and harmonization of laws and regulations can be essential in addressing wildlife crime that crosses borders.[201]

Another critical strategy to combat wildlife crime by corporations is increasing enforcement efforts. This can be achieved by providing law enforcement agencies with the necessary resources, training, and expertise to investigate

199 Ruggiero, V., & South, N. (2010). Critical criminology and crimes against the environment. *Critical Criminology*, *18*, 245–250.

200 The Endangered Species Act of 1973 is an example of significant legislation in the United States. It is a federal law that provides protection to threatened or endangered species, along with their habitats. This law is enforced by two agencies, namely the U.S. Fish and Wildlife Service and the National Oceanic and Atmospheric Administration Fisheries Service. It also covers plants in addition to wildlife and fish. The ESA facilitates listing and delisting of species, recovery plan preparation, and promotes interagency collaboration to prevent harm to the listed species. As per the law, federal agencies are required to ensure that their actions do not pose a threat to these species or their habitats. In this context, the Office of Pesticide Programs plays an important role in implementing the ESA by regulating pesticide use. For more about this legislation, visit Retrieved November 10, 2023, from www.fws.gov/law/endangered-species-act

201 Jiao, Y., Yeophantong, P., & Lee, T. M. (2021). Strengthening international legal cooperation to combat the illegal wildlife trade between Southeast Asia and China. *Frontiers in Ecology and Evolution*, *9*, 645427.

and prosecute wildlife crime.[202] It may also require the development of specialized units or task forces dedicated to addressing wildlife crime by corporations. Promoting corporate social responsibility is also an important strategy in combating wildlife crime by corporations. This can be achieved by encouraging corporations to adopt sustainable business practices, implement robust environmental management systems (EMSs), and engage in regular monitoring and reporting of their environmental performance.[203] Additionally, consumer awareness and activism can be critical in holding corporations accountable for their actions and driving positive change within the corporate sector.[204]

Wildlife crime is a serious issue that requires the involvement of international laws and regulations. To address this issue, several international conventions and agreements have been established. These include the Convention on International Trade in Endangered Species of Wild Fauna and Flora (CITES), the CBD, and the United Nations Convention against Transnational Organized Crime (UNTOC). These conventions and agreements address different aspects of wildlife crime and are crucial in holding corporations accountable for their actions.

CITES is an international agreement that aims to prevent international trade in wild animals and plants from threatening their survival.[205] It provides a global framework for regulating the trade of endangered species and mechanisms for holding corporations accountable for illegal activities related to wildlife trade. The CBD constitutes an international agreement aimed at preserving biodiversity, sustainably managing its components, and guaranteeing that the benefits derived from exploiting living resources are distributed justly and equitably. It emphasizes the importance of corporate responsibility in biodiversity conservation and encourages adopting sustainable business practices.[206] UNTOC is a global instrument that combats transnational organized crime, including wildlife crime. It establishes a framework for international cooperation and assistance in investigating, prosecuting, and preventing

202 O'Connor Shelley, T., & Crow, M. S. (2009). The nature and extent of conservation policing: Law enforcement generalists or conservation specialists? *American Journal of Criminal Justice*, *34*, 9–27.

203 Plumptre, A. J., et al. (2014). The status of wildlife in protected areas compared to non-protected areas of Africa. *Conservation Biology*, *28*(4), 1031–1041. Nurse, A., & Nurse, A. (2015). Theoretical perspectives on wildlife law enforcement. In *Policing wildlife: Perspectives on the enforcement of wildlife legislation* (pp. 83–100). Palgrave Macmillan.

204 Travers, H., Archer, L. J., Mwedde, G., Roe, D., Baker, J., Plumptre, A. J., Rwetsiba, A., & Milner-Gulland, E. J. (2019). Understanding complex drivers of wildlife crime to design effective conservation interventions. *Conservation Biology*, *33*(6), 1296–1306.

205 Chavez, J., Payuse, I. N. A. D., Campera, M., & Nijman, V. (2024). Tourism, international wildlife trade and the (in) effectiveness of CITES. *Environmental Conservation*, *51*(1), 64–70.

206 Ekardt, F., Günther, P., Hagemann, K., Garske, B., Heyl, K., & Weyland, R. (2023). Legally binding and ambitious biodiversity protection under the CBD, the global biodiversity framework, and human rights law. *Environmental Sciences Europe*, *35*(1), 80.

organized crime, including corporate involvement in illegal activities related to wildlife and their products.

Although international laws and regulations provide a valuable foundation for addressing corporate liability in wildlife crime, implementation and enforcement remain challenging.[207] However, there have been successful cases of environmental litigation against corporations, demonstrating that legal action can be an effective tool in holding corporations accountable for wildlife crime and seeking compensation for damages.[208] One such example is the lawsuit against Chevron Corporation for environmental damages in the Ecuadorian Amazon. In 2011, an Ecuadorian court found Chevron liable for widespread pollution and ordered the company to pay $9.5 billion in damages. Despite ongoing legal challenges and appeals, this case serves as an important example of how environmental litigation can hold corporations accountable for their actions.[209] Another successful case of environmental litigation against a corporation is the lawsuit against Volkswagen for its role in the emissions cheating scandal. In 2016, Volkswagen agreed to a $14.7 billion settlement with the U.S. government, which included compensation for affected consumers, environmental remediation efforts, and investments in clean vehicle technology.[210] This case highlights the potential for legal action not only to hold corporations accountable for their actions but also to promote positive change within the corporate sector.

3.2.7 The 'Dieselgate' Scandal

Volkswagen AG, commonly known as VW, has been a prominent player in Europe's automotive sector for many years, ranking among the world's largest auto manufacturers. In the mid-1970s, VW launched the diesel-powered Golf Mk1, which became one of the most-produced vehicles in automotive history and VW's flagship model.[211] VW's diesel technology, mainly its direct injection technology introduced in the 1980s, contributed to its dominance in the diesel market.[212] However, VW started lagging behind competitors like

207 Harris, H. (2023). Corporate liability within the IACC framework-a proposal for enhanced corporate accountability. *Transnational Criminal Law Review*, *2*, 74. Das, R. C., Goswami, J., & Mia, M. E. (2024). Addressing the human rights violation into the corporate criminal accountability under international law. *Jus Corpus Law Journal*, *5*, 343.

208 Okedele, P. O., Aziza, O. R., Oduro, P., & Ishola, A. O. (2024). Climate change litigation as a tool for global environmental policy reform: A comparative study of international case law. *Global Environmental Policy Review*, *8*(2), 104–115.

209 Pellegrini, L., Arsel, M., Orta-Martínez, M., & Mena, C. F. (2020). International investment agreements, human rights, and environmental justice: The Texaco/Chevron case from the Ecuadorian Amazon. *Journal of International Economic Law*, *23*(2), 455–468.

210 Cavico, F. J., & Mujtaba, B. G. (2016). Volkswagen emissions scandal: A global case study of legal, ethical, and practical consequences and recommendations for sustainable management. *Global Journal of Research in Business & Management*, *4*(2).

211 Mujkic, E., & Klingner, D. (2019). Dieselgate: How hubris and bad leadership caused the biggest scandal in automotive history. *Public Integrity*, *21*(4), 365–377.

212 Ibid.

Fiat and BMW in the late 1990s, which embraced a more advanced Common Rail diesel technology.[213]

In 2009, VW decided to penetrate the U.S. market with cars powered by its 2.0-liter EA189 engine, claiming superior fuel efficiency and lower emissions.[214] However, contrary to VW's 'clean diesel' marketing claims, this engine did not meet the new U.S. and EU emissions standards without using Selective Catalyst Reduction technology, which VW did not possess.[215] Diesel engines operate at higher injection pressure and significantly higher temperatures compared to gasoline engines. Although they emit lower amounts of carbon dioxide (CO_2) compared to gasoline engines, they produce higher levels of nitrogen oxides (NOx). Using Selective Catalyst Reduction technology in diesel-run vehicles since the NOx-induced emissions, which do not exist naturally, are carcinogenic.[216] VW's leadership, driven by the primary objective of becoming the world's largest auto manufacturer, made a flawed decision. Instead of investing in the necessary technology to meet the emissions standards, they opted to cheat.[217] With approval from the top echelons of the company, VW began installing 'defeat device' software that could manipulate the emissions output during regulatory tests.[218]

VW's fraudulent practices came to light in 2014 when a team of graduate students from West Virginia University, supported by the International Council for Clean Transportation, started investigating emissions from 'clean diesel' in real-world driving conditions.[219] The tests showed that VW models

213 Ibid.; Mačaitytė, I., & Virbašiūtė, G. (2018). Volkswagen emission scandal and corporate social responsibility–a case study. *Business Ethics and Leadership*, *2*(1), 6–13.

214 Mujkic, E., & Klingner, D. (2019). Dieselgate: How hubris and bad leadership caused the biggest scandal in automotive history. *Public Integrity*, *21*(4), 365–377.

215 Ibid.; Fracarolli Nunes, M., & Lee Park, C. (2016). Caught red-handed: The cost of the Volkswagen Dieselgate. *Journal of Global Responsibility*, *7*(2), 288–302.

216 For details, see Carrington, D., Topham, G., & Walker, P. (2016, April 23). Revealed: Nearly all new diesel cars exceed official pollution limits. *Guardian*. www.theguardian.com/business/2016/apr/23/diesel-cars-pollution-limits-nox-emissions; Ewing, J. (2017). *Faster, higher, farther: The Volkswagen scandal*. W. W. Norton; Ewing, J. (2018, January 25). 10 monkeys and a Beetle: Inside VW's campaign for "clean diesel". *New York Times*. www.nytimes.com/2018/01/25/world/europe/volkswagen-diesel-emissions-monkeys.html

217 Davenport, C., & Ewing, J. (2015, September 18). VW is said to cheat on diesel emissions; US to order big recall. *The New York Times*. Retrieved November 4, 2023, from www.nytimes.com/2015/09/19/business/volkswagenisorderedtorecallnearly 500000vehiclesoveremissionssoftware.html;Schmitt,B.(2017,January12).Dieselgate:13VWmanagersindictedaround the world, big guys unbothered. *Forbes*. www.forbes.com/sites/bertelschmitt/2017/01/12/dieselgate-15-vw-managersindicted-around-the-world-big-guys-unbothered

218 Mujkic, E., & Klingner, D. (2019). Dieselgate: How hubris and bad leadership caused the biggest scandal in automotive history. *Public Integrity*, *21*(4), 365–377.

219 Thompson, G. J. (2014). *In-use emissions testing of light-duty diesel vehicles in the United States*. Center for Alternative Fuels, Engines & Emissions of the West Virginia University; Fracarolli Nunes, M., & Lee Park, C. (2016). Caught red-handed: The cost of the Volkswagen Dieselgate. *Journal of Global Responsibility*, *7*(2), 288–302.

equipped with the EA189 engine were emitting up to 40 times more NOx than what was legally allowed.[220]

The Dieselgate scandal had a huge impact on the environment and public health. VW's excess NOx emissions from their vehicles caused air pollution, which is a leading cause of respiratory diseases like asthma and bronchitis. In fact, air pollution causes seven million premature deaths worldwide every year, according to the WHO. Moreover, the excess emissions also contribute to global warming, which results in rising sea levels, wildfires, and severe weather patterns. VW initially denied any wrongdoing and tried to discredit the research findings.[221] However, persistent investigations by the EPA and the California Air Resources Board (CARB) eventually forced VW to admit its guilt.[222]

Many lawsuits and cases were filed against VW as a result of the Dieselgate scandal.[223] The U.S. EPA and the CARB launched administrative actions against VA under the CAA for violating emissions standards. Thousands of car owners filed lawsuits across the country, and the government began civil and criminal investigations. The controversy came to light around the same time the U.S. government was finalizing a settlement agreement with BP over the

220 Ewing, J. (2016, July 24). Researchers who exposed VW gain little reward from success. *The New York Times*. Retrieved November 4, 2023, from www.nytimes.com/2016/07/25/business/vw-wvu-dieselvolkswagen-west-virginia.html; Kollewe, J. (2015, December 10). Volkswagen emissions scandal – timeline. *The Guardian*. Retrieved November 4, 2023, from www.theguardian.com/business/2015/dec/10/volkswagen-emissions-scandal-timelineevents

221 *Plea Agreement, Exhibit 2 Statement of Facts*, paras. 31–36, United States v. Volkswagen AG, No. 16-CR-20394 (E.D. Mich. Mar. 10, 2017), ECF No. 68. For more, see Cruden, J. C., Engel, B., Cooney, N., & Van Eaton, J. (2018). Dieselgate: How the investigation, prosecution, and settlement of Volkswagen's emissions cheating scandal illustrates the need for robust environmental enforcement. *Virginia Environmental Law Journal*, *36*, 118.

222 Morgan, D. (2015, September 23). West Virginia engineer proves to be a David to VW's Goliath. *Reuters*. Retrieved November 5, 2023, from www.reuters.com/article/ususa-volkswagenresearchersidUSKCN0RM2D720150924; Neate, R. (2015, September 18). Volkswagen under investigation over illegal software that masks emissions. *The Guardian*. Retrieved November 5, 2023, from www.theguardian.com/business/2015/sep/18/epacaliforniainvestigate-volkswagencleanairviolations

223 One of these cases involves Rupert Stadler, the former CEO of Audi and a board member of VW. Stadler has been handed a suspended sentence of one year and nine months for fraud related to the scandal. In addition to Stadler's case, four current or former VW managers and engineers are on trial for group and commercial fraud. Civil proceedings are also underway, including a lawsuit brought by Deka Investment with damages claims amounting to around $9.9bn. It is worth mentioning that the case also involves an Italian antitrust fine levied against VW in 2016. For details, see State of legal cases in VW's diesel scandal. (2023, June 27). *Reuters*. Retrieved November 3, 2023, from www.reuters.com/sustainability/state-legal-cases-vws-diesel-scandal-2023-06-27/; Foo Chee. (2023, September 14). Volkswagen fight against Italian dieselgate fine to be decided by Italian court. *Reuters*. Retrieved November 3, 2023, from www.reuters.com/business/autos-transportation/volkswagen-fight-against-italian-dieselgate-fine-be-decided-by-italian-court-2023-09-14/; Lasarte, D. (2023, September 14). A Volkswagen board member was convicted in the Dieselgate scandal that's costing $38 billion and counting. *Quartz*. Retrieved November 3, 2023, from https://qz.com/volkswagen-dieselgate-scandal-rupert-stadler-audi-1850581201

Deepwater Horizon oil spill, which had caused immense environmental damage and economic loss. The civil complaint by the United States against VW was filed in January 2016, with Judge Charles R. Breyer appointed as presiding judge; former FBI Director Robert S. Mueller III was appointed as Settlement Master. Within a year, the DOJ's Environmental Enforcement Section (EES) obtained three consent decrees, VW was found guilty of four felonies, and seven high-ranking VW officials were indicted.[224] On top of this, there were several class-action lawsuits filed by affected customers seeking compensation for the diminished value of their vehicles.

The scandal caused a huge financial and reputational blow to VW.[225] In the United States, VW agreed to pay $14.7 billion to settle civil and criminal charges related to the scandal. The company also faced legal action in several other countries, including Germany, the UK, and South Korea. The compensation for affected parties in the Dieselgate scandal varied based on the country and the type of impact. In the United States, affected customers were offered buybacks or vehicle repairs, along with cash compensation. In Europe, compensation was more limited and affected customers were offered repairs or software updates. The compensation for investors was also limited, with some receiving settlements while others continued to seek compensation through legal action.[226] VW recalled its vehicles, appointed a new CEO, implemented several reforms, and invested in electric vehicles to reduce its carbon footprint.

224 For a detailed account of the dieselgate litigation in the United States, see Cruden, J. C., Engel, B., Cooney, N., & Van Eaton, J. (2018). Dieselgate: How the investigation, prosecution, and settlement of Volkswagen's emissions cheating scandal illustrates the need for robust environmental enforcement. *Virginia Environmental Law Journal*, *36*, 118; Muller, N. (2018, February 1). Car diesel fume experiments on humans "widespread," scientists say. *Deutsche Welle*. Retrieved from www.dw.com/en/car-diesel-fume-experiments-on-humans-widespread-scientistssay/a-42400407

225 At the end of 2015, Volkswagen faced a loss due to charges from governments and compensations promised to customers. As a result, in 2016, VW announced a $10 billion buyback program for diesel car owners. The program allowed owners to sell their vehicles to VW for amounts ranging from $12,500 to $44,000 based on the model, age, trim, and region. For those who did not want to sell their cars, VW offered compensation ranging from $5,100 to $10,000. In 2017, Volkswagen announced a $1.2 billion program for owners of 2009–2012 Audi Q7 and Volkswagen Touareg models with the Generation 1 engine. Under this program, owners were able to sell their cars back to VW for amounts between $24,755 and $57,157. Overall, the 'Dieselgate' scandal has already cost the company around $30 billion. For details, see Atiyeh, C. (2017). Everything you need to know about the VW diesel-emissions scandal. *Car and Driver*. Retrieved April 7, from www.caranddriver.com/news/a15339250/everything-you-need-to-know-about-the-vw-diesel-emissions-scandal/

226 It is interesting to note that the number of VW vehicles sold did not decrease as much as expected after the scandal. In October 2015, sales of all VW models decreased by 3.5% compared to the same month the previous year, with a total of 136,345 units sold. The following month, sales increased to 133,201 units, up 0.4% compared to November 2014. By the end of 2015, vehicle sales had increased by 1.78% compared to December 2014. In 2015, VW sold approximately 1.7 million vehicles, representing a 5.51% annual growth. For details, see Mačaitytė, I., & Virbašiūtė, G. (2018). Volkswagen emission scandal and corporate social responsibility: A case study. *Business Ethics and Leadership*, *2*(1), 6–13.

The automotive industry has been rocked by other high-profile scandals, such as VW's Dieselgate, General Motors's (GM's) faulty ignition switches, and Takata's exploding airbags, during 2014. GM faced a scandal in 2014 due to a faulty ignition switch that caused several deaths. The company has been aware of the problem since 2003, but it took them a long time to address it.[227] The faulty switches had the potential to turn off car engines and airbags while driving, causing the recall of 30.1 million vehicles in North America, including 2.6 million small cars.[228] These defects resulted in 97 deaths.[229] GM has faced numerous class-action lawsuits over the years due to issues with their ignition switches. They have paid out millions of dollars in settlements, with the most recent settlement being for $120 million. GM contributed $70 million to the settlement, while a bankruptcy trust contributed $50 million.[230] The scandal forced GM to restructure its safety processes and culture. The company created a new position of Vice President of Global Vehicle Safety, established a Safety Field Investigation Team, and introduced a 'Speak Up For Safety' program for employees to report safety concerns.[231] The ultimate goal of these reforms is to prevent future crises and ensure that the leadership is accountable for vehicle quality. Takata's defective airbags have raised significant safety concerns in the automobile industry. These airbags, manufactured by Takata, have been found to explode during deployment, resulting in severe injuries and even fatalities.[232] The root cause of this issue was identified as the use of ammonium-nitrate-based propellant without a chemical drying agent in the airbag inflators. Over 67 million airbags have been recalled across 19 different automakers, out of which 11 million still require replacement.[233] The problem has caused 26 deaths and over 400 injuries in the United States alone. To address the issue, a 'Do Not Drive' warning has been issued for specific models from automakers like Dodge, BMW, and Honda, urging immediate repairs. Car owners are advised to check the recall status of their vehicles using

227 Plumer, B. (2023). The GM recall scandal of 2014. *Vox*. Retrieved April 7, from www.vox.com/2014/10/3/18073458/gm-car-recall.

228 Basu, T. (2014, March 31). Timeline: A history of GM's ignition switch defect. *NPR*. Retrieved April 7, from www.npr.org/2014/03/31/297158876/timeline-a-history-of-gms-ignition-switch-defect; Plumer, B. (2023). The GM recall scandal of 2014. *Vox*. Retrieved April 7, from www.vox.com/2014/10/3/18073458/gm-car-recall

229 Ibid.

230 Lemon Law Experts. (2023). *GMC ignition switch settlement update 2022–2023*. Retrieved November 5, from https://lemonlawexperts.com/gmc-ignition-switch-settlement-update/

231 LaReau, J. (2019, September 6). GM: We encourage employees, dealers to tattle after ignition switch crisis. *The Detroit Free Press*. Retrieved November 5, from www.freep.com/story/money/cars/general-motors/2019/09/06/gm-ignition-switch-nhtsa-recalls-safety-defects/2099289001/

232 National Highway Traffic Safety Administration (NHTSA). (2023). *Takata recall spotlight*. Retrieved November 5, from www.nhtsa.gov/equipment/takata-recall-spotlight

233 Ibid.

their VIN and schedule free repairs at their dealership.[234] The faulty airbags manufactured by Takata have caused numerous lawsuits due to their disastrous impact.[235] The lawsuits typically accuse Takata of negligence and failing to inform consumers of the potential risks. Despite being aware of the airbag inflator issues since 2004, Takata only initiated a nationwide recall in 2015. Unfortunately, this delay in action and misconduct has led to the U.S. DOJ and attorneys general from 44 states imposing penalties on Takata, resulting in $1.65 billion for compensating the injured individuals.[236] Takata became bankrupt in 2017.

These incidents have highlighted the crucial role played by government regulators in enforcing environmental regulations. The Dieselgate scandal, in particular, has led to increased scrutiny of the automotive industry and its regulatory bodies.[237] As a result, governments worldwide have introduced stricter emissions regulations and harsher penalties for those who violate them. The scandal has also emphasized the importance of transparency and accountability in the automotive industry.

The aforementioned cases taught several lessons to the corporate world, regulators, and the general public. First, corporate greed often causes severe environmental damage. The traditional 'shareholder-first' approach, which aims to maximize profits, neglects environmental needs and contributes to issues like CO_2 emissions, plastic pollution, and biodiversity loss.[238] This approach is also criticized for exacerbating wealth inequality, with most benefits going to the top 1%.[239] Former Unilever CEO Paul Polman criticizes this approach and advocates for a shift toward a purpose-driven, net-positive approach. He believes that businesses should become restorative, reparative, and regenerative, contributing positively to society and the environment.[240] This approach, known as Net Positive, presents an opportunity for businesses to grow in the 21st century. Despite the belief that businesses are best equipped to solve

234 Consumer Reports. (2023). *Takata airbag recall: Everything you need to know*. Retrieved November 6, from www.consumerreports.org/cars/car-recalls-defects/takata-airbag-recall-everything-you-need-to-know-a1060713669/

235 Turner, T. (2023). Takata airbag lawsuits and settlement. *Consumer Notice*. Retrieved November 5, from www.consumernotice.org/legal/takata-airbag-lawsuits/

236 Dean, K. (2023). Takata airbag injury lawsuit. *Motley Rice*. Retrieved November 5, from www.motleyrice.com/personal-injury-wrongful-death/takata-airbag

237 Ridley, K., & Sterling, T. (2017, June 13). Dutch, English drivers team up to sue VW over "Dieselgate". *Reuters*. Retrieved from www.reuters.com/article/us-volkswagen-emissions-claims/dutch-english-drivers-team-up-to-sue-vw-over-dieselgate-idUSKBN1940NL

238 Zarnett, B. (2019). How billionaire greed ruined a perfectly good strategy called corporate sustainability. *Toronto Sustainability*. Retrieved November 5, from http://tsss.ca/channels/culture-leadership/how-billionaire-greed-ruined-a-perfectly-good-strategy-called-corporate-sustainability-part-1

239 Ibid.

240 Buckholtz, A. (2022). Countering "a crisis of greed". *International Finance Corporation*. Retrieved November 5, from www.ifc.org/en/stories/2022/making-the-case-for-net-positive-companies

problems, the preference of corporate elites for market-based solutions often benefits themselves, maintains the status quo, and worsens social and environmental issues. It is crucial for companies to shift their focus from profit maximization to implementing sustainable green strategies, which can provide win-win solutions for both the environment and the business.[241] However, this requires a significant shift in corporate culture and the willingness to prioritize long-term sustainability over short-term profits. Corporate greed can lead to environmental damage, but businesses can become part of the solution by changing their approach and focus.

Second, there is a need for greater transparency and accountability in the automotive industry.[242] It is crucial for companies to establish, monitor, and enforce institutional controls.[243] No company is above the law, regardless of its size, which includes the largest automobile manufacturer.[244] Every employee, stockholder, and executive needs to understand this. The compliance culture within the corporation, as a minimum, needs to be compliant, starting with model behavior from senior executives.[245] If present, whistleblowers need to be protected and respond to their complaints in good faith, guiding company staff to take appropriate actions. Every employee in conflict with the policy or the law needs to be subjected to instantaneous discipline at all levels.[246]

Third, they demonstrated the importance of government regulations in safeguarding the environment and public health. It is imperative to implement prompt enforcement actions pertaining to health and safety violations concerning the environment.[247] The enforcement action may include civil or criminal prosecution of individuals or businesses. The federal government has a dominant position in coordinating the litigation and settlements that tend to bundle multiple parties due to its control over the system; thus, it serves an important coordination function for all parties in significant enforcement

241 Clarke, R. A., Stavins, R. N., Greeno, J. L., Bavaria, J. L., Cairncross, D., Esty, D., Smart, B., Piet, J., Wells, R., & Gray, R. (1994). The challenge of going green. *Reader in Business and the Environment*, *45*.

242 Russo-Spena, T., Tregua, M., & De Chiara, A. (2018). Trends and drivers in CSR disclosure: A focus on reporting practices in the automotive industry. *Journal of Business Ethics*, *151*, 563–578.

243 Henk, O. (2020). Internal control through the lens of institutional work: A systematic literature review. *Journal of Management Control*, *31*(3), 239–273.

244 Lupu, A. C. (2020). Evolution of corporate governance in automotive industry. Study case daimler AG. *USV Annals of Economics & Public Administration*, *20*(2).

245 DeStefano, M. (2013). Creating a culture of compliance: Why departmentalization may not be the answer. *Hastings Business Law Journal*, *10*, 71.

246 Cruden, J. C., Engel, B., Cooney, N., & Van Eaton, J. (2018). Dieselgate: How the investigation, prosecution, and settlement of Volkswagen's emissions cheating scandal illustrates the need for robust environmental enforcement. *Virginia Environmental Law Journal*, *36*, 118.

247 Forsyth, M., & Tepper, F. (2024). Environmental enforceable undertakings: An innovative tool to repair and prevent environmental harm. *Journal of Environmental Law*, *36*(3), 385–411.

actions. By exerting this influence, the federal government can maximize the potential for an early resolution.[248] In the case of the multidistrict litigation structure, for instance, the United States filed its civil complaint early on while the structure was still forming.[249] This enabled the government to engage comprehensively in the initial deliberations regarding the case's structure, discovery protocols, and the management framework of the case.[250]

Finally, they highlighted the significance of ethical business practices and CSR. Having a comprehensive and well-publicized CSR program can significantly contribute to both preventive and responsive measures during an incident. However, the mere presence of a CSR program in an organization is not enough to ensure complete compliance with regulations. Nonetheless, it does leave a meaningful impact on the organizational culture, indicating a willingness to comply with regulations. Achieving a culture of compliance requires continuous and intentional efforts from leaders at all levels of the organization.[251]

3.3 Criminal Liability of Corporate Polluters in Major Jurisdictions

The later part of the 19th and 20th centuries witnessed the industrial explosion. The natural consequence of this has been the emergence of big business houses and domestic companies. Today, the social and economic life of the people is greatly influenced by these types of corporations.[252] On the other hand, with the emergence of the concept of the welfare state, the state has sought to regulate the activities of corporations and channel production to cater to the needs of society. In its endeavor to check the operation of corporations, the state has sought to impose criminal responsibility on them,[253] in addition to civil regulations, as a last resort to punish the recalcitrant or egregious corporate bodies.[254] In the last decades, the areas of taxation, antitrust regulation, and newer fields like environmental pollution and security

248 Chopra, R., & Frothman, S. (2025). State enforcement as a federal legislative tool. *Harvard Journal on Legislation*, *62*(1).
249 Ahdout, Z. P. (2021). Enforcement lawmaking and judicial review. *Harvard Law Review*, *135*, 937.
250 Cruden, J. C., Engel, B., Cooney, N., & Van Eaton, J. (2018). Dieselgate: How the investigation, prosecution, and settlement of Volkswagen's emissions cheating scandal illustrates the need for robust environmental enforcement. *Virginia Environmental Law Journal*, *36*, 118.
251 Ibid.
252 See Friedmann, W. (1996). *Law in a changing society* (2nd ed.). Sweet & Maxwell.
253 See Cruden, J. C., Engel, B., Cooney, N., & Van Eaton, J. (2018). Dieselgate: How the investigation, prosecution, and settlement of Volkswagen's emissions cheating scandal illustrates the need for robust environmental enforcement. *Virginia Environmental Law Journal*, *36*, 118.
254 Supra note 20, p. 1229.

exchange have evidenced the increasing use of deterrence by criminal sanction upon the corporation. Lederman puts this change as follows:

> Times however have changed. The last two decades have created a new socio-political-economic reality, characterized by a thriving common market in Europe, changes in the political regimes of Eastern Europe, intensive privatization processes in many countries that shifted many areas of activity to the non-governmental sector, and the creation of mega-multinational-corporations that are the result of acquisitions, mergers and takeovers. In a process that peaked in the second half of this century, legal bodies have actually assumed control of all forms of commerce and industry, to the extent that no economic endeavor is deemed possible without their involvement. This socio-economic reality has dictated, to a large extent, the change in the law's approach to the imposition of penal liability on corporations. Policy setters in various legislative and law enforcement bodies sensed that attaining effective, and mainly trouble-free, control of the economy through criminal law depends on a sweeping subordination of the legal bodies themselves, as far as possible, to criminal proceedings. All this without restricting the scope of the personal criminal liability incumbent on management ranks or on those actually involved in breaking the law.[255]

A corporation is a legal fiction. Deterrence, in the sense of fear, cannot work on it. However, the object of deterrence may be used to put up a front against the corporation's officials responsible for its criminal conduct. Deterrent sanctions against the corporation may take two forms: civil and criminal. Both of these sanctions have some common characteristics but differ in certain respects. The similarity lies in the fact that, in both cases, the liability is imposed upon the corporation, and both aim at restraining the corporation from committing misconduct. On the other hand, dissimilarities lie in the fact that the criminal sanction has stronger procedural protection, more powerful devices that are severe in nature, unique features of its kind (e.g., stigmatization), and 'a greater message-sending role than corporate civil liability.'[256] Lederman summaries the conceptual development of corporate criminal liability as follows:

> Generally, the importance of the independent development of the issue of criminal liability of corporations has grown as a function of the growth of its theoretical base. This process is accompanied by a change from using ideas aimed at emphasizing the possible similarities between imposing criminal liability on individuals and the imposition of such responsibility on legal bodies, toward the formation of constructions underlining

255 Lederman, E. (2000). Models for imposing corporate criminal liability: From adaptation and imitation toward aggregation and the search for self-identity. *Buffalo Criminal Law Review*, *4*(1), 641–708.

256 Supra note 19, p. 1496.

the unique structure of corporations. Consequently, the issue, in recent years, has moved away from the notion of adapting the imposition of criminal liability on a human being to its imposition on corporate bodies. In essence, this is a process of imitation, moving toward the creation of new models of aggregation and self-identity, specifically designed for the unique structure and modes of operations of corporate entities.[257]

A corporation's susceptibility to deterrence is often questioned. When a sanction is imposed on it, its business is affected severely. The consequence may be a loss of production or a decrease in profit. The shareholders who put their money in the corporation are affected by it. So, they can devise plans to regulate the activities of the board of directors or managers and employees.[258] This is a sort of indirect control or indirect liability.[259] Furthermore,

257 Lederman, E. (2000). Models for imposing corporate criminal liability: From adaptation and imitation toward aggregation and the search for self-identity. *Buffalo Criminal Law Review*, *4*, 641–708, p. 644.

258 Such context in corporate governance, a new type of shareholders has emerged, known as 'enlightened shareholders.' These shareholders prioritize the interests of non-shareholders in their decision-making, as opposed to the traditional shareholders whose focus is solely on maximizing their return on investment. However, enlightened shareholders do not abandon the goal of earning a return on their investment, but rather aim to support the society in which the company operates by prioritizing long-term profit-making. This shift in shareholders' objectives is a significant change in traditional corporate governance, and it allows the corporate management to address concerns and expectations about the responsible conduct of the company. For details, see Glac, K. (2010). *The influence of shareholders on corporate social responsibility* (Working Paper No. 2). Center for Ethical Business Cultures; Greenfield, K. (2000). Corporate social responsibility: There's a forest in those trees: Teaching about corporate social responsibility. *Georgia Law Review*, *34*, 1011. For a recent critique of the existing scholarship of corporate regulation thought, see generally, Greenfield, K. (2019). *The failure of corporate law: Fundamental flaws and progressive possibilities.* University of Chicago Press.

259 See Kadish, S. H., Schulhofer, S. J., & Barkow, R. E. (2016). *Criminal law and its processes: Cases and materials* (p. 437). Aspen Publishing. The institutional investors and lenders as shareholders of companies are increasingly being 'enlightened' and putting impacts on governance and business strategies of companies. Among them, public and union pension funds are at the forefront of adding environmental, social, and ethical measures with the core corporate strategies and portfolio risk analysis. These types of shareholders account for a significant percentage of world equity holdings, and hence, their activism usually impacts the aims of shareholders of many companies heavily dependent on external funds. For information, the assets of the pension funds and public pension reserve funds of the OECD countries were $30.2 trillion in 2014. In 2001, the pension and public pension reserve fund was 51.8% of the combined GDP of the OECD countries; this share was raised to 61.9% in 2014. As of 2015, five of the largest pension funds in the world include Stichting Pensioenfonds ($473.6 billion, the Netherlands), California Public Employees' Retirement System ($301.9 billion, the United States), Central Provident Fund ($210.2 billion, Singapore), California State Teachers' Retirement System ($188 billion, the United States) Stichting Pensioenfonds Zorg en Welzijn ($186 billion, the Netherlands). For details, see OECD. (2016). *Annual survey of large pension funds and public pension reserve funds: Reports on pension funds' long-term investment.* Retrieved December 6, from http://www.oecd.org/daf/fin/private-pensions/2015-Large-Pension-Funds-Survey.pdf

liability, in the form of sanctions, may be imposed on the agents of the corporation and the corporation itself.[260] The liability quantum depends on society's harm and the corporation's net profits. It will adversely affect the total profits of the corporation. Imposing criminal liability also has a stigmatizing effect, a strong social sanction against a corporation.[261]

The concept of corporate criminal liability emerged as corporations faced increasing litigation coupled with governments' declining role in society. The frequency of corporate crimes has been on the rise, and with the increasing corporate power, the gravity of such crimes has become far greater than those caused by negligence and recklessness in the past. The change in the notion of a laissez-faire state has also brought about changes in the roles of governments in society – governments rely more on social actors, including corporations, to ensure the welfare of the people. However, this situation has changed as the use and abuse of corporate power are now primary concerns in every social development.[262] Governments are also trying to shift their position by increasing their rule-making power to ensure that corporations are not involved in criminal activities and are performing their obligations to society.[263] In light of these changes, they review the principles necessary to develop frameworks for regulating corporate polluters. These principles are crucial as they set the tone for their substantive laws and, most importantly, indicate the nature of the procedures governments should create to enforce the laws.

3.3.1 The United Kingdom

Under English law, a corporate entity may be subject to criminal liability, although recognizing corporate criminal liability was very slow and

260 Vu, S. N. (2004). Corporate criminal liability: Patchwork verdicts and the problem of locating a guilty agent. *Columbia Law Review, 104*, 459.

261 Supra note 19, p. 1497.

262 Geis, G., & DiMento, J. F. (2001). Empirical evidence and the legal doctrine of corporate criminal liability. *American Journal of Criminal Law, 29*, 341; Logan, W. S. (1901). The use and abuse of corporations. *The American Lawyer, 9*, 158.

263 KKhanna defines this development as the 'substitution theory of corporate crime legislation.' He opines:

> [M]ost corporate crime legislation arises at times when there is a large public outcry over a series of corporate scandals during or around a downturn in the economy. In such a situation, Congress must respond, and corporate crime legislation may be the preferred response for some corporate interests because it satisfies the public outcry while imposing relatively low costs on those corporate interests, avoiding legislative and judicial responses that are more harmful to their interests, and sometimes helping to deflect criminal liability away from managers and executives and onto corporations. In this respect, corporate crime legislation is a substitute for other responses that are less favored by certain corporate interests.

For details, see Khanna, V. S. (2004). Corporate crime legislation: A political economy analysis. *Washington University Law Quarterly, 82*, 95.

unsystematic in the initial years. The legal impediments in the criminal prosecutions of corporate entities have been removed by the doctrine of *ultra vires.* The judicial doctrine has developed that corporate bodies are not natural persons, so the activities (including any criminal act) of a person or persons who are in direct control of it will be the act of a corporation, so they regard the corporation as the *alter ego* of the person or persons. The principles of identification and managing the personalities of the corporation and its controlling individuals have been decisive and influential in the development of English law in this area.[264] In one sense, the identification doctrine had a liberating effect, clearing the way for the imposition of criminal liability on corporate bodies, even in situations where criminal liability was based upon the culpable human mind (i.e., *mens rea*). In other words, it is a limiting doctrine that justifies criminal liability by discovering a 'unity' of the corporation and the person or persons who control it. Thus, corporate criminal liability generally arises in economic offenses, public safety, consumer interest and commercial fair dealings, and environmental offenses. The most straightforward penalty (quantification of criminal liability) that may be imposed on a corporation is pecuniary punishment (i.e., fine).[265] Imprisonment has traditionally been viewed as inappropriate in the case of a corporation, since the corporate person, as such, cannot be physically incarcerated.

3.3.2 The United States

Corporate criminal liability in the United States is established by attributing the contract and culpability of an agent's ostensible conduct to the corporation. This is based on the principle of 'vicarious liability,' which holds that employers or principals should bear responsibility for the wrongful actions of their employees or agents while acting within the scope of their employment or agency. The *respondeat superior*[266] doctrine is the core of vicarious liability.

264 Supra note 35.

265 Smith and Hogan, in their leading work on *English Criminal Law*, stated that a corporation can only be convicted of offenses which are punishable with a fine.

266 For more about this doctrine, see Kadish, S. H. (1979). Developments in the law – Corporate crime: Regulating corporate behaviour through criminal sanctions. *Harvard Law Review*, *92*, 1227; Sayre, F. B. (1930). Criminal responsibility for the acts of another. *Harvard Law Review*, *43*(5), 689–723. This doctrine has its critics. It can be an unsatisfactory basis of liability, as it may result in liability even if the company had prohibited the act. For some critics of this doctrine, see Luskin, R. (2020). Caring about corporate "Due Care": Why criminal respondeat superior liability outreaches its justification. *American Criminal Law Review*, *57*, 303; Sayre, F. B. (1930). Criminal responsibility for the acts of another. *Harvard Law Review*, *43*(5), 689–723. Alschuler, A. W. (2009). Two ways to think about the punishment of corporations. *American Criminal Law Review*, *46*, 1359; Bucy, P. H. (1990). Corporate ethos: A standard for imposing corporate criminal liability. *Minnesota Law Review*, *75*, 1095; Leigh, L. H. (1977). The criminal liability of corporations and other groups. *Ottawa Law Review*, *9*, 247.

In the United States, a corporation, therefore, may be held criminally liable for the activities of its employees and agents where (a) the employee must have been acting within their authorized duties for the corporation to be held criminally liable[267] and (b) the employee's actions were driven, at least in part, by the intention to benefit the corporation.[268] However, if an employee of a company engages in conduct that is clearly outside the scope of their employment, the company as the employer may not be held liable. A corporation can also be held criminally liable if it is proven that the criminal deeds were sanctioned, permitted, or accepted by managerial staff.[269] This modification shifts the principle of vicarious liability to something closer to the identification doctrine.

Under the *respondeat superior* doctrine, companies in this country cannot avoid liability for corruption by demonstrating a compliance program. They may be held accountable for an employee's corrupt actions, even if they did not condone them, as long as they acted within the apparent scope of their employment. However, corporations that implement adequate procedures to prevent bribery have a defense. A corporation's compliance efforts can lead to a reduced sentence. Compliance programs, voluntary disclosures, and a corporation's history can all influence the decision to prosecute a company.

Accordingly, the Model Penal Code of this country permits holding a corporation vicariously liable if 'a legislative purpose of imposing liability on corporations plainly appears' or the 'offense consists of an omission to discharge a specific duty of affirmative performance imposed on corporations.'[270] It provides 'three distinct systems of corporate liability.'[271] The first system applies to ordinary crimes, such as fraud, theft, or manslaughter. Here, the corporation will be liable only if the offense was committed by hiring a management agent. The second system of corporate liability applies in cases like price-fixing or security fraud, which are not crimes of strict liability, yet through legislation,

267 The U.S. Supreme Court endorsed the proposition that 'since a corporation acts by its officers and agents, their purposes, motives, and intent are just as much those of the corporation as are the things done' (*New York Central & Hudson River Co. v. United States*, 1909, 212 U.S. 481, 492). Also, see the decision in *United States v. Route 2*, 60 F.3d 1523, 1527 (11th Cir. 1995).

268 See, for example, *United States v. 7326 Highway 45 North*, 965 F.2d 311, 316 (7th Cir. 1992); *United States v. Cincotta*, 689 F.2d 238, 241–242 (1st Cir. 1982). See generally, Ragozino, A. (1994). Replacing the collective knowledge doctrine with a better theory for establishing corporate *mens rea*: The duty stratification approach. *Southwestern University Law Review*, *24*, 423; Beale, S. S. (2016). The development and evolution of the U.S. law of corporate criminal liability and the Yates memo. *Stetson Law Review*, *46*, 41.

269 See, for example, *State v. Christy Pontiac-GMC Inc.*, 354 N.W.2d 17, 20 (Minn. 1984); Lederman, E. (2000). Models for imposing corporate criminal liability: From adaptation and imitation toward aggregation and the search for self-identity. *Buffalo Criminal Law Review*, *4*(1), 641–708, citing *State v. Christy Pontiac-GMC Inc.*, 354 N.W.2d 17, 20 (Minn. 1984), at 655.

270 American Legal Institute. *Model Penal Code*, § 2.07.

271 Supra note 29, p. 1251.

liability has been explicitly put on the corporation. In these situations, the employee must commit a crime within the scope of their employment. The employee may not be a member of the high management agent of the corporation. A high managerial agent would be someone 'having duties of such responsibility that his conduct may fairly be assumed to represent the policy of the corporation.' The third system is where the corporation is strictly liable for violating regulatory offenses. In federal criminal proceedings, the penalties imposed on corporations include fines, restitution, and non-monetary sanctions such as remedial orders, community service, and probation. These sanctions are now governed by the *Sentencing Reform Act 1984* and the guidelines for sentencing organizations issued by the U.S. Sentencing Commission in 1991. The principles the Sentencing Guidelines set for calculating fines are as follows.

The first principle of determining the fine for an offense involves identifying the 'base fine.' This 'base fine' is calculated by selecting the highest value from three options: the financial gain obtained by the organization from the offense, the financial losses incurred by the offense (if it was intentional, knowing, or reckless), or the values listed in a table provided in the guidelines for over 30 levels of offenses. To determine the organization's 'culpability score,' various aggregation and mitigation factors are considered. The list of aggravating factors approved by the guidelines focuses on whether high-level managers were involved in, condoned, tolerated, or were aware of the wrongdoing; whether the organization has a previous history of similar misconduct; whether the offense involved a violation of a judicial order or injunction; and whether the organization obstructed justice during the proceedings.[272] The mitigating factors center on whether the organization had an adequate program for the prevention and detection of violations and whether the organization self-reported the offense, fully cooperated with the investigation, and took responsibility for its wrongdoing.[273] The third principle is to use the 'culpability score' to find the minimum and maximum 'multipliers' from a table provided in the guidelines. For example, a 'culpability score' of 0 or less produces a minimum multiplier of 0.05 and a maximum multiplier of 0.20. On the other hand, a culpability score of 10 or more produces a minimum multiplier of 2.00 and a maximum multiplier of 4.00. The 'base fine' is then multiplied by these 'multipliers' to obtain a range of fines that may be imposed. Finally, the court selects a fine from that range. The guidelines provide another list of factors to be considered when determining the actual amount of the fine to be imposed.[274] These factors include the severity of the offense, the organization's role in the offense, the

272 Dixon, J. (2019). The organizational context of criminal sentencing 1. In *Criminal courts* (pp. 243–284). Routledge; Murphy, D. E. (2001). The federal sentencing guidelines for organizations: A decade of promoting compliance and ethics. *Iowa Law Review*, *87*, 697.

273 United States Sentencing Commission (2015). Chapter Eight – Sentencing of Organization <2015 Chapter 8 | United States Sentencing Commission>

274 Ibid.

collateral consequences of conviction, non-financial losses caused or threatened by the offense, the vulnerability of the victim, the prior criminal record of the individuals within the organization, and so on.

The U.S. Sentencing Guidelines of 2005 lay down some important principles for the courts while adjudicating corporate offenses.[275] In the first place, the court has the responsibility to instruct the organization to compensate for any harm that may have been caused. The costs incurred to remedy the harm must not be regarded as punitive but as an attempt at victim restoration.[276] Second, if the organization acted primarily for criminal purposes or by criminal means, the fine should be set at a level that completely strips the organization of all its possessions. Third, the fining range set for all other organizations should depend upon the intensity of the offense and the amount of guilt the organization bears. The offense's seriousness is almost always indicated by the maximum monetary value the entity could expect to receive, the monetary value the entity could expect to lose, or the figure given in a guideline offense-level fine scale. Culpability is usually defined by six factors, which the sentencing court has to look at more often than not. Of the six factors, four increase the organizational punishment to a higher degree: (a) the participation in or willful ignorance of the criminal acts, (b) the organization's past offending behavior, (c) the non-compliance with a civil order, and (d) the willful interference with the judicial process. The two factors that lessen the organizational sanction are (a) the existence of an effective compliance and ethics program and (b) self-reporting, cooperation, or acceptance of some responsibility. With regard to sentencing, organizational defendants may be placed on probation when it is necessary to make sure that some other sanction will be implemented or that action will be taken to diminish the likelihood of future criminal conduct. Such policies are effective in motivating organizations to control and eventually eliminate criminal conduct by creating a framework that enables the organization to institute self-policing through an effective compliance and ethics program. This type of program is intended to prevent and detect criminal actions, promote ethical behavior, and ensure compliance with all applicable statutes and regulations.

*3.3.3 **Australia***

In Australia, corporate responsibility development sheds light on how legal doctrine is shaped by corporate theory.[277] For example, the early treatment of

275 United States Sentencing Commission. (2025). Corporate Crime <Corporate Crime | United States Sentencing Commission>

276 United States Sentencing Commission, 2005 Federal Sentencing Guidelines Manuals <2005 Federal Sentencing Guidelines Manual | United States Sentencing Commission>

277 On the question of the influence of the theory on practice, see Horwitz, M. J. (1985). Santa Clara revisited: The development of corporate theory. *West Virginia Law Review*, *88*, 173, 223–224; and Bratton Jr., W. W. (1989). The new economic theory of the firm: Critical perspectives from history. *Stanford Law Review*, *41*, 1471–1527.

the corporation as a *persona ficta*, incapable of intention or *mens rea*, insisted on liability for certain kinds of wrongdoing,[278] an approach that conflicts with some organizational models of the corporation, which confer a greater capacity for distinct corporate accountability. According to this theory, the 'personhood' of the corporation is 'a matter of convenience rather than reality'[279]; the reality is the web of contracts between individual factors of production. The methodological individualism underlying such theories of the corporation seems to offer little scope for recognition of the corporation.

The coordination of a corporate system is considered legitimate in its relation to the corporation's interaction with society as well as the nature of corporations as private enterprises.[280] Within this approach, the possibility of external impacts as a result of corporate actions on the public domain makes those activities of concern to the public, and therefore, corporate responsibility as well as governance and control become necessary.[281] Areas of corporate activity such as environment, consumer, and occupational health and safety contain verifiable evidence of external impacts in the public domain. The need for control is often best accomplished at the corporate level rather than at the individual level. If the sole remedy is the prosecution of individuals, the corporation would readily evade responsibility for the offense, which, under such circumstances, is highly unreasonable.[282] Also, it has been claimed that for greater resources and access to information, corporations are, in fact, more appropriate bearers of responsibility and are more capable of avoiding the commission of offenses than individual persons.[283]

It is interesting to note that concern over the need for accountability for public harms has been echoed in recent times in the area of tortious liability, where commentators have questioned whether limited liability should be available to provide de facto installation to corporations and their shareholders against tortious liability arising from, for example, environmental disasters. In Australia, corporate criminality has long been a feature of work care and

278 See Lederman, E. (2000). Models for imposing corporate criminal liability: From adaptation and imitation toward aggregation and the search for self-identity. *Buffalo Criminal Law Review*, *4*(1), 641–708. See also Mueller, G. O. (1957). Mens rea and the corporations: A study of the Model Penal Code position on corporate criminal liability. *University of Pittsburgh Law Review*, *19*, 21.

279 See also, Macey, J. R. (1991). Agency theory and the criminal liability of organizations. *Boston University Law Review*, *71*, 315.

280 See Buxbaum, R. M. (1984). Corporate legitimacy, economic theory, and legal doctrine. *Ohio State Law Journal*, *45*, 515. See also Teubner, G. (1988). Enterprise corporatism: New industrial policy and the "essence" of the legal person. *The American Journal of Comparative Law*, *36*(1), 130–155.

281 Ibid.

282 See Foerschler, A. (1990). Corporate criminal intent: Toward a better understanding of corporate misconduct. *California Law Review*, *78*, 1287.

283 See McDonald, M. (1987). The personless paradigm. *The University of Toronto Law Journal*, *37*(2), 212–226.

safety legislation, but the 1970s saddled the corporation with quite onerous but, in the mind of most, restraints on marketing, trade practices, and competition behavior. More recently, the corporate form of enterprise has been particularly singled out for attention regarding the care and control of the environment.[284] These developments have extended well beyond any previous endeavor to impose corporate sanctions. In Australia, instead of strengthening corporate criminal liability, the legislation has placed more stress on public awareness about the activities of the corporations so that it can create a public opinion that shall work against corporate wrongdoing.

3.3.4 Canada

Canadian corporate criminal liability is still in its early stages of development and has yet to shift from an orthodox model of liability based on natural person responsibility. In this country, the capacity of corporations for criminal liability is defined solely by exception or variation to this model.[285] Continued adherence to this orthodoxy affirms a deep aversion to legal fiction as the basis of criminal responsibility. Paradoxically, the identification doctrine that lies at the core of Canadian corporate liability itself rests on the fiction that the liability of moral persons can be proved in the acts of our natural person.[286] As there is no distinct theory of collective criminal liability, Canadian law has no model of corporate criminality that reflects the dependence of modern industrial society upon moral persons as agents capable of responsible action. In short, dependence upon the corporation, as a social and economic agent, has

284 Regulation of the environment was initially done at the local level, but enforcement and compliance were inadequate. However, in the late 1960s and early 1970s, Australia witnessed the visible impact of environmental degradation due to rapid industrial advances, which took a toll on the environment. Additionally, more information became available regarding the health risks of pollution. It has also been suggested that the increased leisure time, resulting from economic growth since the Second World War, has provided the community with more time to contemplate and appreciate natural resources. Environmental disasters, which have received international attention such as the gas leak at Union Carbide in Bhopal in 1984, have promoted international regulation and an awareness of environmental issues. Within the last five years, other major factors contributing to the new prominence of environmental regulations have included: Australia's role as party to the most major international conventions on the environment, the terms of which must be implemented through domestic law; increased international monitoring of global environmental problems; the influence of strict U.S. environmental laws in transactions involving multinational corporations; and the instances by Australian banks and financial institutions of 'environmental audits' as a prerequisite to loan approvals for proposed land purchases. The new awareness of the need for environmental regulation has resulted in legislation which focuses on the public interest rather than individual rights and protection.

285 Justice, C. D. O. (2002). *Corporate criminal liability: Discussion paper*. Department of Justice Canada.

286 Quaid, J. A. (1998). The assessment of corporate criminal liability on the basis of corporate identity: An analysis. *McGill Law Journal, 43*(1), 67.

not been matched by decisions to expand the criminal law to reflect the power, both constructive and destructive, that these fictions can exert in reality.[287]

The Supreme Court of Canada has detected three levels of liability as they appear in the Canadian Penal Code: (a) infractions where the prosecution is required to prove some positive state of mind – intent, knowledge, or recklessness – as *mens rea*, and that proof may be either inferred from the actus reus or by supporting evidence[288]; (b) infractions where there is no requirement for the prosecution to establish the existence of *mens rea*: doing the prohibited act is prima facie enough to lead to an offense but the prosecution may be disarmed if the defendant shows that he exercised reasonable care; this line of reasoning requires that such a person to be placed in that situation is a reasonable man; the prosecution becomes endowed with a rebuttal burden if the person in question put forth all reasonable means to avoid the specific event in question; these should properly be referred to as strict liability offenses[289]; and (c) wholly blameworthy offenses, where the defendant cannot be afforded a defense that they were wanting.[290]

The first category includes all conduct viewed as criminal. Public welfare offenses would, on the surface, reside within the second category. The presumption of *mens rea* does not apply to these offenses.[291] This type of offense will only be placed in the first category if the provision creating the offense includes such phrases as 'willfully,' 'with intent,' 'knowingly,' or 'intentionally.'[292] In contrast, the general principle that a punishment should not be inflicted without fault provides an exception.[293] Offenses of absolute liability would be those in relation to which there was a clear statutory provision that guilt would result in proof of nothing more than the proscribed act.[294] The overall system of regulation, which is established by the legislature,

287 Archibald, T., Jull, K., & Roach, K. (2013). Corporate criminal liability: Myriad complexity in the scope of senior officer. *Criminal Law Quarterly*, *60*, 386.

288 Moore, M. (2023). Developments in contract law: The 2021–2022 term – the enduring allure of freedom of contract. *Supreme Court Law Review*, *111*, 3.

289 Shortt, M. (2019). Contractual limitation period clauses in Canada: Drafting and litigation considerations. *The Advocates' Quarterly*, *50*, 257.

290 Khan, S. (2022). Validity of limitation of liability clauses: The Supreme Court of Canada changes the rules and rejects the application of the notion of "fundamental breach" in Quebec civil law. *Lavery Lawyer*. Retrieved March 15, from www.lavery.ca/en/publications/4290-publication-display-PDF.html

291 Singer, R. G. (1988). The resurgence of Mens Rea: III – The rise and fall of strict criminal liability. *BCL Review*, *30*, 337.

292 Chesney, E. J. (1938). Concept of mens rea in the criminal law. *American Institute of Criminal Law and Criminology*, *29*, 627; Perkins, R. M. (1938). Rationale of Mens Rea, A. *Harvard Law Review*, *52*, 905., Pickard, T. (1980). Culpable mistakes and rape: Relating Mens Rea to the crime. *The University of Toronto Law Journal*, *30*(1), 75–98.

293 Omoregie, O. (2008). Strict liability and criminal responsibility: A critique. *Journal of Law and International Security*, *2*(2).

294 Tyagi, A. (2020). *Reiterating the principle of absolute liability in light of Oleum gas leakage case*. SSRN 3697451.

the subject matter of the statute, the significance of the punishment, and the detail of the wording used is what is most relevant for deciding whether the offense belongs to the third category.

*3.3.5 **Finland***

Finland is a civil law country. The Finnish law does not recognize the possibility of punishing a corporate entity.[295] However, they provide different means to control the delinquent behavior of the corporation.[296] For example, a corporation may be subject to forfeiture of assets and payment of damages. Second, several forms of administrative orders may be passed against them. The corporation may also be punished through the prosecution of its individual members, such as executive officers and employees.[297] There are several statutes regulating corporate activities, imposing penalties on the officers and executives of the company for wrongdoing in the course of their employment on behalf of the company. An order to pay damages can be made in addition to a penalty, as a part of criminal procedure, or it can be used alone as a civil sanction. Making a civil claim in criminal proceedings is possible since, in Finland, the two proceedings are 'adhesive.' 'Adhesiveness' of the proceedings means that while the main procedure is criminal, at the discretion of the court, the complainant is allowed to present his compensation claim during the procedure if the claim is based on the offense in question. The court will thereupon decide both the criminal and civil issues at the same time. However, if the compensation claim considerably prolongs the process, the court can divert the civil claim to separate civil proceedings.

Since a corporation as such cannot be made criminally liable for its action, the liability lies on the individual working in or for the corporation. Finding the right person is often difficult due to the complex corporate structure and delegation of authority. And since only a few environmental statutes attribute liability to a certain person, the courts have been forced to look elsewhere for guidance.[298]

A further stimulation toward the formulation of corporate criminal liability has been the public's perception of corporate criminality. Today's Finnish

295 Alvesalo-Kuusi, A., & Lähteenmäki, L. (2016). Legislating for corporate criminal liability in Finland: 22-year long debate revisited. *Journal of Scandinavian Studies in Criminology and Crime Prevention*, *17*(1), 53–69.

296 Alvesalo-Kuusi, A., Bittle, S., & Lähteenmäki, L. (2018). Repositioning the corporate criminal: Comparing and contrasting corporate criminal liability in Canada and Finland. *International Journal of Comparative and Applied Criminal Justice*, *42*(2–3), 215–231.

297 Lahti, R., & Rainiala, M. K. (2019). Alternative investigation and sanctioning systems for corporate and corporate-related crime in Finland. *Revue internationale de droit pénal*, *2019*(1), 131–163.

298 For instance, some log-floating offenses provided in chapter 13 of the Water Act 1961 are attributed to the members of the board of governors of the log-floating association and to the log-floating foreman.

public regards corporations as entities with a definite identity capable of considering risks and consequences. Penalizing corporations has become a generally accepted and even anticipated concept among the public.[299] In Finland, there are two proposed alternative footings for corporate liability. First, the corporation can be made liable when somebody belonging to corporate management participates in the crime. The second footing for liability is a breach of the corporation's duty to prevent criminal conduct in corporate activities. When some or several individuals belonging to a statutory or other body with decision-making power participate in a crime or allow a crime to be committed, the corporation can be sentenced for the crime. The commentary following the above propositions points out that penalizing the corporation is highly justified when the top management of the corporation has been directly involved in the offense. In a sense, the legislator has identified the corporation and its management. Since the highest management is responsible for the corporation's decisions, decisions made by some belonging to management are regarded as representing the corporation directly.[300] At the very top, there was the board of governors, the partners, the chief executive officers, all shareholders that attended the meeting, the auditors, members of the municipal council, and other upper-level managers. The commentary notes explicitly that the provision does not encompass middle management. Drawing a finite line is, however, impossible and is therefore left to the discretion of the courts.

3.3.6 Germany

Significant discourse has emerged within legal circles regarding the incorporation of corporate criminal liability in Germany. This debate stems from the escalating prevalence of economic and environmental crimes perpetrated by corporations, for which the current sanctions and administrative measures are deemed insufficient and exhibit minimal deterrent effect.[301] It is argued that despite evidence of corporations being involved in organized crimes, the criminal justice system in Germany has yet to acknowledge the 'organized absence of responsibility.'[302] Those who oppose including corporate criminal liability in regulations argue that the then regulatory system in Germany was not ready to deal with the criminal liability of an artificial legal person. They claim that

299 Sahramäki, I. (2016). Enforcement and professional constructions of environmental crime in Finland. In *The geography of environmental crime: Conservation, wildlife crime and environmental activism* (pp. 189–216).

300 Tolvanen, M. J. (2012). Trust, business ethics and crime prevention–Corporate criminal liability in Finland. In *Business ethics and crime prevention–corporate criminal liability in Finland (January 16, 2012)*. University of Eastern Finland Legal Studies Research Paper(2).

301 Gutnikov, O. V. (2019). The grounds for development of corporate liability category in civil law. *Law: Journal of Higher School of Economics, 4.*

302 Fieberg, G. (1998, May 4–5). *National development in Germany: An overview.* International Colloquium on Criminal Responsibility of Legal and Collective Entities, Berlin.

an artificial legal person cannot commit a crime, as it is impossible to establish the criminal intent of an artificial person. Their argument is based on the belief that corporate entities are not capable of being culpable. They also argue that punishing a company is not feasible and that it may violate the principle of *non bis in idem*. In 1998, the German government established a working group to address the ongoing debate around corporate criminal liability. The group was tasked with reviewing the current situation and improving the criminal justice system for corporate entities.[303] Instead of using criminal law, Germany has created a complex system of administrative sanctions,[304] including provisions for corporate criminal liability.

In Germany, the core principle in corporate criminal liability regulation is the concept of 'organizational fault' or *organisationsverschulden*. This principle holds corporations and other legal entities criminally liable for offenses committed by their representatives, employees, or agents in the course of their duties for the benefit of the organization. As such, executives and individuals with decision-making authority within the corporation can also face personal liability for their involvement in criminal activities.

The legal framework for corporate criminal liability in Germany is primarily outlined in the German Criminal Code (*Strafgesetzbuch*) and the act on Administrative Offenses (*Ordnungswidrigkeitengesetz*). If found guilty of criminal offenses, corporations in Germany can face sanctions such as fines, exclusion from public procurement, and confiscation of profits. These sanctions, known as *Ordnungswidrigkeiten*, are imposed by administrative bodies. The main provision for penalizing corporations is *Ordnungswidrigkeitengesetz*, § 30,[305] which requires fines to be levied on corporate entities. In recent years, there has been a growing emphasis on corporate compliance and the responsibility of senior management in preventing corporate criminal activities.[306] Additionally, legislative changes have been made to strengthen the legal framework governing corporate criminal liability, aiming to enhance transparency and accountability within corporate entities.[307]

303 This possible departure is due to significant pressure from the latest directives and conventions, both on the EU and OECD level.

304 Administrative sanctions are imposed by an agency of the executive branch, as opposed to being imposed by the judiciary. For more, see Wagner, M. *Corporate criminal liability: National and international response*. Retrieved December 12, 2023, from http://www.icclr.law.ubc.ca/Publications/Reports/CorporateCriminal.pdf

305 Allahverdiyev, S., & Othman, M. (2022). "Verbandssanktionengesetz" – Corporate liability for Germany? *German Law Journal*, *23*(4), 637–649.

306 Momsen, C., & Schwarze, M. (2018, December). The changing face of corporate liability: New hard law and the increasing influence of soft law. *Criminal Law Forum*, *29*, 567–593. Springer Netherlands.

307 Ramos, M. E. G. (2018). Corporate indemnification: Experiences in USA and developments in Germany, Italy and Portugal. *European Company and Financial Law Review*, *14*(4), 723–774.

3.3.7 France

Prior to 1992, France's legal system did not recognize corporate criminal liability.[308] However, it was eventually included in the new Code Pénal in Sections 121–2 despite facing resistance. The Conseil Constitutionnel clarified in 1982 that corporations could be fined without violating the French Constitution.[309] Despite this provision, France follows the directing mind concept, which means that only crimes that specifically mention corporate punishment can be applied. As a result, corporate criminal liability is only applicable to a limited number of crimes.[310] Additionally, only legal representatives or organs of corporations who have acted can be held liable under the French Code Pénal.[311] Nevertheless, violation of supervisory duties is enough to initiate proceedings for corporate criminal liability.

The Sapin II Law, which came into effect in 2016, is a significant piece of regulation aimed at dealing with corporate criminal liability.[312] This law extends the reach of corporate criminal liability and incorporates measures to prevent and detect corruption, influence peddling, and related offenses. According to this law, companies can be held criminally responsible for any offenses committed on their behalf by directors, representatives, or employees. The law goes beyond the actions of senior management and makes it mandatory for companies to introduce compliance programs to prevent and detect corruption and related offenses. These programs include risk assessments, codes of conduct, internal reporting procedures, and whistleblowing mechanisms. Companies found guilty of any offenses can face severe sanctions, such as fines, exclusion from public procurement, and publication of the court's decision. The fines can be significant, running into millions of euros.[313] Furthermore, the law introduces aggravating circumstances for corporate offenses, such as repeat offenses, involvement of public officials, or offenses committed transnationally.[314]

The enforcement of corporate criminal liability regulations in France can pose significant challenges due to the intricacies and interpretations of the

308 Stessens, G. (1994). Corporate criminal liability: A comparative perspective. *International & Comparative Law Quarterly*, *43*(3), 493–520.

309 Ibid.

310 Ibid.

311 Pieth, M., & Ivory, R. (2011). *Emergence and convergence: Corporate criminal liability principles in overview*. In *Corporate criminal liability: Emergence, convergence, and risk* (pp. 3–60). Springer.

312 Lelieur, J. (2023). France's "Sapin II" law. In *Elgar concise encyclopedia of corruption law* (pp. 228–230). Edward Elgar Publishing.

313 Barsan, I. (2017). Corporate accountability: Non-financial disclosure and liability – A French perspective. *European Company and Financial Law Review*, *14*(3), 399–433.

314 Sachs, T., & Tricot, J. (2020). The French law on corporate duty of vigilance: Rethinking corporate governance? *Droit et Société*, *106*, 683.

Sapin II Law.[315] Conducting investigations and prosecuting corporate offenses under this law can be a prolonged and resource-intensive process, often resulting in lengthy legal proceedings. The requirement for companies to establish compliance programs can be a significant administrative and financial burden, particularly for small- and medium-sized enterprises (SMEs). Some provisions of the law, notably those related to the determination of corporate criminal liability and the efficacy of compliance programs, lack clarity and may lead to interpretational difficulties. Additionally, as the Sapin II Law is relatively new, there is limited judicial practice and precedent in its application, which can create uncertainties for companies and legal practitioners alike.

3.3.8 Japan

The regulation of corporate criminal liability in Japan is based on two principles within the country's criminal justice system: *Ryoubatsu-Kitei* and *Kigya-Soshikitai-sekininoron*. While the interpretation of *Ryoubatsu-Kitei* has been the subject of debate, a recent interpretation (post-World War II) avoids the concept of vicarious liability as it conflicts with the fundamental doctrine of criminal responsibility. Those who support the criminal liability of an enterprise explain that the enterprise must be punished because its employee (and through a representative) committed a crime. On the other hand, the theory of *Kigya-Soshikitai-sekininoron* (corporate organization theory) recognizes the difficulties of punishing a large and complex organization, where it can be challenging to determine who committed the alleged crime. As a result, punishing the enterprise is often not pursued.

Historically, Japan's approach to corporate criminal liability was characterized by a limited scope of legal responsibility for corporate entities. However, in response to the need for enhanced corporate governance and accountability, Japan introduced significant reforms to its corporate criminal liability regime.[316] Notably, the 2007 amendment to the act on Penal Provisions for the Prevention of Unfair Competition marked a pivotal moment in strengthening corporate criminal liability regulations. Additionally, the Companies Act sets forth provisions related to corporate governance and the responsibilities of directors and officers, thereby influencing the framework of corporate criminal liability. Under these regulations, corporate criminal liability can be established when criminal offenses are committed for the benefit of the corporation by individuals in positions of authority within the company.[317] Moreover, the principle of 'obligation to supervise' holds corporations accountable for the

315 Sachs, T., & Tricot, J. (2020). The French law on corporate duty of vigilance: Rethinking corporate governance? *Droit et Societe*, *106*, 683.

316 Oda, H. (2021). *Japanese law*. Oxford University Press.

317 Nagata, K. (2013). Fines in the Japanese criminal justice system. *Kansai University Review of Law and Politics*, *34*, 1–16.

actions of their officers and employees, emphasizing the importance of implementing effective compliance and monitoring mechanisms.

When individuals with authority in a corporation commit certain crimes for the benefit of the corporation, the corporation may face criminal responsibility. If found guilty, the corporation may face penalties such as fines, confiscation of property, and legal sanctions.[318] The act on Punishment of Organized Crimes and Control of Crime Proceeds also includes provisions for asset forfeiture and other measures to combat organized crime and money laundering. Japan has taken steps to increase penalties for antitrust violations by corporations, indicating a growing emphasis on corporate criminal liability in competition law.[319]

The case involving the Tokyo Organizing Committee for the Olympic and Paralympic Games is a significant example of the enforcement of corporate criminal liability in Japan.[320] In August 2022, a former director of the Tokyo Organizing Committee for the Olympic and Paralympic Games was taken into custody for allegedly accepting bribes from sponsor companies. This case later expanded into a bid-rigging scandal that involved test competitions, and directors of multiple sponsor companies were also detained.[321] This serves as a significant example of how corporate criminal responsibility is enforced in Japan, where both individuals and corporations can be held accountable for their actions.[322] Japan's legal framework allows business crime cases to be prosecuted, and public prosecutors have the exclusive authority to prosecute any crime, including business crimes.[323] This situation also underscores the significance of compliance measures, and corporations are urged to establish compliance programs to prevent and detect criminal conduct.[324]

In contrast to other jurisdictions, Japan lacks a formal Deferred Prosecution Agreement (DPA) framework to encourage self-reporting and cooperation,

318 Bottomley, S. (2018). Company law in Japan. In *Company law in East Asia* (pp. 39–74). Routledge.

319 Nagata, K. (2013). Fines in the Japanese criminal justice system. *Kansai University Review of Law and Politics*, *34*, 1–16.

320 Wade, S., & Kageyama, Y. (2023, December 15). *Ex-Tokyo Olympics official pleads not guilty to taking bribes in exchange for Games contracts.* The Associated Press. https://apnews.com/article/dentsu-tokyo-olympics-bribery-takahashi-ioc-dccbc9e8fb453f9b139de19ceb17e450; Kaneko, K. (2023, December 14). Former Tokyo Games executive pleads not guilty over bribery. *The Japan Times.* www.japantimes.co.jp/news/2023/12/14/japan/crime-legal/olympics-bribery-1st-hearing/

321 Ohashi, K., & Akahori, J. (2024). *Business crime laws and regulations Japan 2024.* ICLG. https://iclg.com/practice-areas/business-crime-laws-and-regulations/japan

322 Mishra, N. (2022, December 12). *Behind the Tokyo Olympics bribery scandal involving Dentsu, Hakuhodo and ADK. Campaign.* Retrieved April 7, 2023, from www.campaignasia.com/article/behind-the-tokyo-olympics-bribery-scandal-involving-dentsu-hakuhodo-and-adk/482577

323 Ohashi, K., & Akahori, J. (2024). *Business crime laws and regulations Japan 2024.* ICLG. https://iclg.com/practice-areas/business-crime-laws-and-regulations/japan

324 Ibid.

potentially hindering effective incentivization.[325] Japan's corporate culture and business practices, such as consensus decision-making and close government ties, may challenge the impartial enforcement of corporate criminal laws.[326] While compliance programs are encouraged, standardized compliance standards may be necessary to prevent corporate criminal conduct. To promote ethical corporate conduct, Japan must address concerns surrounding liability scope, lack of DPAs, cultural challenges, and compliance measures.[327] The Supreme Court of Japan recognizes business corporations' liability for criminal offenses, providing a legal basis for further developing corporate criminal liability regulation in this country.[328]

3.3.9 China

Before introducing 'unit crime' in Article 30 of the Criminal Code, the Customs Law of the People's Republic of China was the first to establish that 'enterprises, institutions, state organs, or public organizations' could be held accountable for criminal offenses.[329] It was not until 1997, with changes to the Criminal Code, that corporate criminal liability was officially recognized in China. The country's laws hold legal entities, such as businesses and organizations, responsible for offenses committed in their name or for their benefit. If a corporation's directors, executives, or other employees commit an offense in the company's interest, the corporation can be held criminally liable. The law places significant emphasis on implementing due diligence measures and compliance programs within corporations to prevent criminal activities and ensure legal compliance when determining this liability.[330] Corporations can be held accountable for a broad range of criminal offenses, including but not limited to bribery, environmental violations, product safety violations, and other economic crimes. Moreover, the concept of corporate criminal liability promotes corporate compliance and encourages corporate social responsibility within the business environment.

When corporations are found guilty of criminal offenses, they can face various penalties, such as fines, confiscation of illegal profits, and other administrative consequences. More than 50 types of unit crimes have been

325 Takahashi, E., & Shimizu, M. (2005). The future of Japanese corporate governance: The 2005 reform. *Zeitschrift für Japanisches Recht, 10*(19), 35–68.

326 Jimenez, G. A. (2019). Corporate criminal liability: Toward a compliance-oriented approach. *Indiana Journal of Global Legal Studies, 26*, 353.

327 Shishido, Z. (2000). Japanese corporate governance: The hidden problems of corporate law and their solutions. *Delaware Journal of Corporate Law, 25*, 189.

328 Hatashin, O. (2008). Crime and culture. *Corporate and White Collar Crime, 141.*

329 Article 30 of the Chinese Criminal Code reads: 'Any company, enterprise, institution, state organ, or organization that endanger society, which is prescribed by law as a crime committed by a unit, shall bear the responsibility.'

330 Zhang, L., & Liu, Y. (2019). Corporate criminal liability in China: A comparative perspective. *Journal of Corporate Law Studies, 19*(3), 355–372.

established across different criminal, civil, economic, and administrative regulations.[331] However, the extensive range of unit crimes has faced criticism for three main reasons: (1) the uncertainty surrounding individual responsibility in the context of unit crimes; (2) the various designations used to describe unit crimes, such as 'enterprises, institutions, organs, or public organizations,' or 'enterprises and institutions,' or simply 'units'; and (3) inconsistencies in punishments, with the laws implementing both the dual and single systems.[332]

In December 2023, the National People's Congress Standing Committee approved a Criminal Law amendment to increase penalties for bribery and corruption in China. The amendment focuses on enhancing the provisions related to these issues within private enterprises' internal personnel. It formalizes anti-bribery regulations for private companies and imposes harsher penalties for certain bribery-related violations. While the amendment's scope is limited, it demonstrates the government's commitment to tackling private-sector issues.[333] Its goal is to ensure equal treatment for private and state-owned companies, and it may not result in significant changes in how private businesses handle bribery within their own ranks.[334]

3.3.10 India

In the Indian context, 'criminal liability of corporation' has been described in the following manner:

> [I]n the case of torts, the general rule prevails that the corporation may be criminally liable for the acts of an officer or agent, assumed to be done by him when exercising authorized powers, and without proof that his act was expressly authorized or approved by the corporation. In the statutes defining crimes, the prohibition is frequently directed against any 'person' who commits the prohibited act, and in many statutes the term 'person' is defined. Even if the person is not specifically defined, it includes a corporation. It is usually construed to include a corporation to bring it within the prohibition of the statute and subject it to punishment. In most of the statutes, the word 'person' is defined to include

331 See Jiachen, L. (1999). The legislation and judicial practice on punishment of unit crime in China. *Criminal Responsibility of Legal and Collective Entities, Freiburg i. Br., 71.*

332 Ibid.; Wang, H., & Liu, Y. (2020). Corporate criminal liability in China: Legislation, application, and challenges. *Asian Journal of Criminology, 15*(1), 1–19.

333 Gon, Y.-L., & Yan, J. (2023). *Business crime laws and regulations China.* ICLG. https://iclg.com/practice-areas/business-crime-laws-and-regulations/china

334 Huld, A. (2024, January 15). China amends criminal law to strengthen anti-bribery regulation for private companies. *Dezan Shira and Associates.* Retrieved April 7, 2024, from www.china-briefing.com/news/anti-corruption-in-china-criminal-law-amendment-tackle-bribery-private-sector/

a corporation. In Section 11 of the Indian Penal Code, the 'person' is defined thus:

'The word "person" includes any Company or Association or body of persons, whether incorporated or not.'

[A]s regards Corporate Criminal Liability, there is no doubt that a corporation or company could be prosecuted for any offense punishable under law, whether it is coming under the strict liability or under absolute liability.

Inasmuch as all criminal and quasi-criminal offences are creatures of statute, the amenability of the corporation to prosecution necessarily depends upon the terminology employed in the statute. In the case of strict liability, the terminology employed by the legislature is such as to reveal intent that guilt shall not be predicated upon the automatic breach of the statute but on the establishment of the *actus reus*. subject to the defense of due diligence. The law is primarily based on the terms of the statutes. In the case of absolute liability, where the legislature by the clearest intendment establishes an offence where liability arises instantly upon the breach of the statutory prohibition, no particular state of mind is a prerequisite to guilt. Corporations and individual persons stand on the same footing in the face of such a statutory offence. It is a case of automatic primary responsibility. It is only in a case requiring *mens rea*, a question arises whether a corporation could be attributed with requisite *mens rea* to prove the guilt.[335]

The Law Commission of India, in its 47th Report, 1972, made the following recommendation[336]:

In many of the Acts relating to economic offences, imprisonment is mandatory. Where the convicted person is a corporation, this provision becomes unworkable, and it is desirable to provide that in such cases, it shall be competent for the court to impose a fine. This difficulty can arise under the Penal Code also, but it is likely to arise more frequently in the case of economic laws. We, therefore, recommend that the following provision should be inserted in the Penal Code as, say, Section 62:

335 See *Standard Chartered Bank and Other etc. vs. Directorate of Enforcement and Other etc.*, AIR 2005 SC 2622; MANU/SC 0380/2005; see also, *The Assistant Commissioner, Assessment – II, Bangalore and Other vs. Velliappa Textiles Ltd. and Other*, AIR 2004 SC 86; MANU/SC/0721/2003, held that criminal liability cannot be imposed upon corporation under the existing legal frame in India. See also: *Charan Lal Sahu vs. Union of India and Others* (1990) 1 CompLJ 125a (SC), imposition of criminal liability of corporation was argued.

336 See Law Commission of India. (1972). *Forty-seventh report: The trial and punishment of social and economic offences*. Government of India; see also, Law Commission of India. (1969). *Forty-first report: The Code of Criminal Procedure 1898*. Government of India.

> (1) In every case in which the offence is punishable with imprisonment only or with imprisonment and fine, and the offender is a corporation, it shall be competent to the court to sentence such offender to fine only. (2) In every case in which the offense is punishable with imprisonment and any other punishment not being fine, and the offender is a corporation, it shall be competent to the court to sentence such offender to a fine. (3) In this section, 'corporation' means an incorporated company or other body corporate, and includes a firm and other association of individuals.

Corporate criminal regulation in India is primarily governed by statutes such as the *Indian Penal Code 1860*, the *Companies Act 2013*, and the *Prevention of Corruption Act 1988*, among others. Under these laws, corporate entities can be held vicariously liable for the criminal acts of their directors, officers, or employees committed in the course of business, if such acts were done with the consent or connivance of the corporation.[337] They are expected to adhere to compliance standards and exercise due diligence to prevent criminal activities.[338]

Several laws exist in India that enable judges and administrative agencies to impose sanctions on corporations, such as cash fines, probation, debarment, and loss of license. The loss of license is particularly severe as it can prevent a corporation from entering transactions, impacting its profits and acting as a strong deterrent. If a corporation is unable to pay an optimal cash fine, additional penalties such as probation, debarment, and loss of license may be utilized as supplementary sanctions.[339] Corporate criminal liability regulation in India considers debarment especially effective, especially in cases where a corporation is involved in contractual activities with the government.[340]

3.4 Conclusion

Criminal liability refers to the legal responsibility of an individual or corporation for the commission of a criminal offense. In environmental law, criminal liability arises when a corporation, through its employees or representatives, engages in activities that are harmful to the environment and violate the existing environmental laws and regulations. These activities may include illegal

337 Sachdeva, R. (2022). An analytical study on corporate criminal liability: Comparative study of India and USA. *International Journal of Law Management & Humanities*, *5*(1), 2577; Khanna, U. (2021). Corporate criminal liability: An analysis of vicarious imposition of corporate sanctions in India. *International Journal of Law Management & Humanities*, *4*(3), 1653.

338 Dhabhar, A. (2023). An analysis of criminal liability of companies under Indian law. *Journal of Legal Studies & Research*, *9*(2), 109–118.

339 Ibid., p. 1499.

340 Supra note 23, p. 1499; Aneja, A. (2016). Multidimensional aspects of corporate criminal liability: An Indian perspective. *JLJ*, *72*, 34.

dumping of hazardous waste, unauthorized release of pollutants, or failure to obtain necessary permits for certain operations.

The concept of corporate criminal liability in environmental law is based on the idea that corporations, as legal entities, can and should be held accountable for the actions of their employees or representatives. This is particularly important in cases where the corporation has profited from the green crimes or has created a culture of non-compliance within the organization. Green crime refers to criminal activities that cause harm to the environment and violate environmental laws and regulations. Examples of green crimes include illegal logging, poaching, and the illegal trade of endangered species. One of the main reasons green crime is a significant concern is that the environment is a shared resource and damage to the environment often has far-reaching consequences.

It is daunting to ask how to reduce green crimes committed by corporations. We suggest combining the rise of environmental capitalism with the regulation of corporate criminal liability in environmental jurisprudence.

Environmental capitalism refers to incorporating environmental concerns into business strategies and decision-making processes. This can involve the adoption of sustainable practices, investment in green technologies, and compliance with environmental laws and regulations. While environmental capitalism can positively affect the environment and society, it can also play a role in corporate criminal liability for pollution offenses. The pursuit of profit can lead to the creation of opportunities for corporations to exploit loopholes or weaknesses in environmental laws and regulations. For instance, a corporation may take advantage of lax enforcement or regulatory gaps to engage in activities that are harmful to the environment but are not explicitly prohibited by law.

The rise of regulations on corporate criminal liability in many significant jurisdictions globally can help reduce the negative impact of environmental capitalism. Several key concepts support the idea of corporate criminal liability for pollution offenses. Vicarious liability means that a corporation can be held accountable for the criminal acts of its employees or representatives, provided those acts are committed within the scope of their employment or authority. This means that if an employee illegally dumps hazardous waste on behalf of the corporation, the corporation may face criminal charges for the offense. Strict liability means that a corporation can be held criminally responsible for certain environmental offenses, irrespective of whether it intended to cause harm or was negligent in its actions. In other words, the mere fact that a corporation breached an environmental law, such as discharging pollutants without a permit, may be adequate to establish criminal liability. The due diligence defense acknowledges that a corporation may be able to avoid criminal liability for pollution offenses if it can demonstrate that it took reasonable precautions and exercised due diligence to prevent the offense from occurring. This may involve implementing comprehensive environmental compliance programs, conducting regular audits, and training employees on environmental laws and regulations.

The latter part of this chapter discusses the principles or doctrines countries use to incorporate the concept of corporate criminal liability into their regulatory frameworks. This is a difficult subject, often considered one of the most challenging areas of criminal law. While this discussion presents a system for regulating corporate criminal liability, it also indicates that there is no single legal principle or doctrine that every country can use as the basis for this regulatory system. The United States and South Africa follow the vicarious liability approach to attribute corporate criminal liability, whereas the identification doctrine is primarily used by the UK, Canada, and New Zealand. However, the identification doctrine is not the only approach used by these countries. In the UK, the Privy Council expanded the identification doctrine by shifting the focus to a purposive approach toward the relevant statutory offense, instead of just evaluating the 'directing mind and will' of the corporation. Recently, an express statutory attribution method was introduced in the UK for specific offenses under the *Corporate Manslaughter and Corporate Homicide Act 2007*. Australia is reviewing its Commonwealth corporate criminal liability regime to enhance and streamline the current legal frameworks for assigning criminal liability to companies. However, it is worth noting that the lack of judicial consideration of these provisions shows that Commonwealth prosecutors have been hesitant to rely on corporate attribution pursuant to that regime. The discussions in Chapters 4 and 5 would further explain this matter.

References

Agency, U. S. E. P. (2023). What is acid rain? *United States Environmental Protection Agency*. Retrieved April 4, from www.epa.gov/acidrain/what-acid-rain#:~:text=Acid%20 rain%20results%20when%20sulfur, form%20sulfuric%20and%20nitric%20acids

Ahdout, Z. P. (2021). Enforcement lawmaking and judicial review. *Harvard Law Review*, *135*, 937.

Albanese, J. S. (1984). Love Canal six years later: The legal legacy. *Federal Probation*, *48*, 53.

Allahverdiyev, S., & Othman, M. (2022). "Verbandssanktionengesetz" – Corporate liability for Germany? *German Law Journal*, *23*(4), 637–649.

Alschuler, A. W. (2009). Two ways to think about the punishment of corporations. *American Criminal Law Review*, *46*, 1359.

Alvesalo-Kuusi, A., Bittle, S., & Lähteenmäki, L. (2018). Repositioning the corporate criminal: Comparing and contrasting corporate criminal liability in Canada and Finland. *International Journal of Comparative and Applied Criminal Justice*, *42*(2–3), 215–231.

Alvesalo-Kuusi, A., & Lähteenmäki, L. (2016). Legislating for corporate criminal liability in Finland: 22-year long debate revisited. *Journal of Scandinavian Studies in Criminology and Crime Prevention*, *17*(1), 53–69.

Anderson, M. (2001). Transnational corporations and environmental damage: Is tort law the answer? *Washburn Law Journal*, *41*, 399.

Aneja, A. (2016). Multidimensional aspects of corporate criminal liability: An Indian perspective. *Journal of the Legal and Judicial System*, *72*, 34.

Archibald, T., Jull, K., & Roach, K. (2013). Corporate criminal liability: Myriad complexity in the scope of senior officer. *Criminal Law Quarterly*, *60*, 386.

Atiyeh, C. (2017). Everything you need to know about the VW Diesel-emissions scandal. *Car and Driver*. Retrieved April 7, from www.caranddriver.com/news/a15339250/everything-you-need-to-know-about-the-vw-diesel-emissions-scandal/

AUSMEPA. (2015). Ballast water: The issue. *Australian Marine Environment Protection Association*. Retrieved February 10, from www.ausmepa.org.au/pests/default.asp?pageid=33&nav=19

Australian Law Reform Commission. (2019). *Corporate attribution – principled simplicity*. Australian Government. Retrieved March 28, 2019, from www.alrc.gov.au/news/corporate-attribution-principled-simplicity/

Baer, M. H. (2008). Insuring corporate crime. *Indiana Law Journal*, *83*, 1035.

Barsan, I. (2017). Corporate accountability: Non-financial disclosure and liability–A French perspective. *European Company and Financial Law Review*, *14*(3), 399–433.

Basha, O., Alajmy, J., & Newaz, T. (2020). *Bhopal gas tragedy: A safety case study* (Report No. CHEN 455). Texas A&M University at Qatar.

Basu, T. (2014, March 31). Timeline: A history of GM's ignition switch defect. *NPR*. Retrieved April 7, from https://www.npr.org/2014/03/31/297158876/timeline-a-history-of-gms-ignition-switch-defect

Baxi, U. (2017). Writing about impunity and environment: The "silver jubilee" of the Bhopal catastrophe. In *Globalization and common responsibilities of states* (pp. 473–494). Routledge.

Beale, S. S. (2016). The development and evolution of the US law of corporate criminal liability and the Yates memo. *Stetson Law Review*, *46*, 41.

Beck, E. C. (1979, September 22, 2016). The Love Canal tragedy. *US Environmental Protection Agency*. Retrieved April 4, from www.epa.gov/archive/epa/aboutepa/love-canal-tragedy.html

Beyer, J., Trannum, H. C., Bakke, T., Hodson, P. V., & Collier, T. K. (2016). Environmental effects of the Deepwater Horizon oil spill: A review. *Marine Pollution Bulletin*, *110*(1), 28–51.

Bhopal Gas Leak Disaster (Processing of Claims) Act (1985).

Bloch, K. (2016). *Rethinking Bhopal: A definitive guide to investigating, preventing, and learning from industrial disasters*. Elsevier.

Bottomley, S. (2018). Company law in Japan. In *Company law in East Asia* (pp. 39–74). Routledge.

Bratton Jr., W. W. (1989). The new economic theory of the firm: Critical perspectives from history. *Stanford Law Review*, 1471–1527.

Briski, E., Bailey, S. A., Casas-Monroy, O., DiBacco, C., Kaczmarska, I., Levings, C., MacGillivary, M. L., McKindsey, C. W., Nasmith, L. E., & Parenteau, M. (2012). Relationship between propagule pressure and colonization pressure in invasion ecology: A test with ships' ballast. *Proceedings of the Royal Society of London B: Biological Sciences*, rspb20112671.

Britannica. (n.d.). Ozone depletion. *Encyclopædia Britannica*. Retrieved September 28, from www.britannica.com/science/ozone-depletion

Brown, C. (2012). Patterns of management, compliance and geography of ballast water in California. *C. S. L. Commission*. www.slc.ca.gov/About/Prevention_First/2012/California-BallastMgmt.pdf

Buck, E. H. (2010). *Ballast water management to combat invasive species*. Congressional Research Service Reports, 25. https://digitalcommons.unl.edu/crsdocs/25

Bucy, P. H. (1990). Corporate ethos: A standard for imposing corporate criminal liability. *Minnesota Law Review*, *75*, 1095.

Buell, S. W. (2006). The blaming function of entity criminal liability. *Indiana Law Journal*, *81*, 473.

Buxbaum, R. M. (1984). Corporate legitimacy, economic theory, and legal doctrine. *Ohio State Law Journal*, *45*, 515.
Carlton, J. T., Thompson, J. K., Schemel, L. E., & Nichols, F. H. (1990). Remarkable invasion of San Francisco Bay (California, USA), by the Asian clam Potamocorbula amurensis. I. Introduction and dispersal. *Marine Ecology Progress Series*, *66*, 81–94.
Cassels, J. (1991). The uncertain promise of law: Lessons from Bhopal. *Osgoode Hall Law Journal*, *29*, 1.
Chesney, E. J. (1938). Concept of mens rea in the criminal law. *American Institute of Criminal Law and Criminology*, *29*, 627.
Chopra, R., & Frothman, S. (2025). State enforcement as a federal legislative tool. *Harvard Journal on Legislation*, *62*(1).
Chouhan, T. R. (1994). *Bhopal: The inside story*. The Other India Press.
Clarke, R. A., Stavins, R. N., Ladd Greeno, J., Bavaria, J. L., Cairncross, D., Etsy, D., Smart, B., Piet, J., Wells, R., & Gray, R. (1994). The challenge of going green. *Reader in Business and the Environment*, *45*.
Clough, J. (2009). A glaring omission: Corporate liability for negligent manslaughter. *Monash University Faculty of Law Legal Studies Research Paper*, *2007*(41), 29.
Colvin, E. (1995). Corporate personality and criminal liability. *Criminal Law Forum*, *6*, 1.
Covell, T. (1991). The Bhopal disaster litigation: It's not over yet. *North Carolina Journal of International Law and Commercial Regulation*, *16*, 279.
Cruden, J. C., Engel, B., Cooney, N., & Van Eaton, J. (2018). Dieselgate: How the investigation, prosecution, and settlement of Volkswagen's emissions cheating scandal illustrates the need for robust environmental enforcement. *Virginia Environmental Law Journal*, *36*, 118.
Cruden, J. C., O'Rourke, S., & Himmelhoch, S. D. (2016). The Deepwater Horizon oil spill litigation: Proof of concept for the *Manual for Complex Litigation* and the 2015 amendments to the federal rules of civil procedure. *Michigan Journal of Environmental & Administrative Law*, *6*, 65.
David, M., Gollasch, S., & Pavliha, M. (2013). Global ballast water management and the "same location" concept: A clear term or a clear issue? *Ecological Applications*, *23*(2), 331–338.
Davidson, L. M., Baum, A., & Gisriel, M. M. (2020). Toxic exposure and chronic stress at Three Mile Island. In *Advances in environmental psychology* (Vol. 6, pp. 35–46). Routledge.
Davies, K. (2023). *The rise of the US environmental health movement*. Rowman & Littlefield.
Deforestation-risk Companies. (2023). *Deforestation free funds*. Retrieved April 7, 2023, from https://deforestationfreefunds.org/companies
Desai, B. (1993). The Bhopal gas leak disaster litigation: An overview. *Asian Yearbook of International Law*, *3*, 163–179.
Desio, P. (2024). *An overview of the organizational guidelines*. U.S. Sentencing Commission.
Dhabhar, A. (2023). An analysis of criminal liability of companies under Indian law. *Journal of Legal Studies & Research*, *9*(2), 109–118.
Dhavan, R. (1985). For whom – and for what: Reflections on the legal aftermath of Bhopal. *Texas International Law Journal*, *20*, 295.
Diamantis, M. E. (2015). Corporate criminal minds. *Notre Dame Law Review*, *91*, 2049.
DiMento, J. F., & Badiee, A. (2017). Historical pollution and criminal liability in the United States. In *Historical pollution: Comparative legal responses to environmental crimes* (pp. 197–223). Springer.

Dixon, J. (2019). The organizational context of criminal sentencing 1. In *Criminal courts* (pp. 243–284). Routledge.
Dybing, S. S. (2016). Environmental harm: Social causes and shifting legislative dynamics. In *Eco-global crimes* (pp. 273–294). Routledge.
Etzkowitz, H. (1984). Corporate induced disaster: Three Mile Island and the delegitimation of nuclear power. *Humanity & Society, 8*(3), 228–252.
Fieberg, G. (1998, May 4–5). National development in Germany: An overview. In *International colloquium on criminal responsibility of legal and collective entities.* Ed. iuscrim, Max-Planck-Institut für Ausländisches und Internationales Strafrecht.
Foerschler, A. (1990). Corporate criminal intent: Toward a better understanding of corporate misconduct. *California Law Review, 78*, 1287.
Fofonoff, P. W., Ruiz, G. M., Steves, B., & Carlton, J. T. (2003). In ships or on ships? Mechanisms of transfer and invasion for nonnative species to the coasts of North America. In *Invasive species: Vectors and management strategies* (pp. 152–182). Island Press.
Force, R., Davies, M., & Force, J. S. (2010). Deepwater Horizon: Removal costs, civil damages, crimes, civil penalties, and state remedies in oil spill cases. *Tulane Law Review, 85*, 889.
Forsyth, M., & Tepper, F. (2024). Environmental enforceable undertakings: An innovative tool to repair and prevent environmental harm. *Journal of environmental law, 36*(3), 385–411.
Fortun, K. (2000). Remembering Bhopal, re-figuring liability. *Interventions, 2*(2), 187–198.
Fortun, K. (2009). *Advocacy after Bhopal: Environmentalism, disaster, new global orders.* University of Chicago Press.
Fracarolli Nunes, M., & Lee Park, C. (2016). Caught red-handed: The cost of the Volkswagen Dieselgate. *Journal of Global Responsibility, 7*(2), 288–302.
Ganescu, C., & Gangone, A. (2017). A model of socially responsible organizational culture. *Studia Universitatis Vasile Goldis Arad–Economics Series, 27*(2), 45–59.
Geis, G., & DiMento, J. F. (2001). Empirical evidence and the legal doctrine of corporate criminal liability. *American Journal of Criminal Law, 29*, 341.
Geller, J., Carlton, J., & Powers, D. (1993). Interspecific and intrapopulation variation in mitochondrial ribosomal DNA sequences of *Mytilus* spp. (Bivalvia: Mollusca). *Molecular Marine Biology and Biotechnology, 2*(1), 44–50.
Gilles, M. (2011). Public-private approaches to mass tort victim compensation: Some thoughts on the Gulf Coast Claims Facility. *DePaul Law Review, 61*, 419.
Glac, K. (2010). The influence of shareholders on corporate social responsibility. *Center for ethical business cultures* (Working Paper No. 2). Center for Ethical Business Cultures, University of St. Thomas, Minnesota.
Gobert, J. (1994). Corporate criminality: Four models of fault. *Legal Studies, 14*(3), 393–410.
Gon, Y.-L., & Yan, J. (2023). *Business crime laws and regulations China.* ICLG. https://iclg.com/practice-areas/business-crime-laws-and-regulations/china
Greenfield, K. (2000). Corporate social responsibility: There's a forest in those trees: Teaching about corporate social responsibility. *Georgia Law Review, 34*, 1011.
Greenfield, K. (2019). *The failure of corporate law: Fundamental flaws and progressive possibilities.* University of Chicago Press.
Gupta, R. C., & Varma, D. R. (2020). Methyl isocyanate: The Bhopal gas. In *Handbook of toxicology of chemical warfare agents* (pp. 389–402). Elsevier.
Gutnikov, O. V. (2019). The grounds for development of corporate liability category in civil law. *Law: Journal of Higher School of Economics, 4.*
Gyo Lee, Y., Garza-Gomez, X., & Lee, R. M. (2018). Ultimate costs of the disaster: Seven years after the Deepwater Horizon oil spill. *Journal of Corporate Accounting & Finance, 29*(1), 69–79.

Haldar, I. (2011). *Global warming: The causes and consequences*. Readworthy.
Hamworthy. (2016). *Hamworthy: Ballast water management*. Hamworthy. Retrieved February 9, 2016, from www.hamworthy.com/ballast_water_management
Harle, K., Saleh, Z., & Partridge-Smith, S. (2024). Corporate crime: Changes to corporate liability. *Dentons*. Retrieved March 28, 2024, from www.dentons.com/en/insights/articles/2024/march/4/corporate-crime-changes-to-corporate-liability
Hatashin, O. (2008). Crime and culture. *Corporate and White Collar Crime, 141*.
Herdman, R. C., Haughie, G. E., Campbell, L. E., Axelrod, D., Vianna, N., Hennessy, W., Sachs, J., Hoffman, C., Cuddy, M., Hennessy, W., Whalen, R. P., & Grushky, A. (1978). *Love Canal – Public health time bomb*. State of New York. www.health.ny.gov/environmental/investigations/love_canal/lctimbmb.htm
Hewitt, C. L., Gollasch, S., & Minchin, D. (2009). The vessel as a vector–Biofouling, ballast water and sediments. In *Biological invasions in marine ecosystems* (pp. 117–131). Springer.
Himmelhoch, S. D. (1992). Environmental crimes: Recent efforts to develop a role for traditional criminal law in the environmental protection effort. *Environmental Law*, *22*, 1469.
Hopkins, A. (2001). Was three Mile Island a "normal accident"? *Journal of Contingencies and Crisis Management*, *9*(2), 65–72.
Horwitz, M. J. (1985). Santa Clara revisited: The development of corporate theory. *West Virginia Law Review*, *88*, 173.
Houghton, J. (2005). Global warming reports on progress. *Physics*, *68*(6), 1340–1403.
Huld, A. (2024, January 15). China amends criminal law to strengthen anti-bribery regulation for private companies. *Dezan Shira and Associates*. Retrieved April 7, 2024, from www.china-briefing.com/news/anti-corruption-in-china-criminal-law-amendment-tackle-bribery-private-sector/
Hunt, R. (2024). Expansion of corporate criminal liability. *Clyde & Co*. Retrieved March 28, 2024, from www.clydeco.com/en/insights/2024/01/expansion-of-corporate-criminal-liability
Incardona, J. P., & Scholz, N. L. (2018). Case study: The 2010 Deepwater Horizon oil spill and its environmental developmental impacts. *Development and Environment*, 235–283.
International Maritime Organization (IMO). (2015a). *Ballast water management*. Retrieved February 9, 2015, from www.imo.org/OurWork/Environment/BallastWaterManagement/Pages/Default.aspx
International Maritime Organization (IMO). (2015b). *GoBallast partnerships: The problem*. Retrieved February 8, 2015, from http://globallast.imo.org/index.asp?page=problem.htm
International Maritime Organization (IMO). (2016). *GoBallast partnerships: Home*. International Maritime Organization. Retrieved February 9, 2016, from http://globallast.imo.org/index.asp
Issacharoff, S., & Rave, D. T. (2013). The BP oil spill settlement and the paradox of public litigation. *Louisiana Law Review*, *74*, 397.
Jiachen, L. (1999). The legislation and judicial practice on punishment of unit crime in China. *Criminal Responsibility of Legal and Collective Entities, Freiburg i. Br.*, 71.
Jimenez, G. A. (2019). Corporate criminal liability: Toward a compliance-oriented approach. *Indiana Journal of Global Legal Studies*, *26*, 353.
Justice, C. D. O. (2002). *Corporate criminal liability: Discussion paper*. Department of Justice Canada.
Kadish, S. H. (1979). Developments in the law – Corporate crime: Regulating corporate behavior through criminal sanctions. *Harvard Law Review*, *92*, 1227.
Kadish, S. H., Schulhofer, S. J., & Barkow, R. E. (2016). *Criminal law and its processes: Cases and materials*. Aspen Publishing.

Kaneko, K. (2023, December 14). Former Tokyo Games executive pleads not guilty over bribery. *The Japan Times*. www.japantimes.co.jp/news/2023/12/14/japan/crime-legal/olympics-bribery-1st-hearing/

Kanso, A. M., Nelson, R. A., & Kitchen, P. J. (2020). BP and the Deepwater Horizon oil spill: A case study of how company management employed public relations to restore a damaged brand. *Journal of Marketing Communications*, *26*(7), 703–731.

Khan, F. I., & Abbasi, S. (1999). The world's worst industrial accident of the 1990s: What happened and what might have been: A quantitative study. *Process Safety Progress*, *18*(3), 135–145.

Khan, S. (2022). *Validity of limitation of liability clauses: The Supreme Court of Canada changes the rules and rejects the application of the notion of "fundamental breach" in Quebec civil law*. Lavery Lawyer. Retrieved March 15, from www.lavery.ca/en/publications/4290-publication-display-PDF.html

Khanna, U. (2021). Corporate criminal liability: An analysis of vicarious imposition of corporate sanctions in India. *International Journal of Law, Management & Humanities*, *4*(3), 1653.

Khanna, V. S. (2004). Corporate crime legislation: A political economy analysis. *Washington University Law Quarterly*, *82*, 95.

Kleiman, J. (2024). *Love canal: A brief history*. Geneseo. Retrieved April 5, from www.geneseo.edu/history/love_canal_history

Kumar, D. (2021). Legal aspects of the Bhopal gas tragedy. *Legal Service India*. Retrieved April 4, from www.legalservicesindia.com/article/373/Legal-Aspects-of-the-Bhopal-Gas-Tragedy.html

Kwok, R. K., Engel, L. S., Miller, A. K., Blair, A., Curry, M. D., Jackson, W. B., Stewart, P. A., Stenzel, M. R., Birnbaum, L. S., & Sandler, D. P. (2017). The Gulf study: A prospective study of persons involved in the Deepwater Horizon oil spill response and clean-up. *Environmental Health Perspectives*, *125*(4), 570–578.

Lahti, R., & Rainiala, M. K. (2019). Alternative investigation and sanctioning systems for corporate and corporate-related crime in Finland. *Revue internationale de droit pénal*, *2019*(1), 131–163.

Lai, O. (2023). 13 major companies responsible for deforestation. *Earth.Org*. Retrieved April 7, 2023, from https://earth.org/major-companies-responsible-for-deforestation/#

Lederman, E. (2000). Models for imposing corporate criminal liability: From adaptation and imitation toward aggregation and the search for self-identity. *Buffalo Criminal Law Review*, *4*(1), 641–708.

Leigh, L. H. (1977). The criminal liability of corporations and other groups. *Ottawa Law Review*, *9*, 247.

Lelieur, J. (2023). France's "Sapin II" law. In *Elgar concise encyclopedia of corruption law* (pp. 228–230). Edward Elgar Publishing.

Lewis, P. (2024). Corporate criminal liability. *Law Commission of the United Kingdom*. Retrieved March 28, 2024, from www.lawcommission.gov.uk/corporate_criminal_liability

Linnenluecke, M. K., & Griffiths, A. (2010). Corporate sustainability and organizational culture. *Journal of World Business*, *45*(4), 357–366.

Logan, W. S. (1901). The use and abuse of corporations. *American Lawyer*, *9*, 158.

Luskin, R. (2020). Caring about corporate "due care": Why criminal respondeat superior liability outreaches its justification. *American Criminal Law Review*, *57*, 303.

Mačaitytė, I., & Virbašiūtė, G. (2018). Volkswagen emission scandal and corporate social responsibility: A case study. *Business Ethics and Leadership*, *2*(1), 6–13.

Macey, J. R. (1991). Agency theory and the criminal liability of organizations. *Boston University Law Review*, *71*, 315.

Magraw, D. B. (1985). The Bhopal disaster: Structuring a solution. *University of Colorado Law Review*, *57*, 835.
Mah, A. (2020). Toxic legacies and environmental justice. In *Environmental justice* (pp. 121–131). Routledge.
Malmsheimer, L. M. (1986). Three Mile Island: Fact, frame, and fiction. *American Quarterly*, *38*(1), 35–52.
Mandavilli, A. (2018). *The world's worst industrial disaster is still unfolding*. The Atlantic Monthly Group.
McCarthy, S. A., & Khambaty, F. M. (1994). International dissemination of epidemic Vibrio cholerae by cargo ship ballast and other nonpotable waters. *Applied and Environmental Microbiology*, *60*(7), 2597–2601.
McCollin, T., Shanks, A. M., & Dunn, J. (2007). The efficiency of regional ballast water exchange: Changes in phytoplankton abundance and diversity. *Harmful Algae*, *6*(4), 531–546.
McDonald, M. (1987). The personless paradigm. *The University of Toronto Law Journal*, *37*(2), 212–226.
Miller, A. W., Minton, M. S., & Ruiz, G. M. (2011). Geographic limitations and regional differences in ships' ballast water management to reduce marine invasions in the contiguous United States. *BioScience*, *61*(11), 880–887.
Mimura, H., Katakura, R., & Ishida, H. (2005). Changes of microbial populations in a ship's ballast water and sediments on a voyage from Japan to Qatar. *Marine Pollution Bulletin*, *50*(7), 751–757.
Mishra, N. (2022, December 12). Behind the Tokyo Olympics bribery scandal involving Dentsu, Hakuhodo and ADK. *Campaign*. Retrieved April 7, from www.campaignasia.com/article/behind-the-tokyo-olympics-bribery-scandal-involving-dentsu-hakuhodo-and-adk/482577
Mohan, M. R. (2019). *Criminal negligence and directors' liability under Indian Penal Code: The case of Bhopal gas tragedy*. Indian Institute of Management.
Momsen, C., & Schwarze, M. (2018, December). The changing face of corporate liability: New hard law and the increasing influence of soft law. *Criminal Law Forum*, *29*, 567–593. Springer Netherlands.
Moohr, G. S. (2007). Of bad apples and bad trees: Considering fault-based liability for the complicit corporation. *American Criminal Law Review*, *44*, 1343.
Moore, M. (2023). Developments in contract law: The 2021–2022 term – the enduring allure of freedom of contract. *Supreme Court Law Review*, *111*, 3.
Morehouse, W. (1994). Unfinished business: Bhopal ten years after. *The Ecologist*, *24*(5), 164–169.
Mueller, G. O. (1957). Mens rea and the corporations: A study of the Model Penal Code position on corporate criminal liability. *University of Pittsburgh Law Review*, *19*, 21.
Mujkic, E., & Klingner, D. (2019). Dieselgate: How hubris and bad leadership caused the biggest scandal in automotive history. *Public Integrity*, *21*(4), 365–377.
Murphy, D. E. (2001). The federal sentencing guidelines for organizations: A decade of promoting compliance and ethics. *Iowa Law Review*, *87*, 697.
Nagata, K. (2013). Fines in the Japanese criminal justice system. *Kansai University Review of Law and Politics*, *34*, 1–16.
Newman, R. S. (2016). *Love Canal: A toxic history from colonial times to the present*. Oxford University Press.
Oda, H. (2021). *Japanese law*. Oxford University Press.
O'Donovan, G. (2002). Environmental disclosures in the annual report: Extending the applicability and predictive power of legitimacy theory. *Accounting, Auditing & Accountability Journal*, *15*(3), 344–371.
Ohashi, K., & Akahori, J. (2024). *Business crime laws and regulations Japan 2024*. ICLG. https://iclg.com/practice-areas/business-crime-laws-and-regulations/japan

Omoregie, O. (2008). Strict liability and criminal responsibility: A critique. *Journal of Law and International Security*, *2*(2).
O'Neil, B., Giles, E., McEvoy, S., Edwards, A., & Benson, J. (2023). *Reform of the UK identification doctrine – significant expansion of corporate criminal liability for economic crimes*. Allen & Overy. Retrieved March 28, from www.allenovery.com/en-gb/global/blogs/investigations-insight/reform-of-the-identification-principle-significant-expansion-to-corporate-criminal-liability-for-economic-crimes
Organisation for Economic Co-operation and Development (OECD). (2016). *Annual survey of large pension funds and public pension reserve funds: Reports on pension funds' long-term investment*. OECD. Retrieved December 6, from www.oecd.org/daf/fin/private-pensions/2015-Large-Pension-Funds-Survey.pdf
Orland, L., & Cachera, C. (1995). Corporate crime and punishment in France: Criminal responsibility of legal entities (Personnes Morales) under the new French criminal code (Nouveau Code Penal). *Connecticut Journal of International Law*, *11*, 111.
Osif, B. A., Baratta, A. J., & Conkling, T. W. (2004). *TMI 25 years later: The Three Mile Island nuclear power plant accident and its impact*. Penn State Press.
Parisaboina, S. (2021). A critical analysis of absolute liability and its role in environmental law. *International Journal of Law, Management and Humanities*, *4*(3), 405.
Patel, N. A., & Petlakh, K. (2014). Ghandi's nightmare: Bhopal and the need for a mindful jurisprudence. *Harvard Journal on Racial & Ethnic Justice*, *30*, 151.
Pérez, W., Ñahui, M., Ellis, D., & Forbes, G. A. (2014). Wide phenotypic diversity for resistance to *Phytophthora infestans* found in potato landraces from Peru. *Plant Disease*, *98*(11), 1530–1533.
Perkins, R. M. (1938). Rationale of Mens Rea, A. *Harvard Law Review*, *52*, 905.
Phillips, A. S., Hung, Y.-T., & Bosela, P. A. (2007). Love Canal tragedy. *Journal of Performance of Constructed Facilities*, *21*(4), 313–319.
Pickard, T. (1980). Culpable mistakes and rape: Relating mens rea to the crime. *The University of Toronto Law Journal*, *30*(1), 75–98.
Pieth, M., & Ivory, R. (2011). Emergence and convergence: Corporate criminal liability principles in overview. In *Corporate criminal liability: Emergence, convergence, and risk* (pp. 3–60). Springer.
Pimentel, D., Lach, L., Zuniga, R., & Morrison, D. (2000). Environmental and economic costs of nonindigenous species in the United States. *BioScience*, *50*(1), 53–65.
Plumer, B. (2023). *The GM recall scandal of 2014*. Retrieved April 7, from www.vox.com/2014/10/3/18073458/gm-car-recall
Quaid, J. A. (1998). The assessment of corporate criminal liability on the basis of corporate identity: An analysis. *McGill Law Journal*, *43*(1), 67.
Ragozino, A. (1994). Replacing the collective knowledge doctrine with a better theory for establishing corporate *mens rea*: The duty stratification approach. *Southwestern University Law Review*, *43*, 423.
Ramanathan, U. (2019). The Bhopal case: Retrospect and prospect. In *Research handbook on law, environment and the Global South* (pp. 138–145). Edward Elgar Publishing.
Ramos, M. E. G. (2018). Corporate indemnification: Experiences in USA and developments in Germany, Italy and Portugal. *European Company and Financial Law Review*, *14*(4), 723–774.
Ranjan, R. (2008). Special issue: Economics of invasive species management. *Journal of Environmental Management*, *89*(4), 271–349.
Rogovin, M. (1980). *Three Mile Island: A report to the commissioners and to the public* (Vol. 1250). Nuclear Regulatory Commission, Special Inquiry Group.
Ruggiero, V., & South, N. (2010). Critical criminology and crimes against the environment. *Critical Criminology*, *18*, 245–250.

Ruiz, G. M., Rawlings, T. K., Dobbs, F. C., Drake, L. A., Mullady, T., Huq, A., & Colwell, R. R. (2000). Global spread of microorganisms by ships. *Nature*, *408*(6808), 49–50.

Rundle, D. (2023). How will changes to corporate criminal liability impact the banking sector. *Bryan Cave Leighton Paisner LLP*. Retrieved March 28, from www.bclplaw.com/en-US/events-insights-news/how-will-changes-to-corporate-criminal-liability-impact-the-banking-sector.html

Sachdeva, R. (2022). An analytical study on corporate criminal liability: Comparative study of India and USA. *International Journal of Law, Management and Humanities*, *5*(1), 2577.

Sachs, T., & Tricot, J. (2020). The French law on corporate duty of vigilance: Rethinking corporate governance? *Droit et Société*, *106*, 683.

Sahramäki, I. (2016). Enforcement and professional constructions of environmental crime in Finland. In *The geography of environmental crime: Conservation, wildlife crime and environmental activism* (pp. 189–216). Palgrave Macmillan.

Sala, O. E., Chapin, F. S., Armesto, J. J., Berlow, E., Bloomfield, J., Dirzo, R., Huber-Sanwald, E., Huenneke, L. F., Jackson, R. B., & Kinzig, A. (2000). Global biodiversity scenarios for the year 2100. *Science*, *287*(5459), 1770–1774.

Sandman, P. M. (2004). Three mile island – 25 years later. *Safety at Work*, 7–11.

Sayre, F. B. (1930). Criminal responsibility for the acts of another. *Harvard Law Review*, *43*(5), 689–723.

Schoenbaum, T. J. (2012). Liability for damages in oil spill accidents: Evaluating the USA and international law regimes in the light of Deepwater Horizon. *Journal of Environmental Law*, *24*(3), 395–416.

Shishido, Z. (2000). Japanese corporate governance: The hidden problems of corporate law and their solutions. *Delaware Journal of Corporate Law*, *25*, 189.

Shortt, M. (2019). Contractual limitation period clauses in Canada: Drafting and litigation considerations. *The Advocates' Quarterly*, *50*, 257.

Shultz, J. M., Walsh, L., Garfin, D. R., Wilson, F. E., & Neria, Y. (2015). The 2010 Deepwater Horizon oil spill: The trauma signature of an ecological disaster. *The Journal of Behavioral Health Services & Research*, *42*, 58–76.

Singer, R. G. (1988). The resurgence of Mens Rea: III – The rise and fall of strict criminal liability. *BCL Review*, *30*, 337.

Singh, P. (2021). Corporate criminal liability and the environment. *Indian Journal of Law & Legal Research*, *3*, 1.

Smith, J. S., & Fisher, J. H. (1981). Three Mile Island: The silent disaster. *JAMA*, *245*(16), 1656–1659.

Spurgeon, W. A., & Fagan, T. P. (2010). Criminal liability for life-endangering corporate conduct. *Journal of Criminal Law & Criminology*, *100*, xxxi.

Staats, E. B. (1980). *Three Mile Island: The most studied nuclear accident in history* (Comptroller General of the United States report to Congress, Report Number EMD-80-109). https://doi.org/10.2172/6941962

Steinzor, R. (2016). How criminal law can help save the environment. *Environmental Law*, 209–239.

Stessens, G. (1994). Corporate criminal liability: A comparative perspective. *International & Comparative Law Quarterly*, *43*(3), 493–520.

Sturgis, S. (2010). *Investigation: Revelations about Three Mile Island disaster raise doubts over nuclear plant safety: A special facing south investigation by Sue Sturgis*. Sage.

Subramanya, T., & Bhattacharya, S. (2020). The evolution of tort law and related developments in India after the Bhopal gas leak: An assessment. *CMR University's Journal for Contemporary Legal Affairs*, *2*, 31.

Takahashi, E., & Shimizu, M. (2005). The future of Japanese corporate governance: The 2005 reform. *Zeitschrift für Japanisches Recht*, *10*(19), 35–68–35–68.
Teubner, G. (1988). Enterprise corporatism: New industrial policy and the "essence" of the legal person. *The American Journal of Comparative Law*, *36*(1), 130–155.
Thornton, J. C. (2023). *An analysis of the oil pollution act of 1990: Regulatory calibration in anticipation of 21st century environmental disasters*. University of South Florida.
Tilling, M. V., & Tilt, C. A. (2010). The edge of legitimacy: Voluntary social and environmental reporting in Rothmans' 1956–1999 annual reports. *Accounting, Auditing & Accountability Journal*, *23*(1), 55–81.
Titus, V., & Mbaraonye, I. (2023). Blame: Stakeholder judgments that impact organizations and entrepreneurs. In *Oxford research encyclopedia of business and management*. Oxford University Press.
Tolvanen, M. J. (2012). Trust, business ethics and crime prevention–Corporate criminal liability in Finland. In *Business ethics and crime prevention–corporate criminal liability in Finland (January 16, 2012)*. University of Eastern Finland Legal Studies Research Paper (2).
Tompkins, L. (2022, January 20). Hundreds of companies promised to help save forests. Did they? *The New York Times*. www.nytimes.com/2021/12/02/climate/companies-net-zero-deforestation.html
Tyagi, A. (2020). *Reiterating the principle of absolute liability in light of Oleum gas leakage case*. Oxford University Press.
Uhlmann, D. (2020). BP paid a steep price for the Gulf oil spill but for the US a decade later, it's business as usual. *The Conversation*. Retrieved April 6, from https://theconversation.com/bp-paid-a-steep-price-for-the-gulf-oil-spill-but-for-the-us-a-decade-later-its-business-as-usual-136905
Varma, D. R., & Mulay, S. (2009). Methyl isocyanate: The Bhopal gas. In *Handbook of toxicology of chemical warfare agents* (pp. 293–312). Elsevier.
Vu, S. N. (2004). Corporate criminal liability: Patchwork verdicts and the problem of locating a guilty agent. *Columbia Law Review*, *104*, 459.
Waddock, S., & Rasche, A. (2012). *Building the responsible enterprise: Where vision and values add value*. Stanford University Press.
Wade, S., & Kageyama, Y. (2023, December 15). Ex-Tokyo Olympics official pleads not guilty to taking bribes in exchange for Games contracts. *The Associated Press*. https://apnews.com/article/dentsu-tokyo-olympics-bribery-takahashi-ioc-dccbc9e8fb453f9b139de19ceb17e450
Walker, J. S. (2004). *Three Mile Island: A nuclear crisis in historical perspective* (Vol. 41). University of California Press.
Wang, H., & Liu, Y. (2020). Corporate criminal liability in China: Legislation, application, and challenges. *Asian Journal of Criminology*, *15*(1), 1–19.
Weber, J. M., & Crew Jr., R. E. (2000). Deterrence theory and marine oil spills: Do coast guard civil penalties deter pollution? *Journal of Environmental Management*, *58*(3), 161–168.
Weinstein, M. J., & Ball, P. B. (1994). Criminal law's greatest mystery thriller corporate guilt through collective knowledge. *New England Law Review*, *29*, 65.
Wells, C., Morgan, D., & Quick, O. (1999). Disasters: A challenge for the law. *Washburn Law Journal*, *39*, 496.
Widoff, M. P. (1981). The accident at Three Mile Island. *Western New England Law Review*, *4*, 223.
Windsor, C., & McNicholas, P. (2012). *The BP gulf oil spill: Public and corporate governance failures*. 11th Australasian Centre on Social and Environmental Accounting Research (A-CSEAR) Conference, University of Wollongong.

Woolf, T. (1997). The criminal code act 1995 (Cth) – towards a realistic vision of corporate criminal liability. *Criminal Law Journal*, 257–272.
Worthley, J. A., & Torkelson, R. (1981). Managing the toxic waste problem: Lessons from the love canal. *Administration & Society*, *13*(2), 145–160.
Zarnett, B. (2019). *How billionaire greed ruined a perfectly good strategy called corporate sustainability*. Toronto Sustainability. Retrieved November 5, from http://tsss.ca/channels/culture-leadership/how-billionaire-greed-ruined-a-perfectly-good-strategy-called-corporate-sustainability-part-1

4 Global Framework for Regulating Corporate Polluters

4.1 Introduction

The dissemination of global norms of corporate environmental liability is best conceptualized as a dynamic process where international intergovernmental organizations and strong economies play vital roles, often in conjunction with global corporations and non-governmental organizations. The role of these actors and the dynamics surrounding global political and economic governance reflect the growing complexity of regulating global actors like TNCs. It is worth mentioning that nowadays, the provision of the public good is no longer preserved solely by governments and private actors. Rather, it depends on the complex nexus of the capacities of diverse actors and factors. For example, mining industry representatives participate in global public policy decision-making through the United Nations Environment Programme (UNEP) and the World Bank; international NGOs work with governments in global conferences such as the World Summit on Sustainable Development.

There is a concern, however, that the weaknesses in instruments and their inability to lawfully obligate actors may undermine the claims of the normative effectiveness of non-governmental regimes. Scholars even argue that the non-governmental actors are interested in policy setting as this provides them high visibility for their activities, entailing lesser commitment of resources than what would be required to attend to their detailed implementation. Additionally, including jurisprudential principles in the policy framework is not always the core agenda for private regimes.

However, effective regimes are also to be found, although it is vital that the businesses with 'green clubs' effectively seek to enhance market reputation through devising norms while implementing them with appropriate monitoring and enforcement mechanisms to deliver on those commitments. Furthermore, we should not ignore the role and capacity of these regimes in the global policy setting. Actors in private regimes are vital stakeholders of global policies as they possess vital technical knowledge and are wholeheartedly involved in communication. They do not ignore the importance of public organization in global policy settings either. Important empirical evidence has concluded that governments (through their agencies) are central to initiating

DOI: 10.4324/9781003279006-4

and implementing many transnational regulatory activities. But governmental activity is far from being the only show in town. There is a need for the convergence of the capacities of both the private and public organizations for global policy, including the policies for regulating corporate criminal liability for environmental damages. A guiding impetus in such convergence would be the principles established by environmental jurisprudence.

This chapter examines the devaluation of state authority at the international level and the emergence of private authority in creating the political space for regulating corporate polluters. It presents some case studies to explicate the implication of the jurisprudential principles in the dominant environmental policy frameworks at the global level.

4.2 Norms for Settling the Global Framework for Regulating Corporate Polluters

Throughout human history, scientific advancements have been harnessed to achieve dominance over nature and exploit its resources for personal gain. However, the relentless exploitation of the environment has taken its toll on the delicate ecosystems, leading to a multitude of issues such as ecological depletion, frequent acid rain, rising sea levels, atmospheric warming, and ozone layer depletion.[1] The advent of the Industrial Revolution prior to World War II and the utilization of nuclear weapons during and after the war ultimately prompted humanity to re-evaluate how natural resources should be preserved. Even after focused attempts at fostering conservation during the 1950s and 1960s, human activity continues to threaten global biodiversity as well as our survival as a civilization. Against this backdrop, the regulation of corporate pollution has been an area of concern for quite some time, with international standards emerging to deal with the consequences of rampant pollution.

Policies and strategies focused on Global Development are usually designed globally to tackle the complex issues related to development. These policies are aimed at setting the standard or threshold for a particular movement or socio-political movement. They are from diverse spheres and are necessary to regulate conduct and relations across the globe. The Universal Declaration of Human Rights sets forth the basic privileges and rights which should be respected and upheld by every individual regardless of citizenship, race, or other identifiers.[2] Agreements such as the Paris Agreement of 2015, strive to create international standards for mitigating the consequences of climate change and espouse sustainability. The Extractive Industries Transparency Initiative (EITI) and Transparency International work toward anti-corruption

1 See Vibhute, K. I. (1997). Environment, present and future generations: Intergenerational equity, justice, and responsibility. *Journal of the Indian Law Institute, 39*(2/4), 281–288, 184.
2 Martinsson, J. (2011). *Global norms: Creation, diffusion, and limits.* T. I. B. f. R. a. Development.

business and governance – global standards of accountability and transparency.[3] The World Trade Organization (WTO) regulates worldwide commerce by policies on trade, tariffs, and intellectual property. Likewise, institutions such as the Internet Corporation for Assigned Names and Numbers (ICANN) formulates rules and policies for the governance and use of domain names, IP addresses, and internet protocols.

Common global standards have controversy associated with them as they can be viewed from various cultural, ethical, and contextual lenses. The balance of the right to free expression and preventing hate speech or harmful content is a debate that is ongoing. Some people advocate for free speech to the exclusion of everything else. Other people argue that there should be some limits placed on harmful and dangerous speech. The conflict between an individual's right to privacy and the need for surveillance for security purposes raises important questions. Problems like mass surveillance and data collection are extremely controversial. The controversy is the extent to which the rights of the creators are protected through patents and copyrights versus equitable access given to knowledge and innovation, argued by some to impede progress. Gender roles, sexuality, and family structure are norms that can differ from one culture to another.[4] Global norms colliding with local beliefs often creates controversy. Controversy persists on which countries are most responsible for climate change because developing countries argue that emission history from industrialized countries laid upon them should be counted.

Global norms are shaped and transformed by historical events, culture, technology, and other changes within a society. The emergence of certain norms has also resulted from historical occurrences, such as the creation of human rights norms through the Universal Declaration of Human Rights after World War II. Global norms are also impacted by supranational agreements like the Paris Agreement on climate change or the Geneva Conventions. The internet and social media greatly accelerate the dissemination of norms worldwide. Existing social norms are challenged by grassroots movements such as the civil rights movement, LGBTQ+ rights movement, and environmental movements. Cross-border economic relationships influence shared norms, and with the emergence of new global power centers, norms are redefined. The existence of different cultures and ideas helps in the evolution of norms and education encourages the development of awareness and critical thinking, further aiding in the evolution of norms. For example, the attitude toward homosexuality and same-sex marriage has softened in an increasing number of countries resulting in legal recognition of gay marriages.[5] Over the past

3 Ibid., p. 10.

4 Ibid., p. 4.

5 Chloe. (2023, May 24). The evolution of cultural norms: How society's values change over time. *MomentsLog*. Retrieved May 24, 2023, from www.momentslog.com/culture/the-evolution-of-cultural-norms-how-societys-values-change-over-time#google_vignette

century, women have also undergone significant changes, gaining the right to vote, employment, and challenging gender norms.[6] Historical actions, even personal, such as George Washington's decision not to seek a third term in office, changed beliefs about the presidency, establishing the idea of limited presidential tenure.[7]

Global norms for protecting the environment have been established through international agreements and initiatives. The UN has hosted numerous conferences and summits on environmental issues, including the 1992 Earth Summit in Rio de Janeiro and the 2002 Johannesburg Summit. These gatherings set an international agenda for environmental policymaking, resulting in both binding treaties ('hard law') and non-binding resolutions ('soft law').[8] ISO 14001 is a global benchmark for EMSs. It can be applied to businesses of any size, promoting sustainability and waste reduction while improving safety and efficiency.[9] Emerging global meta-norms recognize the rights of nature. Legal provisions exist in various countries, challenging anthropocentric development norms and emphasizing our obligations toward nature.[10] The protection of endangered species was one of the first global environmental norms. Its impact continues to shape environmental policymaking worldwide.[11]

Economic interests significantly influence environmental norms, shaping how societies balance prosperity and ecological well-being. Contrary to the perception that economic growth inevitably harms the environment, history shows that economic progress and environmental protection can harmoniously coexist. Public policies, regulations, and technological advancements have allowed businesses to reduce pollution while maintaining economic growth.[12] Stringent environmental regulations initially increase production costs (e.g., carbon taxes), but they boost long-term productivity. For instance, cleaner technologies enhance efficiency and sustainability.[13] The relationship

6 Ibid.

7 Acemoglu, D., & Jackson, M. O. (2015). History, expectations, and leadership in the evolution of social norms. *The Review of Economic Studies*, *82*(2), 423–456.

8 Bueren, E. V. (2019). Environmental policy: References & edit history. *Britannica*. Retrieved May 24, 2024, from www.britannica.com/topic/environmental-policy

9 ISO (International Organization for Standardization). (2024). *Protecting our planet*. International Organization for Standardization. Retrieved May 24, 2024, from www.iso.org/protecting-our-planet.html

10 Kauffman, C. M., & Martin, P. L. (2018). Constructing rights of nature norms in the US, Ecuador, and New Zealand. *Global Environmental Politics*, *18*(4), 43–62. Kauffman, C. M., & Martin, P. L. (2018). Constructing rights of nature norms in the US, Ecuador, and New Zealand. *Global Environmental Politics*, *18*(4), 43–62.

11 Epstein, C. (2006). The making of global environmental norms: Endangered species protection. *Global Environmental Politics*, *6*(2), 32–54.

12 Cohen, S. (2020, January 27). Economic growth and environmental sustainability. *State of the Planet*. Retrieved January 27, 2020, from https://news.climate.columbia.edu/2020/01/27/economic-growth-environmental-sustainability/

13 Ibid.

between economic growth and environmental quality follows an inverted U-shape. Economic development may lead to environmental degradation in poorer countries, while the association reverses in wealthier nations.[14] Norms vary across cultures, affecting how economic and environmental priorities align. Balancing national economic interests with global environmental cooperation remains a critical challenge.

International institutions play a crucial role in shaping and promoting global norms. Over the past few decades, international organizations (IOs) have integrated various liberal norms into their policy portfolios. The mentioned norms encompass sustainable development, gender equality, human security, good governance, and deregulation.[15] IOs capture or transform the information relevant to these sustainable development goals and norms, as well as the gender equality policies in individual and national life.[16] The more intense commitments of IOs to liberal norms are more often a consequence of internal causes. These causes include democratic memberships and institutional configurations that invite entrepreneurship of norms. External standards of legitimacy, while often cited, primarily explain only superficial recognition or 'talk' about norms from IOs.[17] Understanding the organizations that contribute to building global environmental protection norms is vital, and this is the focus of the rest of this section. Many institutions and organizations are contributing to norm-building at the global level. However, this section will discuss only the Stockholm Conference, Nairobi Declaration, Vienna Convention, Earth Summit, Agenda 21, CBD, Earth Summit +5, Global Judges Symposium, Alien Tort Statute, and the Jurisdiction Regulation of the EU.

4.2.1 Stockholm Conference

The depletion of natural resources, environmental deterioration, and pollution have drawn the serious attention of mankind. The Stockholm Conference

14 Čábelková, I., Smutka, L., Mareš, D., Ortikov, A., & Kontsevaya, S. (2023). Environmental protection or economic growth? The effects of preferences for individual freedoms. *Frontiers in Environmental Science, 11*, 1129236. https://doi.org/10.3389/fenvs.2023.1129236. Čábelková, I., Smutka, L., Mareš, D., Ortikov, A., & Kontsevaya, S. (2023). Environmental protection or economic growth? The effects of preferences for individual freedoms. *Frontiers in Environmental Science, 11*, 1129236.

15 Tallberg, J., Lundgren, M., Sommerer, T., & Squatrito, T. (2020). Why international organizations commit to liberal norms. *International Studies Quarterly, 64*(3), 626–640.

16 Desai, B. H., & Mandal, M. (2022). Role of international institutions in addressing SGBV. In *Sexual and gender-based violence in international law: Making international institutions work* (pp. 205–246). Springer.

17 Tallberg, J., Lundgren, M., Sommerer, T., & Squatrito, T. (2020). Why international organizations commit to liberal norms. *International Studies Quarterly, 64*(3), 626–640.

initiated some positive steps to that effect globally.[18] The theme of the conference was as follows[19]:

> A point has been reached in history when we must shape our actions worldwide with more prudent care for their environmental consequences. Through ignorance or indifference, we can do massive and irreversible harm to the early environment on which our life and well-being depend. Conversely, through fuller knowledge and wiser action, we can achieve for ourselves and our posterity a better life in an environment more in keeping with human needs and hopes. There are broad vistas for the enhancement of environmental quality and the creation of a good life. What is needed is an enthusiastic but calm state of mind and intense but orderly work. For the purpose of attaining freedom in the world of nature, man must use knowledge to build, in collaboration with nature, a better environment. To defend and improve the human environment for present and future generations has become an imperative goal for mankind, a goal to be pursued together with, and in harmony with, the established and fundamental goals of peace and worldwide economic and social development.
>
> Achieving this environmental goal will demand the acceptance of responsibility by citizens and communities and by enterprises and institutions at every level, all sharing equitably in common efforts. Individuals from all walks of life and organizations in many fields, by their values and the sum of their actions, will shape the world environment of the future. Local and national governments will bear the greatest burden for large-scale environmental policy and action within their jurisdictions. International cooperation is also needed to raise resources to support developing countries in their responsibilities in this field. A growing class of environmental problems, because they are regional or global in extent or because they affect the common international realm, will require extensive co-operation among nations and action by international organizations in the common interest. The Conference calls upon Governments and peoples to exert common efforts for the preservation and improvement of the human environment, for the benefit of all the people and their prosperity.

This conference has brought to the attention of the states the pressing issue of environmental preservation and conservation like never before. It

18 The United Nations Conference on the Human Environment was held at Stockholm from June 5 to June 16, 1972. It laid down 26 principles which should be guide line for all the Nation in implementation of Environmental law.

19 Ibid., *Proclamation 6* and *7*.

recognized the significant and indispensable role nature plays in humanity's social, spiritual, and intellectual development. The conference emphasized the crucial importance of both natural and man-made environments in fulfilling basic human rights, including the right to life. As science and technology continue to advance, humanity has gained unprecedented power to shape the environment around us, enabling us to meld it to our needs and desires. Unfortunately, such power has often been misused and abused, significantly harming humanity and the planet. Pollution levels in water, air, and soil have reached critical and alarming levels, disrupting the ecological balance of the biosphere and threatening physical, mental, and social health. In underdeveloped countries, the root of environmental problems lies in poverty and lack of access to necessities like food, shelter, and education, further exacerbating the problem. In contrast, industrialization and technological development have been identified as the main sources of environmental issues in developed countries. Rapid population growth also contributes to pollution and environmental degradation, making it a pressing and urgent issue that must be addressed immediately.

During the Stockholm Conference, it was widely acknowledged that the role of humans in advancing science and technology is of immense significance, particularly in improving the environment. However, it was also emphasized that even the slightest negligence could result in irreversible environmental harm. To ensure a prosperous and sustainable future, individuals, businesses, and institutions must take collective responsibility to preserve and enhance the environment for both the present and future generations. The conference further stressed the need for education and the effective use of mass media to raise awareness about environmental issues. All citizens were called upon to make concerted efforts toward this cause to secure a better tomorrow for all.

During the Conference, it was agreed that states are responsible for planning and managing natural resources in a way that supports development while protecting the fragile ecosystem. Humans must safeguard and wisely manage wildlife and its habitat and employ non-renewable resources judiciously to avoid future depletion.[20] To avoid irreversible environmental harm, toxic substances, and excessive heat should not be released beyond the ecosystem's carrying capacity.[21] The state must take necessary steps to prevent pollution that endangers human health and other living organisms on Earth.[22] Proper planning for economic development is crucial for nature conservation.[23] In accordance with the United Nations Charter and international legal frameworks, bordering states have the right to exercise control over activities which may be

20 See *Principle 4.*
21 See *Principle 5.*
22 See *Principle 6.*
23 See *Principle 7.*

damaging to the environment within a certain radius of their borders.[24] Each state should, at the same time, work with other countries in formulating international laws on liability and compensation regarding pollution and damages to the victims.[25]

In reviewing the documents and resolutions of the Stockholm Conference, it is noticeable that there is a clear need for governments to legislate within their jurisdiction to control pollution. The Conference's objectives contained the essential rules and frameworks. Furthermore, the acknowledgment that the problems of pollution and the destruction of nature are multifaceted, including the forces of population growth, basic social needs for food, clothing, shelter, hygiene, or the non-stop civilizationscape (industrial) technology, is powerful. In looking toward solutions, the spirit of cooperation between countries is deemed necessary alongside the formation of a global policy on the environment tailored to the specific environments of the nations involved. This is critical because it underscores that policies aimed at economic growth should also focus on enhancing and rehabilitating the environment of the nation.

As a result of the recommendations set forth by the Congress, the UNEP was established in December 1972, which had 58 member states.[26] The Stockholm Action Plan focused on three areas: environmental assessment, management, and support. UNEP had the responsibility of providing critical information on the world's environmental patterns, developing issues, and current problem issues. The plan placed great importance on research, monitoring, and information exchange as the support mechanisms for policy construction on the environment. Most importantly, the recommendations called for the pursuit of social and economic development that is environmentally positive and supportive to our planet.

4.2.2 Nairobi Declaration

At the Nairobi meeting commemorating the 10th Anniversary of the Stockholm Conference, the world looked into how far the recommendations and the action plan of the Conference have been put into action. The countries present accepted that the Conference requested actions from governments and people that there was a need to take the human environment of each nation and attempt to preserve it with due regard. They recognized that a lot of progress has been accomplished in that many countries have changed their constitutions and policies to include an 'Environment' section as was recommended in Stockholm. There has also been great advancement in environmental science, education, and training. In addition, various governmental

24 See *Principle 21.*
25 See *Principle 22.*
26 United Nations, United Nations Conference on the Human Environment, June 5–16, 1972, Stockholm. Retrieved from www.un.org/en/conferences/environment/stockholm1972.

and non-governmental organizations have been formed to define and execute national frameworks for the restoration and conservation of natural environment. The declaration reaffirmed the political decisions taken at the Stockholm Conference and underlined the importance of the Conference as a code of laws on an international governorship for Environmental Law.

The Nairobi Declaration, alongside other subsequent efforts, draws attention to the need to step up preventive measures and policies dealing with pollution of the soil and water, deforestation, desertification, ozone layer depletion, carbon emissions, acid rains, and sea and groundwater contamination, as well as the disposal of hazardous waste. These aspects are indeed troubling for the entire international community as they underscore the need for properly crafted policies and programs directed toward socio-economic development in combination with environmental protection and resource management. It is high time that national governments took bold initiatives to strengthen their ecosystems, foster new technological developments, wage wars against poverty, recycle waste, and mitigate the effects of pollution. As for policies, the declaration suggested the need to control the activities of enterprises, especially the multinational ones, which have been shown to deal much damage to sensitive ecosystems, and stressed the need for relevant legislative guarantees in an urgent manner. The declaration underscored the lack of development and the inequitable distribution of resources among countries in terms of the environment, making it possible to say that developed nations need to take serious steps to narrow the gap with less developed countries to establish a sustainable environment.

To implement the Nairobi Declaration, African countries have worked collectively and individually to integrate its principles into their national policies and strategies.[27] This includes developing and strengthening climate change action plans, setting emission reduction targets, and implementing adaptation measures. African governments are also engaging in international negotiations and advocacy to ensure that the concerns and priorities of the continent are adequately addressed in global climate change agreements.[28] Financial mechanisms have also been established to support the implementation of the Nairobi Declaration. This includes establishing the Africa Climate Change Fund, which provides resources for climate change projects and programs on the continent. Additionally, efforts are being made to explore innovative financing options, such as green bonds and climate finance instruments, to mobilize additional resources for climate action in Africa.[29]

27 Muhambe, D. (2018). The paradox of the Nairobi ministerial decision on export competition: Lessons for the future. *Global Trade and Customs Journal*, *13*(2).

28 Desai, B. H. (2002). Mapping the future of international environmental governance. *Yearbook of International Environmental Law*, *13*(1), 43–61.

29 Poorhashemi, A. (2021, November 8–12). Opportunities and challenges facing the future development of international environmental law. In *International conference on natural resources and sustainable environmental management*. Northern Cyprus.

4.2.3 The Vienna Convention

On March 22, 1985, parties to the Vienna Convention[30] met to discuss the protection of the ozone layer in accordance with Principle 21 of 'The Declaration of the United Nations Conference on Human Environment.'[31] Principle 21 asserts that countries can utilize their resources as per their environmental policy, provided that their actions do not infringe upon the environment of other nations or areas outside their national jurisdiction.[32] The Convention stressed the importance of international collaboration and comprehensive action alongside scientific research and observation to understand the consequences human activities inflict on the ozone layer.

The 1985 Vienna Convention on the Protection of the Ozone Layer sought to get nations to commit to 'appropriate actions' to protect the health and environment from damage posed by humans to the Ozone Layer, under the balance of research, cooperation, and information sharing within countries. Although there was some delay in finalizing the convention for four years, resulting in only 20 signatories, most of the countries failed to ratify it in a timely manner. The Convention included provisions for future protocols and outlined procedures for amendments and dispute resolution. While delaying the Convention was deemed necessary, it set a crucial precedence. For the first instance, countries confronted the issue of global environmental degradation before causative impacts were felt, noted, and scientifically verified. Furthermore, there was a demand for stricter laws against the exploitation of the ozone layer due to human activity.[33]

The Vienna Convention primarily focuses on civil liability for nuclear damage rather than corporations' liability. However, it indirectly addresses corporations' liability through its provisions on state responsibility and the obligations of states to ensure compliance with the Convention. The Convention aims to establish minimum standards to compensate for nuclear damage and promote international cooperation.[34] It is important to note that implementing the Vienna Convention involves incorporating its principles and provisions into national legislation, which may vary across countries.[35] Therefore, the extent

30 *The Vienna convention for the protection of the Ozone Layer*, held on March 22, 1985.

31 Supra note 3.

32 Supra note 10.

33 See *Article 2*; see also, *The Montreal Protocol on the Substances That Deplete the Ozone Layer, 1987*.

34 International Atomic Energy Agency. (2023). *Vienna convention on civil liability for nuclear damage*. Retrieved May 25, 2024, from www.iaea.org/topics/nuclear-liability-conventions/vienna-convention-on-civil-liability-for-nuclear-damage

35 Ku, J. G. (2012). The limits of corporate rights under international law. *Chicago Journal of International Law*, *12*(2), 729–754. https://scholarlycommons.law.hofstra.edu/faculty_scholarship/76

of corporations' liability under the Convention may depend on the specific national laws and regulations of each contracting party.[36]

4.2.4 Earth Summit

Leaders from around the world gathered in Rio de Janeiro in 1992, two decades after the Stockholm Conference, to review the state of the environment and propose plans for its preservation.[37] The Stockholm Conference emphasized creating national policies and using sovereign powers to enforce legislation, while the Nairobi Declaration focused on political principles for environmental conservation. The Rio Conference contributed significantly to the development of environmental law by supplementing and modifying the principles adopted in the 1972 Conference. It recognized the need for sustainable development, which emphasized eradicating poverty and meeting the basic needs of all while preserving the environment for future generations.[38] States were encouraged to formulate sound environmental policies to protect their citizens while promoting development. The Conference also recommended incorporating certain IEL principles into domestic law,[39] such as the 'precautionary principle' and 'polluter pays principle.' It advised states to establish tribunals and specialized agencies to address environmental disasters and provide speedy remedies to victims.[40] Additionally, it recommended the implementation of strict EIAs to make the law more effective.[41]

In addition, the inclusion of prior notification and consultation principles acknowledged the state's responsibility to notify neighboring countries of emergencies and consult with them prior to cases of transboundary pollution.[42] The agreement underscores, as it should, the necessity of facilitating the unrestricted exchange of information pertaining to scientific and technological advancements relevant to ecology in order to foster international cooperation.

One of the most important objectives of the Rio Conference was to devise a comprehensive, equitable, and respectful strategy to safeguard the

36 Ku, J. G. (2011). The limits of corporate rights under international law. *Chicago Journal of International Law*, *12*, 729.

37 See *Rio Declaration on Environment and Development*, held at Rio de Janierio.

38 See *Principle 5.*

39 See infra., *Principles 4*, *14* and *15.*

40 See *Principle 13.*

41 The statement goes as follows, 'Environmental Impact Assessment is an exercise of evaluating and predicting future changes caused by proposed project, plans or polices to the quality of environment. Guiding to make informed trade-offs among conflicting aspects of environmental quality and between environmental quality and other social objective, EIA helps administrative agencies to choose correctly from among the various options for making environmentally sound decisions'; see Leelakrishnan, P. (1992). Environmental impact assessment: Legal dimensions. *Journal of the Indian law Institute*, *34*(4), 541–562. see also *Principle 17* of the Rio Declaration on Environment and Development (1992).

42 See *Principle 19.*

environment alongside the global development system.[43] The conference generated five primary documents: a political declaration of principles on forestry, two conventions on biological diversity and climate change through the UNCED process, a declaration of principles on environment policy and development initiatives, and a comprehensive program of action referred to as Agenda 21.[44] The purpose of these documents was to formulate treaties that provide reciprocal advantages and foster collaboration among nations, societies, and peoples.

The Convening of the Rio Conference could be interpreted as marking another gradual milestone in the development chronicles of the international laws pertaining to the distinctly fast-emerging area of environmental law as a system.[45] This information can be found in the Register of International Treaties and Other Agreements in the Field of the Environment, which is maintained by the UNEP and receives periodic updates. Various publications, both formal and informal, have compiled relevant texts and documents. According to the distinction made by the world community, international legal norms for the environment are classified as either 'hard law' or 'soft law,' depending on the existence of criteria for an international treaty.

Using the UNCED's Rio framework, the normative products or outcomes of the conference are clearly distinguished as the 'Rio Instruments.' Both the UN Framework Convention on Climate Change[46] and the CBD are prepared by intergovernmental parallel negotiating committees and were opened for signature in Rio as formal multilateral treaties. Different is the case of the Rio Declaration on Environment and Development (which consists of 27 principles) alongside the more succinct set of 15 Principles for a Global Consensus on the Management, Conservation, and Sustainable Development of All Types of Forests. Both were endorsed by the Conference and adopted by the General Assembly but not as legally binding and merely as neurotic and prefigurative proclamations. Operatively, the conventions shall only come into effect as legally binding three months after the minimum number of ratifications is

43 United Nations. (1992, August 12). *Report of the United Nations conference on environment and development* (Vol. 1, A/CONF.151/26). General Assembly. The report states:

> Among the tangible achievements of the Rio Conference was the signing of two conventions, one on biological diversity and another on climate change. These conventions were signed by 153 Nations. The delegations also approved by consensus between non-binding documents, namely, a Statement on Forestry principles, a Declaration of Principles on Environment Policy and Development Initiatives, and Agenda 21, a program of action into the next century in the areas like property, population, and pollution.

See Agarwal, V. (1998). Sustainable development and environmental protection: Some reflections. *All Indian Reporters Journal Section*, 1–9.

44 Infra.

45 See Sand, P. H. (1993). International environmental law after Rio. *European Journal of International Law*, *4*(3), 377–389. https://doi.org/10.1093/oxfordjournals.ejil.a035836

46 See Supra note 14.

obtained. Regardless, a more in-depth critique of the two conferences must agree based on procedural components that govern the two instituting frameworks of policy that, with the exception of the institutional constitutive provisions, devolve upon the signatories a remote and non-binding set of duties which, for all intents and purposes, appear softer than those formulated in the declarations of intent.

This is, at least, in part because both conventions employ the 'framework approach,' which has become a darling of international environmental lawmaking in recent decades. Rather than attempting to codify a sectoral regime in one fell swoop, they begin with the definition of its normative scope in very general, often vague, terms that will be elaborated in later dynamic 'protocols' sequences. Therefore, Rio conventions are fundamental to the construction of a future climate and biodiversity regime, where the 'interim agreements' can be modified and expanded upon as needed.

In a few cases, the Rio Conference decided to assign some specialized legal issues to competent bodies, such as the International Atomic Energy Agency on the preparation of the Convention on Nuclear Safety and the Sixth Committee of the UN General Assembly on environmental protection in times of armed conflict. The conference purposefully ignored the sweeping concern of 'ecological crimes' raised by the UNCED Preparatory Committee.[47] With respect to a potential conflict of laws between environment and trade law, the Rio Conference did not go further than the deadlock reflected in both chapter 2 and chapter 39 of Agenda 21, which were copied word for word from the earlier Cartagena Commitment of the UN Conference on Trade. Many new initiatives of 'conference diplomacy' under the oceans chapter of Agenda 21 dealing with small island States, straddling fish stocks, and land-based marine pollution may end up having more immediate – though postponed – legal impacts than some of the provisions that claim to promote the development of IEL.

The 'alternative treaties' created by the International NGO Forum during the Global Forum 92 are worth noting.[48] This event saw over 8,000 non-governmental groups and organizations in attendance. The 'alternative treaties' were not intended to be legally binding, nor were they meant to replace the important contributions of NGOs to the official UNCED process and other international environmental lawmaking efforts. Their primary purpose

47 This point was introduced by the EC delegation, and was prompted by a joint declaration of the Russian and German Environment Ministers (Moscow, June 3, 1991) calling for 'international condemnation of crimes against the environment,' and for inclusion of the topic in the UNCED agenda. After further debate of the issue in the UN General Assembly and at PrepCom 4, the Main Committee of the Rio Conference eventually decided to follow proposals by the USA and several developing countries and restricted the scope of para. 39.6 in *Agenda 21* to times of armed conflict.

48 Haigh, M. (2002). Sustaining environmental education: The contribution of non-government organizations (NGOs). *Planet*, *8*(1), 22–24.

was to encourage collaboration between NGOs in defining goals and action plans. Notably, the Forum didn't present final texts as conference products but instead turned them into 'open documents' that could be continuously developed through electronic networking. The Earth Summit did not establish a binding legal framework for corporations' liability, but it initiated efforts to address this issue through initiatives like the UN Global Compact and the advocacy work of civil society organizations.[49]

4.2.5 Agenda 21

The nations in Rio signed the non-binding treaty Agenda 21 to prioritize satisfying basic needs, improved living standards for everyone, better-managed ecosystems, and a safe and prosperous life. Agenda 21 was considered a fundamental tool to enhance the global partnership in addressing common environmental issues across nations.[50]

The plan outlined essential steps to achieve sustainable development, promote fairness, ensure habitability, encourage efficient resource usage, preserve global and regional resources, and manage hazardous wastes.[51] It also addressed the tools necessary to achieve environmentally sustainable development, including developing international legal instruments, institutional arrangements, and financial arrangements promoting environmental preservation. The plan advocated the strengthening and development of compliance programs, the participation of all countries, and the establishment of effective dispute-resolution mechanisms.[52] The institutional arrangements focused on creating an intergovernmental commission at the ministerial level, with regular progress reports sent to the United Nations Economic and Social Council. Non-governmental organizations were encouraged to play an active role in raising public awareness. The plan also recognized the importance of financial stability at the international level in effectively implementing environmental policy.

The program ascertained by Agenda 21 emphasized the problems arising during the economic transition and 'the program areas that constitute Agenda 21

49 Friends of the Earth International. (2024). *Rio+20 summit under corporations' undue influence.* Retrieved May 25, 2024, from www.foei.org/rio20-summit-under-corporations-undue-influence/; Karliner, J., & Bruno, K. (2002). The corporate takeover of sustainable development. *Food First.* Retrieved May 25, 2024, from https://archive.foodfirst.org/publication/earthsummit-biz-the-corporate-takeover-of-sustainable-development/

50 Grubb, M., Koch, M., Thomson, K., Sullivan, F., & Munson, A. (2019). *The 'Earth Summit' agreements: A guide and assessment: An analysis of the Rio '92 UN conference on environment and development* (Vol. 9). Routledge.

51 Dodds, F. (2019). *The way forward: Beyond Agenda 21* (Vol. 3). Routledge.

52 Koch, M. (2019). Agenda 21. In M. Grubb, M. Koch, K. Thomson, F. Sullivan & A. Munson (Eds.), *The 'Earth Summit' agreements: A guide and assessment* (pp. 97–158). Routledge.

describe the basis of action, objective, activities, and means of implementation.'[53] Emphasis was placed on balancing the 'International Economy' and the domestic economy, ultimately setting up an international environment standard.[54]

Agenda 21 had several goals to promote sustainable development, including international cooperation in trading, transferring eco-friendly technologies from developed to developing countries, strengthening the financial resources of host countries, and ensuring national governments preserve domestic environmental conditions through periodic assessments. Additionally, non-governmental organizations were encouraged to actively participate in conserving ecology and the environment, and hazardous industries were to be subjected to reasonable restrictions. Equitable obligations toward future generations and steps for achieving sustainable development were the underpinning features of Agenda 21. It offered detailed guidelines to states to develop and improve their environmental policies.

4.2.6 Convention on Biological Diversity

The members have joined the CBD in order to support the biological diversity of the Earth, which has immense ecological, genetic, social, economic, scientific, educational, cultural, recreational, and aesthetic value.[55] This convention states the obligation of every state to take measures to protect biodiversity within its jurisdiction by formulating suitable environmental policies and laws. Biological diversity is conserved through the protection of ecosystems and natural habitats, the maintenance of, and where necessary, restoration to the viable populations of species to be maintained in their natural environment.[56] A number of Indigenous and local communities that are economically dependent on biological resources and have traditional ways of life deserve to be allocated the benefits that derive from traditional knowledge, innovation, and practices in a fair manner to enable biodiversity and its constituents to be maintained sustainably. This convention underlines the importance of cooperation between states as well as intergovernmental organizations and non-governmental organizations on an international, regional, or global level to eradicate and sustain the constituents of biological diversity. The friendly relations of states and the conservation and sustainable use of biodiversity are factors contributing to world peace.

53 United Nations. (1992). *Agenda 21, Chapter 1 (Preamble)* (p. 2). UN Home, ESA Home Search.

54 United Nations. (1992). *Agenda 21, Chapter 2: Convention on Biological Diversity*. Earth Summit.

55 *Convention on Biological Diversity*, one of the multilateral treaties entered as part of the Earth Summit by the states on June 5, 1992.

56 Ibid., *Principle 2*; 'In-situ conditions' means conditions where genetic resources exist within ecosystems and natural habitats, and, in the case of domesticated or cultivated species, in the surroundings where they have developed their distinctive properties.

The *Convention* comprehensively addresses all aspects of biological diversity.[57] Here are some key points about its contribution to global environmental regulation:

(a) **Conservation of Biodiversity**

The CBD emphasizes protecting biodiversity, including ecosystems, species, and genetic diversity. It recognizes the dependency of Indigenous peoples and local communities on biological diversity and their unique role in conserving life on Earth.[58]

(b) **Sustainable Use of Biological Resources**

The CBD promotes the sustainable use of biological resources. It encourages practices that maintain ecological balance while allowing for human development and economic activities.[59]

(c) **Equitable Benefit Sharing**

The CBD aims to ensure the fair and equitable sharing of benefits from genetic resource use. This includes sharing benefits with local communities and Indigenous peoples with traditional biodiversity-related knowledge.[60]

(d) **Global Targets and Frameworks**

Negotiations are underway to develop the CBD's post-2020 Global Biodiversity Framework (GBF), which will set international targets for environmental action over the next decade.[61]

The CBD plays a crucial role in shaping policies, strategies, and actions to safeguard our planet's biodiversity and promote sustainable development. Its impact extends beyond national boundaries, contributing to global

57 Glowka, L., Burhenne-Guilmin, F., Hugh, M., Jeffrey, A., & Gündling, L. (1994). *A guide to the convention on biological diversity*. International Union for Conservation of Nature and Natural Resources (IUCN). Retrieved May 18, from www.iucn.org/resources/publication/guide-convention-biological-diversity

58 International Union for Conservation of Nature and Natural Resources (IUCN). (2024a). *UN convention on biological diversity (CBD)*. Retrieved May 18, from www.iucn.org/our-work/informing-policy/international-policy/un-convention-biological-diversity-cbd

59 Secretariat of the Convention on Biological Diversity. (2009). *Sustaining life on earth: How the convention on biological diversity promotes nature and human well-being*. Retrieved May 18, from www.cbd.int/convention/guide

60 Secretariat of the Convention on Biological Diversity. (2011). *Convention on Biological Diversity*. United Nations Environment Programme. Montreal. Diversity, S. O. T. C. O. B. (2011). *Convention on biological diversity*. United Nations Environment Programme.

61 Australian Government, Department of Agriculture, Water and the Environment. (2021). *National and international agreements and policy*. Retrieved May 18, from https://soe.dcceew.gov.au/biodiversity/management/national-and-international-agreements-and-policy

environmental regulation. The Convention has established a separate secretariat to monitor global activities.

4.2.7 Earth Summit +5

Heads of state, governments, and delegations from international institutions and non-governmental organizations convened on September 19, 1997, for the Nineteenth Special Session of the United Nations General Assembly to assess the progress made in the 'program area' of Agenda 21. The objectives of this Special Session were to accelerate the implementation of Agenda 21 and to reaffirm 'that Agenda 21 remains the fundamental program of action for achieving sustainable development.'[62] It was contended that several positive results had been achieved, but overall trends concerning sustainable development had declined. Developing countries generally suffer from poverty, low social development, inadequate infrastructure, and low per capita income. It was also noted that the economic conditions of many countries had worsened, and the gap between the developing and developed countries had widened, which had a debilitating effect on the environment. It was contended that 'Significant environmental problems remain deeply embedded in the socio-economic fabric of countries in all regions.'[63]

The Special Session showed its deep concern for areas requiring the immediate implementation of Agenda 21. The scheme pinpointed by it was an integrated approach toward economic, social, and environmental objectives, sections, issues, and means of implementation. The most notable feature, with respect to industrialized countries, was their unsustainable production and consumption patterns. Such patterns of industrialization, when adopted by the developing countries, enabled them to more than adequately fulfill their basic needs but posed a danger to environmental conservation. Reaffirmation was, therefore, made toward the transmission of eco-friendly technology from industrialized countries to developing countries. To successfully implement the policies of Agenda 21, it was decided that the industrialized countries should encourage such policies that promote sustainable consumption and production patterns. A recommendation was also made to eliminate subsidies for environmentally deleterious activities.[64] International cooperation within the institutional framework of the countries, as outlined under Chapter 38 of Agenda 21, was said to be of immense importance, and international arrangements in the area of sustainable development were intended to march toward the goal of a progressive society.

For the implementation of the commitments of Agenda 21, the Commission on Sustainable Development[65] assesses and reviews the implementation of

62 United Nations. (1997). *Nineteenth special session, agenda item 8*, General Assembly, September 19, 1997, Dists. GENR (A1), p. 3.

63 Supra note 23.

64 Supra note 23.

65 General Assembly *Resolution 47/191.*

environmental policies. The Commission collaborates with the Social and Economic Council, other organizations, and institutional bodies. Efforts are made to strengthen the participation of ministers and high-level national policymakers in its work and to exchange national experiences and best practices in sustainable development. The Commission considers the effective modalities, with appropriate emphasis on the means of implementation,[66] to achieve the goals of Agenda 21.

4.2.8 The Global Judges Symposium[67]

The Symposium for Global Judges on Sustainable Development and the Role of Law offered suggestions and direction for creating a plan to enhance the skills of judicial officers in developing nations and countries undergoing economic transitions.[68] As noted earlier, the Symposium also directed legal practitioners such as prosecutors, enforcement officers, advocates, public interest litigation groups, and civil society organizations who focus on the enforcement of national laws as well as safeguarding the environmental rights of people. The training needs of the judiciary are already within UNEP's work program derived from the Montevideo Programme for the Development and Periodic Review of Environmental Law for the First Decade of the Twenty-First Century.[69] At the Global Judges Symposium, over 120 senior judges from different jurisdictions together with chief justices, adopted the recommendations on the need for active participation of the judiciary and other stakeholders toward more effective implementation and enforcement of national environmental law. The symposium renewed discussions on the need for a global initiative to enhance the effectiveness of critical groups of actors engaged in the implementation, compliance, and enforcement of domestic environmental law. The symposium developed 25 principles for strengthening environmental jurisprudence around the world.[70]

The Symposium, in 2022, together with the Asian Development Bank (ADB), the Global Judicial Institute on the Environment (GJIE), and the

66 Supra note 23.

67 The global Judges symposium on the sustainable development and the role of law was held on 18–22, 2002 at Johannesburg, South Africa.

68 United Nations Environment Programme. (2002). *Report of the global judges symposium on sustainable development and the role of law: Note by the executive director*. United Nations. https://digitallibrary.un.org/record/484610?v=pdf

69 United Nations Environment Programme. (2020). *Montevideo environmental law programme: A decade of action on environmental law*. United Nations. www.unep.org/resources/factsheet/montevideo-environmental-law-programme-decade-action-environmental-law#:~:text=The%20Montevideo%20Environmental%20Law%20Programme%20is%20a%20ten,involves%20a%20wide%20range%20of%20environmental%20law%20stakeholders

70 United Nations Environment Programme. (2002). *Global judges symposium on sustainable development and the role of law*. United Nations. Retrieved May 25, from https://stg-wedocs.unep.org/handle/20.500.11822/30024

International Association of Judges, organized a conference for reflection on the implications of the Stockholm Declaration for the development of global environmental law and jurisprudence. This conference was important to tackle the following specific matters: (a) the role of judges in the domestication of environmental laws, agreements, and declarations vis-a-vis national and sub-national law, (b) the need to strengthen the independence and integrity of the Judiciary as essential components of the Environmental Rule of Law, and (c) judicial training in the area of Environmental Law and the challenge of Judicial Education.[71]

As cited, the concern has been noted that the Fourth Judicial Revolution instills novel human principles from the United Nations Millennium Declaration into humanity's civilization through further respect for the rule of law in the international and national systems.[72] The Symposium further justified that the independent Judiciary and judicial process is crucial for the execution, cultivation, and advancement of environmental law. This makes judicial officers and other stakeholders in the judicial process at the global, regional, and national levels critical allies of international and national environmental law compliance, implementation, as well as enforcement.

4.2.9 The Alien Tort Statute

The Alien Tort Statute has the potential to hold individuals and corporations accountable for human rights abuses and other violations of international law.[73]

This remarkable litigation strategy has been employed in many notable cases like Mark B.C. Goda's case in 2013.[74] The ATCA or Alien Tort Claims Act hails from the United States and is part of the *Judiciary Act 1789*. It mandates U.S. federal courts to take jurisdiction over civil suits brought by non-Americans for torts committed in violation of international law or United States treaty. This statute enables individuals who are not U.S. citizens to seek justice in U.S. courts for human rights violations, not committed within the bounds of the United States, provided that there exists some relationship to the United States.[75]

The ATS originated together with the first section of the *Judiciary Act 1789* which was intended to create a federal court system in the United States.[76] As a young and relatively weak nation, the United States sought

71 Ibid.
72 Ibid.
73 Legal Information Institute. (2022). *Alien Tort statute*. Wex. Retrieved May 25, from www.law.cornell.edu/wex/alien_tort_statute
74 Golove, D. (2020). *The Alien Tort statute and the law of nations: Newly uncovered* (HRP 21–001). Harvard University.
75 Ibid.
76 Service, C. R. (2022). *The Alien Tort statute: A primer*. L. O. Congress.

to avoid potential conflicts with other countries by ensuring that foreign plaintiffs had access to effective remedies for violations of international law.[77] Consequently, the ATS was designed to allow federal courts to hear claims by foreign citizens against U.S. citizens for intentional torts to persons or personal property.[78]

Meanwhile, the ATS remained largely dormant for almost two centuries until the case *Filartiga v. Peña-Irala* in 1980.[79] This case involved a Paraguayan father who sued a Paraguayan police officer for the alleged torture and murder of his son in Paraguay. The U.S. Court of Appeals for the Second Circuit ruled that within the scope of the ATS, significant human rights abuses such as torture could be claimed because these acts featured universal condemnation and were violations of the law of nations. Following the Filartiga case, U.S. courts have permitted ATS lawsuits for various human rights violations such as genocide, crimes against humanity, summary execution, torture, slavery, war crimes, and state-sponsored sexual violence. The Supreme Court, however, has restricted the types of claims that can be litigated under the ATS. In *Sosa v. Alvarez-Machain*, the Supreme Court ruled that the international legal standards constituting a cause of action under the ATS must be 'specific, universal, and obligatory.'[80] In other words, only the most egregious and internationally accepted breaches of law can be litigated under the statute. Furthermore, in *Kiobel v. Royal Dutch Petroleum*, the Supreme Court held that the ATS, in general, does not apply to torts occurring in other nations, with the exception of cases where the claims 'touch and concern' the United States with 'sufficient force.'[81]

The developments of international human rights law have been significant with the expansion of the ATS to encompass human rights abuses perpetrated by non-state actors like multinational corporations. With the turn of the 1990s, a number of corporate-led cases began surfacing against corporations under the ATS, accusing them of turning a blind eye to human rights and environmental violations. Some of these include *Doe v. Unocal*, where Burmese villagers litigated against an American oil company for alleged human rights violations concerning the Burmese security forces' abuse during the construction of a natural gas pipeline.[82] In a similar manner, *Wiwa v. Royal Dutch*

77 Ibid.

78 Ibid.

79 See Encyclopaedia Britannica. (n.d.). *Filartiga v. Pena-Irala*. www.britannica.com/topic/Filartiga-v-Pena-Irala

80 See Encyclopaedia Britannica. (n.d.). *Sosa v. Alvarez-Machain*. www.britannica.com/topic/Sosa-v-Alvarez-Machain

81 See Encyclopaedia Britannica. (n.d.). *Kiobel v. Royal Dutch Petroleum*. www.britannica.com/topic/Kiobel-v-Royal-Dutch-Petroleum

82 See Earth Rights International. (n.d.). *Doe v. Unocal*. https://earthrights.org/case/doe-v-unocal/

Petroleum Co. saw Nigerians suing the company on the basis of their perceived perpetration of human rights abuses regarding the Ogoni people in Nigeria.[83]

The Alien Tort Statute has demonstrated its strength in the protection of human rights and in the regulation of corporate power. ATS's provisions enabling foreign citizens to litigate in U.S. courts for breaches of international law have certainly helped bring to light the damaging actions of some individuals and corporations who would otherwise remain hidden.

4.2.10 Jurisdiction Regulation of the European Union

Navigating the legal landscape can be daunting for a multinational corporation. Each country has its own set of laws and regulations that govern how businesses operate within its borders. To complicate matters further, the EU has its jurisdiction regulations that multinational corporations must comply with. The Jurisdiction Regulation is a set of rules determining which courts have jurisdiction over legal disputes within the EU.[84] The regulation aims to provide a clear and predictable legal framework for resolving disputes. It applies to civil and commercial matters, including disputes between businesses. The regulation is designed to prevent forum shopping, where parties choose a court more favorable to their case. It has established rules that determine which courts have jurisdiction over cross-border disputes.[85] These rules prevent conflicting judgments and resolve disputes fairly and efficiently.

Article 4 of the Jurisdiction Regulation sets out the rules for determining the domicile of a natural person or a company. Domicile is where a person or company is considered to have their permanent home or base. The regulation provides that a person is domiciled in the member state where they have their habitual residence. The regulation states that the companies are located in the member state where their registered office, central administration, or headquarters are situated. Article 7(5) of Jurisdiction Regulation allows for additional jurisdiction in some cases. These include situations where a contract has been concluded or performed within a certain member state or where the dispute is about interpreting a contract. The regulation states that the court of the member state where the contract was performed or ought to have been performed has authority over the dispute. Article 7(2) of the Jurisdiction Regulation is about disputes arising out of a contract. It states that a person may be sued in the courts of the member state where they are domiciled or in the courts of the member state where the obligation constituting the cause of

83 See Center for Constitutional Rights. (n.d.). *Wiwa et al. v. Royal Dutch Petroleum et al.* https://ccrjustice.org/home/what-we-do/our-cases/wiwa-et-al-v-royal-dutch-petroleum-et-al

84 Hartley, T. C. (2022). Basic principles of jurisdiction in private international law: The European Union, the United States and England. *International & Comparative Law Quarterly*, *71*(1), 211–226.

85 Kazazi, E., & Çela, E. (2015). Jurisdiction in the European Union. *International Journal of Academic Research and Reflection*, *3*(4), 48–54.

action was discharged. This means that if an agreement has been entered into by a multinational company and a supplier in a particular member state, then that company can be sued in the courts of that member state if any dispute arises regarding the contract.

The Jurisdiction Regulation has a cross-border aspect to it. It covers a dispute with a non-EU party if the dispute bears some relation to the EU. This implies that a multinational's dispute with an off-EU party having an EU connection may be covered by the regulation, for example, the dispute may concern a contract executed in the EU or the defendant is a local person with interests in the EU. For example, TNCs are transnational corporations which operate in multiple jurisdictions and have to pay attention to the laws of each jurisdiction they operate in. This often poses a problem, especially for smaller businesses that do not have the means to engage legal professionals in every country. If a dispute occurs that violates the regulation, the business is subjected to further expenses and delays. Therefore, businesses must be aware of the processes for determining the domicile status and guarantee that they are incorporated in the right member state. They must ensure that their contracts have no less than jurisdictional clauses that comply with the regulation.

A complicated system of Jurisdiction rules results from the complex nature of the EU's Jurisdiction Regulation which can be hard to comprehend for large-scale companies. Nonetheless, failure to follow these requirements may lead to legal action, litigation, or reputational damage. Businesses operating within the EU need to have a legal counsel and strategize on how to determine the jurisdiction of their matters. This should help them ensure compliance with the law and avoid unnecessary legal disputes.[86]

4.2.11 OECD's Due Diligence Guidance for Responsible Business

The OECD Due Diligence Guidance for Responsible Business Conduct sets the requirements for companies willing to conduct ethical business and is regarded as a main regulatory framework for cross-national company dynamics. This is vital for the management of international business supply chains as the impact of one business's actions in these supply chains can be felt internationally.

The OECD Due Diligence Guidance is rooted in the OECD Guidelines for Multinational Enterprises on Responsible Business Conduct, which were first issued in 1976 and have been revised over the years to incorporate contemporary norms of responsible business conduct (RBC) that address human rights, labor, and environmental issues. One of the significant influences in developing the OECD Due Diligence Guidance was the UN Guiding Principles on Business and Human Rights (UNGPs) adopted by the UN Human Rights Council in 2011. The frameworks that assist

86 Ibid.

businesses in the mitigation and prevention of human rights violations relevant to them are rooted in Ruggie's principles. With regard to the development of the OECD Due Diligence Guidance, one must also consider the historical development of the evolution of due diligence in corporate social responsibility and business conduct.[87] There has been growing recognition that companies need to exercise due diligence in identifying, preventing, and mitigating the impact of their activities on society, which has motivated the OECD's work in this area.[88]

The OECD Due Diligence Guidance is anchored on the key elements of RBC, which include (a) respect for human rights, (b) labor, (c) environment, and (d) non-discrimination and anti-corruption.[89] These elements and others are derived from the UNGPs, the International Labour Organization (ILO) core conventions, and the UN Global Compact.[90]

The scope of application of the guidance covers a variety of sectors, including, but not limited to, the extractive and manufacturing sectors, agriculture, finance, and technology. Due diligence is required at every level in the procurement and production cycle, in other words, from the mining of raw materials to the consumption of finished goods. Furthermore, the OECD Due Diligence Guidance promotes participation from different groups to solve the intricate problems pertaining to RBC that involve multiple parties working together to form a cohesive solution

Numerous case studies and reports have demonstrated the tangible impact of the OECD Due Diligence Guidance on business practices.[91] Companies that have embraced the principles outlined in the guidance have enhanced their reputations, mitigated risks, and contributed to sustainable development.[92] Implementing the guidance, however, is not without challenges. It requires significant organizational commitment, capacity building, and, in some cases, the overhaul of existing business practices.

87 Organization for Economic Co-operation and Development (OECD). (2020). *OECD due diligence guidance for responsible business conduct.* OECD Publishing.

88 Ventura, L. (2023). Corporate sustainability due diligence and the new boundaries of firms in the European Union. *European Business Law Review*, *34*(2); Ventura, L. (2023). Corporate sustainability due diligence and the new boundaries of the firms in the European Union. *European Business Law Review*, *34*(2).

89 OECD. (2024). *OECD due diligence guidance for responsible business conduct.* OECD. Retrieved May 25, from https://mneguidelines.oecd.org/due-diligence-guidance-for-responsible-business-conduct.htm

90 Ibid.

91 Kryczka, K., Lambooy, T., & Beckers, S. (2012). Importance of due diligence practices for the future of business operations in Fragile States. *The Europe Company Limited*, *9*, 125. Oldenziel, J., & Wilde-Ramsing, J. (2010). *10 years on: Assessing the contribution of the OECD guidelines for multinational enterprises to responsible business conduct.* SSRN. https://ssrn.com/abstract=1641036

92 Oldenziel, J., & Wilde-Ramsing, J. (2010). *10 years on: Assessing the contribution of the OECD guidelines for multinational enterprises to responsible business conduct.* SSRN 1641036.

The OECD Due Diligence Guidance for Responsible Business Conduct has received various constructive criticisms. Some stakeholders have suggested that enhancing the enforcement mechanisms could further promote widespread compliance by businesses.[93] Additionally, there is an opportunity to simplify the guidance for easier implementation, especially for smaller businesses with limited resources, thus facilitating its effective adoption. Furthermore, expanding the scope of the guidance to address a broader range of issues, such as the rights of marginalized groups, environmental conservation, and the impacts of business conduct on local communities, could enhance its overall effectiveness. Addressing these concerns could strengthen the monitoring and reporting mechanisms, ensuring better tracking and addressing non-compliance.

4.2.12 UN's Business and Human Rights Guidelines

The UN has played a pivotal role in establishing guidelines to ensure businesses respect human rights. The UN Human Rights Council endorsed the UNGPs in 2011, representing a significant milestone in corporate responsibility.[94]

The evolution of the discourse on corporate accountability in regard to human rights forms the basis for why the UN Business and Human Rights Guidelines, or succinctly the UNGPs, were created. These guidelines were developed in response to attempts to harmonize the human rights consequences of business activities at a global level. Before the UNGPs were published, there was a heightened focus on corporate social responsibility, where firms started acknowledging their responsibility toward social and environmental issues in addition to economic ones. At the same time, human rights abuses associated with corporate activities were becoming the focal point of concern for many advocacy groups, and there were calls for increased accountability from corporations. In 2005, the UN Secretary-General appointed John Ruggie as Special Representative on business and human rights, hoping to better define the expectations and responsibilities of states and corporations regarding human rights. He consulted broadly with governments, businesses, civil society, and other directly affected people to capture their views on the relationship between business and human rights. After six years of research and dialogue, John Ruggie delivered the UNGPs to the UN Human Rights Council in 2011, and they endorsed it.[95]

The Guidelines have significantly influenced companies' awareness and adoption of human rights strategy in their operations, including on their supply

93 Schleper, M. C., & Bernaz, N. (2019). The international framework for business and human rights: A critical appraisal. *Journal of Business Ethics, 155*(2), 451–467.

94 Mares, R. (2011). *The UN guiding principles on business and human rights: Foundations and implementation* (Vol. 39). Martinus Nijhoff Publishers.

95 Ruggie, J. G. (2020). The social construction of the UN Guiding Principles on Business and Human Rights. In *Research handbook on human rights and business* (pp. 63–86). Edward Elgar Publishing.

chains and at the level of decision-making.[96] This has heightened the concern for human rights issues and responsibility among legal persons. Businesses are now more active in mitigating the human rights threats posed by their activities, which has resulted in the formulation of competent management systems and due diligence frameworks.[97] Additionally, the UNGPs have influenced the development of regulatory frameworks in various countries, prompting governments to enact laws and policies that align with corporate respect for human rights principles. This has resulted in several countries adopting National Action Plans (NAPs) on business and human rights, outlining specific measures to implement the UNGPs within their jurisdictions, which is a significant step forward. Moreover, the UNGPs have become a reference point for standard-setting organizations, industry initiatives, and multistakeholder partnerships, influencing the formulation of codes of conduct, certification schemes, and industry standards that emphasize human rights, due diligence, and RBC.

The UNGPs rest on three pillars: the state's duty to protect, the corporate responsibility to respect, and the need for access to a remedy by victims of human rights violations.[98] In this regard, the UNGPs emphasize the provision of information to potentially affected communities about their environment, which enhances accountability for the stewardship of nature. This has helped establish the nexus of human rights as well as environmental protection by building the case for the mitigation of corporate activities that infringe on the rights of individuals or communities concerning ecosystem degradation. Adoption of the UNGPs has been widespread among governments, businesses, and members of civil society. They act as the primary basis for encouraging business enterprises to observe and respect human rights.[99] A number of states have drafted NAPs in regard to the UNGPs in their specific situations. These documents contain strategies aimed at promoting responsible business practices and the protection of human rights. Through ongoing interactions and academic discourse, they have aimed at strengthening the implementation and usefulness of the plans in a changing world of business.

96 Addo, M. K. (2014). The reality of the United Nations guiding principles on business and human rights. *Human Rights Law Review*, *14*(1), 133–147.

97 Scherer, A. G., Palazzo, G., & Baumann, D. (2006). Global rules and private actors: Toward a new role of the transnational corporation in global governance. *Business Ethics Quarterly*, *16*(4), 505–532.

98 Bonnitcha, J., & McCorquodale, R. (2017). The concept of 'due diligence' in the UN guiding principles on business and human rights. *European Journal of International Law*, *28*(3), 899–919; Mares, R. (2011). *The UN guiding principles on business and human rights: Foundations and implementation* (Vol. 39). Martinus Nijhoff Publishers.

99 Faracik, B. (2017). *Implementation of the UN guiding principles on business and human rights*. European Parliament, PE 578.

4.3 Organizations for Implementing Global Norms Against Corporate Pollution

Multinational entities have a powerful impact on the protection of the environment through their international technical assistance, research, and analysis. They facilitate the active participation of governments and local communities in decision-making regarding the policies within the framework of the environmental issues that build the skills and knowledge of the individual and organizational players in the environmental protection system. Also, they promote environmental and ecological civil rights and help sustain environmental protection through advocacy campaigns. They promote the circulation of ideas and strategies by documenting and disseminating relevant materials as well as enabling countries and communities to adopt effective measures against pollution by corporations. Their worldwide presence allows for more coordinated action and integration beyond the borders of nations to carry out joint activities for solving problems that require cooperation.

Various international institutions have successfully campaigned against corporate pollution. One example is the Clean Air Initiative Campaign run by the WHO. This campaign aims to reduce air pollution levels and improve the air quality in metropolitan areas because air pollution is a serious health hazard. The advocacy, research, and policy efforts of the initiative have persuaded several governments and corporations to adopt cleaner technologies and more stringent emissions policies. Another one worth noting is Detox Fashion by Fashion Revolution. This campaign actually mobilizes the public about the environmental devastation caused by the fashion industry. The Fashion Revolution has engaged different stakeholders like consumers and policymakers to successfully compel many fashion brands to endorse transparent chemical and labor practices in their supply chains.

Various international bodies are now opposing corporate pollution. The UNEP is one of the foremost international bodies attempting to safeguard the environment. UNEP works side by side with the government, industries, and the public to promote measured economic growth and prevent pollution. Another strong organization is Greenpeace, which is popular for its campaigns and intervention in solving environmental issues. Noise-free demonstrations, in addition to lobbying and scientific studies, prove corporate pollution and push for change. There are many additional accomplishments, like getting rid of certain dangerous chemicals and saving some species from extinction. The following part discusses these world organizations in more detail, also providing a summary of other world organizations such as the International Union for Conservation of Nature (IUCN), Greenpeace, UNEP, UNFCCC, and Global Reporting Initiative (GRI).

4.3.1 The International Union for Conservation of Nature

IUCN is an international body devoted to furthering and protecting the environment. It has over 1,400 member organizations and more than 16,000 experts on issues of conservation, making it the largest and most varied environmental network in the world.[100] IUCN's biggest strength is its ability to mobilize all stakeholders and address environmental challenges globally. Additionally, the IUCN can offer governments and other institutions consulting services regarding policies and management strategies and provide technical expert aid. Additionally, the IUCN can leverage its global network to raise awareness about environmental issues and advocate for change at the international level.

The IUCN has taken several steps to reduce corporate pollution.[101] One of its most important initiatives is the Business and Biodiversity Program, which works with companies to integrate biodiversity into their operations and supply chains. The tools are designed to assist companies in effectively decreasing the environmental impacts of their businesses and enhancing eco-friendly practices. The IUCN has developed corporate guidelines for preventing ecosystem or biodiversity impacts. For example, it has collaborated with the airline sector to create an emissions reduction framework for air travel. It has also worked on emissions reductions for shipping and other industries, sustainable forestry, hazardous materials, chemical waste reduction, and waste minimization.

The impact of IUCN's corporate pollution monitoring policy is felt by the business world. In dealing with the issues, the IUCN has prompted many corporations to adopt new policies by advocating for sustainable policies. For instance, some large companies pledged to cut down on GHG emissions largely because of pressures from the IUCN and other groups. It has collaborated with the mining sector to formulate a responsible mining policy. It has also collaborated with the fishing industry to develop policies on sustainable fish capture. Furthermore, IUCN has been active in the conservation of threatened species like the African elephant and the black rhinoceros.

Even though the IUCN has had some success, it still has numerous challenges to overcome in tackling corporate pollution.[102] The lack of willingness

100 International Union for Conservation of Nature (IUCN). (2024b). *United for life & livelihoods*. International Union for Conservation of Nature. Retrieved May 20, from https://iucn.org/sites/default/files/2023-04/iucn-brochure-2023-cor_0.pdf

101 Beumer, C., & Martens, P. (2013). IUCN and perspectives on biodiversity conservation in a changing world. *Biodiversity and Conservation*, *22*, 3105–3120; Atkins, J., & Maroun, W. (2018). Integrated extinction accounting and accountability: Building an ark. *Accounting, Auditing & Accountability Journal*, *31*(3), 750–786.

102 Keith, D. A., Rodríguez, J. P., Brooks, T. M., Burgman, M. A., Barrow, E. G., Bland, L., Comer, P. J., Franklin, J., Link, J., & McCarthy, M. A. (2015). The IUCN Red List of ecosystems: Motivations, challenges, and applications. *Conservation Letters*, *8*(3), 214–226; Beumer, C., & Martens, P. (2013). IUCN and perspectives on biodiversity conservation in a changing world. *Biodiversity and Conservation*, *22*, 3105–3120; Rodríguez-Rodríguez, E. J., Beltrán, J., El Mouden, E., Slimani, T., Márquez, R., & Donaire-Barroso, D. (2020). Climate change challenges IUCN conservation priorities: A test with western Mediterranean amphibians. *SN Applied Sciences*, *2*, 1–11; Dudley, N., Parrish, J. D., Redford, K. H., & Stolton, S. (2010). The revised IUCN protected area management categories: The debate and ways forward. *Oryx*, *44*(4), 485–490.

to change practices from some companies is perhaps the greatest challenge. Many firms do not want to adopt sustainable approaches since they view environmental regulations as expensive and burdensome. Furthermore, an absence of political will, especially concerning economic powers, tends to highly prioritize growth and will take action on issues of the environment as a secondary concern.

The IUCN has an integral responsibility to ensure corporate pollution is kept in check.[103] Besides being able to gather the stakeholders, the IUCN's technical expertise and knowledge of the environmental issues help in creating concern on a global level. The IUCN has changed the perception of many businesses through its programs on sustainable supply chains, GHG emissions, and other environmental concerns campaigns. Although there are sustaining challenges, the work done by IUCN is indeed very crucial. As individuals and governments, we need to get actively involved in supporting the IUCN's environmental strategies and shifts to sustain it for the coming generations.

Greenpeace

In 1971, a group of activists in Vancouver, Canada, founded a non-profit organization known as Greenpeace, which initially focused on opposing the nuclear weapons testing in Alaska.[104] Today, the organization single-handedly deals with most issues relating to the environment.[105]

Greenpeace has been active in fighting corporate pollution since its inception.[106] It has launched campaigns against Shell, BP, and Nestlé, among many others. In the 1970s, they began focusing on the U.S. nuclear weapons industry

103 Robinson, N. A. (2005). IUCN as catalyst for a law of the biosphere: Acting globally and locally. *Environmental Law*, *35*, 249; McCormick, J. (2023). The role of environmental NGOs in international regimes. In *The global environment* (pp. 52–71). Routledge; Holdgate, M. W. (1995). Pathways to sustainability: The evolving role of transnational institutions. *Environment: Science and Policy for Sustainable Development*, *37*(9), 16–42.

104 Greenpeace. (2024). *Our history, victories and successes*. Greenpeace. Retrieved May 20, from www.greenpeace.org/international/about/founders/?_gl=1*1625il1*_up*MQ.*_ga*NTQxMzY0MzY3LjE3MTYxODEzNjk.*_ga_94MRTN8HG4*MTcxNjE4MTM2OS4xLjAuMTcxNjE4MTQyOS4wLjAuMTA1NjU1MTgzNw.*_ga_0CCB1GTVV6*MTcxNjE4MTM2OC4xLjEuMTcxNjE4MTQyOS4wLjAuMA.*_ga_99CSX66YC1*MTcxNjE4MTM2OC4xLjEuMTcxNjE4MTQyOS4wLjAuMA.www.greenpeace.org/international/about/founders/?

105 Novis, J. (2021, November 29). Greenpeace: Half a century on the frontline of environmental photo activism. *The Guardian*. www.theguardian.com/environment/2021/nov/29/greenpeace-half-a-century-on-the-frontline-of-environmental-photo-activism; See also, Weyler, R. (2004). *Greenpeace: How a group of ecologists, journalists, and visionaries changed the world*. Rodale.

106 Butler, R. A. (2010, July 22). How Greenpeace changes big business. *Mongabay*. https://news.mongabay.com/2010/07/how-greenpeace-changes-big-business/

and then shifted toward toxic waste disposal in the 1980s.[107] Greenpeace has, and is, fighting against fashion industries for their lack of concern for the environment.[108] The 'Detox' campaign made many important clothing manufacturers cut down on the poisonous chemicals they use.[109]

All of these and more are made possible by the efforts of Greenpeace using social media to gain support and awareness for their campaigns. One of their most effective strategies to change corporate practices is direct action that includes physically blocking and occupying polluting activities or facilities. This approach has worked remarkably well in campaigns against coal mining and oil drilling in the Arctic.[110] Their campaign against using PVC in children's toys led to major toy companies switching to safer materials. Their campaign against Nestle's use of palm oil led to the company committing to use only sustainable palm oil by 2020. Greenpeace's campaigns have also led to increased public awareness about the impact of corporate pollution, which has, in turn, put pressure on governments and corporations to act.[111]

Greenpeace faces many challenges in its fight against corporate pollution. One of the biggest challenges is the power and influence of corporations, which can make it difficult to effect change.[112] Corporations often have deep pockets and extensive legal resources, which they can use to fight back against Greenpeace and other environmental groups. Another challenge is the lack of political will to address environmental issues, making it difficult for Greenpeace to achieve its goals. Greenpeace also faces challenges in terms of funding and resources, as they rely on donations from supporters to fund their campaigns.

The future of Greenpeace in corporate pollution reduction is bright.[113] The organization continues to grow and expand its reach, constantly developing new campaigns and tactics to address the issue of corporate pollution. Greenpeace's campaigns have already had a significant impact on reducing

107 Greenpeace. (2024b). *Nuclear campaign*. Greenpeace. Retrieved May 20, from https://history.greenpeace.org/aotearoa/nuclear/
108 Jordan, G. (2001). *Shell, greenpeace and the brent spar*. Springer.
109 Greenpeace. (2024a). *Destination zero*. Greenpeace International. Retrieved May 20, from www.greenpeace.org/international/publication/17612/destination-zero/
110 Pacific, G. A. (2018, January 11). *Arctic oil: The verdict in*. Greenpeace International. Retrieved May 20 from; Glaser, A. (2015). *You did it! Shell abandons Arctic drilling*. Greenpeace. Retrieved May 20 from www.greenpeace.org/international/story/7022/you-did-it-shell-abandons-arctic-drilling/
111 Taylor, L. (2014, August 7). Five Greenpeace campaigns against companies: Lego, Barbie, and Shell. *The Guardian*. www.theguardian.com/sustainable-business/blog/greenpeace-campaigns-companies-lego-mattel-barbie-shell
112 Bendell, J., & Bendell, M. (2007). Facing corporate power. In *The debate over corporate social responsibility* (pp. 59–73); Murphy, P., & Dee, J. (1992). Du Pont and Greenpeace: The dynamics of conflict between corporations and activist groups. *Journal of Public Relations Research*, *4*(1), 3–20.
113 Plourde, Y. (2015). *Engaging with the future: A historical investigation of greenpeace*. The University of Western Ontario (Canada).

corporate pollution, and they will undoubtedly continue to play a major role in this area for many years to come.

4.3.2 *United Nations Environment Programme*

The UNEP was formed in 1972 as the world's foremost authority on environmental matters, which sets international environmental policy and advocates the implementation of the environmental aspect of development in the United Systems as well as advocating interactively for the environment. UNEP is responsible for providing leadership and stimulating partnerships in the environmental field, which inspires, informs, and enables people and nations to enhance their quality of life while safeguarding it for coming generations.

UNEP has tackled issues directed toward pollution by corporations.[114] UNEP has focused on pollution from corporations by studying the impact of their emissions, creating policies that guide their operations, and working with other stakeholders to enhance environmental stewardship. In addition, UNEP works with other stakeholders, including government, civil society, and business, to achieve development and environmental sustainability.

UNEP has developed legal frameworks and the capacity to punish corporate polluters. UNEP's legal frameworks include the Basel Convention on the Control of Transboundary Movements of Hazardous Wastes and Their Disposal,[115] which regulates the movement of hazardous wastes across borders, and the Stockholm Convention on Persistent Organic Pollutants,[116] which aims to eliminate or restrict the production and use of persistent organic pollutants. It also can punish corporate polluters through its Compliance and Enforcement Programme, which investigates and prosecutes environmental crimes.

UNEP has recorded some success stories in punishing corporate polluters.[117] One notable example is Trafigura, a multinational oil trading company

114 Borowy, I. (2019). Before UNEP: Who was in charge of the global environment? The struggle for institutional responsibility 1968–72. *Journal of Global History*, *14*(1), 87–106; Ivanova, M. (2021). *The untold story of the world's leading environmental institution: UNEP at fifty*. MIT Press; Ivanova, M. (2020). Coloring the UN environmental: The catalytic role of the UN environment programme. *Global Governance: A Review of Multilateralism and International Organizations*, *26*(2), 307–324.

115 Ahmed, I. (2019). The Basel convention on the control of transboundary movements of hazardous wastes and their disposal: A legal misfit in global ship recycling jurisprudence. *Washington International Law Journal*, *29*, 411; Islam, M. (2020). The Basel convention on the control of transboundary movements of hazardous wastes and their disposal: Critical analysis. *International Journal of Multidisciplinary Research and Growth Evaluation*, *1*(2), 11–16.

116 United Nations Environment Programme (UNEP). (2011). *Stockholm convention on persistent organic pollutants*. Geneva.

117 Ivanova, M. (2020). Coloring the UN environmental: The catalytic role of the UN environment programme. *Global Governance: A Review of Multilateralism and International Organizations*, *26*(2), 307–324.

that dumped toxic waste in Cote d'Ivoire in 2006. UNEP investigated the incident, and Trafigura was fined $200 million.[118] Another example is the Ogoni people in Nigeria, who were affected by oil spills from Shell's activities. UNEP conducted an environmental assessment of the Ogoni region, and Shell was forced to pay $15.5 million in compensation.[119]

Despite UNEP's efforts to curb corporate pollution, the organization still faces challenges. One major challenge is the government's lack of political will to enforce environmental regulations. Another challenge is the limited resources available to UNEP to carry out its mandate effectively. Additionally, the lack of public awareness and participation in environmental issues challenges UNEP's efforts to promote environmental protection. To face these challenges, UNEP relies mainly on collaboration with other organizations to tackle corporate pollution. One notable collaboration is the UNEP and the World Wildlife Fund (WWF) partnership for the implementation of programs in the marine and coastal areas of the western Indian Ocean region.[120] UNEP recently built partnerships with some other leading environmental organizations like the Center for Large Landscape Conservation, Climate Chance, the CBD, the Convention on Wetlands, the World Wide Fund for Nature, and the International Council for Local Environmental Initiatives (ICLEI) to fight against the destruction, degradation, and fragmentation of natural habitat.[121] Another notable collaborative initiative is the promotion of sustainable production and consumption patterns. UNEP is working to promote adopting sustainable production and consumption patterns by governments, businesses, and individuals to reduce the impact of human activities on the environment.[122]

UNEP plays a crucial role in the fight against corporate pollution. UNEP's legal frameworks and capacity to punish corporate polluters, collaborations with other organizations, and future initiatives to combat corporate pollution are essential in achieving sustainable environmental practices.

118 Amnesty International. (2016, April). *Trafigura: A toxic journey*. Amnesty International. Retrieved May 19, from www.amnesty.org/en/latest/news/2016/04/trafigura-a-toxic-journey/

119 Pilkington, E. (2009, June 9). Shell pays out $15.5m over Saro-Wiwa killing. *The Guardian*. www.theguardian.com/world/2009/jun/08/nigeria-usa

120 WWF (World Wide Fund for Nature). (2024b). *World wide fund for nature (WWF)*. Retrieved May 20, from www.unep.org/explore-topics/oceans-seas/what-we-do/working-regional-seas/partners/world-wide-fund-nature-wwf

121 WWF (World Wide Fund for Nature). (2024a). *Major new global initiative to protect and connect natural areas launched at UN wildlife meeting*. World Wide Fund for Nature. Retrieved May 20, from https://wwf.panda.org/wwf_news/?10698416/Convention-on-the-Conservation-of-Migratory-Species-of-Wild-Animals

122 UNEP (United Nations Environment Programme). (2024). *Sustainable consumption and production policies*. United Nations Environment Programme. Retrieved May 20, from www.unep.org/explore-topics/resource-efficiency/what-we-do/sustainable-consumption-and-production-policies

4.3.3 United Nations Framework Convention on Climate Change

The UNFCCC is a global environmental treaty whose purpose is to combat the problem of anthropogenic climate change.[123] Founded in 1992, the UNFCCC has been one of the law international treaties aimed at uniting cooperation on persistent world challenges such as climate change and sustainable development. The UNFCCC has also induced important agreements like the Kyoto Protocol and the Paris Agreement which set distinct protocols for decreasing GHG emissions.[124]

The 1980s were marked by new scientific research that, alongside the existing worries about global warming, triggered the idea of international collaboration to solve and address climate change. The Intergovernmental Panel on Climate Change (IPCC) was established in 1988 by the World Meteorological Organization (WMO) and the UNEP for the sole purpose of assembling scientific evidence and providing advisory recommendations for the policy decisions concerning climate change mitigation or adaptation. Following the advice from IPCC during the 1990 Second World Climate Conference in Geneva, global efforts commenced toward establishing a legally binding convention to tackle GHG emissions.

The UNFCCC was adopted on May 9, 1992, and opened for signatories at the UNCED in Rio de Janeiro. It was opened for signature on May 9, 1992, at the UN Conference for Environment and Development, which took place in Rio de Janeiro.[125] It is primarily aimed at the population to try to limit their GHG emissions in a way that dangerous human alterations to climate systems could be avoided. The convention further underlines the idea of responsibilities being both common and differentiated. Moreover, it recognizes the

123 Hickmann, T., Widerberg, O., Lederer, M., & Pattberg, P. (2021). The United Nations framework convention on climate change secretariat as an orchestrator in global climate policymaking. *International Review of Administrative Sciences, 87*(1), 21–38. https://doi.org/10.1177/0020852320941055; Ford, J., Maillet, M., Pouliot, V., Meredith, T., Cavanaugh, A., & Harper, I. R. (2016). Adaptation and indigenous peoples in the United Nations Framework Convention on Climate Change. *Climatic Change, 139*, 429–443. https://doi.org/10.1007/s10584-016-1704-3; Tompkins, E. L., & Amundsen, H. (2008). Perceptions of the effectiveness of the United Nations Framework Convention on Climate Change in advancing national action on climate change. *Environmental Science & Policy, 11*(1), 1–13.

124 Human activities have significantly contributed to the rising levels of greenhouse gases in the atmosphere, increasing global average temperatures. These anthropogenic emissions have increased by 70% between 1970 and 2004, according to the IPCC 4th Assessment Report. The greenhouse gas effect is a naturally occurring phenomenon that helps regulate the Earth's temperature. However, human activities such as burning fossil fuels, deforestation, and industrial processes have amplified the greenhouse gas effect, caused global warming and posing a severe threat to the planet's ecosystems.

125 Johnson, S. P. (2001). *The earth summit: The United Nations conference on environment and development (UNCED)*; Linnér, B.-O., & Selin, H. (2013). The United Nations conference on sustainable development: Forty years in the making. *Environment and Planning C: Government and Policy, 31*(6), 971–987. https://doi.org/10.1068/c12287

specific needs and concerns of some vulnerable countries and regions like small island states and other developing countries. It classifies the treaty signatory countries into three main groups, namely: Annex I countries or developed nations; Annex II countries, which refers to developed nations who bear special financial obligations; and Non-Annex I countries, or developing nations. Member states in Annex I are to impose national policies and measures to mitigate GHG emissions by undertaking activities and monitoring systems to limit the emission of GHGs into the atmosphere/imposition of limitation emission policies on the monitoring systems which need to be implemented and reported in intervals. On the other hand, member states in Annex II are to support Non-Annex I member states with exact expenditure and specialized aid for the purpose of enabling the Non-Annex I members to meet their compliance and mitigation or adaptation of the climate change.

Through the years, the UNFCCC has developed numerous crucial worldwide treaties and protocols to confront issues arising from climate change. The Kyoto Protocol signified the first legally binding framework agreement within the UNFCCC system. The Protocol, which was adopted in 1997, set emission reduction target benchmarks for the Annex I countries to lower their emissions by at least 5% below the 1990 spewed level within the set commitment period of 2008–2012. In 2016, the Kyoto Protocol was replaced by the Paris Agreement. Aiming to bolster the world response to climate change, the Paris Agreement strives to ensure that global temperature rise remains well below 2°C above the pre-industrial level while endeavors are made to limit the increase to 1.5°C, both surpassing 2015 targets. It establishes a global stocktake meeting to assess the progress toward fulfilling the goals of the agreement and mandates every Nation to prepare national climate action plans, which are referred to as Nationally Determined Contributions (NDCs). The COP, which is the UNFCCC's highest decision organ, sustains annual gatherings to evaluate climate change advancement, needing decisions endorsed on the execution of the agreement. These summits have resulted in the endorsement of a number of key decisions and agreements, like the initiation of the Kyoto Protocol, the creation of the Green Climate Fund, and the acceptance of the Paris Agreement.

During the 1980s, scientific advancements and growing concerns about global warming led to calls for international collaboration to address climate change. In 1988, the WMO and the UNEP established the IPCC to provide policymakers with the latest scientific research and policy implications for climate change mitigation and adaptation. Following the recommendations of the IPCC and the 1990 Second World Climate Conference in Geneva, the international community began working on a legally binding convention to address the issue of GHG emissions.

The UNFCCC was adopted on May 9, 1992, and opened for signatories at the UNCED in Rio de Janeiro.[126] The Convention's main objective is to stabilize GHG concentrations in the atmosphere at a level that would

126 Ibid.

prevent dangerous anthropogenic interference with the climate system. It also emphasizes the principle of 'common but differentiated responsibilities' and recognizes vulnerable countries' specific needs and concerns, such as small island states and developing nations. The UNFCCC divides its signatory countries into three categories: Annex I countries (developed nations), Annex II countries (developed nations with special financial responsibilities), and Non-Annex I countries (developing nations). Annex I countries must adopt national policies and measures to limit their GHG emissions and report their progress regularly. Annex II countries must provide financial resources and technical assistance to Non-Annex I countries to help them meet their reporting requirements and implement climate change mitigation and adaptation measures.

Over the years, the UNFCCC has created several significant global agreements and protocols to address climate change. The Kyoto Protocol was the first legally binding agreement from the UNFCCC framework. Adopted in 1997, the Protocol established specific emission reduction targets for Annex I countries, to reduce overall emissions by at least 5% below 1990 levels during the commitment period of 2008–2012. The Kyoto Protocol was superseded by the Paris Agreement in 2016. Intended to reinforce the global response to the climate crisis, the Paris Agreement was signed in 2015, ratified in 2016, and targets a reduction of global temperature increase to 2°C relative to pre-industrial levels – with an aspirational limit of 1.5°C. Additionally, the agreement stipulates that all countries must present NDCs, detailing their climate mitigation strategies. These documents outline milestones and benchmarks to be achieved by each party, providing a means to evaluate their efforts cumulatively through the established periodic global stocktake. The COP is their supreme organ and meets on an annual basis for a convention on climate change. Through these conventions, a number of landmark decisions have been made, including – but not limited to – the Paris Agreement, the Kyoto Protocol, and the establishment of the Green Climate Fund.

Critics have pointed out that the UNFCCC has not adequately addressed global GHG emission mitigation, which remains a central issue in need of focus. Many feel that the principle of 'common but differentiated responsibilities' has caused an unequal gap in the allocation of emission reduction responsibilities. Furthermore, the slow pace of progress toward more ambitious climate targets is often attributed to the fact that international negotiations are multifaceted and countries have competing domestic priorities. It is clear that sustained cooperation by countries under the UNFCCC framework will be vital to address these criticisms and challenges that arise as a result of business waste capitalism-driven climate change.

4.3.4 Global Compact

The United Nations Global Compact, also referred to as UNGC, is an initiative that seeks for businesses around the world to adopt sustainable and socially responsible measures, and report them.[127] Launched in 2000, the UNGC's intention is to align business and corporate activities with ten fundamental human rights, labor, environmental, and anti-corruption principles.

The ten principles of the UNGC are based on the Universal Declaration of Human Rights, the ILO's Declaration on Fundamental Principles and Rights at Work, the Rio Declaration on Environment and Development, and the United Nations Convention Against Corruption. They promote human rights, labor, environmental, and anti-corruption policies.[128] These principles are meant to help businesses adopt ethical policies by becoming socially and environmentally responsible.

In order to take part in the UNGC, member companies and organizations have to incorporate all of the principles and policies of the UNGC into their business plans, everyday operations, and even the culture of the organization. Moreover, they are encouraged to take up efforts that are in furtherance of social purposes. Additionally, signatories have to self-evaluate annually and report on their initiatives and actions taken in order to implement the principles, thus fostering transparency. For instance, Novo Nordisk, a global healthcare company, has made strong commitments toward UNGC's principles.[129] Novo Nordisk has depended heavily on international corporations for its global expansion, which has resulted in the internalization of sustainability in the core operations of the company. The company's policies toward non-communicable diseases and improving access to healthcare in developing nations fulfill the UNGC's fundamental human rights and sustainable development principles. Unilever has also been known to advance environmental sustainability and social responsibility. With its Sustainable Living Plan, Unilever promises to lessen its environmental effects, all while improving the lives of millions around the world.[130] It is claiming to reach these goals within a set timeframe, which fosters accountability and makes great strides toward social responsibility. This action falls under the UNGC's demand regarding responsibility toward the environment, labor, and human rights.

127 See About the UN Global Compact. (2024). *United Nations Global Compact*. Retrieved May 19, 2024, from https://unglobalcompact.org/about

128 Compact, G. (2024). *The ten principles of the UN global compact*. United Nations. Retrieved May 19, from https://unglobalcompact.org/what-is-gc/mission/principles https://unglobalcompact.org/what-is-gc/mission/principles

129 Novo Nordisk, N. (2023). *Human rights report*. https://au.search.yahoo.com/yhs/search?hspart=mnet&hsimp=yhs-001&type=type9043493-spa-796-84469&param1=796&param2=84469&p=Novo+Nordisk%2C+a+global+healthcare+company%2C+has+demonstrated+a+strong+commitment+to+the+UNGC+principles.+ www.novonordisk.com/content/dam/nncorp/global/en/sustainable-business/pdfs/esg-portal/2024/novo-nordisk-human-rights-report-2023.pdf

130 Unilever. (2024). *Leading and delivering on sustainability through our Compass commitments*. Unilever. Retrieved May 19, from www.unilever.com/news/news-search/2023/leading-and-delivering-on-sustainability-through-our-compass-commitments/

Through the promotion of sustainability and responsible business practices the UNGC has tremendously influenced the global business community. It has prodded businesses to devise their operations using social and environmental sustainability as frameworks.[131] Moreover, the UNGC fostered interaction and collaboration among businesses, governments, and civil society, which has facilitated the sharing of great ideas and innovative practices to tackle global issues.[132] The UNGC, like any other organization, has its challenges which include low participation from developing countries' businesses, enforcement of principles, impact measurement, and several others.[133] Looking ahead, the UNGC aims to expand its reach and influence, focusing on engaging SMEs and driving progress toward the Sustainable Development Goals.

4.3.5 Corporate Sustainability Due Diligence Directive

The Corporate Sustainability Due Diligence Directive (CSDDD) originating from the European Commission was passed in March 2024.[134] It is an attempt to improve business responsibility and sustainability frameworks in the EU. The directive tries to mitigate social and destructive environmental effects of business activities, especially with regard to human impact and labor, and eco-sensitive issues.[135] The CSDDD seeks to achieve responsible international business behavior and foster sustainable development within the EU.

The directive would obligate some businesses to undertake due diligence to identify, prevent, and mitigate human rights, environmental, and

131 Rasche, A. (2020). The United Nations Global Compact and the sustainable development goals. In *Research handbook of responsible management* (pp. 228–241). Edward Elgar Publishing.

132 Brown, J. A., Clark, C., & Buono, A. F. (2018). The United Nations global compact: Engaging implicit and explicit CSR for global governance. *Journal of Business Ethics, 147*, 721–734. Gilbert, D. U., & Behnam, M. (2013). Trust and the United Nations global compact: A network theory perspective. *Business & Society, 52*(1), 135–169; Nelson, J., Anesa, M., & Grayson, D. (2017). United Nations global compact (UNGC). In *Corporate responsibility coalitions* (pp. 328–346). Routledge.

133 Andrews, N. (2020). The UN global compact: An overview of the promise and pitfalls. In *The Palgrave handbook of corporate social responsibility* (pp. 1–21). Palgrave Macmillan; Williams, O. F. (2014). The United Nations global compact: What did it promise? *Journal of Business Ethics, 122*, 241–251.

134 Kilsby, R., & Puzniak-Holford, M. (2024, April 19). The EU corporate sustainability due diligence directive is final. What now for your organisation? *Deloitte.* Retrieved May 19, 2024, from www2.deloitte.com/uk/en/blog/emea-centre-for-regulatory-strategy/2024/the-eu-corporate-sustainability-due-diligence-directive-is-final-what-now-for-your-organisation.html; Patz, C. (2022). The EU's draft corporate sustainability due diligence directive: A first assessment. *Business and Human Rights Journal, 7*(2), 291–297.

135 European Commission. (2024). *Corporate sustainability due diligence.* Retrieved May 19, 2024, from https://commission.europa.eu/business-economy-euro/doing-business-eu/corporate-sustainability-due-diligence_en

corporate governance issues relating to their operations and value chains.[136] Corporations would need to evaluate the risk their operations pose to society and the environment and implement appropriate actions to avert or lessen such impacts. The CSDDD has increased transparency and reporting requirements which include disclosure on due diligence measures and risk sustainability actions taken. The directive provides that local communities, local workers, and other civil society organizations that are impacted by these business activities have access to adequate remedy processes when there are negative impacts.[137]

Like any policy, the CSDDD has its supporters and critics.[138] Supporters claim that the directive serves as an important step toward sustainable and responsible businesses, upholding human rights, and mitigating the impacts of harmful activities on nature. They argue that it will enable fair competition among businesses while strengthening the EU's position as a forerunner in corporate sustainability on an international level. On the other hand, some critics have pointed out the potential compliance burden on businesses, especially SMEs.[139] They claim it may lead to higher administrative burdens and costs for companies, especially those working within intricate supply chains.

4.3.6 National Action Plan on Responsible Business Conduct

The National Action Plan on Responsible Business Conduct is a framework that outlines how governments, private-sector companies, and other stakeholders can promote responsible business practices.[140] It aims to positively

136 Corporate Sustainability Due Diligence Directive (CSDDD). (2024). *ERM.* Retrieved May 19, 2024, from www.erm.com/insights/corporate-sustainability-due-diligence-directive-csddd/

137 Kilsby, R., & Puzniak-Holford, M. (2024, April 19). The EU corporate sustainability due diligence directive is final. What now for your organisation? *Deloitte.* Retrieved May 19, 2024, from www2.deloitte.com/uk/en/blog/emea-centre-for-regulatory-strategy/2024/the-eu-corporate-sustainability-due-diligence-directive-is-final-what-now-for-your-organisation.html

138 Ventura, L. (2023). Corporate sustainability due diligence and the new boundaries of the firms in the European Union. *European Business Law Review, 34*(2); Andersen, P. K., Arvidsson, N., Bartkus, G., Bergþórsson, A. F., Bité, V., Hansen, S. F., Hansen, J. L., Johansson, S., Kinander, M., & Knuds, M. (2022). Response to the proposal for a directive on corporate sustainability due diligence by Nordic and Baltic company law scholars. *Nordic and European Company Law Working Paper Series* (22–01).

139 Delille, T., Fillmann, A., Seranne, M., Giovannini, V., & Economides, C. (2024). The highly debated Corporate Sustainability Due Diligence Directive at risk of a definitive block. *Squire Patton Boggs.* Retrieved May 19, 2024, from www.squirepattonboggs.com/en/insights/publications/2024/03/the-highly-debated-corporate-sustainability-due-diligence-directive-at-risk-of-a-definitive-block

140 U.S. Department of State. (2024). *The U.S. Government's national action plan on responsible business conduct.* United States of America. Retrieved May 19, 2024, from www.state.gov/responsible-business-conduct-national-action-plan/

impact communities, ensure transparency, respect human rights, and promote good governance.[141] The key components of an *NAP* can vary depending on the context. The most common components, however, are as follows.

(a) Forming the Federal Advisory Committee on Responsible Business Conduct

The Department of State will collaborate with relevant private-sector constituents, affected communities, unions, civil society, academia, and other entities to support the further development and implementation of RBC policies and initiatives. The Federal Advisory Committee on Responsible Business Conduct will significantly contribute toward advancing RBC concerns and facilitating the realization of the NAP.[142]

(b) Amending Federal Procurement Policies and Processes to Enhance Respect for Human Rights

The U.S. Government Hotlines Working Group led by the Departments of Health, Human Services, Homeland Security, and Justice will have the mandate to explore ways of enhancing the reporting of human trafficking violations by federal contractors. The Department of State will undertake an initial contracting of high-risk contracts with a human trafficking risk mapping process. Guidance will be developed by Customs and Border Protection of the Department of Homeland Security to refrain from doing business with the federal government for forced labor violations. The Department of Defense will review sponsoring the International Code of Conduct Association for Private Security Providers for its private security vendors.[143]

(c) Strengthening Access to Remedy

In the United States, the Department of State undertakes negotiations with stakeholders to outsource initiatives for the National Contact Point (NCP) of the OECD National Guidelines for Multinational Enterprises on Responsible Business Conduct. Suggested reforms involve establishing an advisory committee, lifting the mandated confidentiality clause, and amending the rules of procedures. Furthermore, the NCP will create a complete policy on reprisals, enhance the accessibility of the website, and look for ways to strengthen its functions. The Department of Labor is focused on encouraging social compliance services that are initiated by the workers, as well as safeguarding labor

141 U.S. Department of State. (2024). *U.S. Government's national action plan on responsible business conduct*. U.S. Department of State. Retrieved May 25, 2024, from www.state.gov/u-s-governments-national-action-plan-on-responsible-business-conduct/
142 Ibid.
143 Ibid.

rights within international production networks. The Export-Import Bank of the United States is working to strengthen remedy procedures and improve access to remedy and the effectiveness of project-based grievance mechanisms.[144]

(d) Providing Resources to Businesses

The U.S. Department of Labor is establishing the Responsible Business Conduct and Labor Rights InfoHub, an online resource that promotes better labor rights outcomes in business operations and value chains. The U.S. government will release business guidance for Tribal Consultation and Engagement with Indigenous and Affected Communities, and issue crucial guidance for online platforms to protect human rights defenders. Additionally, guidance will be developed to encourage investors to conduct due diligence for investments in technologies impacting human rights. Lastly, the U.S. government will provide business advisories for companies, investors, and stakeholders in specific countries and sectors.[145]

The NAP clearly outlines expectations for companies regarding RBC. It helps businesses understand their obligations and encourages them to align their practices with human rights, labor rights, and environmental standards.[146] By leveraging the influence of U.S. government financial resources, the NAP encourages companies to adopt responsible practices, leading to better risk management and improved sustainability across value chains. The commitment to robust enforcement of U.S. law ensures that companies are held accountable for their actions, deterring unethical behavior and promoting responsible conduct.[147] The NAP emphasizes communication with external stakeholders, fostering transparency and collaboration. Companies engaging in RBC can build trust with customers, investors, and communities.[148]

4.3.7 Global Reporting Initiative

With growing knowledge of the impact humanity has placed on the world, corporations are often expected to roll back on their pollution damages.[149] The GRI is a major player in sustaining these efforts by providing businesses

144 Ibid.
145 Ibid.
146 United States Government. (2024). *National action plan on responsible business conduct.*
147 Ibid.
148 Ibid.
149 Reporting, S. (2022). *Global reporting initiative.*

an opportunity to report on their sustainability projects and assess their developments.[150]

An independent international non-profit organization, GRI actively advances the reporting of sustainability and assists businesses in the assessment and disclosure of their ESG (environmental, social, and governance) performance.[151] GRI provides businesses with a system to effectively monitor and report on their sustainability activities and evaluate their improvement over periods of time.[152] This system consists of particular frameworks and a range of guidelines and indicators that enable businesses to report on their ESG performance.

One of the primary headways made by GRI mechanisms that concentrate on contending with corporate pollution is the 'polluter pays' rule. This rule asserts that the responsible company must take care of monitoring, controlling, and restoring pollution done by them. Companies must be accountable for their contribution toward solving the problem. GRI has come up with a method for managing this mechanism by making companies report the level of pollution they cause alongside the garnering efforts made to mitigate it. In order to accomplish this framework, GRI has developed pollution indicators for companies and industries to follow for boasting about their level of pollution and pollution control efforts they have put in. These indicators cover all aspects of the environment such as air, water, and waste. With regard to reporting, companies have to account for not only emissions and discharges and waste generation but also control measures undertaken as well as investment in pollution reduction efforts. A company can use the underlying framework to gauge pollution levels, control efforts made, and mitigate further pollution increments. A company's initiative of reporting emissions can shed light on environmental performance, which stakeholders can leverage to make favorable decisions with regard to operating or investing in the company.

The adoption of such reporting frameworks has increased, which is evidence of change with regard to the impact of this approach and its mechanisms.

In 2020, more than 10,000 organizations from 160 countries used GRI's framework to report on their sustainability activities. By 2022, four out of five of the largest global companies reported using GRI for their reports.[153]

150 Global Reporting Initiative (GRI). (2024b). *The global leader for impact reporting*. Global Reporting Initiative. Retrieved May 19, 2024, from www.globalreporting.org/

151 Woods, M. (2003). The global reporting initiative. *The CPA Journal*, *73*(6), 60; Willis, A. (2003). The role of the global reporting initiative's sustainability reporting guidelines in the social screening of investments. *Journal of Business Ethics*, *43*(3), 233–237.

152 Boshoff, A. (2023, June 19). An overview of the GRI standards. *BDO Australia*. Retrieved May 19, 2024, from www.bdo.com.au/en-au/insights/esg-sustainability/an-overview-of-the-gri-standards#!

153 Global Reporting Initiative (GRI). (2022, October 31). *Four-in-five largest global companies report with GRI*. Global Reporting Initiative. Retrieved May 19, 2024, from www.globalreporting.org/news/news-center/four-in-five-largest-global-companies-report-with-gri/

This indicates that companies are beginning to acknowledge the importance of sustainability reporting and the need to combat pollution. As an example, Nestlé has resorted to using GRI's framework to report on its sustainability efforts and pollution control measures. Nestlé is setting targets to reduce GHG emissions, water consumption, and waste generation and is reportedly making strides. Another example is the multinational consumer goods company Unilever. Unilever has taken up GRI's framework in reporting sustainable corporate social responsibility efforts such as pollution control measures. Unilever is also setting targets to reduce GHG emissions, water consumption, and waste generation, and it is reportedly making strides. GRI has also contributed to the creation of other sustainability reporting frameworks like sustainability accounting standards board and the task force on climate-related financial disclosures.

Companies aiming to reduce pollution through GRI's reporting framework should be guided by a few best practices.[154] First, it is recommended that companies define the goals to be achieved in terms of pollution reduction and assess the journey toward accomplishing these goals. Furthermore, companies need to adopt efficient and effective measures for controlling pollution. In addition, the companies should participate actively with their stakeholders and report their environmental performance honestly and accurately. This way, stakeholders are instrumental in assisting and implementing the GRI reporting framework within the pollution control domain. It is especially important for stakeholders to hold companies to greater standards of transparency and accountability regarding pollution levels. The stakeholders are also in a position to give companies feedback on their performance on environmental issues and offer suggestions on how to improve.

GRI's expansion in its use has been very encouraging, particularly as more companies seem to be adopting its reporting framework.[155] The resolution made by GRI regarding corporate pollution is beginning to have an impact, given the increasing stakeholder pressures for transparency and accountability. GRI is expected to enhance the pollution control policy in corporations as well as expand its focus on the economy toward cleaner low-carbon systems. The reporting framework designed by GRI may assist firms in locating avenues for emission mitigation and the adoption of renewable energy, in

154 Global Reporting Initiative (GRI). (2024c). *Premium tools for better reporting*. Global Reporting Initiative. Retrieved May 19, 2024, from www.globalreporting.org/reporting-support/reporting-tools/

155 Vigneau, L., Humphreys, M., & Moon, J. (2015). How do firms comply with international sustainability standards? Processes and consequences of adopting the global reporting initiative. *Journal of Business Ethics*, *131*, 469–486; Halkos, G., & Nomikos, S. (2021). Corporate social responsibility: Trends in global reporting initiative standards. *Economic Analysis and Policy*, *69*, 106–117; Rimmel, G. (2020). Global reporting initiative. In *Accounting for sustainability* (pp. 111–125). Routledge.

addition to assisting the transition to these systems.[156] On the other hand, GRI faces challenges and constraints to boundaries that explain the reporting framework. One constraint is that GRI lacks mandatory stipulations, meaning not all corporations have to adopt the framework. This particular voluntary aspect limits the efficiency of GRI's initiatives pertaining to pollution control. Another limitation is that the comprehension complexity of GRI's reporting framework makes it easier to manipulate and create inconsistencies instead of seamlessly integrating them into the company's processes. The stakeholders who desire to evaluate the firm's position with regard to the environment end up having a hard time because of the disparity in reporting.

4.4 'Voluntarism,' 'Collaboration,' and 'Partnership' in Global Environmental Regulation

VOLUNTARISM

The social dimension of global governance of voluntarism is captured by the notion of non-state actions and initiatives undertaken by non-state actors, which include non-governmental organizations, business entities, and local actors. It allows decision-making based on individual conditions and goals, often resulting in non-binding commitments that complement traditional regulations.[157] Voluntarism for a business corporation is distributing resources to benefit society and the company.[158] It is believed that there is a positive correlation between voluntarism and value creation, as proactive behavior leads to innovation, ultimately improving the value generated by the firm.[159]

The neo-liberal school of thought provides the conceptual foundation of 'voluntarism' in regulation. Neoliberalism is characterized by its core principles of individualism, market freedom, and deregulation. Individualism underscores the significance of personal autonomy in the pursuit of self-interest, which is evident in the belief in independent legal entities within the framework of neoliberalism. In this context, a business is regarded as a distinct artificial person, allowing it to pursue its own objectives without being constrained by government regulations.[160] Neoliberalism emphasizes the concept

156 Global Reporting Initiative (GRI). (2024a). *Business reporting on the SDGs*. Global Reporting Initiative. Retrieved May 19, 2024, from www.globalreporting.org/goals-and-targets-database/

157 United Nations Volunteers. (2014). *Environmental sustainability and voluntarism: Considerations for post-2015 development agenda*. United Nations.

158 Burke, L., & Logsdon, J. M. (1996). How corporate social responsibility pays off. *Long Range Planning*, *29*(4), 495–502.

159 Ibid.

160 Hanrahan, P., Ramsay, I., & Stapledon, G. (2002). *Commercial applications of company law*. CCH Australia.

of 'market freedom,' which prioritizes the reliance on unfettered market forces for efficient resource allocation, free from political intervention.[161] This concept is closely associated with deregulation, which advocates for the gradual relaxation or elimination of legal business regulations to foster entrepreneurial activity within society.[162] Milton Friedman argues against mandatory social responsibilities for businesses, stating that they exist to serve the monetary interest of their investors.[163] According to the Coase theorem, setting market standards is unnecessary for achieving the social optimum, as private economic players can resolve difficulties through negotiation when property rights are well-established.[164]

4.4.1 Collaboration

In global environmental governance, collaboration entails the active participation of diverse stakeholders such as governments, intergovernmental organizations, non-governmental organizations, and businesses, uniting to confront environmental challenges and promote sustainable management of natural resources. This concept embodies the principles of joint decision-making, shared accountability, and concerted efforts to address intricate environmental issues that extend beyond national borders.[165]

Collaboration in environmental governance can be initiated in various ways. It can be self-initiated by individuals or groups.[166] IOs, citizen groups, business corporations, stakeholders, or a combination of these parties can also

161 Fourcade, M., & Healy, K. (2007). Moral views of market society. *Annual Review of Sociology*, *33*, 285–311.

162 See generally, Mudge, S. L. (2008). What is neo-liberalism? *Socio-Economic Review*, *6*(4), 703–731.

163 Friedman, M. (1970). A Friedman doctrine: The social responsibility of business is to increase its profits. *New York Times Magazine*, *13*, 33; Windsor, D. (2006). Corporate social responsibility: Three key approaches. *Journal of Management Studies*, *43*(1), 93–114.

164 Coase, R. (1960). The problem of social cost. *The Journal of Law and Economics*, *3*(October), 1–44; Peters, M., & Turner, R. K. (2004). SME environmental attitude and participation in local-scale voluntary initiatives: Some practical applications. *Journal of Environmental Planning and Management*, *47*(3), 451.

165 Emerson, K., & Nabatchi, T. (2015). *Collaborative governance regimes*. Georgetown University Press; Imperial, M. T. (2005). Using collaboration as a governance strategy: Lessons from six watershed management programs. *Administration & Society*, *37*(3), 281–320. Milward, H. B., & Provan, K. G. (2000). Governing the hollow state. *Journal of Public Administration Research and Theory*, *10*(2), 359–380.

166 Berthod, O., Blanchet, T., Busch, H., Kunze, C., Nolden, C., & Wenderlich, M. (2023). The rise and fall of energy democracy: 5 cases of collaborative governance in energy systems. *Environmental Management*, *71*(3), 551–564; Lakshmisha, A., & Thiel, A. (2022). Bridging actors and their role in co-managing lakes: Cases from Greater Bengaluru Metropolitan Region (GBMR). *Sustainability*, *14*(10), 5865.

initiate collaborations.[167] Government agencies, funders, or other 'top-down' forces can also encourage or compel members to participate in a collaborative governance regime.[168] Furthermore, external organizations can serve as a convener and catalyze the initiation of a collaborative process.[169]

Including 'collaboration' in the post-2015 environmental development framework is crucial. When properly facilitated, collaboration supports environmentally sustainable outcomes and promotes long-term processes. Integrating human development, poverty eradication, and environmental objectives is highlighted in these processes. 'Collaboration' can help connect these dimensions, especially in addressing climate change and disaster risk. Natural disasters, often linked to climate change, significantly affect human and economic development.[170]

How global organizations have structured their environmental protection initiatives and developed their policies for engaging with environmental stakeholders demonstrates the need for comprehensive, cross-sector, and multi-stakeholder approaches to address the pressing environmental challenges of the 21st century.[171] Collaboration is a valuable resource in all societies, uniting communities worldwide to tackle environmental issues. Well-facilitated collaboration contributes to sustainable environmental outcomes and fosters long-term processes. It aids in strengthening community resilience, enhancing local self-sufficiency, empowering grassroots movements, and creating lasting changes in attitudes and mindsets, all of which are essential for sustaining environmental progress.

Collaboration is important, and in fact critical, toward solving complex problems in the environment, such as dealing with ambiguities and feedback loops. The ability to solve these problems is located among the stakeholders at different degrees of the government and organizations, which means they must decide and coordinate together.[172]

167 Moore, E. A., & Koontz, T. M. (2003). Research note a typology of collaborative watershed groups: Citizen-based, agency-based, and mixed partnerships. *Society &Natural Resources*, *16*(5), 451–460; Ulibarri, N., Emerson, K., Imperial, M. T., Jager, N. W., Newig, J., & Weber, E. (2020). How does collaborative governance evolve? Insights from a medium-n case comparison. *Policy and Society*, *39*(4), 617–637.

168 Emerson, K., & Nabatchi, T. (2015). *Collaborative governance regimes*. Georgetown University Press.

169 Ansell, C., & Gash, A. (2018). Collaborative platforms as a governance strategy. *Journal of Public Administration Research and Theory*, *28*(1), 16–32.

170 Ibid.

171 United Nations Volunteers. (2014). *Environmental sustainability and voluntarism: Considerations for post-2015 development agenda*. United Nations.

172 Ulibarri, N., Imperial, M. T., Siddiki, S., & Henderson, H. (2023). Drivers and dynamics of collaborative governance in environmental management. *Environmental Management*, *71*(3), 495–504.

Global governance covers the cooperation of many units to provide for or control international problems like the environment, human rights, or economic imbalances. In this scenario, voluntarism and collaboration are driving concepts which shape how stakeholders deal with these multifaceted problems. To start with, voluntarism defines actions and obligations undertaken voluntarily by non-state actors who take unilateral decisions, often leading to non-committal declarations and actions termed as initiatives, while collaboration implies partnerships and coordinated work among state and non-state actors that result in binding contracts or shared duties. Freedom of choice – or individuation – encapsulated in voluntarism becomes decision-making and joint action, or collaboration, among the stakeholders. In spite of what might appear as contradictions, voluntarism and collaboration are two ideas that, in fact, can coexist without excluding each other. In numerous such case scenarios, both can work together, where voluntarism nurtures innovation and flexibility, while collaboration acts as a plateau for fostered, cooperative actions put forth collectively.

4.4.2 Partnership

The term partnership underscores the need for active inclusion and participatory decision-making in the context of environmental protection and sustainable management of natural resources. In business management, a partnership is defined as a profit-oriented economic entity organized and run by two or more persons who contribute capital, real estate, work, or expertise and share in the profits and losses.[173] In environmental governance, partnership involves multiple parties working toward shared objectives but with unequal distribution of costs and profits.[174] It signifies a collaborative and mutually beneficial relationship between diverse actors, such as governments, IOs, and the private sector, to address environmental challenges and promote sustainable development.

Partnerships in global environmental regulation have a transformative impact, driving collaboration, innovation, accountability, and sustainable practices to address environmental challenges and promote responsible stewardship of the planet's resources.[175]

They stimulate economic activity, create jobs, and capture investments from various sources, in addition to aiding the development of green technologies

173 Ladonko, L., Kosach, I., Mykhailovska, O., & Filipova, N. (2022). Partnership as a specific form of business integration. *Scientific Horizons, 25*(2), 20–28. Scientific Horizons: Dnipro, Ukraine. https://doi.org/10.48077/scihor.25(2).2022.20-28

174 Ivashchenko, N., & Isaeva, L. (2021). Basic principles of partnership as the factor of sustainable development in the context of business ecosystems. *E3S web of conferences.*

175 Witte, J. M., Benner, T., & Streck, C. (2017). Partnerships and networks in global environmental governance: Moving to the next stage. In *Governance and sustainability* (pp. 141–152). Routledge.

and infrastructures.[176] Furthermore, alliances foster resourcefulness and environmentally sustainable technologies and practices, resulting in cost reduction for companies and the government, thus stimulating economic growth in renewable energies, clean transportation, and sustainable agriculture.

The rise of 'voluntarism,' 'collaboration,' and 'partnership' as norms in global environmental governance has further established the base of a private ordering system in this governance.

4.4.3 Private Ordering System

In the past three decades, utilitarian and libertarian philosophers have called for a complete separation of state and law, also known as the privatization-of-law paradigm.[177] This has reignited the long-running debate about the theoretical concept of the state of nature. The paradigm suggests that without state law, 'market communities' would naturally work to establish law and order.[178] Proponents of this view cite private-ordering literature – empirical studies that claim to have found instances where market communities supply their own law and order without government interference.[179]

Most analyses of private ordering provide specific case-based explanations for their development.[180] However, some scholars put forth a more general hypothesis about the growth of private orders.[181] These scholars, often legal economists, explain extralegal ordering in terms of cost-benefit analysis (CBA), if communities choose private ordering for efficiency and maximization of utility. Furthermore, they view organizations implementing private orders as homogeneous entities, regardless of how incentives are distributed among group members.[182]

176 Witte, J. M., Streck, C., & Benner, T. (2003). The road from Johannesburg: What future for partnerships in global environmental governance. In *Progress or Peril* (pp. 59–84).

177 Sagy, T. (2011). What's so private about private ordering? *Law & Society Review*, *45*(4), 923–954.

178 Fisher, T. (2008). Nomos without narrative. *Theoretical Inquiries in Law*, *9*(2), 473–502, 488.

179 Benson, B. L. (2013). *The enterprise of law: Justice without the state.* Independent Institute; Friedman, L. M. (1975). *The legal system: A social science perspective.* Russell Sage Foundation; Osterfeld, D. (2017). Freedom, society, and the state: An investigation into the possibility of society without government (excerpt). In *Anarchy and the law* (pp. 504–537). Routledge; Schofield, N. (1985). Anarchy, altruism, and cooperation: A review. *Social Choice and Welfare*, *2*(3), 207–219.

180 Bernstein, L. (2013). Opting out of the legal system: Extralegal contractual relations in the diamond industry. In *Contract-freedom and restraint* (pp. 359–403). Routledge; Feldman, E. A. (2006). The Tuna Court: Law and norms in the world's premier fish market. *California Law Review*, *94*, 313.

181 Ellickson, R. C. (1991). *Order without law: How neighbors settle disputes.* Harvard University Press.

182 Sagy, T. (2011). What's so private about private ordering? *Law & Society Review*, *45*(4), 923–954, 925.

Private disputes often arise within socially stratified groups, where individuals are unequally classified based on their social capital (money, position, and power).[183] These groups, whether industries or cultural communities, are interested in establishing an internal process for resolving conflicts among their members. The hierarchical social structure enables leaders to incentivize others to use the private conflict resolution system. When access to resources or participation in the community depends on using privately established conflict resolution mechanisms, individuals not only 'choose' to use these private forums but also comply with their decisions due to the risk of losing access to resources.[184] As mentioned, organizations that create and utilize private conflict resolution systems typically have a hierarchical, diverse incentive structure.

Recognizing that incentive structures are shaped by individuals' positions within the social hierarchy rather than distributed randomly among group members enhances our ability to explain how the group selects controllers and adopts substantive norms.[185] When a private order emerges, those in positions of power often rely on it to maintain their authority by upholding and establishing norms that reinforce intragroup stratification, thus ensuring the continuity of the private legal system and their control over the group.[186] This section highlights how conflict resolution procedures and their governing rules perpetuate the power structures from which they originated.

Private orders can be viewed as strategies that uphold social hierarchy within a specific framework. They enable dominant group members to maintain power by establishing norms, resolving disputes, and exerting influence over others. This dominance allows them to enforce decisions and punishments, thus solidifying their role as conflict resolution professionals. By controlling group norms, they can preserve the existing social structure. This perspective presents private ordering as a means for societies to preserve their hierarchical structure and private methods of conflict resolution without necessitating a deliberate structure and plotting by the group's leadership.[187]

The private ordering system in environmental governance involves private entities participating in environmental regulation. This participation can manifest in various ways, including private organizations developing voluntary environmental standards, delegating environmental monitoring and enforcement to private companies, and forming public-private partnerships to address environmental issues.

Within the private ordering system of global environmental regulation, 'collaboration' refers to the cooperation and coordination among private entities, such as corporations, industry associations, NGOs, and other non-state

183 Ibid., p. 931.
184 Ibid.
185 Ibid., p. 932.
186 Ibid.
187 Ibid.

actors, to establish rules, standards, and practices for environmental protection and sustainability. This collaboration often occurs outside of traditional government-led regulatory frameworks and involves self-regulation and voluntary initiatives within the private sector. 'Self-regulation' in this context refers to the voluntary decision-making capacity of private entities. It involves voluntary actions and initiatives that private entities undertake to develop and adopt environmental standards and codes of conduct to guide their operations and supply chains toward sustainable and environmentally responsible practices. Self-regulated corporations seek assistance from independent organizations to demonstrate compliance with environmental standards, using eco-labels to inform consumers about environmentally friendly products. They also form partnerships to tackle common environmental challenges, such as reducing carbon emissions, managing water resources, and conserving biodiversity.

4.5 Transnational Corporations and the 'Private Ordering System' in Global Environmental Regulation

The development of the private ordering system in global environmental regulation is a topic that requires extensive research.[188] There are several reasons behind the creation of this system.[189] Two of the most important reasons include the increasing influence of TNCs and the inability of sovereign states to regulate development partners effectively. States have failed to establish a suitable regulatory system for holding corporations accountable as key partners in development initiatives. Another contributing factor to the development of this system is the success of large corporations in influencing the policy decisions of major countries and organizations.

The UN's Draft Code of Conduct for Transnational Corporations was a significant topic of discussion within the UN system for many years. It emphasized the responsibility of TNCs and their home countries to establish health and safety standards for workers in their subsidiaries in developing

188 For a detailed discussion about this system, see generally, Appel, P. A., & Irvin, T. R. (2012). 11. Public regulatory encouragement to the adoption of private ordering systems to achieve environmental protection through sustainable commerce. In *How public regulation changes corporate governance practice–corporate board reform in Taiwan* (p. 251); Vogel, D. (2008). Private global business regulation. *Annual Review of Political Science*, *11*, 261–282; Héritier, A., Mueller-Debus, A. K., & Thauer, C. R. (2009). The firm as an inspector: Private ordering and political rules. *Business and Politics*, *11*(4), 1–32; Perez, O. (2012). International environmental law as a field of multi-polar governance: The case of private transnational environmental regulation. *Santa Clara Journal of International Law*, *10*, 285; Wai, R. (2005). Transnational private law and private ordering in a contested global society. *Harvard International Law Journal*, *46*, 471.

189 Rimmel, G. (2020). Global reporting initiative. In *Accounting for sustainability* (pp. 111–125). Routledge; Macey, J. R. (1996). Public and private ordering and the production of legitimate and illegitimate legal rules. *Cornell Law Review*, *82*, 1123; West, M. D. (1999). Private ordering at the world's first futures exchange. *Michigan Law Review*, *98*, 2574.

countries. The UN formally started discussions for a draft of the Code in the early 1970s. It created the Commission on Transnational Corporations in 1974, and three years later, it presented the draft text of the Code to an Inter-governmental Working Group of the Commission.[190] The UN abandoned this initiative in 1992 due to significant conflicts among member countries.[191] Nonetheless, the debate established that TNCs have moral obligations to society, and crafting a global code or binding framework for TNCs is exceptionally challenging.

The OECD Guidelines for Multinational Enterprises, developed in 1977, are intended for TNCs operating in or from any OECD member country.[192] The updated OECD Guidelines outline non-binding principles and benchmarks for responsible business practices promoting socio-economic and environmental development, presenting a comprehensive social responsibility code for TNCs.[193] The purpose of the Guidelines is to standardize the regulation of TNC activities and remove any obstacles that may hinder their operations.[194] Although they serve as a non-binding model for safeguarding investment treaties, there are inconsistencies in the foreign direct investment's approach and regulation among member countries. Due to the absence of an effective enforcement mechanism, voluntary compliance, and confidentiality provisions, the global acceptance of the guidelines as a framework for TNCs

190 On request of the Economic and Social Council through its 1982/68 of October 27, 1982, number resolution, the Inter-Governmental Working Group prepared the draft code of conduct. This draft also considers a variety of resolutions adopted by the General Assembly and Economic and Social Council. It applies the ILO Tripartite Declaration of Principles concerning Multinational Enterprises.

191 "The most controversial part of the draft code was its section dealing with the general treatment of MNEs by host countries. It differed most significantly from the spirit of the OECD guidelines. The provisions under this heading reiterated the sovereignty of (host) states and described great importance to governmental rights rather than their responsibilities toward MNEs. Countries 'determine the role that such cooperation may be called to play in economic and social development'" (ECOSOC-CTC 1978, p 11), from Hajduk, T. (2019). An "instrument of moral persuasion" – Multinational enterprises and international codes of conduct in the 1970s. In M. M. Rahim (Ed.), *Code of conduct on transnational corporations: Challenges and opportunities* (pp. 23–43). Springer.

192 Some scholars argue that the OECD Guideline was a 'counter attack' to the UN initiative for a code on TNCs. See Hajduk, T. (2019). An "instrument of moral persuasion" – Multinational enterprises and international codes of conduct in the 1970s. In M. M. Rahim (Ed.), *Code of conduct on transnational corporations: Challenges and opportunities* (pp. 23–43). Springer, p. 33. See also Muchlinski, P. (2007). *Multinational enterprises and the law*. Oxford University Press.

193 The current text was enriched with the entirety of social responsibilities after a revision. The revision added a number of issues to the main text including an extension of labor rights, a direct referral to human rights assigning the multinational responsibilities, and a reference to their responsibility to the supply chain (i.e., business partners, suppliers, and sub-contractors). More importantly, the applicability guidelines cover extraterritorial activities of TNCs.

194 Hamilton, G. (1984). *The control of multinationals: What future for international codes of conduct in the 1980s?* Institute for Research and Information on Multinationals.

has been limited. Deva (2012) evaluated the strengths, weaknesses, and progress of this framework and ultimately concluded that despite some potential, specifically after the 2011 update, the OECD Guidelines are insufficient in ensuring TNCs uphold their human rights responsibilities across all their operations.[195]

All the roles the UNEPs have taken so far in promoting international cooperation on environmental issues have been based on 'voluntarism' and 'participation.' While the UNGC exists, some critics feel it lacks effective monitoring and enforcement protocols, causing many to perceive corporate participation as opportunistic. According to Nolan (2005) and Knudsen (2011), some companies may use the Compact to improve their public image without altering their behavior.[196] Additionally, the UN's facilitative approach, rather than enforcement, has led to concerns that companies can take advantage of the Compact without adhering to its principles. Sethi and Schepers (2014) even claim that publicly available data shows the Compact has not successfully encouraged signatory companies to integrate its principles into their policies and reports.[197] Schembera (2018) utilized stakeholder, network, and institutional theories to examine the impact of the Compact on companies.[198] While his findings showed some positive effects, they were significantly smaller than previous practitioner studies had revealed. Schembera also identified flaws in the Compact's accountability structure, as the implementation of its principles relies heavily on continuous stakeholder dialogue, which many scholars and studies have deemed insufficient for incentivizing companies toward its objectives. Scholars like Berliner and Prakash (2015), Deva (2006), and Rasche et al. (2013) have all highlighted this issue and urged more focus on the development of the UNGPs.[199]

The UNGP is a UN framework that was adopted in June 2011. It is widely recognized as the most authoritative document promoting the human rights

195 Deva, S. (2012). *Regulating corporate human rights violations: Humanizing business* (p. 88). Routledge.

196 Nolan, J. (2005). With power comes responsibility: human rights and corporate accountability. *University of New South Wales Law Journal*, *28*(3), 581–613. Knudsen, J. S. (2011). Company delistings from the UN Global Compact: Limited business demand or domestic governance failure? *Journal of Business Ethics*, *103*, 331–349.

197 Sethi, S. P., & Schepers, D. H. (2014). United Nations global compact: The promise–performance gap. *Business and Society Review*, *122*, 193–208.

198 Schembera, S. (2018). Implementing corporate social responsibility: Empirical insights on the impact of the UN Global Compact on its business participants. *Business & Society*, *57*(5), 783–825.

199 Berliner, D., & Prakash, A. (2015). "Bluewashing" the firm? Voluntary regulations, program design, and member compliance with the United Nations Global Compact. *Policy Studies Journal*, *43*(1), 115–138. Deva, S., & Bilchitz, D. (2013). *Human rights obligations of business: Beyond the corporate responsibility to respect?* Cambridge University Press; Rasche, A., Waddock, S., & McIntosh, M. (2013). The United Nations global compact: Retrospect and prospect. *Business & Society*, *52*(1), 6–30.

and responsibilities of both state and corporate enterprises. The significance of the UNGPs lies in its three core principles. First, it requires governments to safeguard human rights (Pillar 1), and second, it demands businesses to respect human rights (Pillar 2). Lastly, the third pillar focuses on providing access to remedy, which is the final step in enabling harmed individuals to seek justice through efficient legal and non-legal pathways.[200] The access to remedy pillar encompasses both legal and non-legal solutions and seeks to establish innovative institutional mechanisms for addressing grievances that involve the business and stakeholders at risk of human rights violations due to its activities.[201]

Deva and Bilchitz (2013) have raised concerns about the integrity of the implementation mechanism for the UNGPs.[202] They argue that the framework places excessive importance on consensus, devaluing the principles and enabling a 'consensus without content.' Similarly, Nolan (2013) points out that the language used in the UNGPs lacks authority and strength, emphasizing dialogue and consensus over ambition.[203] The UNGPs have not established mandatory global regulations or platforms for individuals affected by corporate practices to lodge complaints.[204] This UN initiative reinforces the voluntary nature of incorporating business and human rights and CSR into business operations rather than mandating compliance.[205]

Neither are the initiatives of the Advanced Global Initiative for Regulating Corporate Polluters (GIRCP) such an all-encompassing effort as this. It has come out as one of the main initiatives in the enforcement of regulation of practices of corporations on a global scale. It understands the importance of bringing all stakeholders in addressing the issue of corporate polluters. The initiative intends to mobilize all governments, NGOs, and relevant bodies across the globe to join forces and fight against corporate polluters and ensure that these corporate entities do not escape responsibility.[206]

The GIRCP has several distinguishing features that mark it as unique from other initiatives of environmental concern. One of the more apparent is the

200 (Justice, 2021).

201 Muchlinski, P. (2007). *Multinational enterprises and the law*. Oxford University Press.

202 Deva, S., & Bilchitz, D. (2013). *Human rights obligations of business: Beyond the corporate responsibility to respect?* Cambridge University Press.

203 Nolan, J. (2013). The corporate responsibility to respect rights: Soft law or not law? In *Human rights obligations of business: Beyond the corporate responsibility to respect* Cambridge University Press.

204 Muchlinski, P. (2021). The impact of the UN Guiding Principles on business attitudes to observing human rights. *Business and Human Rights Journal*, *6*(2), 212–226.

205 Muchlinski defines this voluntarism as a middle ground between stricter procedural requirements to manage human rights risks in corporate activities, which may be supported by national legal obligations, but falling short of complete international legal accountability for human rights violations (2021, p. 219).

206 West, M. D. (1999). Private ordering at the world's first futures exchange. *Michigan Law Review*, *98*, 2574.

strategy of harnessing the collective efforts of disparate actors against any single corporate polluter. The initiative aims to effectively assemble all the necessary tools from all NGOs in an attempt to create a powerful coalition that ensures that corporate entities take responsibility. It focuses on promoting sustainable practices and encouraging corporations to adopt environmentally friendly technologies. This is done through various measures, including incentives for corporations to adopt sustainable practices and penalties for those that do not. One notable example is the Montreal Protocol, established in 1987 to regulate the use of ozone-depleting substances. The protocol is claimed to have been effective in cutting down the use of controlled substances and preventing millions of cases of melanoma and other skin cancers. Another illustration is the EU Emission Trading System (ETS) created in 2005 to manage GHG emissions. The system has managed to reduce emissions and has been a model for other similar systems across the globe.[207]

As with any initiative, each government is free to enforce within its borders the policies mandated by the initiative. Moreover, governments have the freedom to determine the policies and foster innovation in sustainability within their jurisdictions. Unfortunately, so do other governments, which may undermine the success of the initiative. In some situations, businesses may lobby governments to become unwilling to control some business activities in the name of economic growth. It is vital for the government because they need to appreciate the fact that there are limits to how much a corporation should be allowed to pollute before control is needed and that such a unit is joint with the initiative.

GIRCP has many obstacles and critics. The most predominant issue is the one regarding the focus of the initiative, which seems to be too punitive toward businesses and not enough to foster the implementation of sustainable practices. Critics of the initiative also argue that it does not go far enough in regulating corporate practices. Some argue that non-compliance penalties are insufficient to deter corporations from engaging in environmentally damaging practices. This has also been the case for international treaties such as the Paris Agreement on Climate Change and the Basel Convention on the Control of Transboundary Movements of Hazardous Wastes and their Disposal. These treaties are often not enforced, and corporations continue to engage in harmful practices.

All global organizations and their initiatives for regulating TNCs' environmental performance at the global level are based on either or all these three

207 Utting, P. (2002). Regulating business via multistakeholder initiatives: A preliminary assessment. In *Voluntary approaches to corporate responsibility: Readings and a resource guide* (p. 61130); Sato, M., Rafaty, R., Calel, R., & Grubb, M. (2022). Allocation, allocation, allocation! The political economy of the development of the European Union Emissions Trading System. *Wiley Interdisciplinary Reviews: Climate Change*, *13*(5), e796.

themes: voluntarism, collaboration, and partnership.[208] These three themes have been established as guiding norms for global environmental regulation. As discussed, this has generated a private ordering system – a dominant system for regulating TNCs' social and environmental performances.

A private ordering system is a term used to describe the efforts of non-governmental organizations, industry associations, and other stakeholders to set voluntary standards and certification programs that hold corporations accountable for their environmental impact. These standards are created through a collaborative process involving input from diverse stakeholders, including corporations, civil society organizations, and governments. The main aim of private regulation is to encourage corporations to adopt sustainable practices and reduce their carbon footprint.

Private regulation is the cornerstone of this system. It involves depending on the capability and integrity of the regulated party without any influence from the government. In private regulation, the private party can self-regulate or seek assistance from another private entity to regulate a subject. Companies use several strategies viz-a-viz their self-regulation strategies to respond to their needs within the private ordering system. On the verge of the general public's increasing focus on ethical business practices, they formalized their communication strategies to inform the stakeholders about their ethical standing in operations. This is evident in the rise of corporate codes of conduct. Companies are increasingly integrating their values and standards into formalized codes of conduct to navigate the complex landscape of modern business.

A company's code of conduct outlines the organization's values, principles, and ethical standards, guiding employees and stakeholders on expected behavior and decision-making. A code of conduct also helps companies ensure compliance with legal requirements. This is particularly relevant in data privacy, anti-corruption, and environmental sustainability. A well-defined code of conduct helps safeguard the company's reputation by setting clear guidelines for responsible business practices. This is vital for companies using global supply chains. They need consistent ethical standards across diverse geographies as they operate in increasingly globalized markets. A code of conduct helps align practices across borders and within the supply chain.[209]

208 Kolk, A., Van Tulder, R., & Welters, C. (1999). International codes of conduct and corporate social responsibility: Can transnational corporations regulate themselves? *Transnational Corporations*, *8*(1), 143–180; Berry, M. A., & Rondinelli, D. A. (1998). Proactive corporate environmental management: A new industrial revolution. *Academy of Management Perspectives*, *12*(2), 38–50; Utting, P. (2002). Regulating business via multistakeholder initiatives: A preliminary assessment. In *Voluntary approaches to corporate responsibility: Readings and a resource guide* (p. 61130).

209 Compa, L., & Hinchliffe-Darricarrere, T. (1995). Enforcing international labor rights through corporate codes of conduct. *Columbia Journal of Transnational Law*, *33*, 663; Pati, R. (2018). Global regulation of corporate conduct: Effective pursuit of a slave-free supply chain. *American University Law Review*, *68*, 1821; Short, J. L., Toffel, M. W., & Hugill, A. R. (2016). Monitoring global supply chains. *Strategic Management Journal*, *37*(9), 1878–1897.

The criticism of the reach and effectiveness of codes of conduct is also increasing. Critics argue that some codes of conduct are too vague and lack specific guidelines, making it difficult for employees to understand what is expected of them. Some codes of conduct are criticized for not being effectively enforced, leading to a lack of accountability and inconsistent application of the rules. There is criticism that some companies only implement a code of conduct as a PR stunt without a genuine commitment to ethical business practices. Many codes of conduct contradict the actual performance of the companies, which leads to blame on companies' accusations of hypocrisy and lack of sincerity.[210]

These days, companies communicate their performance on their commitment (generally found in their code of conduct) related to society and the environment through their sustainability reports. By checking their sustainability reports, people get a general idea of the gaps between the set codes and the efforts enacted to meet the set codes. With growing awareness of the environmental impact of purchasing decisions, consumers are increasingly seeking sustainable products and practices. Therefore, the future of private regulation regarding global corporate pollution depends on corporations' commitment to embracing sustainable practices and consumers' demand for sustainable products. At this juncture, companies adopted reporting on environmental sustainability.[211]

Sustainability reporting is a crucial communication tool firms utilize to signal their commitment to sustainable development to various stakeholders. It involves providing financial and non-financial information transparently and reliably, catering to the growing interest of shareholders and the financial market in sustainable practices.[212] Sustainability reporting has experienced exponential growth, moving from a 'paucity' stage in 2000 to the 'saturation' stage in 2022, indicating its ongoing significance.[213] It is a widely recognized and accepted practice, with approximately 96% of the largest 250 companies producing sustainability reports in 2020.[214]

210 Zakaria, M., Garanča, Z., & Sobeih, A. (2012). Cultural and legal challenges in implementing code of conduct in supply chain management of mobile phone industries: Sony Ericsson case study. *Social Responsibility Journal*, *8*(2), 227–241; Basu, R. (2023). *Managing global supply chains: Contemporary global challenges in supply chain management*. Routledge.

211 Dixon, R., Mousa, G. A., & Woodhead, A. (2005). The role of environmental initiatives in encouraging companies to engage in environmental reporting. *European Management Journal*, *23*(6), 702–716. Alazzani, A., & Wan-Hussin, W. N. (2013). Global reporting initiative's environmental reporting: A study of oil and gas companies. *Ecological Indicators*, *32*, 19–24; Cowan, D. M., Dopart, P., Ferracini, T., Sahmel, J., Merryman, K., Gaffney, S., & Paustenbach, D. J. (2010). A cross-sectional analysis of reported corporate environmental sustainability practices. *Regulatory Toxicology and Pharmacology*, *58*(3), 524–538.

212 Benameur, K. B., Mostafa, M. M., Hassanein, A., Shariff, M. Z., & Al-Shattarat, W. (2023). Sustainability reporting scholarly research: A bibliometric review and a future research agenda. *Management Review Quarterly*, 1–44.

213 Ibid., p. 859.

214 Threlfall, R., King, A., Shulman, J., & Bartels, W. (2020). *The time has come: The KPMG survey of sustainability reporting 2020*. KPMG. https://kpmg.com/xx/en/home/insights/2020/11/the-time-has-come-survey-of-sustainability-reporting.html

It was hoped that sustainability reporting can be understood as a dynamic and essential tool for firms to communicate their sustainable development commitment to stakeholders, while also meeting the growing interest in sustainable practices within the financial market and beyond.[215] Kenneth P. Pucker, a former COO of Timberland, among many others, found nonstandard metrics, unreliable ESG ratings, and more, emphasizing that real progress requires better measurement and reporting practices and changes in regulations, investment incentives, and corporate mindsets.[216] Pucker suggests that reporting is riddled with problems, and sustainable investing is overhyped while environmental threats continue to mount and inequality continues to grow.[217] A critical discourse analysis of the oil and gas industry's sustainability reporting revealed that several global upstream oil and gas companies still have potential biases in sustainability reporting. The research also identified a lack of understanding of social responsibility in detailed sustainability reporting for several oil and gas industry actors, indicating that the industry is prone to CSR practices and sustainability reporting violations.[218]

A major bone of contention is that companies have been granted more leeway than originally envisaged to decide which environmental and social factors they consider relevant to *sustainability* reporting following so-called materiality assessments. Companies can omit data for some standards if they can justify that action.[219] As such, if companies may voluntarily decide what to report, they tend to disclose only the positive aspects of certain activities while omitting the negative. As a result, sustainability reports do not necessarily reflect a company's real performance, bringing into question the report's value. The format, clarity, and presentation of the document also play an important role. These issues have led academics, NGO officials, corporate representatives, and social activists to ascertain whether the voluntary approach to global environmental regulation is reliable.[220] Voluntarism in sustainability reporting has questioned the effectiveness of the recently

215 Ibid., p. 824.

216 Pucker, K. P. (2021). Overselling sustainability reporting. *Harvard Business Review*. Retrieved May 18, from https://hbr.org/2021/05/overselling-sustainability-reporting

217 Ibid.

218 Kwarto, F., Nurafiah, N., Suharman, H., & Dahlan, M. (2024). The potential bias for sustainability reporting of global upstream oil and gas companies: A systematic literature review of the evidence. *Management Review Quarterly*, *74*(1), 35–64.

219 Lewis, I. (2023). Final EU sustainability reporting rules trigger fresh wave of criticism. *Impact Investor*. Retrieved May 18, from https://impact-investor.com/final-eu-sustainability-reporting-rules-trigger-fresh-wave-of-criticism/

220 Anderson, H., & Gumley, W. (2008). Corporate social responsibility: Legislative options for protecting employees and the environment. *The Adelaide Law Review*, *29*(1), 29–77; Thirarungrueang, K. (2013). Rethinking CSR in Australia: Time for binding regulation? *International Journal of Law and Management*, *55*(3), 173–200. Halkos, G., & Skouloudis, A. (2016). National CSR and institutional conditions: An exploratory study. *Journal of Cleaner Production*, *139*, 1150–1156.

introduced European Sustainability Reporting Standards (ESRS). The ESRS reporting standard will affect 50,000 companies and might allow them to practice greenwashing.[221] Based on data collected from disclosure documents between 2009 and 2020, it has been discovered that major oil companies such as Chevron, ExxonMobil, BP, and Shell frequently discussed transitioning to clean energy in their annual reports. However, they have not made significant changes to facilitate a company-wide transition.[222] These companies have been responsible for over 10% of global carbon emissions since 1965 and have pledged to transition to clean energy or at least reduce their carbon footprint.[223] Despite these promises, their actions and investments do not align with their goals. For example, Shell has expanded its oil and gas exploration activities, while ExxonMobil has not generated clean energy over the past decade. Additionally, BP, which has the largest global renewables capacity among the four major companies, only has a capacity equivalent to two large gas-fired power plants, totaling 2,000 MW.[224]

Social auditing has been touted as a mechanism to counter this disconnect. It can check corporate self-regulation performance against social commitments through greater stakeholder engagement. Social auditing is at the core of the standardization regime, aimed at improving the alignment between corporate intentions declared in their codes and their performance.[225] It is also a process by which a business can ascertain its impacts on society, and report its responsibility performance in social issues to the wider community. This is important because irresponsible firm behavior may harm legitimacy and gain a social license to operate.[226]

Social audits are not mandatory for companies, and the adoption of these audits has not yet reached a convincing level. A study examined ESG reports of companies on *The Wall Street Journal*'s and *Investor's Business Daily*'s top 100 sustainable companies. Only 58% sought external assurance services for

221 Lewis, I. (2023). Final EU sustainability reporting rules trigger fresh wave of criticism. *Impact Investor*. Retrieved May 18, from https://impact-investor.com/final-eu-sustainability-reporting-rules-trigger-fresh-wave-of-criticism/; Haigh, M., & Jones, M. T. (2006). The drivers of corporate social responsibility: A critical review. *The Business Review*, *5*(2), 245–251.

222 Li, M., Trencher, G., & Asuka, J. (2022). The clean energy claims of BP, Chevron, ExxonMobil and Shell: A mismatch between discourse, actions and investments. *PLoS ONE*, *17*(2), e0263596.

223 Domonoske, C. (2021, June 8). Big oil (probably) isn't going away anytime soon. But it's definitely changing. *NPR*. www.npr.org/2021/06/08/1002448099/big-oils-transition-3-takeaways-on-how-the-industry-is-and-isnt-going-green

224 Ibid., p. 18.

225 Rahim, M. M., & Idowu, S. O. (2015). *Social audit regulation: Development, challenges and opportunities*. Springer.

226 Fiaschi, D., Giuliani, E., & Nieri, F. (2017). Overcoming the liability of origin by doing no-harm: Emerging country firms' social irresponsibility as they go global. *Journal of World Business*, *52*(4), 546–563.

some of their reports, with limited assurance primarily provided.[227] A possible problem with social auditing, that can discourage its effective use, is the ability of the management of a firm to control the entire process. This can happen when management is not accountable to society and strategically collects and disseminates only the information necessary to progress its corporate image.[228] Therefore, there is a risk that this audit system can often be limited to being used as a management strategy to claim legitimacy for global buying firms' sourcing operations, rather than as a mechanism for promoting social responsibility performance in supply firms in weak economies.[229] Private auditors' lack of independence and capacity to reflect the true account of corporate social and environmental responsibility further raised the usefulness of this audit practice.[230] Auditors struggle to record labor rights violations due to the pressure from the auditing firms that pay them, the companies reviewing the inspection, and the suppliers themselves.[231] Incidents such as the Rana Plaza collapse in Bangladesh and the Ali Enterprises fire in Pakistan, both of which were audited shortly before the tragedies happened, have drawn attention to the pitfalls of social auditing in the textile sector.[232] A sense of gamification resulting from such auditing practices has already been shown to be detrimental and regressive to creating social value within industries.[233]

227 Bakarich, K. M., Baranek, D., & O'Brien, P. E. (2023). The current state and future implications of environmental, social, and governance assurance. *Current Issues in Auditing*, *17*(1), A1–A21.

228 Owen, D. L., Swift, T. A., Humphrey, C., & Bowerman, M. (2000). The new social audits: Accountability, managerial capture or the agenda of social champions? *European Accounting Review*, *9*(1), 81–98.

229 O'Dwyer, B., & Owen, D. L. (2005). Assurance statement practice in environmental, social and sustainability reporting: A critical evaluation. *The British Accounting Review*, *37*(2), 205–229.

230 Rahim, M. M., & Vicario, V. (2015). Social audit: A mess or means in CSR assessment? In *Social audit regulation: Development, challenges and opportunities* (pp. 1–13). Springer; Rahim, M. M., Kuruppu, S. C., & Islam, M. T. (2023). Social auditing in the supply chain: Business legitimisation strategy rather than a change agent. *Meditari Accountancy Research*, *31*(6), 1606–1633.

231 Dreier, H. (2023, December 28). They're paid billions to root out child labor in the U.S. why do they fail? *The New York Times*. www.nytimes.com/2023/12/28/us/migrant-child-labor-audits.html

232 *Beyond Social Auditing*. (2024). Business & Human Rights Resource Centre. Retrieved May 19, from www.business-humanrights.org/en/big-issues/labour-rights/beyond-social-auditing/; Sinkovics, N., Hoque, S. F., & Sinkovics, R. R. (2016). Rana Plaza collapse aftermath: Are CSR compliance and auditing pressures effective? *Accounting, Auditing & Accountability Journal*, *29*(4), 617–649.

233 Wilks, S., Blankenbach, J., & Manschot, A. (2023, June 16). Respecting human rights: Why the CSDDD needs to go beyond social auditing. *Business & Human Rights Resource Centre*. Retrieved May 19, from www.business-humanrights.org/en/blog/respecting-human-rights-why-the-csddd-needs-to-go-beyond-social-auditing/

4.6 Conclusion

Civil society and grassroots movements have been vital in addressing global corporate pollution. Examples of such movements include Greenpeace, Friends of the Earth, and the Extinction Rebellion. These movements have played a crucial role in establishing a form of global private regulation of the harmful effects of pollution. As part of this system, various guidelines and voluntary best practices have existed for years, such as the OECD's Due Diligence Guidance for Responsible Business and the UN's Business and Human Rights Guidelines. The failure of global initiatives and the increasing demand for mandating TNCs to be socially and environmentally responsible has led to the development of a private ordering system with the assistance of private vendors. This system has successfully promoted sustainability reporting. Social auditing and a partnership between corporate bodies and private vendors have been promoted to legitimize this approach. However, this has also failed as pollution, environmental damage, and reckless corporate behavior have continued to increase. This has undermined the acceptance and effectiveness of voluntarism, collaboration, and partnership as the basis of current global environmental regulation.

With legislation in place in some countries – for example, the 2023 German Supply Chain Due Diligence Act – the environmental rules are moving from 'good to have' to 'must have' from a compliance perspective.[234] Based on the Kyoto Conference, the Environmental Protection Authority of the United States has set new federal GHG emission standards for passenger cars and light trucks for Model Years 2023 through 2026, with plans for multi-pollutant emission standards for heavy-duty vehicles from MY 2027.[235] In March 2024, the European Council approved the CSDDD.[236] Shortly thereafter, the Biden-Harris administration issued the United States' revised NAP on RBC.

234 A study conducted in China from 2005 to 2015 found that mandatory CER disclosure policies can decrease environmental pollution, while environmental pollution has a positive impact on CER. The study suggests finding a balance between environmental regulations and CER to effectively reduce pollution and increase firms' enthusiasm for environmental responsibility activities. For details, see Wang, M., Liao, G., & Li, Y. (2021). The relationship between environmental regulation, pollution and corporate environmental responsibility. *International Journal of Environmental Research and Public Health, 18*(15), 8018. Ben-David, I. Z., Kleimeier, S., & Viehs, M. (2019). When environmental regulations are tighter at home, companies emit more abroad. *Harvard Business Review*. https://hbr.org/2019/02/research-when-environmental-regulations-are-tighter-at-home-companies-emit-more-abroad

235 *Regulating air quality: The first global assessment of air pollution legislation*. (2021). U. N. Organization. www.unep.org/resources/report/regulating-air-quality-first-global-assessment-air-pollution-legislation

236 Burrow, S., & Bloomer, P. (2024). Step change for corporate accountability as EU member states endorse due diligence directive. *Business & Human Rights Resource Centre*. Retrieved May 19, from www.business-humanrights.org/en/blog/step-change-for-corporate-accountability-as-eu-member-states-endorse-due-diligence-directive/; Vass, M. (2023, April 25). Corporate sustainability: Firms to tackle impact on human rights and environment. *European Parliament*. www.europarl.europa.eu/news/en/press-room/20230424IPR82008/corporate-sustainability-firms-to-tackle-impact-on-human-rights-and-environment; Vervynckt, M. (2024, May 13). Sweden's CSDDD U-turn crucial step forward. *Business & Human Rights Resource Centre*. Retrieved May 19, from www.business-humanrights.org/en/blog/sweden-csddd/

Global organizations have been calling for stricter regulations on corporate activity to reduce ecological destruction and promote human rights. Greenpeace, for example, has put forward ten principles for corporate accountability to end corporate capture and close the governance gap.[237] The UN has also recommended mandatory due diligence laws to standardize corporate responsibility. With the aim of a Legally Binding Instrument to Regulate Transnational Corporations,[238] the Human Rights Council of this global organization has passed two resolutions resulting in the creation of an Intergovernmental Working Group to 'elaborate an international legally binding instrument to regulate, in international human rights law, the activities of TNCs and other business enterprises.'[239]

References

Addo, M. K. (2014). The reality of the United Nations guiding principles on business and human rights. *Human Rights Law Review*, *14*(1), 133–147.

Agarwal, V. (1998). Sustainable development and environmental protection: Some reflections. *All Indian Reporters Journal Section*, 1–9.

Agency, I. A. E. (2023). *Vienna convention on civil liability for nuclear damage*. Retrieved May 25, from www.iaea.org/topics/nuclear-liability-conventions/vienna-convention-on-civil-liability-for-nuclear-damage

Alazzani, A., & Wan-Hussin, W. N. (2013). Global reporting initiative's environmental reporting: A study of oil and gas companies. *Ecological indicators*, *32*, 19–24.

Ansell, C., & Gash, A. (2018). Collaborative platforms as a governance strategy. *Journal of Public Administration Research and Theory*, *28*(1), 16–32.

Appel, P. A., & Irvin, T. R. (2012). 11. Public regulatory encouragement to the adoption of private ordering systems to achieve environmental protection through sustainable commerce. In *How public regulation changes corporate governance practice–corporate board reform in Taiwan* (p. 251). Edward Elgar Publishing.

Basu, R. (2023). *Managing global supply chains: Contemporary global challenges in supply chain management*. Routledge.

Benameur, K. B., Mostafa, M. M., Hassanein, A., Shariff, M. Z., & Al-Shattarat, W. (2023). Sustainability reporting scholarly research: A bibliometric review and a future research agenda. *Management Review Quarterly*, 1–44.

Berliner, D., & Prakash, A. (2015). "Bluewashing" the firm? Voluntary regulations, program design, and member compliance with the United Nations Global Compact. *Policy Studies Journal*, *43*(1), 115–138.

Bernstein, L. (2013). Opting out of the legal system: Extralegal contractual relations in the diamond industry. In *Contract-freedom and restraint* (pp. 359–403). Routledge.

Berry, M. A., & Rondinelli, D. A. (1998). Proactive corporate environmental management: A new industrial revolution. *Academy of Management Perspectives*, *12*(2), 38–50.

237 Mittler, D. (2018). How do we make corporations more accountable? *Greenpeace*. Retrieved May 19, from www.greenpeace.org/international/story/14185/how-do-we-make-corporations-more-accountable/

238 Boyd, D. R. (2022, July 4). Human rights and environmental due diligence laws crucial to combat irresponsible business activities – UN expert. *Office of the High Commissioner for Human Rights*. www.ohchr.org/en/press-releases/2022/07/human-rights-and-environmental-due-diligence-laws-crucial-combat

239 Human Rights Council. (2014, June 26). *37th Meeting*.

Berthod, O., Blanchet, T., Busch, H., Kunze, C., Nolden, C., & Wenderlich, M. (2023). The rise and fall of energy democracy: 5 cases of collaborative governance in energy systems. *Environmental Management*, *71*(3), 551–564.
Beumer, C., & Martens, P. (2013). IUCN and perspectives on biodiversity conservation in a changing world. *Biodiversity and Conservation*, *22*, 3105–3120.
Bonnitcha, J., & McCorquodale, R. (2017). The concept of "due diligence" in the UN guiding principles on business and human rights. *European Journal of International Law*, *28*(3), 899–919.
Borowy, I. (2019). Before UNEP: Who was in charge of the global environment? The struggle for institutional responsibility 1968–72. *Journal of Global History*, *14*(1), 87–106.
Brown, J. A., Clark, C., & Buono, A. F. (2018). The United Nations global compact: Engaging implicit and explicit CSR for global governance. *Journal of Business Ethics*, *147*, 721–734.
Burke, L., & Logsdon, J. M. (1996). How corporate social responsibility pays off. *Long Range Planning*, *29*(4), 495–502.
Burrow, S., & Bloomer, P. (2024). *Step change for corporate accountability as EU member states endorse due diligence directive*. Business & Human Rights Resource Centre. Retrieved May 19, from www.business-humanrights.org/en/blog/step-change-for-corporate-accountability-as-eu-member-states-endorse-due-diligence-directive/
Čábelková, I., Smutka, L., Mareš, D., Ortikov, A., & Kontsevaya, S. (2023). Environmental protection or economic growth? The effects of preferences for individual freedoms. *Frontiers in Environmental Science*, *11*, 1129236.
Chloe. (2023, May 24). *The evolution of cultural norms: How society's values change over time*. www.momentslog.com/culture/the-evolution-of-cultural-norms-how-societys-values-change-over-time#google_vignette
Coase, R. (1960). The problem of social cost. *The Journal of Law and Economics*, *3*(October), 1–44.
Cohen, S. (2020, January 27). Economic growth and environmental sustainability. *State of the Planet*. https://news.climate.columbia.edu/2020/01/27/economic-growth-environmental-sustainability/
Compact, G. (2024). *The ten principles of the UN global compact*. United Nations. Retrieved May 19, from https://unglobalcompact.org/what-is-gc/mission/principles
Cowan, D. M., Dopart, P., Ferracini, T., Sahmel, J., Merryman, K., Gaffney, S., & Paustenbach, D. J. (2010). A cross-sectional analysis of reported corporate environmental sustainability practices. *Regulatory Toxicology and Pharmacology*, *58*(3), 524–538.
Diversity, S. O. T. C. O. B. (2011). *Convention on biological diversity*. United Nations Environment Programme.
Dixon, R., Mousa, G. A., & Woodhead, A. (2005). The role of environmental initiatives in encouraging companies to engage in environmental reporting. *European Management Journal*, *23*(6), 702–716.
Domonoske, C. (2021, June 8). Big oil (probably) isn't going away anytime soon. But it's definitely changing. *NPR*. www.npr.org/2021/06/08/1002448099/big-oils-transition-3-takeaways-on-how-the-industry-is-and-isnt-going-green
Dreier, H. (2023, December 28). They're paid billions to root out child labor in the U.S. why do they fail? *The New York Times*. www.nytimes.com/2023/12/28/us/migrant-child-labor-audits.html
Dudley, N., Parrish, J. D., Redford, K. H., & Stolton, S. (2010). The revised IUCN protected area management categories: The debate and ways forward. *Oryx*, *44*(4), 485–490.
Epstein, C. (2006). The making of global environmental norms: Endangered species protection. *Global Environmental Politics*, *6*(2), 32–54.
Feldman, E. A. (2006). The Tuna Court: Law and norms in the world's premier fish market. *California Law Review*, *94*, 313.

Friedman, M. (1970). A Friedman doctrine: The social responsibility of business is to increase its profits. *New York Times Magazine*, *13*, 33.

Glaser, A. (2015). *You did it! Shell abandons Arctic drilling*. Greenpeace. Retrieved May 20, from www.greenpeace.org/international/story/7022/you-did-it-shell-abandons-arctic-drilling/

Golove, D. (2020). *The Alien tort statute and the law of nations: Newly uncovered* (HRP 21–001). Harvard University.

Greenpeace. (2024). *Our history, victories and successes*. Greenpeace. Retrieved May 20, from www.greenpeace.org/international/about/founders/?_gl=1*1625il1*_up*MQ.*_ga*NTQxMzY0MzY3LjE3MTYxODEzNjk.*_ga_94MRTN8HG4*MTcxNjE4MTM2OS4xLjAuMTcxNjE4MTQyOS4wLjAuMTA1NjU1MTgzNw.*_ga_0CCB1GTVV6*MTcxNjE4MTM2OC4xLjEuMTcxNjE4MTQyOS4wLjAuMA.*_ga_99CSX66YC1*MTcxNjE4MTM2OC4xLjEuMTcxNjE4MTQyOS4wLjAuMA

GRI. (2024). *Premium tools for better reporting*. Global Reporting Initiative. Retrieved May 19, from www.globalreporting.org/reporting-support/reporting-tools/

Hajduk, T. (2019). An "instrument of moral persuasion' – multinational enterprises and international codes of conduct in the 1970s. In M. M. Rahim (Ed.), *Code of conduct on transnational corporations: Challenges and opportunities* (pp. 23–43). Springer.

Halkos, G., & Nomikos, S. (2021). Corporate social responsibility: Trends in global reporting initiative standards. *Economic Analysis and Policy*, *69*, 106–117.

Hamilton, G. (1984). *The control of multinationals: What future for international codes of conduct in the 1980s?* Institute for Research and Information on Multinationals.

Héritier, A., Mueller-Debus, A. K., & Thauer, C. R. (2009). The firm as an inspector: Private ordering and political rules. *Business and Politics*, *11*(4), 1–32.

Hickmann, T., Widerberg, O., Lederer, M., & Pattberg, P. (2021). The United Nations framework convention on climate change secretariat as an orchestrator in global climate policymaking. *International Review of Administrative Sciences*, *87*(1), 21–38.

Imperial, M. T. (2005). Using collaboration as a governance strategy: Lessons from six watershed management programs. *Administration & Society*, *37*(3), 281–320.

Ivanova, M. (2020). Coloring the UN environmental: The catalytic role of the UN environment programme. *Global Governance: A Review of Multilateralism and International Organizations*, *26*(2), 307–324.

Ivashchenko, N., & Isaeva, L. (2021). Basic principles of partnership as the factor of sustainable development in the context of business ecosystems. *E3S web of conferences*. EDP Science.

Johnson, S. P. (2001). *The earth summit: The United Nations conference on environment and development (UNCED)*. Kluwer Law International.

Justice, E. Q. F. C. (2021). *Justice delayed: 10 years of UN guiding principles*. European Coalition for Corporate Justice. Retrieved April 26, from https://corporatejustice.org/news/justice-delayed-10-years-of-un-guiding-principles/

Kauffman, C. M., & Martin, P. L. (2018). Constructing rights of nature norms in the US, Ecuador, and New Zealand. *Global Environmental Politics*, *18*(4), 43–62.

Kazazi, E., & Çela, E. (2015). Jurisdiction in the European Union. *International Journal of Academic Research and Reflection*, *3*(4), 48–54.

Kilsby, R., & Puzniak-Holford, M. (2024, April 19). *The EU corporate sustainability due diligence directive is final. What now for your organisation?* Deloitte. Retrieved May 19, from www2.deloitte.com/uk/en/blog/emea-centre-for-regulatory-strategy/2024/the-eu-corporate-sustainability-due-diligence-directive-is-final-what-now-for-your-organisation.html

Kolk, A., Van Tulder, R., & Welters, C. (1999). International codes of conduct and corporate social responsibility: Can transnational corporations regulate themselves? *Transnational Corporations*, *8*(1), 143–180.
Kryczka, K., Lambooy, T., & Beckers, S. (2012). Importance of due diligence practices for the future of business operations in Fragile States. *The Europe Company Limited*, *9*, 125.
Ku, J. G. (2011). The limits of corporate rights under international law. *Chicago Journal of International Law*, *12*, 729.
Kwarto, F., Nurafiah, N., Suharman, H., & Dahlan, M. (2024). The potential bias for sustainability reporting of global upstream oil and gas companies: A systematic literature review of the evidence. *Management Review Quarterly*, *74*(1), 35–64.
Lakshmisha, A., & Thiel, A. (2022). Bridging actors and their role in co-managing lakes: Cases from greater Bengaluru metropolitan region (GBMR). *Sustainability*, *14*(10), 5865.
Leelakrishnan, P. (1992). Environmental impact assessment: Legal dimensions. *Journal of the Indian Law Institute*, *34*(4), 541–562.
Lewis, I. (2023). Final EU sustainability reporting rules trigger fresh wave of criticism. *Impact Investor*. Retrieved May 18, from https://impact-investor.com/final-eu-sustainability-reporting-rules-trigger-fresh-wave-of-criticism/
Li, M., Trencher, G., & Asuka, J. (2022). The clean energy claims of BP, Chevron, ExxonMobil and Shell: A mismatch between discourse, actions and investments. *PLoS ONE*, *17*(2), e0263596.
Linnér, B.-O., & Selin, H. (2013). The United Nations conference on sustainable development: Forty years in the making. *Environment and Planning C: Government and Policy*, *31*(6), 971–987.
Mares, R. (2011). *The UN guiding principles on business and human rights: Foundations and implementation* (Vol. 39). Martinus Nijhoff Publishers.
Martinsson, J. (2011). *Global norms: Creation, diffusion, and limits*. T. I. B. F. R. A. Development.
Moore, E. A., & Koontz, T. M. (2003). Research note a typology of collaborative watershed groups: Citizen-based, agency-based, and mixed partnerships. *Society & Natural Resources*, *16*(5), 451–460.
Muchlinski, P. (2021). The impact of the UN Guiding Principles on business attitudes to observing human rights. *Business and Human Rights Journal*, *6*(2), 212–226.
Nelson, J., Anesa, M., & Grayson, D. (2017). United nations global compact (UNGC). In *Corporate responsibility coalitions* (pp. 328–346). Routledge.
Nolan, J. (2005). With power comes responsibility: Human rights and corporate accountability. *University of New South Wales Law Journal*, *28*(3), 581–613.
Nordisk, N. (2023). *Human rights report*. https://au.search.yahoo.com/yhs/search?hspart=mnet&hsimp=yhs-001&type=type9043493-spa-796-84469&param1=796&param2=84469&p=Novo+Nordisk%2C+a+global+healthcare+company%2C+has+demonstrated+a+strong+commitment+to+the+UNGC+principles.+
O'Dwyer, B., & Owen, D. L. (2005). Assurance statement practice in environmental, social and sustainability reporting: A critical evaluation. *The British Accounting Review*, *37*(2), 205–229.
OECD. (2024). *OECD due diligence guidance for responsible business conduct*. OECD. Retrieved May 25, from https://mneguidelines.oecd.org/due-diligence-guidance-for-responsible-business-conduct.htm
Oldenziel, J., & Wilde-Ramsing, J. (2010). *10 Years on: Assessing the contribution of the OECD guidelines for multinational enterprises to responsible business conduct*. Available at SSRN 1641036.

Owen, D. L., Swift, T. A., Humphrey, C., & Bowerman, M. (2000). The new social audits: Accountability, managerial capture or the agenda of social champions? *European Accounting Review*, *9*(1), 81–98.

Pacific, G. A. (2018, January 11). *Arctic oil: The verdict in in*. Greenpeace International. Retrieved May 20, from https://www.greenpeace.org/international/story/15193/arctic-oil-the-verdict-is-in

Pati, R. (2018). Global regulation of corporate conduct: Effective pursuit of a slave-free supply chain. *American University Law Review*, *68*, 1821.

Perez, O. (2012). International environmental law as a field of multi-polar governance: The case of private transnational environmental regulation. *Santa Clara Journal of International Law*, *10*, 285.

Peters, M., & Turner, R. K. (2004). SME environmental attitude and participation in local-scale voluntary initiatives: Some practical applications. *Journal of Environmental Planning and Management*, *47*(3), 451.

Plourde, Y. (2015). *Engaging with the future: A historical investigation of Greenpeace*. The University of Western Ontario (Canada).

Pucker, K. P. (2021). Overselling sustainability reporting. *Harvard Business Review*. Retrieved May 18, from https://hbr.org/2021/05/overselling-sustainability-reporting

Rahim, M. M., & Vicario, V. (2015). Social audit: A mess or means in CSR assessment? In *Social audit regulation: Development, challenges and opportunities* (pp. 1–13). Springer.

Rasche, A. (2020). The United Nations Global Compact and the sustainable development goals. In *Research handbook of responsible management* (pp. 228–241). Edward Elgar Publishing.

Sustainability Reporting (2022). *Global reporting initiative*. Global Reporting Initiative (GRI)

Ruggie, J. G. (2020). The social construction of the UN Guiding Principles on Business and Human Rights. In *Research handbook on human rights and business* (pp. 63–86). Edward Elgar Publishing.

Sagy, T. (2011). What's so private about private ordering? *Law & Society Review*, *45*(4), 923–954.

Sato, M., Rafaty, R., Calel, R., & Grubb, M. (2022). Allocation, allocation, allocation! The political economy of the development of the European Union Emissions Trading System. *Wiley Interdisciplinary Reviews: Climate Change*, *13*(5), e796.

Scherer, A. G., Palazzo, G., & Baumann, D. (2006). Global rules and private actors: Toward a new role of the transnational corporation in global governance. *Business Ethics Quarterly*, *16*(4), 505–532.

Service, C. R. (2022). *The Alien Tort statute: A primer*. L. O. Congress.

Sethi, S. P., & Schepers, D. H. (2014). United Nations global compact: The promise–performance gap. *Journal of Business Ethics*, *122*, 193–208.

Short, J. L., Toffel, M. W., & Hugill, A. R. (2016). Monitoring global supply chains. *Strategic Management Journal*, *37*(9), 1878–1897.

Sinkovics, N., Hoque, S. F., & Sinkovics, R. R. (2016). Rana Plaza collapse aftermath: Are CSR compliance and auditing pressures effective? *Accounting, Auditing & Accountability Journal*, *29*(4), 617–649.

Tallberg, J., Lundgren, M., Sommerer, T., & Squatrito, T. (2020). Why international organizations commit to liberal norms. *International Studies Quarterly*, *64*(3), 626–640.

Thirarungrueang, K. (2013). Rethinking CSR in Australia: Time for binding regulation? *International Journal of Law and Management*, *55*(3), 173–200.

Threlfall, R., King, A., Shulman, J., & Bartels, W. (2020). *The time has come: The KPMG survey of sustainability reporting 2020*. KPMG. https://kpmg.com/xx/en/home/insights/2020/11/the-time-has-come-survey-of-sustainability-reporting.html

Tompkins, E. L., & Amundsen, H. (2008). Perceptions of the effectiveness of the United Nations Framework Convention on Climate Change in advancing national action on climate change. *Environmental Science & Policy*, *11*(1), 1–13.

Ulibarri, N., Emerson, K., Imperial, M. T., Jager, N. W., Newig, J., & Weber, E. (2020). How does collaborative governance evolve? Insights from a medium-n case comparison. *Policy and Society*, *39*(4), 617–637.

Ulibarri, N., Imperial, M. T., Siddiki, S., & Henderson, H. (2023). Drivers and dynamics of collaborative governance in environmental management. *Environmental Management*, *71*(3), 495–504.

UNEP. (2002). *Global judges symposium on sustainable development and the role of law*. United Nations. Retrieved May 25, from https://stg-wedocs.unep.org/handle/20.500.11822/30024

Unilever. (2024). *Leading and delivering on sustainability through our Compass commitments*. Unilever. Retrieved May 19, from www.unilever.com/news/news-search/2023/leading-and-delivering-on-sustainability-through-our-compass-commitments/

Utting, P. (2002). Regulating business via multistakeholder initiatives: A preliminary assessment. In *Voluntary approaches to corporate responsibility: Readings and a resource guide* (p. 61130). United Nations Non-Governmental Liaison Service and the United Nations Research Institute for Social Development.

Ventura, L. (2023). Corporate sustainability due diligence and the new boundaries of the firms in the European Union. *European Business Law Review*, *34*(2).

Volunteers, U. N. (Ed.). (2014). *Environmental sustainability and voluntarism: Considerations for post-2015 development agenda*. United Nations.

Wai, R. (2005). Transnational private law and private ordering in a contested global society. *Harvard International Law Journal*, *46*, 471.

Wang, M., Liao, G., & Li, Y. (2021). The relationship between environmental regulation, pollution and corporate environmental responsibility. *International Journal of Environmental Research and Public Health*, *18*(15), 8018.

Williams, O. F. (2014). The United Nations global compact: What did it promise? *Journal of Business Ethics*, *122*, 241–251.

Willis, A. (2003). The role of the global reporting initiative's sustainability reporting guidelines in the social screening of investments. *Journal of Business Ethics*, *43*(3), 233–237.

Witte, J. M., Benner, T., & Streck, C. (2017). Partnerships and networks in global environmental governance: Moving to the next stage. In *Governance and sustainability* (pp. 141–152). Routledge.

Witte, J. M., Streck, C., & Benner, T. (2003). The road from Johannesburg: What future for partnerships in global environmental governance. *Progress or Peril*, 59–84.

WWF. (2024). *World wide fund for nature (WWF)*. Retrieved May 20, from www.unep.org/explore-topics/oceans-seas/what-we-do/working-regional-seas/partners/world-wide-fund-nature-wwf

Zakaria, M., Garanča, Z., & Sobeih, A. (2012). Cultural and legal challenges in implementing code of conduct in supply chain management of mobile phone industries: Sony Ericsson case study. *Social Responsibility Journal*, *8*(2), 227–241.

5 Domestic Framework for Regulating Corporate Polluters

5.1 Introduction

Corporations operating with extreme negligence or reckless attitude toward risk management can bring disastrous environmental consequences. In 2020, Chevron was ranked as the fourth most polluting company, emitting 43.35 billion metric tons of CO_2 equivalent since 1965. Additionally, it released 900,218 metric tons of carbon dioxide equivalent per capita.[1] On the other hand, Saudi Aramco was ranked fifth, emitting 59.26 billion metric tons of CO_2 equivalent and releasing 750,126 metric tons of per capita carbon dioxide equivalent.[2] An annual audit by Break Free from Plastic has named Coca-Cola the world's worst plastic polluter for the fifth straight year. The audit involved 200,000 citizen scientists across 87 countries. Mondelez International, Unilever, Nestle, and PepsiCo also ranked in the top five.[3] These companies are facing the risk of litigation for their contribution to plastic pollution. A recent report has unveiled that a mere 100 companies have been accountable for over 70% of the world's GHG emissions since 1988. Notably, ExxonMobil, Shell, BP, and Chevron have been recognized as the leading investor-owned companies that emit the most.[4] The report emphasizes systemic change and calls for transparency among fossil fuel producers. It warns that if fossil fuel extraction continues at the same rate, global temperatures could rise by 4°C by the end of the century, leading to catastrophic consequences. Some oil and gas companies have started investing in renewables, but more action is needed to address the climate crisis.[5]

1 Howell, B. (2023). The top 14 most polluting companies. *The Eco Expert*. Retrieved May 29, from www.theecoexperts.co.uk/blog/most-polluting-companies

2 Ibid.

3 Gallagher, T. (2022, November 18). Coca-Cola revealed as world's worst plastic polluter for fifth year in a row. *Euronews*. www.euronews.com/green/2022/11/18/coca-cola-revealed-as-worlds-worst-plastic-polluter-for-fifth-year-in-a-row

4 Riley, T. (2017, July 10). Just 100 companies responsible for 71% of global emissions, study says. *The Guardian*. www.theguardian.com/sustainable-business/2017/jul/10/100-fossil-fuel-companies-investors-responsible-71-global-emissions-cdp-study-climate-change

5 Ibid.

DOI: 10.4324/9781003279006-5

Several examples exist of global companies being punished for damaging the environment through domestic legal systems. One such example is the case of Chevron in Ecuador. In 2011, a court in Ecuador ordered Chevron to pay $9.5 billion in damages for polluting the Amazon rainforest. The company was found guilty of causing significant environmental harm through oil drilling operations, resulting in soil and water contamination, deforestation, and harm to local communities. Another example is the Volkswagen (VW) case in the United States. VW was fined billions of dollars in 2015 for intentionally cheating on emissions tests, leading to excessive air pollution from their vehicles. These cases demonstrate that domestic legal systems have the power to hold global companies accountable for their environmental damage.[6] However, the regulations about ecological damage caused by companies can vary domestically. Different countries have their own set of policies and laws in place to regulate and mitigate the impact of corporate polluters on the environment. The specifics of these regulations can differ significantly from one country to another. Some nations have implemented strict environmental policies and laws to hold companies accountable for pollution. These regulations may include emission standards, waste management regulations, and penalties for non-compliance. Other countries may rely on international cooperation and agreements to address environmental issues caused by corporations. The regulatory framework can also be influenced by factors such as the level of industrialization, economic priorities, and the political will of a country. The 'polluter pays' principle is often applied, meaning companies are held financially responsible for the environmental damage they cause. Additionally, the idea of a global carbon price has been proposed as a potential solution to regulate and reduce GHG emissions on a global scale.

While most countries have plans for protecting their environment and laws against polluters, the diversity of their regulatory frameworks is striking. This chapter delves into the dominant principles of some of these countries' environmental jurisprudence, highlighting the significant differences that impact the effectiveness of their regulatory frameworks against corporate polluters. The examination and explanation in this chapter focus on the regulatory approaches of countries such as the UK, the United States, Australia, Canada, Finland, Germany, Japan, China, and India. Ultimately, this chapter aims to provide a comprehensive understanding of why some domestic frameworks are more effective in preventing corporate pollution than others.

6 Bundesamt für Umwelt [Federal Environment Agency]. (2024). *Laws of environmental liability, harm and criminal actions*. www.umweltbundesamt.de/en/environm-liability-a-environm-damage-law-envir#harmonisation-of-compensation-for-environmental-harm; Márquez, D. I. (2015). Legal avenues for holding multinational corporations liable for environmental damages in a globalized world. *ARACÊ–Direitos Humanos em Revista*, *2*(3), 58–74.

5.2 Regulating Corporate Polluters in the UK

The UK is the first industrialized nation and the sixth largest economy by Gross Domestic Product (GDP).[7] The country depended heavily on its natural gas, coal, and oil reserves to achieve its current economic progress. Although these reserves have declined, it is still one of the countries with the highest GHG emissions in the world.

The UK witnessed a rapid environmental downfall due to its reliance on industrialization during the Industrial Revolution, which caused numerous catastrophic events. However, with time, the UK's awareness and understanding of environmental issues have grown, along with its regulatory frameworks for protecting the environment. It has a complex environmental regulation framework encompassing international, regional, and national obligations. The nation has demonstrated a high level of maturity in its regulatory approach, characterized by multi-layered governance systems and diverse legal strategies.[8]

To understand the present situation of the laws to control corporate polluters in the UK, it is crucial to study the evolution of this country's environmental policies. This evolution can be divided into three phases: (a) the pre-EU Era – 1800 to the mid-20th century; (b) the EU Era and Brexit – 1972 to 2020; and (c) the post-Brexit Era – 2020 to present.

5.2.1 The Pre-European Union Era

The evolution of the UK's environmental law is rooted in its heavy industrialization in the 1800s. The Industrial Revolution, beginning in the late 18th and 19th centuries in Britain, contributed to the country's economic growth and had a colossal impact on the environment of the UK. Along with air pollution, other environmental problems started to increase because of industrialization. However, as early as the 1950s, the awareness of environmental and ecological issues grew in the UK. As the OECD's 2002 Country Review on environmental performance postulated, 'Since the early 1990s, the UK has made noteworthy progress in decoupling several environmental pressures from economic growth. It achieved strong decoupling for major air pollutants and CO_2, water withdrawals, and agrochemical consumption.'[9]

7 WorldData. (2024, May 29). *Biggest economies in 2022 by gross domestic product*. www.worlddata.info/largest-economies.php

8 Lees, E., & Viñuales, J. E. (Eds.). (2018). *The Oxford handbook of comparative environmental law* (1st ed.). Oxford University Press.

9 Organization for Economic Co-operation and Development (OECD). (2002). *OECD environmental performance reviews: United Kingdom 2002*. OECD Publishing. https://doi.org/10.1787/9789264161078-en

The UK environmental law has ancient roots.[10] However, the evolution of environmental protection through laws is relatively young. The first-ever legislation on any environmental issue was rooted back in the series of epidemics of the early 1800s due to the rigorous and unrestrained industrialization and urbanization of various cities. Published in 1842, Sir Edwin Chadwick's seminal work – *Report on the Sanitary Condition of the Labouring Population of Great Britain*[11] – assisted the government in preparing and passing the *Public Health Act* 1848. This legislation established a Central Board of Health, albeit limited in powers and without money. Though imperfect, it is considered the first step to improving public health in the UK. The legislation conferred powers upon central and local governments to safeguard public health, signifying the commencement of a proactive approach to public health within the nation.[12] This approach, however, was subject to criticism as scholars found that 'the legal system, represented by the courts, compromised with the Industrial Revolution, leaving little room for the successful legal initiative by the individuals and communities adversely affected by it.'[13]

The next significant threat to the environment of the UK was air and water pollution, as coal was used excessively for energy. The waste assemblage produced by the industries also contributed to air and water pollution. By the mid-19th century, some 250,000 tons of salt were being decomposed yearly in alkali works in the UK, releasing about 115,000 tons of acid gas.[14] Judicial proceedings against such polluters did not help, as attributing damages from gas, especially from acid gas, was difficult. In the meantime, the laws for controlling nuisance did not provide sufficient protection against environmental harm.[15]

10 The Book of Deuteronomy, written circa 7th century BCE, provides evidence that rules and regulations to keep a clean and safe environment existed even in the ancient period. There was even rudimentary local control over pollution which was considered small-scaled, in medieval England. See also, Etherington, L. (2016). Canons of environmental law: Pollution of churches and the regulation of the medieval "environment". *Legal Studies*, *36*(4), 566–587.

11 Chadwick, E. (1842). *Report on the sanitary condition of the labouring population of Great Britain* (pp. 23–24). Clowes and Sons.

12 Christman, B. (2013). A brief history of environmental law in the UK. *Environmental Scientist*, *22*(4), 4. Queen's University Belfast Law Research Paper No. 2014–03.

13 McLaren, J. P. S. (1983). Nuisance law and the industrial revolution: Some lessons from social history. *Oxford Journal of Legal Studies*, *3*(2), 155–221. It is worth mentioning the court decision in the *St Helen's Smelting Co v. Tipping* case. Although the decision in this case assisted in shaping the nuisance law in this country, it is criticized for its lenience toward the corporate pollutant (as defendant in this case). For details of this decision, see Mine, C. (2024). *St. Helen's smelting company v tipping*. Gauge Data Solutions Pvt. Ltd. www.casemine.com/judgement/uk/5a938b3d60d03e5f6b82ba20

14 Reed, P. (2014). 150th anniversary of the establishment of the Alkali Inspectorate. *ECG Bulletin*, July 2014, 16.

15 Holder, J., & Lee, M. (2007). *Environmental protection, law and policy: Text and materials* (2nd ed., p. 330). Cambridge University Press.

Realizing that the absence of penalties for actions adversely affecting others provided little incentive for polluters to address their behavior, the government acknowledged the necessity of imposing restrictions on property rights and regulating self-interested conduct.[16] Though the *Smoke Nuisance Abatement Act of 1853* was the first-ever law to control pollution, it was ineffective. The most effective response against pollution was made by the introduction of the *Alkali Act of 1863*. One significant provision of this legislation was the employment of an Alkali Inspector (AI) to oversee the effective operation of the legislation and enforce the emission limit.[17] The legislation mandated that all alkali plants condense at least 95% of the harmful gas. However, compliance with this requirement resulted in a significant increase in water pollution, as the focus on effectively controlling air pollution led to the discharge of liquid by-products from the condensation of noxious gas into rivers and streams.[18] To solve this problem, the subsequent amendments of this legislation expanded its scope to cover air, water, and land pollution from industrial chemical production. The CAA was enacted in 1956. This legislation empowered local authorities to regulate the emissions of smoke, dust, fumes, etc., from industrial premises and furnaces. The legislation also introduced smokeless zones throughout the large cities of this country.

The other major initiatives taken in the mid-20th century were enacting the *Deposit of Poisonous Waste Act 1972* and participating in the United Nations Conference on the Human Environment in 1972. The act was enacted to deal with those who deposit waste on land, which is poisonous, harmful, or polluting in nature and is liable to give rise to environmental hazards. In the same year, the UK joining the EU was another pivotal moment, and it began a new era of the evolution of environmental laws in the UK.

5.2.2 The Era of the European Union and Brexit

The UK officially joined the EU in 1973. The EU played a pivotal role in implementing the UK's environmental policy.[19] The EU policies on air and water pollution control, waste disposal and recycling, chemicals and dangerous substances, biodiversity, environmental impact, and liability have shaped and improved the UK's environmental protection standards. They have also provided the UK with a platform to pursue its environmental objectives

16 Coyle, S., & Morrow, K. (2004). *The philosophical foundations of environmental law: Property, rights and nature* (p. 134). Hart Publishing.

17 Reed, P. (2016). *Entrepreneurial ventures in chemistry: The Muspratts of Liverpool, 1793–1934*. Routledge.

18 Supra note 11, p. 331.

19 Bennet, C. (2016, January 25). Outside the EU, the UK could again be the "dirty man of Europe". *The Ecologist*. https://theecologist.org/2016/jan/25/outside-eu-uk-could-again-be-dirty-man-europe.

internationally and access a valuable knowledge pool.[20] The EU has directed the UK to more robust environmental protection by introducing new procedures or amending existing environmental policies.[21] Due to the escalating amount of legislation, the architecture of modern environmental policy in the UK took shape during this period.

The *Environmental Protection Act 1990* was significant legislation after the UK joined the EU. It was enacted to improve the control of waste management and emissions into the environment. It was the first act to initiate legal responsibilities for pollution control. However, the act was amended by the *Environment Act 1995*. The 1995 Act established the Environment Agency and the Scottish Environment Protection Agency (SEPA).

Stepping into the 21st century, the country's approach to democratizing environmental law by increasing public involvement in environmental matters has altered environment and ecological policymaking into a participatory one, though in a limited way. Such an approach was ushered by various international agreements, most significantly, the Aarhus Convention.[22] This convention boosted the growth of various environmental agencies, for example, Client Earth, Friends of Earth, Green Alliance, which have contributed to forming the modern structure of the environmental frameworks in the UK.

The EU has had a tremendous impact on the UK's current environmental policies. For instance, the Marine Strategy Framework Directive was transposed into the Marine Strategy Regulations 2010. The Directives were to improve the protection of marine water.[23] The waste policies of the UK are based on an EU concept known as the 'waste hierarchy.'[24] The Waste Framework Directive,[25] and the Landfill Directive are the two notable EU directives based on this concept. The Landfill Directive assisted the UK in creating its legislation – the *Landfill (England and Wales) Regulations* in 2002. The impact of this legislation is impressive, as the EU Environmental Implementation Review 2017

20 House of Commons Environmental Audit Committee. (2016). *EU and UK environmental policy: Third report of session 2015–16*. https://publications.parliament.uk/pa/cm201516/cmselect/cmenvaud/537/537.pdf

21 Ibid.

22 The United Nations Economic Commission for Europe's (UNECE). *Convention on access to information, public participation in decision-making and access to justice in environmental matters*, also known as the 'Aarhus Convention,' was ratified by the UK in February 2005.

23 Office for National Statistics. (2021). *Marine accounts, natural capital, UK: 2021*. www.ons.gov.uk/economy/environmentalaccounts/bulletins/marineaccountsnaturalcapitaluk/2021

24 The waste hierarchy is the foundation of EU waste management. It was established in the Waste Management Framework. The hierarchy consists of five steps to create an order of preference for the management and disposal of waste.

25 HM Government. (n.d.). *Review of the balance of competences between the United Kingdom and the European Union environment and climate change*. https://assets.publishing.service.gov.uk/government/uploads/system/uploads/attachment_data/file/284500/environment-climate-change-documents-final-report.pdf

found that the percentage of waste being landfilled had significantly dropped in this country.[26]

The UK showed its strong commitment to mitigating climate change-induced environmental problems by introducing the *Climate Change Act* in 2008. It is the first regulatory framework to legally bind a country to the global commitment against climate change-induced environmental hazards, targeting it as the first legislation of this kind in the world.[27] The legislation mandates the Secretary of State for Energy and Climate Change[28] to ensure that the UK reduces its net GHGs by 26% and 80% from the 1990 baseline by 2020 and 2050, respectively.[29] This legislation seems impactful as it has been found that from 2005 to 2022, there was a 60% decrease in nitrogen oxide emissions, an 83% decrease in sulfur dioxide emissions, a 7% decrease in ammonia emissions, and a 59% decrease in carbon monoxide emissions.[30]

5.2.3 The Brexit Initiative[31]

The UK had been a key player of higher climate ambition within the EU (and beyond to international negotiations in the UN) and a greener Common Agricultural Policy (CAP).[32] Therefore, environmental agencies and experts have repeatedly criticized the UK's decision to leave the EU. Many opine that departing from the EU will have significant consequences for the existing and proposed environmental and ecological frameworks, as the UK's legislations are heavily influenced and shaped by the EU.[33] Colin T. Reid opines that the EU laws are entangled with the UK laws in many ways, and it won't be easy

26 European Commission. (2017). *EU environmental implementation review 2017 factsheet: Country highlights: The United Kingdom.* https://ec.europa.eu/environment/eir/pdf/country-reports-archive/factsheet_uk_en.pdf

27 Organisation for Economic Co-operation and Development (OECD). (n.d.). *The United Kingdom's pioneering climate change act.* www.oecd.org/climate-action/ipac/practices/the-united-kingdom-s-pioneering-climate-change-act-c08c3d7a/.

28 Previously known as Secretary of State.

29 Christman, B. (2013). A brief history of environmental law in the UK. *Environmental Scientist, 22*(4), 4. Queen's University Belfast Law Research Paper No. 2014–03.

30 National Atmospheric Emissions Inventory. (2022). *UK informative inventory report (1990 to 2020.* https://uk-air.defra.gov.uk/assets/documents/reports/cat09/2203151456_GB_IIR_2022_Submission_v1.pdf; European Environment Agency. (2015). *SOER 2015: The European environment report: State and outlook.* www.eea.europa.eu/soer/2015/countries/united-kingdom

31 Brexit refers to Britain exiting the EU.

32 Ibid.

33 Burns, C., Gravey, V., & Jordan, A. (2018). *UK environmental policy post-Brexit: A risk analysis: A report commissioned by Friends of the Earth England, Wales and Northern Ireland.* ESRC UK in a Changing Europe Initiative. www.brexitenvironment.co.uk/wp-content/uploads/2018/04/Environment-and-Brexit-Risk-Analysis-C-Burns-Et-al-2018.pdf

to untangle.[34] He emphasizes the stability and accountability provided by EU laws, contrasting them with older UK domestic instruments.[35] Critics also worry that the UK government could modify environmental regulations in areas not governed by the European Economic Area, threatening the UK's ecological framework.[36]

The government's White Paper on the 2017 Repeal Bill emphasized that the Great Repeal Bill would ensure the continuity of all existing EU environmental laws in UK legislation, providing certainty for businesses and stakeholders as the UK exited the EU.[37] To achieve this, the *European Union (Withdrawal) Act 2018* introduced the Retained EU Law (REUL) concept.[38] This act outlined the procedure for retaining existing EU laws or 'EU-derived domestic legislation.' The EU (Withdrawal) Bill, Factsheet number 8, which addresses environmental principles, assured that the UK's long-standing environmental protection would not be weakened by leaving the EU and committed to upholding all obligations under international environmental treaties.[39] The British government has emphasized that leaving the EU will enable the implementation of an improved environmental policy tailored to the country's needs.[40] Additionally, the British government has published the *25-Year Environment Plan*, outlining the country's plan for environmental development.

5.2.4 *Post-Brexit Era*

The UK officially removed all its ties with the EU in December 2020, ushering in a new era for the environmental law of this country. No diaristic change has been made since the official date of the transition. However, the UK has

34 Reid, C. T. (2016). Brexit and the future of UK environmental law. *Journal of Energy & Natural Resources Law*, *34*(4), 407–415. https://doi.org/10.1080/02646811.2016.1218133

35 Ibid.

36 Burns, C., Jordan, A., Gravey, V., Berny, N., Bulmer, S., Carter, N., Cowell, R., Dutton, J., Moore, B., Oberthür, S., Owens, S., Rayner, T., Scott, J., & Stewart, B. (2016). *The EU referendum and the UK environment: An expert review. How has EU membership affected the UK, and what might change in the event of a vote to remain or leave? Executive Summary*. http://environmentEUref.blogspot.co.uk/

37 Department for Exiting the European Union. (2017). *Policy paper: Legislating for the United Kingdom's withdrawal from the European Union*. www.gov.uk/government/publications/the-repeal-bill-white-paper/legislating-for-the-united-kingdoms-withdrawal-from-the-european-union

38 REUL refers to *Retained EU Law*, which includes laws the UK has kept to provide legislative continuity immediately after Brexit.

39 Department for Exiting the European Union. (2018). *EU (withdrawal) bill: Factsheet 8: Environmental principles*. https://assets.publishing.service.gov.uk/government/uploads/system/uploads/attachment_data/file/714379/180511_EUWB_Environmental_Protections_factsheet_10_May_18.pdf

40 Ibid.

taken a few initiatives to improve its environment by implementing new legislation. The Environment Act 2021 is the first-ever legislation passed by the British government after Brexit. The legislation has been enacted to provide much-improved ecological protection now that the UK has finally left the EU. It contains mechanisms to protect the natural environment, especially in four priority areas: air quality, water, waste management, and biodiversity.

This legislation also requires a long-term environmental improvement plan to ensure that the *25-Year Environment Plan* can transition into reality from ambition. It empowers the government to set new legally binding targets. It included five environmental principles: (a) environmental integration, (b) prevention, (c) rectification at source, (d) polluter pays, and (e) precautionary principle.

The most significant feature of this legislation is the founding of a new environmental regulator – the Office for Environmental Protection (OEP). The main objectives of this office are to hold the government and other public bodies accountable and ensure that environmental laws are complied with.[41]

5.2.5 Covid-19 Pandemic

The Covid-19 pandemic has had a profound impact on the country's economy. However, it also resulted in a notable decrease in air pollution. Data from ten cities in the UK during the lockdown indicated that nitrogen dioxide levels and small particle pollution were significantly lower than usual for spring, according to the UK Research and Innovation report.[42] Ally Lewis, Director of Science at the National Centre for Atmospheric Science, suggests that while the improvement in air quality may have had only a minor impact during the pandemic, it will undoubtedly benefit the environment in the long term.[43] The UK Centre for Ecology & Hydrology (UKECH) opines that 'air pollution levels during the lockdown period provided valuable evidence on how air quality might change as sources are reduced, for example, as part of the UK's transition to net zero greenhouse gas emissions.'[44]

Through its commencement of the environmental policy and profound changes in legislation, along with similarly remarkable policies and regulations in other areas of the environment, the UK has emerged as a leading nation in decreasing pollution and improving the environment among its European

41 ClientEarth. (2022). *The UK environment act – what's happening now?* www.clientearth.org/latest/latest-updates/news/why-the-uk-environment-bill-matters

42 UK Research and Innovation. (2021). *Impact on the environment.* www.ukri.org/news-and-events/tackling-the-impact-of-covid-19/researching-the-impact-of-coronavirus/impact-on-the-environment/

43 Ibid.

44 UK Centre for Ecology & Hydrology. (n.d.). *UKCEH supports UK's emergency response to COVID-19.* www.ceh.ac.uk/news-and-media/news/ukceh-supports-uk-emergency-response-covid-19

peers. According to the OECD Environmental Performance Review 2022, among the G7 countries, the UK was the first to legislate net-zero GHG emissions by 2050 to follow the Paris Agreement.[45] The review praised the UK's significant reduction of GHGs with the shift to renewable energy and the change of power production from coal to gas. However, the study noted the slow progress rate outside the energy industry.

The ecological condition of the UK is progressing, but there are still some areas in which the country needs to focus more. Air pollution is still the UK's most significant environmental risk to health. To top it up, carbon-intensive industries and waste produced by many industries regularly contribute to issues like climate change, disturbance in the marine ecosystem, debris, and soil contamination. The same concern was pondered upon in the OECD Environmental Performance Review 2022, which contemplates:

> Over the past decade, the United Kingdom has reduced several environmental pressures while growing its economy. Protected areas, especially marine areas, significantly expanded. However, concerns include air pollution, deteriorating natural assets, and missed biodiversity targets. Further efforts are needed to achieve net zero greenhouse gas (GHG) emissions by 2050, prepare for climate change, reverse biodiversity loss, and ensure a more resource-efficient circular economy.[46]

The current climate and environment in the UK are generally improving, but the long-term impact of Brexit is still uncertain. Widespread changes are happening in the UK's environment, with the average temperature now 1.2°C higher than before industrialization.[47] However, 'the 2020 Ten Point Plan for a Green Industrial Revolution,' 'the 2021 Plan to Build Back Better,' 'Net Zero Strategy to Build Back Greener and the Fairer,' 'Greener Scotland Programmer for government 2021–2022,' to name a few, the government's interest on green recovery. It's important to note that while the new *Environment Act 2021* seems promising for the ecological improvement of the UK, future environmental progress relies on the proper implementation of this legislation.

5.3 Regulating Corporate Polluters in the United States

The Industrial Revolution began in the United States in the 1820s. The first ever corporation was built in the 1790s and gradually became the United

45 Organisation for Economic Co-operation and Development. (2022). *OECD environmental performance reviews: United Kingdom 2022*. OECD Publishing. https://doi.org/10.1787/b6a2be87-en

46 Ibid.

47 Supra note 54.

States' primary source of economic development. Though corporations were functioning in Europe in the early 19th century – especially in Great Britain and the Netherlands – the United States took corporate development to a new level.[48] The overwhelming progress in America through the expansion of corporations took its toll on the environment. Due to the sudden growth of industrialization, acres of forests were destroyed, and numerous natural landscapes were radically transformed, causing an alarming level of harm to the environment. With 11% of the world's total GHG emissions, it is the second-largest GHG emitter after China.[49]

The United States took environmental issues seriously only in the late 20th century. The notion that ecosystems, water bodies, and air masses should be designated as geographical units warranting special legal protection was not prevalent until the late 19th and early 20th centuries.[50] At this time, the U.S. government started to initiate various legal frameworks in the environmental context, mainly to cut back on the constant ecological destruction and pollution. Since the 1970s, Congress has passed several significant legislations to pull the reins on corporate pollution. This was also the time when the United States faced backlash from various corporations. They highlighted the high cost of implementing regulations for environmental protection against the low budgetary capacity of the government. Despite these gridlocks, the United States has achieved significant success in controlling pollution in areas like air and water, waste management, and wildlife protection during this time.

5.3.1 Before the 1970s

The oldest federal environmental law in the United States is the *Rivers and Harbors Appropriation Act 1899*. This legislation made discharging any refuse matter in any navigable water or excavating, filling, or shifting the course of any port, harbor, and channel without the permission of the U.S. government a misdemeanor. Although superseded mainly by the *Clean Water Act*, some of its provisions are still in operation. Other than this legislation, before the late 20th century, there were no notable legal frameworks to protect the environment against corporate pollution. Most of the significant legal frameworks were passed during the 1960s to 1980s.

48 Investopedia. (2021). *What is the history of corporations in America?* Retrieved June 20, 2022, from www.investopedia.com/ask/answers/041515/what-history-corporations-america.asp

49 Rhodium Group. (2021). *China's greenhouse gas emissions exceeded the developed world for the first time in 2019*. Retrieved June 20, 2022, from https://rhg.com/research/chinas-emissions-surpass-developed-countries/

50 Tarlock, A. D., & Dernbach, J. C. (2009). *Environmental laws and their enforcement* (p. 42). Macmillan Publishers.

Rachel Carson's 1962 book – *Silent Spring* – is considered a milestone in developing the environmental movement in the United States.[51] The book documented the deadly effect of synthetic pesticides on birds and other wildlife and eventually on humans, having a massive impact on public opinion. Various environmental crises that began in the late 1960s – the Santa Barbara Oil Spill,[52] smog in New York City and Los Angeles,[53] and the Cuyahoga River fires[54] – informed Americans about the frightening consequences of ecological imbalance. *The Population Bomb* by Paul Ehrlich, published in 1968, threw

51 Chemistry for Life. (2022). *Legacy of Rachel Carson's silent spring*. Retrieved June 23, 2022, from www.acs.org/content/acs/en/education/whatischemistry/landmarks/rachel-carson-silent-spring.html

52 The Santa Barbara oil spill transpired between the years 1969 and 1970, resulting in the discharge of approximately 3.4–4.2 million U.S. gallons of crude oil into the Channel and along the beaches of Santa Barbara County, located in Southern California. This event had a significant impact on marine life, resulting in the deaths of an estimated 3,500 sea birds and various marine animals. The economic consequences of the spill were severe, leading to the suspension of all commercial fishing in the affected area and a decline in tourism. The spill also caused property damage along the shoreline, resulting in class-action lawsuits against Union Oil to recover damages, which were settled within about five years. For details, see Thulin, L. (2019, April 22). *How an oil spill inspired the first Earth Day*. Smithsonian. www.smithsonianmag.com/history/how-oil-spill-50-years-ago-inspired-first-earth-day-180972007/; Hamilton, J. (2019, January 28). *How California's worst oil spill turned beaches black and the nation green*. NPR. www.npr.org/2019/01/28/688219307/how-californias-worst-oil-spill-turned-beaches-black-and-the-nation-green

53 Los Angeles has been consistently ranked number one for ozone pollution, posing a threat to public health and the environment. Its air quality has been impacted by increased heat, more active wildfire seasons, and particle pollution from devastating wildfires. New York is one of the ten cities with the worst smog-fouled air. Like Los Angeles, New York is facing challenges related to unhealthy air, necessitating measures to mitigate the impact of pollution on public health. For details, see Daniels, J. (2019, April 24). *Los Angeles is still the smoggiest US city, report says*. CNBC. www.cnbc.com/2019/04/24/los-angeles-is-still-the-smoggiest-us-city-report-says.html; American Lung Association. (2024). *New York*. www.lung.org/research/sota/city-rankings/msas/new-york-newark-ny-nj-ct-pa#ozone; Margaritoff, M. (2021, October 2). *The story of the New York City smog of 1966 that killed 200 people*. All That's Interesting. https://allthatsinteresting.com/new-york-city-smog-1966

54 The Cuyahoga River had a history of pollution due to industrial waste and sewage being dumped into the river. The fires, particularly the 1969 fire, highlighted the severe pollution of the Cuyahoga River and the detrimental impact of industrial waste on water quality and aquatic life. It brought national attention to the issue of water pollution and the environmental movement in the United States. For more about this incident, see Blackmore, E. (2023, October 4). *The shocking river fire that fueled the creation of the EPA*. History. Retrieved June 21, 2022, from www.history.com/news/epa-earth-day-cleveland-cuyahoga-river-fire-clean-water-act; National Park Service. (n.d.). *The 1969 Cuyahoga River fire*. U.S. Department of the Interior. Retrieved June 21, 2022, from www.nps.gov/articles/story-of-the-fire.htm; Boissoneault, L. (2019, June 19). The Cuyahoga River caught fire at least a dozen times, but no one cared until 1969. *Smithsonian*. www.smithsonianmag.com/history/cuyahoga-river-caught-fire-least-dozen-times-no-one-cared-until-1969-180972444/

further light on the bourgeoning environmental crisis.[55] All these events led to an outraged public demanding a balance between safeguarding the environment and economic growth. As an outcome of this demand, the government of this country passed the *Clean Water Act in 1963*. The *Wilderness Act* was passed in 1964. It provided a new definition of wilderness, protected numerous wilderness areas, and laid the base for creating the National Wilderness Preservation System in this country.

5.3.2 From the 1970s

The United States' environmental policy underwent a noteworthy shift in the 1970s. The legislative work during this period showed the impact of the environmental movement in the late 1960s. Amid the environmental crisis in the late 1960s, Congress drafted a new law to promote environmental improvement. The law, known as the *NEPA*, was passed in 1969 and finally signed into law on January 1, 1970. The act is the world's first legislation for EIA.[56] It assisted in creating a national policy to protect the environment against any action taken by the federal government and the Council of Environmental Quality (CEQ) to monitor the implementation of the legislation. NEPA obliges federal agencies to evaluate the environmental effects of their planned actions before making decisions by preparing an EIA.[57] The NEPA mechanism significantly transformed government engagement with ecological issues, and this model has been replicated in 23 states.[58] Created in the mid-1970s, the EPA consolidated the duties of all other agencies and state governments regarding environmental protection. The Agency is responsible for implementing, maintaining, and enforcing environmental legislation and creating legal provisions to meet Federal requirements on ecological protection.

The CAA, initially passed in 1963 and later amended in 1970, is a landmark instance of environmental protection legislation in the United States. Like the NEPA, this act established a federal program within the U.S. Public Health Service to extend research on controlling air pollution. The act underwent two more significant amendments in 1977 and 1990, with the latter

55 University of Michigan: Michigan in the World. (n.d.). *"Environmental crisis" in the late 1960s.* Retrieved June 23, 2022, from https://michiganintheworld.history.lsa.umich.edu/environmentalism/exhibits/show/main_exhibit/origins/-environmental-crisis-in-the-.

56 Environmental Impact Assessment (EIA) is a systematic decision-making tool that compares various alternatives for a project and selects the one which offers the best combination of economic and environmental costs and benefits. Simply put, it is a study to predict the consequences of any potential action on the environment. Many countries have EIA interposed in their domestic law to enhance environmental protection.

57 United States Environmental Protection Agency (EPA). (n.d.). *What is the national environmental policy act?* Retrieved June 21, 2022, from www.epa.gov/nepa/what-national-environmental-policy-act

58 Gad, S. E., & Gad, S. C. (2005). National environmental policy act, US. In S. E. Gad (Ed.), *Encyclopedia of toxicology* (2nd ed., p. 193). Elsevier.

notably increasing the capacities of governmental agencies in controlling environmental hazards.[59] Among the other legislations introduced in the 1970s, the amendment of the *Clean Water Act* stands out. This amendment and the *Ocean Dumping Act* played a significant role in establishing a robust structure to regulate pollution discharges into the waters and ensure quality standards for surface waters. These legislations, with their stringent regulations, have been instrumental in protecting the nation's water resources, a testament to the effectiveness of U.S. environmental policy in the 1970s.

The *Endangered Species Act* was passed in 1973. It aims to protect wildlife in danger of extinction due to extensive economic growth. It sets obligations for both federal and state governments to protect all rare species and has established a program to conserve endangered animals and plants in their habitats. The U.S. Supreme Court finds this legislation 'the most comprehensive of its type to be enacted by any nation.'[60]

The *Toxic Substance Control Act* and the *Resource Conservation and Recovery Act* were passed in 1976. The *Toxic Substance Control Act* was designed to test, regulate, and screen all chemicals manufactured or imported into the United States. It gives EPA the authority to require reporting, testing, and keeping track of chemical substances and mixtures. It also authorized EPA to put restrictions on certain chemical substances if necessary. Nonetheless, it was repelled in 2016 by the *Lautenberg Chemical Safety Act.* The Resource Conservation and Recovery Act was enacted to tackle the rising problems of the increasing quantity of municipal and industrial waste faced by the United States. It gives the EPA authority to control and regulate hazardous waste management. It also provides a structure for managing non-hazardous solid wastes.

The CERCLA *of 1980* was another critical legislation that addressed the responses to processing deserted harmful waste sites, accidental spills, and other emergency discharges of toxins. Under the act, a federal superfund was created to clean up abandoned harmful waste sites and accidents, spills, and other emergency discharges of toxins into the environment.[61] The act is also known as the 'Superfund' act. The *Emergency Planning and Community Right-to-Know Act* was passed in 1986 to amend the CERCLA. It is also known as SARA Title III.[62] The act was enacted to help communities make plans for emergencies caused by chemicals. It also obliges the industry to

59 Organisation for Economic Co-operation and Development (OECD). (2006). *OECD environmental performance reviews: United States 2005.* OECD Environmental Performance Reviews. OECD Publishing. https://doi.org/10.1787/9789264013179-en

60 See the judgment of the US Supreme Court in *Tennessee Valley Authority v. Hill*, 437 U.S. 153 (1978).

61 United States Environmental Protection Agency (EPA). (n.d.). *Summary of the comprehensive environmental response, compensation, and liability act (superfund).* Retrieved June 23, 2022, from www.epa.gov/laws-regulations/summary-comprehensive-environmental-response-compensation-and-liability-act.

62 SARA means *Superfund Amendments and Reauthorization Act.*

report the storage, use, and release of harmful substances to the government at the federal, state, and local levels.

The *Pollution Prevention Act* of 1990 was established to create a national policy to promote the prevention and reduction of pollution at its source through changes in production and operation processes and how raw materials are used. The *Oil Pollution Act* was passed the same year, enhancing the EPA's ability to prevent and respond to major oil spills. The EPA is now authorized to require detailed plans from both public and private companies regarding large oil reserves and discharges. Since 1990, there haven't been any significant new laws enacted for environmental protection and pollution control, although the EPA has been continuously introducing new regulations to manage corporate pollution as needed.

5.3.3 U.S. Constitution and Judiciary on Expanding Environmental Policy

It would be inaccurate to claim that the U.S. Constitution plays no role in expanding environmental protection, even though it does not have a direct provision to grant such a right. Before the late 1960s, environmental protection was not a primary concern, and as a result, the Constitution did not contain a direct clause guaranteeing the right to environmental protection. However, *Article I, Clause 8* of the Constitution, also known as the commerce clause, is considered a crucial mechanism for protecting the environment. Most primary environmental legislation in the United States relies on this clause, which federal courts have extensively interpreted to justify federal control of environmental pollution issues. Furthermore, the federal government's taxing power is another mechanism that enables the government to levy fees and fines to control corporate polluters.[63]

The treaty-making power is another important source of constitutional authority for environmental protection. The federal government can make an environmental treaty with another country through this power. In *Missouri v. Holland*,[64] the Court had sustained the *Migratory Bird Treaty Act of 1918*.[65]

63 A federal carbon tax would generate significant federal revenues, potentially bringing in hundreds of billions of dollars per year. The revenues raised by the tax are contingent on the tax rates, scope, and other design options. For instance, the Deutch Bill suggests that carbon tax revenues would increase from $70 billion in 2020 to $400 billion in 2030. For more about this, see Kaufman, N. (2019, June 6). What you need to know about a federal carbon tax in the United States. *Center on Global Energy Policy at Columbia University*. Retrieved June 21, 2022, from www.energypolicy.columbia.edu/publications/what-you-need-to-know-about-a-federal-carbon-tax-in-the-united-states

64 *Missouri v. Holland*, 252 U.S. 416 (1920).

65 The *Migratory Bird Treaty Act* (MBTA) is a federal law in the United States that was enacted in 1918. The primary purpose of the *Migratory Bird Treaty Act* is to protect migratory birds, their nests, and their eggs from being taken, possessed, imported, exported, transported, sold, purchased, or bartered, except under the terms of a valid permit.

According to the Supreme Court, the Supremacy Clause (*Article VI*, *Clause 2*) recognizes that treaties are the 'supreme law of the land' and thus cannot be struck down. The Court upheld the *Migratory Bird Act*, although a similar act, which was not based on a treaty, had earlier been considered invalid as beyond the scope of congressional power.

The judiciary also played a crucial role in expanding the legislative framework for ecological protection. In this regard, the *Scenic Hudson Preservation Conference v. Federal Power Commission*[66] is one of the earliest cases, where the Court upheld the action brought by the environmental group to stop building a power plant on Strom King Mountain on the grounds of public interest. Judge Paul R. Hays divulged:

> To ensure that the Federal Power Commission will adequately protect the public interest in the aesthetic, conservational, and recreational aspects of power development, those who by their activities and conduct have exhibited a special interest in such areas, must be held to be included in the class of 'aggrieved' parties under § 313(b). We hold that the Federal Power Act gives petitioners a legal right to protect their special interests.[67]

In 2004, the U.S. Supreme Court clarified the power and scope of EPA to protect the environment.[68] The Court concurs that the CAA 1990 authorizes the EPA to examine whether a company uses the 'best available controlling technology' to stop pollution. EPA is also allowed to stop building a new facility that emits pollutants, as permitted by a state environmental regulator if such a facility does not have the 'best available controlling technology' to avert pollution.

5.3.4 *Massachusetts v. Environmental Protection Agency*[69]

The case was a landmark in the United States' control of GHGs. In this case, the Supreme Court regarded carbon dioxide and GHGs as air pollutants under the CAA. The pollutants could be controlled by the EPA.[70] However, the U.S.

66 *Scenic Hudson Preservation Conference v. Federal Power Commission*, 354 F.2d 608 (2d Cir. 1965).

67 Justia. (n.d.). Scenic Hudson preservation conference, town of Cortlandt, Town of Putnam Valley and Town of Yorktown, Petitioners, v. Federal Power Commission, Respondent, Andconsolidated Edison Company of New York, Inc., Intervener, 354 F.2d 608 (2d Cir. 1965). *Justia Law*. Retrieved June 23, 2022, from https://law.justia.com/cases/federal/appellate-courts/F2/354/608/151121/

68 *Alaska Department of Environmental Conservation v. EPA*, 540 U.S. 461 (2004).

69 *Massachusetts v. Environmental Protection Agency*, 549 U.S. 497 (2007).

70 Ballotpedia. (n.d.). *Massachusetts v. environmental protection agency*. Retrieved June 23, 2022, from https://ballotpedia.org/Massachusetts_v._Environmental_Protection_Agency

Supreme Court recently promulgated a controversial decision regarding carbon dioxide emission regulation by EPA.[71] In this case, the Court ruled that the EPA has no authority to take any new action or regulate unless Congress specifically authorized it. In this case, some states and coal industries challenged the EPA's power to regulate existing power plants under Section 7411(d) of the CAA *1990*. The Supreme Court ruled in favor of the coal industries by stating that regulating existing power plants in Section 7411(d) falls under the major questions doctrine. As per this doctrine, Congress did not grant the EPA jurisdiction to regulate emissions from existing plants based on the principles of generation shifting. Chief Justice John Roberts stated that under the 'major questions doctrine,' neither the EPA nor any other agency can approve rules that have a 'transformational' impact on the economy unless Congress has explicitly endorsed such a rule to address a specific issue, such as climate change.[72] J. Kagan, the dissenting Judge, pointed out:

> [T]he majority says it is simply 'not plausible' that Congress enabled EPA to regulate power plants' emissions through generation shifting. . . . But that is just what Congress did when it broadly authorized EPA in Section 111 to select the 'best system of emission reduction' for power plants. . . . The 'best system' full stop – no ifs, ands, or buts of any kind relevant here.[73]

Many environmental organizations opine that this new ruling by the Supreme Court has curtailed the EPA's power to control GHG emissions. UN Spokesperson Stéphane Dujarric commented that the ruling by the U.S. Supreme Court against the EPA is an obstacle in the global fight against climate change.[74] The ruling of the Supreme Court will impact the ecological balance of an already imbalanced atmosphere of the United States, which is considered one of the world's biggest polluters. The decision also creates more challenges for other environmental agencies. The verdict also put the United States in a backward position on its promise to cut carbon dioxide emissions to 32% below its 2005 emissions by 2030. While this case can devastate environmental protection, this is not the first time the U.S. Supreme Court has favored the corporation against environmental agencies. The same pattern can

71 *West Virginia v. EPA*, 2022 WL 2347278.

72 NPR (National Public Radio). (2022, June 30). ***Supreme Court restricts the EPA's authority to mandate carbon emissions reductions.*** Retrieved July 2, 2022, from www.npr.org/2022/06/30/1103595898/supreme-court-epa-climate-change

73 Supreme Court of the United States. (2022). ***West Virginia et al. v. Environmental protection agency.*** Retrieved July 2, 2022, from www.supremecourt.gov/opinions/21pdf/20-1530_n758.pdf

74 United Nations. (2022, June 30). US Supreme Court ruling on environmental protection "a setback in our fight against climate change". *UN News*. Retrieved July 1, 2022, from https://news.un.org/en/story/2022/06/1121782

be seen in the 2015 case, *Michigan v. EPA*,[75] where the court decision favored the corporation. The case was criticized for not considering the health impact of corporate emissions.

5.3.5 Pollution Control and Ecological Structure

As mentioned earlier, the United States is the second-largest GHG emitter in the world. The United States has some praiseworthy legislation to control its already mountain-high pollution emissions. The OECD, in its 2005 *Environmental Performance Review*, remarked: 'the National Environmental Policy Act, together with other sectoral acts, sets environmental protection as an overarching goal and establishes the framework of environmental federalism, within which specific environmental management responsibilities are shared among federal, state and local authorities.'[76] Some mechanisms, such as implementing laws and regulations through cost-effective methods and funding, have effectively helped the country reduce its pollution rate.

The recent data published by the EPA[77] shows that, in 2020, total GHG emissions were equivalent to 5,981.4 million metric tons of carbon dioxide. According to the data, emissions decreased by 7.3% from 1990 to 2020. From 2019 to 2020, 10.6% of net emissions decreased, while 21.5% decreased from 2005 to 2020. The data further noted that the sharp fall in emissions during 2019 and 2020 is mainly due to the impacts of the COVID-19 pandemic on travel and economic activity.

The United States has made significant progress in reducing GHG emissions. The government implemented various mechanisms to continue this trend, such as the Clean Power Plan 2015. Under this plan, each state was given a goal to reduce carbon dioxide emissions, and they had the flexibility to choose their methods for achieving this. The EPA was authorized to intervene if a state failed to submit a plan. The ultimate aim was to cut carbon dioxide emissions by 32% by 2030. However, in 2017, the Trump administration repealed the plan and withdrew the United States from the Paris Agreement. In 2019, under the Trump administration, the EPA introduced a new plan called the 'Affordable Clean Energy Rule,' which was challenged in the *American Lung Association v. EPA* case.[78] The court criticized the plan as a fundamental misunderstanding of environmental laws and ruled that the

75 *Michigan v. Environmental Protection Agency*, 576 U.S. 743 (2015).

76 Organization for Economic Co-operation and Development (OECD). (2006). *OECD environmental performance reviews: United States 2005.* OECD Environmental Performance Reviews. OECD Publishing. https://doi.org/10.1787/9789264013179-en

77 U.S. Environmental Protection Agency (EPA). (2022). *Inventory of U.S. greenhouse gas emissions and sinks: 1990–2020* (EPA 430-R-22-003). U.S. Environmental Protection Agency. Retrieved June 28, 2022, from www.epa.gov/ghgemissions/draft-inventory-us-greenhouse-gas-emissionsand-sinks-1990-2020

78 *American Lung Association v. Environmental Protection Agency*, 19–1140 (D.C. Cir. 2021).

industry-friendly climate regulation for power plants violated federal laws.[79] While this ruling was a win for environmental protection, the 2022 Supreme Court ruling in *West Virginia v. EPA* curbed the environmental movement in the United States.

The energy sector is a significant source of GHG emissions. In the United States, this sector accounts for 84% of GHG emissions, 80% of nitrogen oxide (NOx) emissions, and 96% of sulfur dioxide, the primary precursor of sulfate aerosol.[80] Meanwhile, coal-based power plants are reviving in the United States due to the inflation of natural gas prices in recent years, increasing GHG emissions. The new Supreme Court ruling has restricted the EPA's capability to limit the emission rate by coal-based power plants. An analysis of EPA data by the Environment Department of Texas shows that the coal plant Martin Lake in Tatum, Texas, released 13.5 million metric tons of GHG in 2020.[81] The energy plant was among the top ten highest GHG-emitting energy plants. Meanwhile, the overall temperature level of the United States is rising every year, causing catastrophic environmental disasters like drought, heat waves, and wildfires. It has been revealed in the Fourth National Climate Assessment Report that the annual average temperatures in the United States have increased by 1.8°F since the start of the 20th century.[82] In recent years, the country has also experienced increasing heat waves and wildfires.

If the United States fails to reduce its GHG emissions level to a more tolerable level, no matter how successful its previous environmental mechanism was, it would not be enough to balance a healthy environment and economic growth. The crucial problem in implementing the environmental frameworks is the lack of coherence and cooperation between federal and state agencies. Also, the non-cooperation of state governments is pushing back the environmental progress of the United States.

79 Bloomberg Law. (2021). EPA's industry-friendly climate rule struck down by court. *Bloomberg Law*. Retrieved June 27, 2022, from https://news.bloomberglaw.com/environment-and-energy/epas-industry-friendly-climate-rule-struck-down-by-court

80 U.S. Global Change Research Program (USGCRP). (2018). *Impacts, risks, and adaptation in the United States: Fourth national climate assessment, Volume II: Report-in-brief* (D. R. Reidmiller, C. W. Avery, D. R. Easterling, K. E. Kunkel, K. L. M. Lewis, T. K. Maycock, & B. C. Stewart, Eds.). U.S. Global Change Research Program. https://doi.org/10.7930/NCA4.2018.RiB

81 The Texas Tribune. (2022). *U.S. Supreme Court ruling limits EPA's authority in regulating greenhouse gases*. The Texas Tribune. Retrieved July 2, 2022, from www.texastribune.org/2022/06/30/environment-epa-supreme-court/

82 See U.S. Global Change Research Program. (2018). *Fourth national climate assessment, volume II: Impacts, risks, and adaptation in the United States*. https://nca2018.globalchange.gov/

5.4 Regulating Corporate Polluters in Australia

Australia, known for its diverse ecosystem, started witnessing environmental degradation in the 1970s. During the same period, the environmental movement gained substantial momentum nationwide. This movement generated awareness among Australians regarding the necessity of environmental protection, leading to notable changes in the country's political landscape and prompting reinterpretations of constitutional structures that influenced Australian environmental law.[83] This movement is recognized as the world's first significant political environmental movement and played a pivotal role in shaping Australia's environmental policy.

Australia operates as a federal state similar to the United States. However, unlike the United States, each state independently manages its environmental regulation framework. State legislation serves as the primary mechanism for environmental regulation in Australia. Nevertheless, the federal government, known as the Commonwealth government, also has the authority to create policy guidelines and public organizations to assist the states in regulating corporate polluters and industrial pollution.

The Commonwealth does not possess direct legislative power over environmental protection. When the Australian constitution was established in the 1900s, environmental protection was not a primary concern for the legislators.[84] As a result, the authority to legislate on environmental protection is held by both the Commonwealth and the States, resulting in a dual legislative framework for environmental protection in Australia. This means that laws and policies at both the Commonwealth and state levels aim to protect the environment and address climate change. These laws are designed to balance maintaining a healthy ecosystem and promoting economic growth.

5.4.1 Commonwealth Laws and Policies to Control Corporate Pollution

Before the 1900s, Australia did not prioritize ecological conservation, resulting in limited environmental activism. Despite this, the Commonwealth introduced several laws to address environmental issues. Notable legislation enacted in the 1970s include the *Environment Protection (Impact of Proposals) Act 1974*, the *National Parks and Wildlife Conservation Act 1975*, and the *Great Barrier Reef Marine Park Act 1975*. The latter was instrumental

83 Godden, L., Peel, J., & McDonald, J. (2018). *Environmental law* (p. 110). Oxford University Press.

84 Crawford remarked that 'the drafters of the Constitution would have emphasized the immensity of the continent, the difficulties in "overcoming" it, rather than the fragility of many of its ecosystems or the problems in managing it once it had been overcome' (as cited in Bates, G. M., 1992). For details, see Bates, G. M. (1992). *Environmental law in Australia*. LexisNexis Butterworths.

in safeguarding the reef from marine oil drilling and mineral mining while permitting activities like fishing and tourism in specific zones. It was one of the earliest regulations overseeing corporate activities. Furthermore, the key legislation for environmental protection, the *Environment Protection and Biodiversity Conservation Act*, was passed in 1999, replacing the *National Parks and Wildlife Conservation Act 1975*.

The *Environment Protection and Biodiversity Conservation Act 1999* is the legal foundation for safeguarding and managing flora, fauna, ecological communities, and heritage places of national environmental importance. The Australian Government is responsible for tackling issues of national environmental significance, while the states and territories oversee matters of state and local importance. The Department of Agriculture, Water, and the Environment administers this legislation. It identifies eight matters of national environmental importance, including world heritage properties, national heritage sites, internationally significant wetlands, migratory species protected by global treaties, listed threatened species and ecological communities, Commonwealth marine areas, the Great Barrier Reef Marine Park, and nuclear actions like uranium mining. The act criminalizes any action that is likely to significantly impact matters protected by the legislation unless it has the approval of the Environment Minister of Australia.[85] Section 522A of the act requires independent statutory review every ten years. Graeme Samuel recently conducted an independent study on the act and submitted an interim report with his findings. The report concludes that the existing environmental course is unsustainable, and fundamental reform of the *Environment Protection and Biodiversity Conservation Act 1999*, focusing on restoration, is essential to cease the decline.[86] The report has criticized the act for not clearly outlining its intended outcomes, and it states that the act is complex and cumbersome and has little benefit for the environment and economic growth.

Australia has a comprehensive environmental protection law, with separate frameworks for climate change and pollutant emissions at the Commonwealth level. Currently, the Commonwealth has three major frameworks for addressing climate change and reducing pollutant emissions, including the *Carbon Credits (Carbon Farming Initiative) Act 2011*. This act was enacted to fulfill Australia's commitments under the UNFCCC and the Kyoto Protocol and to incentivize projects that help cost-effectively reduce carbon emissions. The

85 Australian Government: Department of Climate Change, Energy, the Environment and Water. (2022). *Local government and Australian environment law*. Retrieved July 16, 2022, from www.dcceew.gov.au/environment/epbc/publications/local-government-and-australian-environment-aw

86 Pacey, K., & Back, O. (2021). Fundamental reform recommended for "ineffective and inefficient" EPBC Act. *Clayton Utz*. Retrieved July 16, 2022, from www.claytonutz.com/knowledge/2021/february/fundamental-reform-recommended-for-ineffective-and-inefficient-epbc-act

act also established the Australian Carbon Credit Unit (ACCU) Scheme,[87] allowing landholders, communities, and businesses to undertake projects in Australia that prevent GHG emissions or capture and store carbon from the atmosphere.

The National Greenhouse and Energy Reporting Act 2007 was enacted to establish the National Greenhouse and Energy Reporting (NGER) scheme,[88] which requires companies to report information about their GHG emissions, energy production, and consumption, as well as other details specified in the act. The *Climate Change Authority Act 2011* also established the Climate Change Authority, responsible for reviewing and recommending changes to the Carbon Farming Initiative under the ACCU Scheme.

Australia ranks 17th as a GHG emitter globally, with a total CO_2 emission of 393 metric tons in 2022.[89] It emitted 376 mt of carbon dioxide in 2020, and 615,380 kilotons of GHG in 2018.[90] This country's per capita CO_2 emissions are relatively high, at 15.12 tons in 2022.[91] This places Australia among the countries with higher per capita emissions, significantly impacting GHG levels and population size.

The consistent reduction in carbon pricing in Australia presents a significant challenge in regulating carbon dioxide emissions. Australia's average effective carbon rate is only 19.23 euros, considerably lower than many other G20 countries.[92] Furthermore, revenue from environmentally related-taxes

87 The Australian Carbon Credit Unit (ACCU) Scheme is a vital component of the Australian carbon market, promoting initiatives by individuals and businesses to implement projects that reduce emissions or sequester carbon. Through this scheme, participants can earn one ACCU for every ton of carbon dioxide equivalent (t CO_2-e) emissions their project sequesters or avoids. These ACCUs can be sold on the secondary market or to the Australian Government via a carbon abatement contract. For details of this Scheme, see Clean Energy Regulator. (2024). *Australian carbon credit unit scheme*. Australian Government. Retrieved June 21, 2024, from https://cer.gov.au/schemes/australian-carbon-credit-unit-scheme

88 The NGER is a secure online system used by corporations to submit their annual reports and manage their obligations under the *National Greenhouse and Energy Reporting Act 2007*. Corporations that meet the threshold criteria are required to provide information on their GFC emissions and energy security in their reports. This data is used to inform the Australian Government's climate change policy development. For more about this Scheme, see Clean Energy Regulator. (2024). *National greenhouse and energy reporting scheme*. Australian Government. Retrieved June 21, 2024, from https://cer.gov.au/schemes/national-greenhouse-and-energy-reporting-scheme

89 World Population Review. (2024). *Carbon footprint by country 2024*. Retrieved June 21, 2024, from https://worldpopulationreview.com/country-rankings/carbon-footprint-by-country

90 World Population Review. (2022). *Greenhouse gas emissions by country 2022*. Retrieved July 17, 2022, from https://worldpopulationreview.com/country-rankings/greenhouse-gas-emissions-by-country

91 World Population Review. (2024). *Carbon footprint by country 2024*. Retrieved June 21, 2024, from https://worldpopulationreview.com/country-rankings/carbon-footprint-by-country

92 Organization for Economic Co-operation and Development (OECD). (2021). *Carbon pricing in times of Covid-19*. OECD Publishing. Retrieved July 17, 2022, from www.oecd.org/tax/tax-policy/carbon-pricing-australia.pdf

has been declining since 2014. As per the OECD *Environmental Performance Review 2019*, Australia's energy taxes do not adequately reflect climate costs: fuels remain largely untaxed outside of transport, and coal is completely untaxed.[93]

The surge in industrial pollution, which has been on the rise since 2015, can be attributed to the government's decision to permit major corporations to increase their emissions limits under a program known as the 'safeguard mechanism.' This mechanism was initially implemented to reduce emissions from industries. It mandates that Australia's largest GHG emitters keep their net emissions below a specified limit, known as the baseline. However, the policy relies on outdated emissions ratings, and no updated mechanism has been introduced to address the current environmental crisis. Most legislations in this country to protect the environment and control corporate pollution are outdated. Nevertheless, Australian states are amending or repealing their old legislation to keep up with the constant threat of an imbalanced ecological system and climate change. Below is a synopsis of the environmental regulation frameworks of the Australian states.

5.4.2 The Australian Capital Territory

The *Environment Protection Act 1997* is the primary law safeguarding the environment against pollution. This legislation outlines rules and regulations for environmental protection and waste management in the Australian Capital Territory. However, an independent study conducted in 2004 identified a lack of implementation and enforcement mechanisms. According to the report, there is a need to adjust the act to enhance the compliance and enforcement functions of the Authority. This will help develop a more coherent and comprehensive strategy for protecting the environment from pollution while maintaining an appropriate balance of environmental, economic, and social considerations. The strategy aims to further strengthen existing partnerships with the community and industry.[94]

The Planning and Development Act 2007 is crucial legislation designed to protect the environment of the Australian Capital Territory. Its primary objective is establishing a planning and land system that contributes to sustainable development. This legislation also incorporates provisions for conducting EIAs.

In 2010, the Australian Capital Territory introduced the Climate Change and Greenhouse Gas Reduction Act 2010 to address climate change and

93 Organization for Economic Co-operation and Development (OECD). (2019). *OECD environmental performance reviews: Australia 2019*. OECD Publishing. https://doi.org/10.1787/9789264310452-en

94 National Competition Policy. (2022). *Review of the environment protection act 1997*. Retrieved July 16, 2022, from http://ncp.ncc.gov.au/docs/ACT%20Review%20of%20Environmental%20Protect%20Act%201997%2C%20June%202004.pdf

reduce emissions. The act aims to raise the policies and practices to combat climate change, establish targets to reduce GHG emissions, and implement monitoring and reporting mechanisms to track progress toward those targets.

5.4.3 New South Wales

In New South Wales (NSW), the *Protection of the Environment Operations Act 1997* serves as the primary legislation for environmental protection. This legislation is designed to safeguard, restore, and enhance the environment of NSW while also promoting public access to information and participation in environmental protection efforts. The Environment Protection Authority[95] is responsible for ensuring the effective implementation of this legislation, which encompasses defining offenses against the environment and establishing penalties. It also includes provisions for voluntary and compulsory environmental audits and procedural guidelines for conducting investigations.

The *Environmental Planning and Assessment Act 1979* is the principal statute governing land use planning in NSW. This act regulates environmental administration in NSW, assesses ecological development, and enforces various environmental rules and regulations within the state. Its primary objective is to foster the economic growth of the community and promote a healthy environment through responsible management and conservation of NSW's natural and other resources. Furthermore, the act establishes the Independent Planning Commission to provide impartial expert advice upon request by the state government, conduct public hearings for development matters, and adjudicate development applications from any party.

While NSW lacks general legislation addressing climate change and pollution emissions, the state has developed the Climate Change Policy Framework to mitigate the ongoing threats posed by climate change and pollutant emissions. The framework outlines objectives aimed at achieving net-zero emissions by 2050 and enhancing the state's resilience in the face of the evolving challenges of a changing climate. The net-zero plan is funded by a $2 billion agreement between the NSW and Commonwealth Governments to reduce emissions and improve the reliability and affordability of electricity in NSW.[96]

95 Environmental Protection Authority (EPA). (n.d.). The EPA's vision is 'Healthy Environment, Healthy Community, and Healthy Business,' aligning with the Protection of the Environment Administration Act 1991. This act aims to protect, restore, and enhance the quality of the environment in New South Wales (NSW), reduce risks to human health, and prevent environmental degradation. The EPA administers various NSW environmental laws, including the Protection of the Environment Operations Act 1997, a principal legislative framework for environmental protection in NSW. For more information, visit www.epa.nsw.gov.au/.

96 Environmental Protection Authority (EPA). (2024). *Climate change and NSW: Overview*. New South Wales Government. Retrieved June 24, 2024, from www.epa.nsw.gov.au/your-environment/climate-change/climate-change-nsw-overview

5.4.4 *The Northern Territory*

In the Northern Territory, the *Environment Protection Act 2019* is the primary framework for protecting the environment against pollution. The act repealed the *Environment Assessment Act 1982*. Implementing the act is considered to start a new era of environmental protection in the Northern Territory. It is because the *Environment Assessment Act 1982*, the predecessor of the *Environment Protection Act*, was full of problems and failed to provide adequate safeguards against severe environmental, social, and cultural impacts from development in the Territory. Under the new act, an environmental approval process is necessary whenever a proposed development could significantly affect the environment. The Northern Territory Environment Protection Authority (NTEPA) must approve the development regardless of its type.

The Northern Territory has yet to enact legislation to reduce emissions and address climate change. Nonetheless, it is developing a Climate Response Strategy to control emissions in the area. The Northern Territory Climate Change Response aims to decrease GHG emissions in all sectors, achieve a long-term aspirational target of net-zero emissions by 2050, and proactively respond to climate change's impacts.

5.4.5 *Queensland*

The *Environment Protection Act 1993* is the primary legislation to control environmental pollution in Queensland. The act provides obligations and duties to prevent environmental harm, nuisances, and contamination. It also provides for enforcement tools to be used against offenses and non-compliance with the act. For ecological assessment, the Planning Act was enacted in Queensland in 2016. The act establishes Queensland's planning framework to support the operation of the three central systems under the act: plan-making, development assessment, and dispute resolution.

Instead of enacting any climate change and emission reduction legislation, Queensland has opted for a Queensland Climate Adaptation Strategy (Q-CAS) and Queensland Climate Transition Strategy. The Q-CAS is a crucial element of Queensland's Climate Change Response and the Queensland Climate Transition Strategy, which directs the state's shift toward a zero net emissions economy. The Q-CAS aims to assist Queenslanders in preparing for both current and future climate changes by understanding impacts, managing risks, and seizing opportunities.[97] On April 18, 2024, the Queensland Government passed the *Clean Economy Jobs Act 2024*, enshrining emissions reduction targets into law as part of

97 Web, P. (2017). *Australia: Queensland climate adaptation strategy 2017–2030*. United Nations Office for Disaster Risk Reduction (UNDRR). Retrieved June 24, 2024, from www.preventionweb.net/publication/australia-queensland-climate-adaptation-strategy-2017-2030

the pathway to a clean economy. The targets include reducing emissions by 30% below 2005 levels by 2030, 75% below 2005 levels by 2035, and achieving net-zero emissions by 2050.[98]

5.4.6 *Northern Territory*

In South Australia, the *Environment Protection Act 1993* is the primary legislation for safeguarding the environment, covering land, air, and water. This act establishes a regulatory framework and entrusts the Environment Protection Authority with enforcing its rules and regulations. In 2016, this state enacted the *Planning, Development, and Infrastructure Act*, replacing the *Development Act 1993*. This new act introduces a refreshed planning and development scheme, along with provisions for infrastructure planning and funding to support environmental protection efforts in South Australia.

South Australia enacted the *Climate Change and Greenhouse Emissions Reduction Act in 2007* to combat climate change and reduce emissions. The act put forward measures to battle climate change, achieve a sustainable future for South Australia, and set targets to decrease GHG emissions by encouraging the use of renewable energy. It is the first legislation in Australia that provides a legally binding emission target: reduce carbon emissions within the state by at least 60% to an amount equal to or less than 40% of 1990 levels by December 31, 2050.

5.4.7 *Tasmania*

Tasmania has two key laws aimed at protecting the environment and reducing emissions. The *Environmental Management and Pollution Control Act 1994* is the primary legislation for safeguarding Tasmania's environment. This performance-based law is designed to prevent, reduce, and address environmental harm, specifically to prevent ecological damage caused by pollution and waste. The *Climate Change (State Action) Act 2008* is Tasmania's climate change legislation, providing guidelines for the government's response to climate change. However, an independent study conducted in 2021 criticized the act for not explicitly promoting action on climate change mitigation or adaptation. Instead, the act offers a narrative and broad framework to encourage and support such efforts.[99]

98 Queensland Government. (2024). *Queensland's 2035 clean economy pathway: 75% by 2035*. Retrieved January 5, 2025, from https://statements.qld.gov.au/statements/100137

99 Department of Premier and Cabinet Tasmanian Climate Change Office. (2021). *Independent review of the climate change (State Action) Act 2008*. Tasmanian Government. Retrieved July 17, 2022, from https://recfit.tas.gov.au/__data/assets/pdf_file/0010/348940/INDEPE~1.PDF

5.4.8 Victoria

Victoria has implemented two significant laws to safeguard its environment from harm: the *Environment Protection Act 2017* and the *Climate Change Act 2017*. The *Environment Protection Act 2017* serves as the primary law for environmental protection in Victoria. It replaced the *Environmental Protection Act* of 1970 to establish a more equitable and balanced framework for environmental regulation of businesses in the region. This act is based on the general environmental duty (GED), which mandates all Victorians to reduce activities that could potentially harm the environment or human health through pollution or waste. It encompasses provisions for GED, environmental permissions, environmental plans, and assessment, as well as enforcement and offenses. The *Climate Change Act 2017* was enacted by the Victorian government to provide a legal foundation for managing climate change risks and leveraging opportunities arising from decisive action. It aims to steer the transition toward a climate-resilient society and economy with net-zero emissions by 2050. The legislation sets a firm target of achieving net-zero emissions by 2050[100] and requires the implementation of 'five-yearly interim targets' to meet the act's long-term goal.

5.4.9 Western Australia

The *Environmental Protection Act 1986* serves as the primary legislation safeguarding Western Australia's environment. This comprehensive act encompasses provisions for preventing, controlling, and reducing pollution and other environmental harm, while also promoting environmental conservation, preservation, protection, enhancement, and management. Additionally, the act established the Environmental Protection Authority to oversee EIAs and other designated responsibilities. In 2020, the act underwent revision through the *Environmental Protection Amendment Act 2020*, aiming to enhance regulatory efficiency and effectiveness and to facilitate the implementation of bilateral agreements under the *Commonwealth Environment Protection and Biodiversity Conservation Act 1999*. At present, Western Australia does not possess specific legislation about climate change and emission reduction. However, in 2020, a Climate Change Policy was introduced to address this crucial matter. The policy's objective is to collaborate with all sectors of the economy to achieve zero GHG emissions by 2050.

5.5 Regulating Corporate Polluters in Canada

Canada, the second-largest country globally, is also one of the largest GHG emitters, ranking fourth globally according to OECD data.[101] The country's

100 Victoria State Government. (2017). *Climate change act 2017*. Victorian Government. Retrieved July 17, 2022, from www.climatechange.vic.gov.au/legislation/climate-change-act-2017
101 Organization for Economic Co-operation and Development (OECD). *OECD environmental performance reviews: Canada 2017*. OECD Publishing. https://doi.org/10.1787/9789264279612-en

economy heavily relies on industrialization, which can be traced back to the first industrial revolution in British North America from the 1780s to the 1860s. This period facilitated the connection of Ontario, Québec, and the Maritime Provinces, significantly shaping Canada's economic development. The subsequent second industrial revolution, spanning from the 1860s to the 1950s, further influenced Canada's economic trajectory and environmental landscape.

Following the Industrial Revolution, Canada has faced various environmental challenges, including high GHG emissions, escalating temperatures, and air pollution. To mitigate these issues and promote ecological stability, Canada has adopted diverse approaches, such as implementing legislation and environmental policies focused on curtailing industrial pollution. The environmental movement in Canada dates back to the early 1900s, driven by an increasing awareness of the need to conserve the country's expansive wilderness. However, Canada's perception of boundless natural resources persisted longer than the United States.

Notably, in 1909, the United States initiated the North American Conservation Conference, extending invitations to Mexico and Canada. This conference led to the establishment of Canada's Commission of Conservation, symbolizing the modernization of the country's environmental movement. In 1971, Canada formally established the Department of the Environment, presently known as Environment and Climate Change Canada (ECCC), with a mandate to craft environmental policies and programs aimed at pollution control, as well as the preservation and enhancement of nature and renewable resources. Since its establishment, Canada has enacted a series of legislations and ratified a host of international environmental protection instruments.

Canada is structurally a Federal State. The Constitution divides the law and policymaking power of the country between the federal government and the regional governments. The Constitution also postulates the areas where the federal government can pass laws and regulations. The ability to enact any environment-related framework has not been exclusively assigned to the federal or provincial government. The environment and pollution are not intrinsically listed in the Constitution.[102] The meaning of environment, 'all that is around us,' has a broad interpretation, so it has not been assigned by the Constitution exclusively to one level of government.[103] It comprises comprehensive matters within various classes of issues, some within federal and others within provincial jurisdiction.[104]

Federal and state governments share the power to create frameworks for environmental issues. The Constitution grants the federal government authority to

102 Cotton, R., & Zimmer, J. S. (1992). Canadian environmental law: An overview. *Canada-United States Law Journal*, *18*(1), 63. https://scholarlycommons.law.case.edu/cuslj/vol18/iss/10

103 *Friends of Oldman River Society v. Canada [1992]* 1 S.C.R. 3, 63, 64, 70.

104 Hogg, P. W. (1977). *Constitutional law of Canada* (3rd ed., p. 730). Carswell Co.

enact laws regarding fisheries, shipping, interprovincial trade and commerce, and criminal law. According to Section 91(12) of the Constitution, the federal government can regulate the environment related to fish.[105] Section 91(10) authorizes the federal government to regulate the ships' activities on marine water, such as releasing oil or other harmful waste. Under Section 91(1A), the federal government is also authorized to control activities of industries within federal jurisdiction, which lets the federal government take steps to reduce emissions from industries in federal lands. Meanwhile, the taxing power conferred to the federal government is a valuable tool to deter activities that cause pollution by incorporating taxes and fines.[106] The ability to pass legislation to keep the peace, order, and good government in Canada also gives the federal government the authority to legislate environmental frameworks.[107]

During the 1980s and 1990s, whether the federal or provincial government had the authority to pass laws and policies on environmental issues was ubiquitous. The court, in the Hydro-Québec[108] case was called on to decide on such a question. In this case, Hydro-Québec was liable for dumping some chemical substances. However, an interim order was issued against the company under the Canadian *Environmental Protection Act 1985*. The authority of the federal government to charge the company with an offense under the act was challenged by the Hydro-Québec company on the ground that the federal government had no such power, as Justice La Forest mentioned in his judgment:

> [T]this Court has recently been increasingly called upon to consider the interplay between federal and provincial legislative powers relating to environmental protection. Whether viewed positively as strategies for maintaining a clean environment or negatively as measures to combat the evils of pollution, there can be no doubt that these measures relate to a public purpose of superordinate importance and one in which all levels of government and numerous organs of the international community have become increasingly engaged.[109]

Most of the Supreme Court of Canada opined that the authority to pass environmental legislation was within the federal government's jurisdiction under the criminal law power conferred by the Constitution. The national

105 Becklump, P. (2019). *Federal and provincial jurisdiction to regulate environmental issues*. Economics, Resources and International Affairs Division. Retrieved March 15, from https://lop.parl.ca/sites/PublicWebsite/default/en_CA/ResearchPublications/201386E

106 Kirikkaleli, D. (2023). Environmental taxes and environmental quality in Canada. *Environmental Science and Pollution Research, 30*(55), 117862–117870.

107 Kennett, S. A. (1992). Federal environmental jurisdiction after Oldman. *McGill Law Journal, 38*, 180.

108 *R. v. Hydro-Québec*, [1997] 3 S.C.R. 213, at para 85.

109 Ibid.

residuary power to legislate on general issues for the 'Peace, Order, and Good Government of Canada' also justifies environmental legislation.

The provincial government is authorized to enact the law on all matters of local nature, property, and civil rights within its area. It also holds jurisdiction over agriculture, forestry, mining, etc. Section 92(13) of the Constitution gives the provincial government the power to pass laws regarding property and civil rights in the province. Following this power, a provincial government has the authority to regulate the use of land, mining affairs, manufacturing, and other activities, including controlling emissions that could contaminate the environment.[110] Under these jurisdictions, the provincial government can enact legal frameworks to protect the environment. Laws on water and air pollution are now also covered by most provinces.

5.5.1 Federal Laws

The federal government of Canada has enacted multiple laws and policies to protect the environment and reduce emissions of pollutant substances. The Canadian *Environmental Protection Act 1999* is the primary federal legislation to prevent pollution and protect the environment and human health. The main object of the act is to maintain sustainable development by preventing pollution. The act makes pollution prevention the foundation of national measures to decrease toxic substances in the environment. It also provides processes and mechanisms to assess chemical substances' environmental and human health risks and imposes timeframes for managing toxic substances. To implement this act, the central government introduced the Reduction of Carbon Dioxide Emissions from Coal-Fired Generation of Electricity Regulations in 2012; the ultimate aim of this organization is to minimize carbon dioxide emissions while producing electricity using coal as fuel. In 2018, an amendment was introduced to this regulation to lessen carbon dioxide emissions and accelerate the phaseout of conventional coal-based power generation from 2050 to 2030.

The *Fisheries Act* is the key legislation to protect fish, fish habitat, and water in Canada. The act prohibits carrying out activities that may result in the harmful alteration, disruption, or destruction of fish habitats. Moreover, under the act, releasing any toxic substance in water frequented by fish is an offense. In 2019, the government amended the *Fisheries Act*. The latest amendment protects all fish, whereas the previous law only protected commercial or Indigenous species and fisheries. The new act also focuses on habitat restoration and rebuilding fish stocks.

In 2003, the federal government of Canada passed the *Antarctic Environmental Protection Act* to protect the Antarctic environment from harmful environmental effects due to Canadian activities in the region. The

110 Supra note 119.

act safeguards the Antarctic environment by employing the Protocol on Environmental Protection to the *Antarctic Treaty*, also known as the Madrid Protocol. Before the *Antarctic Environmental Protection Act*, the *Arctic Waters Pollution Prevention Act* was enacted in 1985 to protect the Arctic's water. The act was passed to stop pollution in Arctic waters. It is a 'zero discharge' act, which states, 'no person or ship shall deposit or permit the deposit of waste of any type in the Arctic waters.'[111]

The *Species at Risk Act* was enacted in 2002 by the federal government to prevent the extinction of wildlife species and secure the necessary actions for their recovery. The act has measurements for the legal protection of wildlife and preserving their natural habitat. It is the key legislation to protect the endangered species of Canada.

In 2012, the *Canadian Environmental Assessment Act* was passed to create a legislative framework for environmental assessment in most regions. Under the act, federal departments and agencies were liable to conduct environmental assessments for any proposed projects. However, the act was repealed by the *Impact Assessment Act* in 2019. An Impact Assessment Agency is established under the act to conduct the impact assessments.

Moreover, in June 2021, the federal government passed the *Canadian Net-Zero Emissions Accountability Act*. The act legislated Canada's commitment under the Paris Agreement to net-zero emissions by 2050 and upheld the country's commitments to mitigate climate change. The act lays out frameworks for planning, reporting, and third-party evaluations by independent experts to accomplish the net-zero goal.

5.5.2 Provincial Laws

Every Canadian province has environmental laws. Pollution prevention and environmental protection were the main goals of British Columbia's (BC's) 2003 *Environmental Management Act*. The act covers waste, hazardous waste, contaminated sites, air contamination, GHG emission reduction, spill prevention, etc. The act also assesses BC pollution overall. The *Environmental Management Amendment Act 2021* improves the province's corporate pollution regulation. BC's Ministry of the Environment oversees the act. Alberta's main industrial pollution and environmental protection law is the *Environmental Protection and Enhancement Act*. The act regulates air, water, land, and biodiversity issues. The act requires companies and agencies to approve or register proposed activities. It encourages ecological resource protection, enhancement, and wise use. Alberta Environment and Sustainable Resource Development administers the act.

111 Government of Canada. (2022). *Arctic waters pollution prevention act (AWPPA)*. Retrieved July 19, 2022, from https://tc.canada.ca/en/marine-transportation/arctic-shipping/arctic-waters-pollution-prevention-act-awppa

The *Environmental Management and Protection Act 2010* is Saskatchewan's main environmental law. It governs environmental conservation and management and is overseen by the Ministry of Environment. Saskatchewan's Act governs air, water, land, and biodiversity and requires environmental assessments and reports.

The *Environment Act* governs Manitoba's environmental protection, which is administered by the Department of Conservation and Water Stewardship. Environmental activities must be licensed under the act. It also issues Environmental Protection Orders to combat environmental pollution. The *Environment Act* is Manitoba's primary environmental law, but the *Water Protection Act* governs water quality, wastewater treatment, invasive species management, and so on.

The main environmental laws in Ontario are the *Environment Protection Act* and the *Ontario Water Resources Act* (OWRA). These laws are enforced by Ontario's Ministry of Environment, Conservation, and Parks. The Environmental Protection Act empowers the Ministry of Environment, Conservation, and Parks to address pollutant discharges. It prohibits the release of hazardous substances into the environment. According to the act, some approved contaminants must not exceed limits, and pollutant leaks must be reported and cleaned immediately. The OWRA prohibits pollutants that degrade water quality.

The main environmental law in Quebec is the *Environment Quality Act*, which is administered by the Ministry of Sustainable Development, Environment, and Climate Change. The act applies to Quebec's air, water, land, waste, and GHG emissions. The Ministry also conducts environmental assessments for government-regulated programs, including Administration strategies, plans, and guidelines.

The CAA and the *Clean Environment Act* are significant environmental legislations in New Brunswick. These legislations are enforced by the New Brunswick Department of Environment and Local Government.[112] The CAA protects the environment from pollution. The act mandates Air Quality Approvals to control airborne contaminants.[113] Meanwhile, the *Clean Environment Act* protects the land from waste and contaminants.[114] Land restoration, wetland, and coastal designation, solid waste commissions, and electricity generation are all discussed.

Pollution control in Nova Scotia is governed by the *Environment Act* and managed by the Department of Environment and Climate Change. The act protects Nova Scotia's ecological system and covers waste management,

112 For the core legislations, visit Environmental Legislation List

113 Brunswick, G. O. N. (2025). *About the clean air act.* Retrieved March 15, from www2.gnb.ca/content/gnb/en/departments/elg/environment/content/air_quality/clean_air/act.html

114 For a copy of this legislation, visit 2021-76.pdf.

contaminated site management, air, water, and land quality, GHG mitigation, and more. It also requires industry assessment reports and qualification certificates.

The *Environmental Protection Act* governs environmental matters on Prince Edward Island. The Department of Labor, Justice, and the Environment enforces the act, which manages, protects, and enhances the island's atmosphere. This law regulates land, water, and waste management and the cleanup of polluted areas. Ministers are also required to conduct EIAs under the act.

Canada has vast natural resources. However, industrialization is putting pressure on the country's environment. Canada is among the top ten countries in the world in terms of GHG emissions. The country also produces significant waste annually, mainly from industrial emissions. In 2014, Canada generated approximately 34 million tons of non-hazardous waste.[115] Nonresidential waste, including industrial waste, accounted for 57% of total generated waste in 2014.[116] However, the country does not have a legal framework at the federal level to address waste management. The provincial governments manage the waste management section entirely.

Canada has ranked 49 on the Environmental Performance Index 2022, scoring only 50.[117] The country has also constantly ranked lowest on the Climate Change Performance Index (CCPI). In 2022, it ranked 61 on the CCPI ranking,[118] among the lowest-rated countries on the list. The country is among the top ten GHG emitter countries according to the CCPI index and has been performing very low on the GHG emissions rating since 2007. The same tendency has been reported in the OECD Environmental Performance Review 2017. The country emitted almost 700 mt of GHGs from 2000 to 2015, as per the OECD report,[119] and is way too far from its 2030 goal to reduce GHG emissions by 30%. However, the country's primary sources of GHG emissions are not electric power plants. The mounting demand for energy in Canada is mainly fulfilled by nuclear power, and since late 2000, Canada has remarkably expanded its wind power. By the end of 2016, Canada produced the eighth-largest wind power globally.[120]

The country's GHG emissions are primarily from heavy industries, mainly mining and treating minerals and fossil fuels for exports. This country withdrew from the Kyoto Protocol in 2011, another significant driver of its continuous increase in GHG emissions. Under the Protocol, Canada was obliged to decrease its GHG emissions to 6% from 1990 levels between 2008 and 2012. Despite this target, the emission levels increased by over 30%. The then Prime Minister of Canada argued that the goal set by the Protocol was impractical

115 Supra note 116.
116 Ibid.
117 Environmental Performance Index. (2022). *Environmental performance index 2022*. Retrieved June 10, 2022, from https://epi.yale.edu/epi-results/2022/component/epi.
118 Supra note 113.
119 Supra note 116.
120 Ibid.

and unattainable for Canada. Hence, the country was saddled with an avoidable $14 billion in penalties for not achieving its goals.[121] However, after the new government came into power in 2015, it promised to update Canada's environmental policies to battle climate change and protect the environment. Signing the Paris Agreement in 2015 was the first step toward the pledge made by the government. Since then, the new government has taken effective approaches to address the issue of climate change. The *Canadian Net-Zero Emissions Accountability Act* was enacted in 2021 to accelerate GHG emissions.[122] Many other extensive efforts have been made by enacting multiple policies and frameworks, which include the Pan-Canadian Framework on Clean Growth and Climate Change (2016), the Strengthened Climate Plan (2020), and Canada's enhanced 2030 target (2021). The government is also incorporating green taxes to regulate GHG emissions. As part of the initiative, the *Greenhouse Gas Pollution Pricing Act* was passed in 2018 to integrate carbon prices. To ensure that carbon pricing is applicable throughout Canada, the federal government has made carbon pollution pricing applicable in any province that requests it or does not have an implementation system to meet the federal requirements.[123] Furthermore, to support the global community to phase out coal-based electric plants, the Prime Minister of this country has announced an investment of up to one billion dollars in the Climate Investment Funds Accelerated Coal Transition Investment Program for developing countries to help them transition to clean power from coal-fired electricity.[124]

Notwithstanding all the initiatives the Canadian government took to combat climate change, significant success depends entirely on properly implementing the legislative frameworks. Likewise, coherence in environmental frameworks between federal and provincial levels is necessary. The CCPI country experts have remarked:

> [T]he entering into law of Canada's 2050 net-zero targets in 2021 is fundamental for the country's long-term climate ambition. It also signals a significant shift in climate ambition. While policy lacks coherence for delivery and achieving the target, detailed plans are on the way.[125]

121 The Guardian. (2011, December 13). *Canada pulls out of Kyoto protocol.* Retrieved July 18, 2022, from www.theguardian.com/environment/2011/dec/13/canada-pulls-out-kyoto-protocol

122 Wright, D. V. (2023). Canadian net-zero emissions accountability act: A bridge over the implementation gap? *UNBLJ*, *74*, 59.

123 Dobson, S., Winter, J., & Boyd, B. (2019). *The greenhouse gas emissions coverage of carbon pricing instruments for Canadian provinces*; Yazdani, H. Q. (2021). No Carbon Left behind: Carbon pricing and the role of supplementary policies. *Texas Environmental Law Journal*, *51*, 357.

124 Winter, J. (2020). Carbon pricing in a federal state: The case of Canada. *ifo DICE Report*, *18*(1), 13–19.

125 Climate Change Index. (2022). *Countries: Canada.* Retrieved July 17, 2022, from https://ccpi.org/country/can/

Hence, it is clear that despite performing low on numerous environmental reviews, Canada can still uphold its net-zero emissions goal if the laws and policies are implemented correctly.

5.6 Regulating Corporate Polluters in Finland

Finland is among the healthiest environments in the world. The country is considered a frontrunner in climate policy.[126] Unlike most developed countries in Europe, the industrial revolution in Finland began in the mid-20th century. Though the Industrial Revolution started late in Finland, the Finnish economy has proliferated and become one of the most prosperous economies in Europe.[127] Industrial growth has created some pressure on the environment in Finland, like declining biodiversity, the water quality of the Baltic Sea, and air and water pollution. The Finnish government has legislated multiple frameworks to control industrial emissions and reduce the impact of such pollutant emissions, efforts that were enhanced when Finland became an EU member in 1995. So, many of Finland's environmental policies are influenced by the EU environmental frameworks.[128] In this part of the chapter, we will study the Finnish frameworks and policies to control corporate polluters to limit emissions.

The Finnish government has one of the best regulatory frameworks for controlling industry pollutant emissions.[129] Though most legislation is enacted nationally, as an EU member State, many laws and regulations are also derived from EU legislation. These laws are either directly applicable to Finland or made applicable through the implementation of EU laws.[130] Apart from these laws, the Finnish government has laid out numerous other plans, policies, and regulations to prevent pollutant emissions and climate change.[131]

The primary legislation for protecting the environment and reducing industrial pollution in Finland is the *Environmental Protection Act*, passed in

126 Tikkakoski, P., Aulake, M., & Paloniemi, R. (2024). Towards just transition: Tackling inequity and structural causes of vulnerability in key environment, health and climate related policies in Finland. *Environmental Science & Policy*, *156*, 103736.

127 Sahrakorpi, T. (2024). Working life, industrial loyalty, and environmental degradation in small-town Finland, 1950s–1980s. *The Historical Journal*, 1–24.

128 Leskinen, P., Belinskij, A., & Saarela, S. R. (2024). Integrating climate change into legislative drafting: An analysis of regulatory impact assessment obligations and practices in the EU and Finland. *Review of European, Comparative & International Environmental Law*, *33*(1), 45–56.

129 Similä, J. (2007). *Regulating industrial pollution: The case of Finland.* University of Helsinki.

130 Leskinen, P., Belinskij, A., & Saarela, S. R. (2024). Integrating climate change into legislative drafting: An analysis of regulatory impact assessment obligations and practices in the EU and Finland. *Review of European, Comparative & International Environmental Law*, *33*(1), 45–56.

131 Huttunen, R., Kuuva, P., Kinnunen, M., Lemström, B., & Hirvonen, P. (2022). *Carbon neutral Finland 2035–national climate and energy strategy.*

2014. The act repealed the *Environmental Protection Act 2000*. The act aims to prevent and reduce air, water, and land emissions, prevent environmental damages, make conservation center stage for the various ecological systems, and promote sustainable use of natural resources. The act also provides for the assessment of the effects of economic activities on the environment. The act has been legislated to enhance environmental protection and meet the requirements of the EU legislation, including the Industrial Emissions Directive (2010/75/EU). The most significant reforms made by the new act are the adoption of binding best available technique (BAT) conclusions, compulsory baseline reporting in case of activities with contamination risks, alterations to the legal position of large combustion plants, as well as rules on the protection of nature values applicable on peat production.[132]

For waste management, the key legislation is the *Waste Act of 2011*. The act aims to prevent harm to humans and the environment caused by hazardous waste. The act mainly manages hazardous waste on land. Different legislations govern emissions of waste in air and water.[133] The negative environmental impacts of waste are also addressed in the Environmental Protection Act 2011.[134] The legislation for managing harmful waste in Finland has primarily been based on EU waste directives.[135] However, in some cases, the Waste Act of Finland has taken more stern approaches than the EU's.

In 2011, the *Water Act* was enacted to safeguard water resources and mitigate water pollution. Its purpose is to encourage sustainable water resource management, minimize adverse water-related impacts, and enhance the overall state of water resources and the aquatic environment. Additionally, the act on the Organization of River Basin Management and the Marine Strategy of 2004 includes provisions for the governance of water resources and marine areas.

The *Nature Conservation Act of 1996* is a vital instrument for safeguarding Finland's biodiversity. Its primary objective is maintaining Finland's natural diversity by preserving or restoring favorable conservation statuses for various natural habitat types and native species. Currently, there are considerations for amending the act to bolster its protection and address the decline of biodiversity in Finland. The *Chemical Act 2013* has been enacted to prevent the

132 Castrén & Snellman. (2014). *Overhaul of Finnish environmental legislation progressing*. Retrieved July 24, 2022, from www.lexology.com/library/detail.aspx?g=53c77b19-9c8d-4f94-be2b-b26242cd65a1

133 Mayanti, B., & Helo, P. (2023). Monetary and environmental damage cost assessment of source-separated biowaste collection: Implications of new waste regulation in Finland. *Waste Management & Research*, *41*(3), 664–675.

134 Airaksinen, J., & Albrecht, E. (2019). Arguments and their effects–a case study on drafting the legislation on the environmental impacts of peat extraction in Finland. *Journal of Cleaner Production*, *226*, 1004–1012.

135 For details of the legislations related to waste regulation, visit Waste legislation – Ministry of the Environment.

environmental impacts of chemicals on human health and the environment. This act aims to protect health and the environment from the hazards and harm caused by chemicals. Apart from this act, all the EU directives relating to chemical safety also apply in Finland.

In 2015, the Finnish government introduced the *Climate Change Act*, which mandated Finland to reduce GHG emissions by at least 80% by 2050 compared to 1990. However, Prime Minister Sanna Marin set a more ambitious goal for Finland to achieve carbon neutrality by 2035. To achieve this, the *Climate Change Act 2015* was replaced by the new *Climate Change Act 2022*, which aims to ensure that Finland achieves carbon neutrality by 2035. The new act includes provisions for climate change policy planning and monitoring and sets national climate goals. It also assigns responsibilities to the authorities. The updated *Climate Change Act* sets emission reduction targets for 2030 and 2040 and revises the target for 2050. The new targets are more ambitious than the previous ones, with reduction targets of –60% by 2030, –80% by 2040, and at least –90% (aiming for –95%) by 2050 compared to 1990 levels, based on the recommendations of the Finnish Climate Change Panel.[136] The act introduces four major national climate change policy plans, which are expected to reduce GHG emissions in Finland and contribute to climate change adaptation.[137] The Finnish government also enacted legislation to levy compensation for environmental damages. The act on *Compensation for Environmental Damages* was passed in 1994 to assess compensation from the party who causes any damages to the environment. The act provides for compensation for losses that are defined as environmental damages in the act resulting from water, air, or soil pollution. Apart from these significant acts, Finland has multiple other legislations and frameworks for protecting the environment from corporate pollution.

Finland's environmental interventions have assured its ecological sanctity. According to the Environmental Performance Index 2022, this country has the world's third cleanest environment. Finland has also ranked fifth in the Sustainable Government Index for environmental policies.[138] According to CCPI, Finland has high Renewable Energy and Climate Policy ratings.[139] The Finnish government has set a goal of carbon neutrality by 2030. To achieve this goal, it has enacted legislation supplemented by multiple policies. The data provided by the CCPI shows that Finland is on its way to being a carbon-neutral country by 2030. It imposed a carbon tax in 1990, which helped to

136 State Treasury: Republic of Finland. (2022). *Climate neutral Finland 2035*. Retrieved July 25, 2022, from www.treasuryfinland.fi/investor-relations/sustainability-and-finnish-government-bonds/climate-neutral-finland-2035/

137 Ministry of the Environment. (2022). *New climate change act into force in July*. Retrieved July 25, 2022, from https://ym.fi/en/-/new-climate-change-act-into-force-in-july

138 Sustainable Government Index. (2020). *Environmental policies*. Retrieved July 26, 2022, from www.sgi-network.org/2020/Sustainable_Policies/Environmental_Policies

139 Climate Change Performance. (2022). *Country: Finland*. Retrieved July 25, 2022.

slash GHG emissions by about a fifth.[140] In 2019, taxes related to the environment raised revenue equal to 2.8% of GDP, which was well above the OECD average.[141] To reach its 2030 carbon-neutral goal, the Finnish government has also announced the Taxation for Development Action Programme 2020–2023. This program has been introduced to make green economic growth while maintaining tax revenue. In Finland, carbon tax applies uniformly across almost every sector that emits carbon. It considers emissions happening when the fuel is used, during production, and disposal.[142] This mechanism eradicates the need for special tax discounts for liquid biofuels. Also, the minimal carbon tax rate is among the highest in the OECD countries.[143] As per Statista data, Finland has the sixth highest carbon price in the world.

One of the significant environmental issues for Finland was the water pollution caused by oil spills. The water quality of the Baltic Sea is also a substantial concern for Finland. Oil Spills on seawater were among the primary causes of water pollution. However, the number of oil spills at sea has reduced over the years. In the State of Environment Report – Finland (2013), it was reported that the oil discharges at sea by the Finnish government have reduced by 50% from 2007 to 2013.[144] According to the report, only 54 oil spills were recorded in 2012, compared to over 100 in 2007. The amount of spilled oil has also decreased noticeably. In 2012, the average amount of an oil spill was 25 liters, while in 2007, it was 170 liters. Fewer spills are also being identified elsewhere in the Baltic Sea.[145]

Finland raised its water quality through efficient surveillance flight operations, enacting new laws, and enabling the faster imposition of an oil pollution payment. The *Oil Pollution Response Act*, passed in 2009, positively impacted the control of oil spills on seawater. Meanwhile, the Finnish Oil Pollution Compensation Fund compensates for the costs of oil spills and oil spill measures on land and at sea when the party that initiated the accident is unknown, or the guilty party cannot compensate the costs. In 2012, the Finnish Border Guard investigated only two oil contamination payment incidents, while in 2007, the corresponding figure was 13.[146]

Industrial waste prevention and recycling are now the most problematic issues for Finland's ecological balance. According to the EU Environmental Implementation Review 2019, the volume of municipal waste generated in Finland amounted to 510 kg per capita in 2017, which is above the average in

140 Ibid.
141 Supra note 141.
142 Ibid.
143 Ibid.
144 Finnish Environment Institute. (2013). *State of the environment report – Finland.* https://wedocs.unep.org/20.500.11822/9471
145 Ibid.
146 Ibid.

the EU (487 kg per year per capita in 2017) and has varied over past years. As reported in the OECD Environmental Performance Review 2019:

> [The] total waste generation has grown by about 20% and municipal solid waste (MSW) generation by 24% since 2010. Per capita, MSW generation also grew and is well above the OECD-Europe average. Finland missed its goal of reversing the trend of growing MSW generation by 2016. Without strong policy measures, MSW volumes are expected to continue to increase alongside economic growth.[147]

Nonetheless, the sanction on filling the land with organic waste and a superior landfill tax reduced waste in landfills. A new *Waste Act* is still underway to better manage the country's waste policy. The OECD Environmental Performance Review 2019 has also observed that Finland's approach to balancing its economic growth and healthy environment is in a leading position. Despite this growth rate, Finland must take additional approaches to reach its 2030 carbon emission goal. Both OECD and the EU have provided the same advice. The Finnish government has announced implementing several policies and frameworks to accelerate carbon emissions. Only time will tell how these new policies and frameworks will affect Finland's economic and ecological balance.

5.7 Regulating Corporate Polluters in Germany

Germany is one of the leading economies in the world. It is the fourth-largest economy in the world and the largest economy in the EU.[148] Germany is a highly industrialized country. At least 23.4% of its economy is based on industries.[149] Industrialization began in Germany during the 1840s with the development of coal mining and iron and steel production. Owing to its rapid industrialization, the country has become densely polluted. The historically significant industries of this country – coal, iron, steel, textiles, petrochemicals, machinery, paper, and pulp – are all major consumers of natural resources and contribute significantly to the pollution of Central Europe's air, land, and water.[150]

In the 1840s, numerous German states transitioned from wood to coal as their primary fuel source. This shift profoundly impacted Germany's economy,

147 Supra note 141.

148 Facts about Germany. (2022). *A strong hub.* Retrieved July 28, 2022, from www.tatsachen-ueber-deutschland.de/en/germany-glance/strong-hub

149 European Union. (2022). *Country profile: Germany.* Retrieved July 27, 2022, from https://european-union.europa.eu/principles-countries-history/country-profiles/germany_en

150 Cioc, M. (1998). The impact of the coal age on the German environment: A review of the historical literature. *Environment and History*, *4*(1), 105–124.

as the nation possessed extensive coal reserves in the territories under Prussian control.[151] Mark Cioc has postulated the following:

> [C]oal mining caused ground depressions, altered the natural hydrology, and pockmarked the landscape. Coal dust, phenol (carbolic acid), and other coal pollutants washed into Germany's rivers and streams. Acid rain from burning coal became a major source of forest death. Coal-tar derivatives also produced the first artificial dyes, giving rise to Germany's mammoth chemical plants – Bayer, BASF, Hoechst, AGFA – companies which today are still among the greatest polluters of Germany's environment.[152]

In the late 19th century, citizens in Germany became aware of environmental degradation.[153] In the 1960s, concern about the depletion of natural resources and environmental pollution led to the emergence of an environmental movement in Germany.[154] During the 1970s, the German government passed several environmental legislations despite opposition from policymakers, industries, and businesses who feared that the environmental movement would hinder economic progress and lead to unemployment.[155] Nevertheless, Germany became a leader in environmental policymaking.[156] As a member of the EU since 1958, Germany's ecological laws and policies are also influenced by EU environmental directives.[157] While Germany was once considered a pioneer in environmental policies in Europe and played a significant role in shaping EU environmental policies, the country's implementation suffered in the 2000s.[158] However, in recent years, Germany has made significant strides in improving its environmental policy implementation.

151 Cioc, M. (1998). The impact of the coal age on the German environment: A review of the Historical Literature. *Environment and History*, *4*(1), 105–124; Životić, D., Jovanovski, G., Simić, V., Boev, I., Cvetkov, V., Makreski, P., Polomčić, D., & Ristić Vakanjac, V. (2024). Coal: exploration, reserves, and utilization. *ChemTexts*, *10*(1), 1.

152 Ibid.

153 Uekotter, F. (2017). *The greenest nation?: A new history of German environmentalism*. MIT Press.

154 Caradonna, J. L. (2014). Eco-warriors: The environmental movement and the growth of ecological wisdom, 1960s–1970s. In *Sustainability*. Oxford University Press.

155 Milder, S. (2022). Re-interpreting west Germany's ecological revolution: Environmental politics, grassroots activism, and democracy in the long 1970s. *European History Quarterly*, *52*(3), 332–351.

156 Weidner, H. (2002). Environmental policy and politics in Germany. In *Environmental politics and policy in industrialized countries* (pp. 149–201).

157 Rung, N. (2022). *Europeanization of environmental policy in Germany: To what extent is the German environmental policy as illustrated in the case of the Rhineland Europeanized?* University of Twente.

158 Seht, H. V., & Ott, H. E. (2000). *EU environmental principles: Implementation in Germany*.

5.7.1 Constitution of Germany and Environmental Protection

The German Constitution has defined environmental protection as a state object. The Federal Constitution and the Constitution of most of the states recognize environmental and climate change policy as a constitutional value.[159] Article 20a of the Federal German Constitution lays the base of environmental protection in Germany, which states that the State must protect the natural foundations of life and animals by legislative, executive, and judicial actions within the framework of the constitutional order for the benefit of the future generation.[160] Because of this provision, any environmental issue can be challenged in the Federal Constitutional Court of Germany.[161] Though Article 20a has been representing the constitutional right of environmental protection since 1994, the Federal Constitutional Court of Germany has recently enhanced the concept of fundamental rights to climate protection based on this Article in a recent landmark judgment.[162]

5.7.2 Key Legislations to Control Corporate Pollution

Germany's environmental protection frameworks and policies are mainly regulated through national legislation despite being influenced by EU directives. The legislative power for environmental laws is shared between the federal and state governments. The German government attempted to introduce a uniform Environmental Code in 2009, but this effort failed and has not been revisited since. As a result, industrial operators are subject to various relevant EU, federal, state, and occasionally local regulations.[163]

The *Federal Emission Control Act* is the primary law in Germany at the national level aimed at preventing air and noise pollution caused by industries. It was enacted in 1974 and has undergone several amendments to address current environmental challenges. The act includes provisions such as Technical Instructions on Air Quality Control and Technical Instructions on Noise Abatement. Additionally, the German government has incorporated

159 ICLG.com. (2022). *Environment & climate change laws and regulations Germany*. Retrieved July 28, 2022, from https://iclg.com/practice-areas/environment-and-climate-change-laws-and-regulations/germany

160 Seht, H. V., & Ott, H. E. (2000). *EU environmental principles: Implementation in Germany*.

161 Krämer-Hoppe, R. (2021). The climate protection order of the federal constitutional court of Germany and the north-south divide. *German Law Journal*, *22*(8), 1393–1408.

162 Winter, G. (2022). The intergenerational effect of fundamental rights: A contribution of the German federal constitutional court to climate protection. *Journal of Environmental Law*, *34*(1), 209–221.

163 Lexology. (2019). *Environmental law in Germany*. Retrieved July 28, 2022, from www.lexology.com/library/detail.aspx?g=26c602be-adca-472a-aba4-ba3190820d3e

various EU directives and international conventions into the act to further its objectives.[164]

The *Federal Soil Protection Act* mainly regulates contaminated soil and the subsequent contamination of groundwater. The Federal law has provisions for protecting the soil and groundwater from potential pollution and administers the liability and remediation of contaminated land. According to the act, the polluter is held accountable and obliged to remediate harmful soil changes, including any groundwater contamination, and to avert any dangers, substantial difficulties, or nuisances for the individual or the public.[165] The *Federal Soil Protection and Contaminated Sites Ordinance* supplements the act. The act provides the power to undertake essential measures to investigate any conceivable sign of pollution.

The *Federal Water Act* was adopted in 1957 to protect water from pollution. The act was amended in 2010 to transpose the EU Water Framework Directive. The amendment aims to procure decent status for all water bodies by reducing pollutant levels in Germany by 2017. The act also implemented several other EU water directives, including the EU Floods Directive, the Marine Strategy Framework Directive, and the provisions of the Industrial Emissions Directive.[166] To properly implement the act, the German government has passed multiple ordinances such as the Surface Water Ordinance, the Ground Water Ordinance, and the Wastewater Ordinance.

The *Federal Nature Conservation Act* was passed in 1977 to conserve, preserve, and develop nature and landscapes.[167] The act provides rules and regulations for land planning to safeguard nature and its resources. The act aims to maintain the usefulness of nature's resources, conserve fauna and flora, protect and care for wild fauna and wild flora, and protect the marine environment.[168]

The *Chemicals Act 2002* was enacted to protect people and the environment from the harmful effects of hazardous substances and their synthetic production, particularly in detecting, preventing, and averting their proliferation.[169]

164 Martines, F. (2014). Direct effect of international agreements of the European Union. *European Journal of International Law*, *25*(1), 129–147.

165 Mueller, H. (2022). *The Legal 500 country comparative guides: Germany – environment.* www.legal500.com/guides/chapter/germany-environment/?export-pdf

166 Andrés Sáenz De Santa María, P. (2019). The European Union and the law of treaties: A fruitful relationship. *European Journal of International Law*, *30*(3), 721–751.

167 Hausotte, M., & Benisch, C. (2017). *Federal nature conservation and species protection legislation in Germany.* www.kerbtier.de/Pages/Themenseiten/enRechtslage.html. Federal Ministry for the Environment, N. C., Nuclear Safety and Consumer Protection. (2025). *Federal nature conservation act.* Government of Germany. www.bmuv.de/en/law/federal-nature-conservation-act-bnatschg/

168 von Haaren, C., & Vollheyde, A.-L. (2019). Landscape planning in Germany: Not loved by all, but badly needed. *International Review for Spatial Planning and Sustainable Development*, *7*(4), 148–166.

169 *Chemicals Act*, Article 1. (1980).

The act is based on multiple EU directives on managing hazardous chemicals. It outlines provisions for manufacturers, importers, and downstream users of specific substances and restricts their use, distribution, labeling, and registration.

The *EIA Act 1990* (last amended in 2023) has been passed to assess the environmental impact of any actions taken by corporations or individuals. The act aims to determine and describe in a report the impact a project will have on human health and ecosystems. It guarantees adequate preventive environmental protection based on uniform principles under the Constitution. The *Federal Environmental Damage Act* was enacted in 2007 to create environmental liabilities and to prevent and remedy ecological damages. The act institutes stringent liability for industries if their activities adversely impact soil, water bodies, and biodiversity.

Germany, being a highly industrialized country, has been affected by climate change. In 2019, the German government passed the *Climate Change Act* as part of its commitment to combat climate change and adhere to the Paris Agreement. The act set a target for Germany to reduce its GHG emissions by 55% by 2030 compared to 1990 levels, with the ultimate goal of achieving net-zero GHG emissions by 2050. However, the law did not provide specific details on how emissions reductions beyond 2030 would be achieved, instead empowering the government to determine reduction levels through an executive order in 2025. Following the decision in *Neubauer, et al. v. Germany [2020]* from the Federal Constitutional Court, the *Climate Change Act* was amended, and the revised version came into effect in August 2021.

5.7.3 *Neubauer, et al. v. Germany [2020]*

Several young climate activists lodged a complaint in the Constitutional Court, challenging the *Climate Change Act of 2019.* They argued that the act's target of reducing GHG emissions by 55% by 2030 from 1990 levels was inadequate and did not align with Germany's and the EU's commitments under the Paris Agreement to control universal temperature increase to 'well below 2°C.' In its ruling, the court found the act to be partially unconstitutional and set a deadline for it to be amended by the end of 2022.[170] The Court based its decision on Article 20a of the German Federal Constitution, which imposes a constitutional duty on the state to achieve climate neutrality and limits political discretion on environmental issues.[171] Additionally, the court declared unconstitutional the provisions of the *Climate Change Act* regarding national climate targets. According to the judgment, 'national climate targets

170 Douhaire, C. (2024). The climate decision of the German constitutional court and its implications on soil management. In *International yearbook of soil law and policy 2022* (p. 35).

171 Krämer-Hoppe, R. (2021). The climate protection order of the federal constitutional court of Germany and the north-south divide. *German Law Journal, 22*(8), 1393–1408.

and the annual emission amounts allowed until 2030 are incompatible with fundamental rights as they lack sufficient specifications for further emission reductions from 2031 onwards.'[172] The court further observed that the act's current provisions did not guarantee the climate neutrality goal in time. The court then ordered the legislature to amend the act and specify in detail the procedure to reduce targets of GHG emissions by the time set by the court.

The German government introduced a revised *Climate Change Act 2021* based on this ruling. This new legislation set a legally binding obligation to reduce GHG emissions by 65% within 2030 compared to 1990 and a 2040 GHG emissions cutback goal of 88%.[173] As for 2050, the goal is to reduce harmful emissions. Under the act, the federal government must pass regulations detailing the annual amounts allowed for each sector for 2031–2045.[174]

5.7.4 *Environmental Policies*

The environmental policy of Germany has been highly regarded, with the country ranking 12th on the *Sustainable Governance Indicator for Environmental Policies.*[175] Germany also ranked 13th for having the cleanest air in the world in the EPI 2022.[176] Germany was a leader in environmental policymaking and implementation during the 2000s. However, a shift in the ecological movement in 2014 led to a rapid decline in the country's environmental quality. Germany is also among the top emitters of GHGs in the world and has been performing poorly despite being obligated by the Paris Agreement to reduce GHG emissions by 2050. Looking at the trends in the CCPI rankings from 2007 to 2022, it is evident that Germany's performance in environmental protection was at its peak in its earlier days, consistently ranking among the top ten performers. However, in 2014, Germany's CCPI rating dropped to 19 from the previous year's ranking of 8,[177] and it continued to decline, reach-

172 Library of Congress. (2021). *Germany: Amendment of climate change act codifies climate neutrality goal by 2045.* Retrieved July 29, 2022, from www.loc.gov/item/global-legal-monitor/2021-09-28/germany-amendment-of-climate-change-act-codifies-climate-neutrality-goal-by-2045/

173 Lachmayer, K. (2024). The constitutional context of climate change litigation. A comparative analysis of Germany and Austria. In Ivano Alogna, Carole Billet, Matteo Fermeglia & Alina Holzhausen (Eds.), *Climate change litigation in Europe. Regional, comparative and sectoral perspectives*; Wang, D., Dong, L., & Mei, J. (2023). An advanced review of climate change mitigation policies in Germany, France, and the Netherlands. *Environmental Research Letters, 18*(10), 103001.

174 Von Hirschhausen, C. (2018). German energy and climate policies: A historical overview. In *Energiewende "made in Germany" low carbon electricity sector reform in the European context* (pp. 17–44).

175 Supra note 137.

176 Supra note 126.

177 See *Climate change performance index 2014.* (2014). https://ccpi.org/wp-content/uploads/CCPI-2014.pdf

ing its lowest point in 2017 with a rank of 29 on the CCPI.[178] In addition to the decline in overall environmental performance, GHG emission levels were also higher during these periods. According to the CCPI 2018 GHG emissions ratings, Germany ranked 40, marking the country's lowest environmental performance.

The low performance was a result of increasing demand for fossil fuels and the government's emphasis on economic growth over environmental concerns. After the Fukushima nuclear disaster in Japan, the government of Germany decided to abandon the country's nuclear power plants, leading to an increase in coal-based energy production. This has resulted in extensive coal mining and deforestation, including a recent battle between environmentalists and coal miners to save the Hambach, an ancient forest in Germany. The attempt to protect the forest failed, and the Tagebau Hambach, a large open-pit coal mine, continues to operate in the area. This forest has significant value to the coal industry due to the presence of rare brown coal, and only a small portion of the 12,000-year-old forest remains intact.[179]

Germany's industries not only contribute to GHG emissions but also produce nearly half of the country's waste.[180] According to data from the European Environment Agency, 85.9% of hazardous waste is generated by various industrial sectors.[181] Industrial emissions, particularly from coal mining, are leading to significant water pollution in Germany. The problem is most severe in East Germany, where decades of opencast mining have caused substantial water pollution.[182] Water in these areas was drained for mining purposes, and even though the mines are no longer operational, the damage caused by the mining is almost irreparable. The Spree River is facing the issue of brown sludge buildup, which is harming the wildlife in the area.[183]

Despite these challenges, the German government has implemented new and more effective environmental policies to address environmental

178 See *Climate change performance index 2017.* (2017). https://ccpi.org/wp-content/uploads/CCPI-2017.pdf.

179 United Nations Environment Programme (UNEP). (2018). *Forest or fuel: Decision time for Germany.* Retrieved July 29, 2022, from www.unep.org/news-and-stories/story/forest-or-fuel-decision-time-germany

180 IREES, I. F. R. E. A. E. S. (2016). *Process emissions in German industries and their relevance for Germany's national climate mitigation targets – an outlining of the problem and first options for action* N. C. A. N. S. B. Federal Ministry for the Environment. www.bmuv.de/fileadmin/Daten_BMU/Download_PDF/Ressourceneffizienz/irees_prozessemissionen_en_bf.pdf

181 Panagiotopoulou, V. C., Stavropoulos, P., & Chryssolouris, G. (2022). A critical review on the environmental impact of manufacturing: A holistic perspective. *The International Journal of Advanced Manufacturing Technology*, 1–23.

182 Khoo, S.-M., & Rau, H. (2013). Movements, mobilities and the politics of hazardous waste. In *Environmental movements and waste infrastructure* (pp. 144–164). Routledge.

183 Uhlig, U., Radigk, S., Uhlmann, W., Preuß, V., & Koch, T. (2026). Iron removal from the Spree River in the Bühlow pre-impoundment basin of the Spremberg reservoir. *IMWA*, 182–190.

issues. In 2019, the government passed the *Climate Change Act* to reduce GHG emissions, which was amended in 2021 to provide stricter goals for emission reduction. Additionally, in 2016, the government adopted the Climate Action Plan 2050, showing Germany's commitment to the Paris Agreement. The Plan aims to achieve widespread GHG neutrality by 2050. The climate goals are continuously monitored to ensure the success of the *Climate Change Act* and Climate Action Plan. Every two years, the Council of Experts for Climate Matters will report on goals achieved, measures taken, and trends. If budgets are insufficient, the Federal Government will adjust its tactics immediately.[184]

Numerous environmentalists have lauded Germany's ambitious environmental initiatives, but they have also expressed concerns about the inadequacy of current policies to achieve these goals. Experts at CCPI have pointed out that government studies indicate that Germany is likely to fall short of its targets with the current policies and may even miss the previous 55% reduction target. They have advised the country to take more significant measures to achieve its goals.[185] The recent announcement by Germany's economy ministry to revert to using coal-based energy plants to conserve its natural gas reserve due to the Russia-Ukraine war has raised additional concerns. While the German Chancellor has stated that the phaseout of coal power is temporary and will not impact GHG reduction goals, many specialists worry that it will further delay the already challenging target of carbon neutrality.

5.8 Regulating Corporate Polluters in Japan

Japan is one of the top ten largest GHG emitters in the world. According to World Bank data, it is also one of the most powerful economies, with the third-highest GDP.[186] It is a leading economy in Asia and played a significant role in the second industrial revolution in Asia. The Industrial Revolution began in Japan in the Meiji era, during the 1870s, and grew rapidly. Japan began to compromise its environment to keep up with Western modernization. Environmental destruction became a part of Japan's progressive economy.[187] However, Japan paid a high price for its constant environmental destruction.

184 German Federal Government. (2021). *Climate change act 2021: Intergenerational contract for the climate.* www.bundesregierung.de/breg-de/themen/klimaschutz/climate-change-act-2021-1936846

185 Climate Change Performance Index. (2022). *Countries: Germany.* Retrieved July 28, 2022, from https://ccpi.org/country/deu/

186 The World Bank. (2022). https://data.worldbank.org/indicator/NY.GDP.MKTP.CD?end=2021&locations=JP&most_recent_value_desc=true&start=2021&view=map

187 Bichler, R. M. (2023). Harm and Harmony – concepts of nature and environmental practice in Japan. *Histories, 3*(2), 62–75; Fujikawa, K. (2012). The social structure of the environmental destruction caused by the Fukushima Nuclear Disaster. *Japanese Association for Environmental Sociology, 18*, 45–59.

Environmental problems like lead and mercury poisoning began to surface all over Japan, starting with the Ashio copper mine poisoning and Watarase River pollution. This resulted in outbreaks of diseases like Minamata, Itai-Itai, and Yokkaichi asthma.[188] In response to these catastrophic environmental problems, various anti-pollution campaigns were launched in Japan by its citizens, who were the victims of these disasters.[189] The movement spread across the country, and public awareness grew. Due to the pressure from the anti-pollution movement, the Japanese government introduced laws and policies to control industrial pollution.[190]

5.8.1 Key Legislations to Control Corporate Pollution in Japan

In Japan, the primary law to control corporate pollution and protect the environment is the *Basic Environment Law of 1993.* The act works as the foundation of environmental law in Japan. It establishes the basis of Japan's environmental laws and policies. The law includes basic principles of environmental policy, a definition of the responsibilities of each actor in society and a prescription of the policy instruments to protect the domestic and global environment.[191] The legislation establishes three basic environmental principles: (1) both present and future generations should enjoy the natural resources; (2) a sustainable society should be created where human activities minimize environmental loads; and (3) Japan should work globally for environmental conservation through international cooperation. The legislation deals with air and water pollution and basic environmental conservation policies. The act provides for establishing the Basic Environment Plan, which is subject to review every six years.

The *Air Pollution Control Act* was passed in 1968 in Japan to reduce air pollution. The act aims to protect people's health by controlling pollutant emissions in the air caused by soot and smoke, volatile organic compounds, and activities carried out by industries.[192] This legislation promotes the implementation of measures and, in necessary cases, implements penalties for industry

188 Ahmed, F., Ali, I., Kousar, S., & Ahmed, S. (2022). The environmental impact of industrialization and foreign direct investment: empirical evidence from Asia-Pacific region. *Environmental Science and Pollution Research*, 1–15.

189 Avenell, S. (2017). Transnational environmental activism and Japan's second modernity. *Asia-Pacific Journal-Japan Focus, 15*(14).

190 Moshkal, M., Akhapov, Y., & Ogihara, A. (2024). Sustainable Waste management in Japan: Challenges, achievements, and future prospects: A review. *Sustainability (2071–1050), 16*(17); Muraki, H. (1999). Environmental laws of Japan: Selected environmental issues of the 1990s and the new millennium. *Asia Pacific Journal of Environmental Law, 4*, 317.

191 Ministry of the Environment, Government of Japan. (2022). *The basic environment law – outline.* www.env.go.jp/en/laws/policy/basic.html

192 Botta, E., & Yamasaki, S. (2020). Policies, regulatory framework and enforcement for air quality management: The case of Japan. *OECD Environment Working Papers, 156*, 0_1–60.

operators for damages.[193] It sets emissions standards for industries for hazardous air pollutants. It also stipulates regulations to govern specific dangerous substances produced by industries.[194]

The *Water Pollution Prevention Act 1970*, also known as the *Water Pollution Control Law*, was employed to regulate water pollution caused by domestic and industrial usage.[195] The act aims to prevent water pollution in public water areas by regulating waste released by factories or establishments into water bodies.[196] It set forth stipulations to govern the emissions of harmful substances into public water bodies to protect human health and the living environment of the water areas. It provides for compensation or damages if human health is harmed by contaminated water or wastewater released from factories or establishments. It obliges the emitters to register with the local government, comply with the emissions limit set by this legislation, and take appropriate measures to monitor and report the level of pollutant discharge.

To prevent the degradation and contamination of soil, Japan passed the *Soil Contamination Countermeasures Act* in 2002. The main object of the act is to guarantee the implementation of countermeasures against soil contamination.[197] The act provides measures to govern the release of specified hazardous substances that cause soil contamination. It also stipulates measures to protect human health from soil contamination.[198] The act defines rules for soil contamination investigation in necessary cases. The Ministry of Environment has been given the authority to conduct the investigation.[199] The act was amended in 2009 to battle the increasing number of inappropriate treatments of contaminated soil. The new amendment introduced the following provisions: (1) measures to prevent removal excavation and proper management of contaminated soil taken out by such excavation; (2) expansion of investigation opportunities under the act and introduction of voluntary investigation; and (3)

193 Tsai, W.-T. (2016). Toxic volatile organic compounds (VOCs) in the atmospheric environment: Regulatory aspects and monitoring in Japan and Korea. *Environments, 3*(3), 23.

194 Barrett, B. F., & Therivel, R. (2019). *Environmental policy and impact assessment in Japan*. Routledge.

195 Kumagai, H., & Kuba, T. (2016). Water purification by reducing the pollution burden. In *Basic studies in environmental knowledge, technology, evaluation, and strategy: Introduction to East Asia environmental studies* (pp. 105–121).

196 Teranishi, S. I. (2023). A brief history of environmental pollution in Japan. In *Environmental pollution and community rebuilding in modern Japan* (pp. 1–16).

197 Ishimaki, M. (2024). Soil protection law in Japan. In *International yearbook of soil law and policy 2022* (p. 227).

198 Kobayashi, H. (2002). Japanese law for remediation of soil contamination. *Asia Pacific Journal of Environmental Law, 7*, 25.

199 Fujikura, M. (2011). Japan's efforts against the illegal dumping of industrial waste. *Environmental Policy and Governance, 21*(5), 325–337.

clarification of zones and necessary countermeasures for managing found soil contamination correctly.[200]

One of the significant environmental issues in Japan is waste management.[201] The *Waste Management and Public Cleansing Act* was introduced in 1970 for waste management in Japan.[202] Article 1 of the act states that 'this law is enacted to preserve the living environment and improve public health through the restriction of waste discharge, appropriate sorting, storage, collection, transport, recycling, disposal, or the like of waste and conservation of a clean-living environment.'[203] The act stipulates the responsibilities of both central and local governments for proper waste management. It also orders the Minister of the Environment to create a fundamental policy for promoting measures comprehensively and systematically restraining waste discharge, waste reduction by recycling, and other proper waste management.[204]

The *Nature Conservation Act 1972* and the *Natural Parks Act 1957* aim to protect Japan's biodiversity. The *Nature Conservation Act* has been passed to ensure diversity in areas where it is essential to conserve the natural environment.[205] This law obligates the country to conduct a biological and environmental conservation survey every five years. It establishes a regional designation system to protect the natural environment by restricting actions within the designated areas.[206] According to Article 1 of the act, the purpose of the act is to make sure citizens, in general, can enjoy the benefits of the natural environment and for the next generation to inherit those benefits by systematically promoting proper conservation of the natural environment, including safeguarding biodiversity in areas where this is particularly necessary; these measures would contribute to securing a healthy and civilized lifestyle for current and future citizens.[207]

The *EIA Act* is the primary law governing EIAs in Japan. The EIA laws were first introduced in Japan in the 1980s. After numerous bills and follow-ups,

200 Ebisu, M., & Hagihara, K. (2019). Methods of environmental risk management for land contamination problems: Suggestions for Japan. *Building Resilient Regions*, 149–175.

201 Hosoda, E. (2016). Waste policies and related legislation in Japan. In *The Economics of Waste Management in East Asia* (pp. 3–37).

202 Fujioka, S. (2019). Overviews of waste management policies in Japan. *Building Resilient Regions*, 125–147.

203 *Waste Management and Public Cleansing Act*, Act No. 137 of 1970, Article 1 (Japan).

204 Mekonnen, G. B., & Tokai, A. (2020). A historical perspective of municipal solid waste management and recycling system in Japan: Learning for developing countries. *Journal of Sustainable Development*, *13*(3), 85.

205 Hiwasaki, L. (2005). Toward sustainable management of national parks in Japan: Securing local community and stakeholder participation. *Environmental Management*, *35*, 753–764.

206 Ibid.

207 Japanese Law Translation. (n.d.). *Nature conservation act. Japanese law translation*. Retrieved August 4, 2022, from www.japaneselawtranslation.go.jp/en/laws/view/3745

the *EIA Act* was finally enacted in 1997 in Japan. The primary purposes of the act are promulgated in Article 1 of the act, which states the following:

> [T]he purpose of this Act is, in recognition of the fact that it is extremely important, in terms of protecting the environment, that the project proponent conduct an environmental impact assessment in advance of a project that changes the shape of the terrain or that involves the construction of a new structure, or that is engaging in other similar activities, to set forth procedures and other provisions designed to define clearly the responsibilities of the government, etc., regarding environmental impact assessments and to ensure that the environmental impact assessments are conducted properly and smoothly with respect to large-scale projects that could have a serious impact on the environment, and to ensure proper consideration for environmental conservation in related to the project, by prescribing process to reflect the result of the environmental impact assessment in determining the measures for environmental conservation in implementing the project and in determining the other contents of the project, thereby contributing to the healthy and cultural life of the Japanese people, both now and in the future.[208]

5.8.2 Key Ecological Structure and Policies

As one of the largest and most powerful economies in the world, it is not surprising that Japan is also one of the highest GHG emitters.[209] This country does not have separate legislation for GHG emissions and climate change.[210] However, it is required to decrease its GHG releases by 6% from its 1990 level and has ratified the Paris Agreement. The fourth Basic Environmental Plan sets a goal for Japan to reduce its GHG emissions. The increase in CO_2 emissions was due to the increasing amount of coal burning in the country. The Japanese national experts find that the promotion of coal-based power plants and the lack of an effective and compulsory emission trading scheme

208 Japanese Law Translation. (n.d.). *Environmental impact assessment act. Japanese law translation.* Retrieved August 4, 2022, from www.japaneselawtranslation.go.jp/en/laws/view/3375/en

209 Aruga, K., Islam, M. M., & Jannat, A. (2024). Assessing the CO_2 emissions and energy source consumption nexus in Japan. *Sustainability, 16*(13), 5742; Kudo, Y., Noborio, K., Shimoozono, N., & Kurihara, R. (2014). The effective water management practice for mitigating greenhouse gas emissions and maintaining rice yield in central Japan. *Agriculture, Ecosystems & Environment, 186*, 77–85; Watabe, A., Leaver, J., Ishida, H., & Shafiei, E. (2019). Impact of low emissions vehicles on reducing greenhouse gas emissions in Japan. *Energy Policy, 130*, 227–242.

210 Kawakatsu, T., Lee, S., & Rudolph, S. (2017). The Japanese carbon tax and the challenges to low-carbon policy cooperation in East Asia. In *Tax law and the environment: A multidisciplinary and worldwide perspective* (pp. 85–103).

are responsible for this rise.[211] However, from 2018 onward, the country is again on track to reducing GHG emissions. The Basic Environment Plan 2018 stipulates Japan's goal to reduce 26% of GHG emissions by 2030 to the base level (1990). The Japanese government has taken multiple measures to achieve this goal. Meanwhile, in October 2020, Japan's Prime Minister Suga announced it would be a carbon-neutral Japan by 2050. Consequently, the Prime Minister announced Japan's goal to decrease GHG emissions by 46% by 2030 compared to its 2013 level. Environmental experts around the world have welcomed this approach. Nonetheless, Japan has not stipulated any clear plan for delivering its ambitious goals, which is concerning and might cause delays in reaching the targeted mark. Moreover, the current GHG per capita and the targeted GHG levels are aligned with the well-below-2°C mark bound by the Kyoto Protocol. Furthermore, to reform its tax policy, Japan was the first Asian country to initiate a carbon tax in 2012. The aim of implementing the tax is to decrease GHG emissions to 80% by 2050.[212] Since 2018, the price of carbon has been increasing in Japan. The OECD has observed that explicit carbon prices have increased to an average of EUR 2.29 per ton of CO_2, up by EUR 0.12 since 2018 (in real 2021 euros). In 2021, fuel excise taxes were EUR 29.3 on average, up by EUR 1.87 relative to 2018 (in real 2021 euros).[213] According to the OECD data, Japan has the seventh highest carbon rate, 31.59 EUR.[214] However, as mentioned earlier, without more clarification and concurrent and coherent measures, Japan will not be able to decrease GHG emissions to the targeted level of 46% by 2030. The 2020 National Greenhouse Gas Inventory Report of Japan reported that the country could reduce only 2.8% of GHG emissions compared to 1990 emissions.[215]

Despite its commitment to reducing GHG emissions, Japan is currently far from reaching its target. The country's plan to increase natural gas consumption and develop new sectors for hydrogen demand to achieve its goals is a cause for concern among experts, who doubt whether this strategy will be sufficient to reduce emissions to the desired level. Moreover, this country's total primary renewable energy supply is quite low. Experts recommend that in order to meet its medium- and long-term climate goals, Japan should raise

211 Burck, J., Marten, F., Bals, C., & Höhne, N. (2015). *The climate change performance index 2016*. Germanwatch, Climate Action Network, & New Climate Institute. https://ccpi.org/wp-content/uploads/The-Climate-Change-Performance-Index-2016.pdf

212 Gokhale, V. (2021). Japan's carbon tax policy: Limitations and policy suggestions. *Current Research in Environmental Sustainability*, *3*, 100082. https://doi.org/10.1016/j.crsust.2021.100082

213 Organization for Economic Co-operation and Development. (2021). *Carbon pricing in times of Covid-19*. OECD. Retrieved July 17, 2022, from www.oecd.org/tax/tax-policy/carbon-pricing-japan.pdf

214 Supra note 111.

215 National Institute for Environmental Studies. (2020). *National greenhouse gas inventory report of Japan 2020*. NIES. Retrieved August 5, 2022, from www.nies.go.jp/gio/archive/nir/jqjm1000000pcibe-att/NIR-JPN-2020-v3.0_GIOweb.pdf

its carbon tax, increase investments in renewable energy sources, cease the construction of new coal power stations, and establish a date for phasing out coal.[216]

5.9 Regulating Corporate Polluters in India

In ancient India, although there were no formal legal systems in place, the people had a strong environmental consciousness. The concept of *dharma* was integral to their lives, guiding them to revere nature. Ancient texts such as *Manu Samhita*, *Brihat Parasar Samhita*, and *Brihaspati Samhita* outlined penalties for those who harmed trees, animals, or polluted water.[217] However, the importance of environmental preservation was overshadowed during the medieval period. It wasn't until the late 19th century, under colonial rule, that India began passing legislation that indirectly contributed to environmental conservation. Presently, around 200 legislations in India directly or indirectly address environmental pollution and degradation.[218] These laws can be divided into two broad categories: (a) supportive legislation and (b) anti-pollution legislation or environmental *lex specialis*.

5.9.1 *Constitution of India and Protection of Environment*

The Indian Constitution places significant importance on environmental conservation. Although it does not explicitly mention the word 'environment,' it addresses comprehensive aspects related to it.[219] The Constitution mandates the promotion of balanced development alongside a sustainable environment. The state and citizens must protect the environment and preserve the country's natural resources. The 'Fundamental Duties' chapter imposes the responsibility on every citizen to safeguard the country's natural resources.[220] Article 48A, added to Chapter IV (Directive Principles) of the Constitution through the *Constitution (Amendment) Act 1976*, directs the state governments to preserve the national environment.[221] Additionally, the Constitution addresses

216 Supra note 113.
217 Chakrabarti, N. K. (1994). *Environmental protection and the law* (S.B. Wangia, Ed., p. 122); see also, Pal, R. (1998). *Legislative measure for environmental protection in India* (3 SCJ 46, pp. 46–47). Eastern book Company.
218 Singh, C. (n.d.). Legal policy for the control of environmental pollution. In P. Diwan & P. Diwan (Eds.), *Environmental Law, Policy, Administration* (Vol. 1). Deep & Deep Publications.
219 Khan, R. (1995). Environment v. development revisited: Contribution of India's judiciary to the conflict resolution. *Asian Year Book of International Law*, *2*, 11.
220 Article 51A (9) states, 'to protect and improve the natural environment including forests, lakes, rivers and wildlife, and to have compassion for living creatures.'
221 Article 48-A states, 'the state shall endeavor to protect and improve the environment and to safeguard the forests and wildlife of the country.'

various environmental issues, such as public health,[222] the organization of agriculture and animal husbandry, and the protection of monuments, places, and objects of national importance.[223]

Articles 252 and 253 of the Indian Constitution delineate the constitutional provisions about the environment. Article 252 confers authority upon the Union Government to enact national legislation upon the request of two or more states. Meanwhile, Article 253 grants the Union Government jurisdiction over matters in the state list to implement decisions made by global institutions or a statement adopted by an international conference. This provision was stated in 1981 when the Union Government enacted the *Air (Prevention and Control of Pollution) Act.*

5.9.2 Key Legislations for Protecting the Environment

For discussion, the legislation supporting the protection of the environment in India can be divided into two groups: (a) pre-independence and (b) post-independence.

The *Indian Penal Code 1860* was crucial legislation before India gained independence. Surprisingly, the word 'environment' was not mentioned in the code. According to Section 268 of the *Penal Code*, a person is considered guilty of a public nuisance if they commit any act or illegal omission that causes harm, danger, or annoyance to the public or people living or owning property nearby or if it causes obstruction or annoyance to those using public rights. The absence of environmental issues in this definition may be due to the unfamiliarity of the concept of environmental preservation to the framers of the code. Nevertheless, several provisions of this Code effectively addressed environmental conservation.

Negligent acts that result in dangerous infections, as well as the adulteration of food, drinks, and drugs, are offenses that carry varying punishments.[224] Examples include contaminating public water sources or poisoning the air in a way that harms people nearby.[225] Negligence in handling poisonous substances, fire, combustible materials, explosives, and machinery is also punishable if it endangers human life.[226] Disobeying a public authority's order becomes a criminal offense if it causes or tends to cause danger.[227] Knowledge of the consequences, rather than intent, is sufficient to constitute the offense. This legal code continues to be highly relevant in modern times. Other environmental

222 Article 47.

223 Article 49. See Kaur, D. (n.d.). Environmental protection in India: Constitutional concepts. In P. Diwan & P. Diwan (Eds.), op. cit.

224 See *Sections* 269, 270, and 272–276 of the *Penal Code* (1860).

225 See *Sections* 277 and 278.

226 See *Sections* 284–287.

227 See *Section* 188.

preservation legislation, such as the *Orient Gas Company Act 1857*,[228] the *Northern Indian Canal and Drainage Act 1873*,[229] the *Indian Ports Act 1908*,[230] and the *Motor Vehicles Act 1939*,[231] also originated from similar concerns.[232]

The legislation following independence shows a strong commitment to preserving the environment. Before the Stockholm era, several laws inadvertently helped protect the environment. The *Factories Act 1948*,[233] the *Damodar Valley Corporation Act 1948*, the *Merchant and Shipping Act 1958*, the *Insecticides Act 1968*, etc., are examples of this kind. In the post-Stockholm period, many regulations were amended and framed to suit the needs of the changing times, for example, the *Wild Life (Protection) Act 1972*, the *Code of Criminal Procedure (Amendment) Act 1973*,[234] the *Water (Prevention and Control of Pollution) Cess Act 1977*, the *Forest (Conservation) Act 1980*, the *Motor Vehicles Act 1938* (amended in 1988), and the *Public Liability Insurance Act 1991*.

Following the Stockholm Conference 1972, the Indian Parliament enacted three major anti-pollution laws. These Environmental *Lex Specialis*, namely, the *Water (Prevention and Control of Pollution) Act 1974*[235] (*Water Act*), the *Air (Prevention and Control of Pollution) Act 1981*[236] (*Air Act*), and the *Environmental Protection Act 1986*[237] (*Environmental Act*), were enacted

228 See *Section* 15.
229 See *Section* 70.
230 See *Section* 6.
231 See *Section* 70.
232 See Prasad, P. S. N. (1999). An overview of march of environmental and pollution control law – Indian scenario. *AIR Journal*, *121*, 122. See also, Bansal, V. K., & Gupta, N. K. Environmental protection: A constitutional obligation. In P. Diwan & P. Diwan (Eds.), op. cit., p. 36.
233 See *Section 12*.
234 See *Section 133* of the *Code of Criminal Procedure, 1973*, which provides,

> wherever a District Magistrate or a Sub-Divisional Magistrate or any other Executive Magistrate or specially empowered in this behalf by the State Government, on receiving the report of a police officer as other information and on such taking evidence (if any) as he thinks fit, considers: (a) that any unlawful obstruction or nuisance should be removed from any public place or from any bay, rivers or channels which is or may be lawfully used by the public – such Magistrate may make a conditional order requiring the person causing such obstruction or nuisance, as carrying on such trade and occupation, or keeping any such goods as merchandise, as owning, possessing, or controlling such building, tent, structure, substance, tank, well, or excavation, or possessing such animal as tree, within a time to be fixed in the order – (1) to remove such obstruction or nuisance; or (ii) to prevent or stop the construction of such building, or to alter the disposal of such substance; or, if he objects, to appear before himself or some other Executive Magistrate subordinate to him at a time and place to be fixed by the order, and show cause, in the manner hereinafter provided, why the order should not be made absolute.

235 *Act No. 60 of 1974.*
236 *Act No. 14 of 1981.*
237 *Act No. 29 of 1986.*

to reduce environmental deprivation and rebuild a clean environment. The *Water Act* was passed on the recommendations of a committee set up in 1962 to arrest the pollution problem of the river and streams due to the growth of massive industrialization and urbanization. The underlying objective was that the domestic and industrial effluents would not be released into the water without treatment. The Parliament introduced and ratified the *Air Act* and *Environment Act* to honor the commitments made at the Stockholm conference. Their primary objectives were to uphold environmental quality and reinstate the natural environment's equitable quality. The implementation of special legislation, like the *Environment Act*, was intended to facilitate coordinating activities within the various regulatory agencies. Against this backdrop, the titles of these anti-pollution acts held substantial significance. The inclusion of the words 'prevention' and 'control' in the *Water* and the *Air Acts*' titles indicated their focus on addressing new and existing sources of pollution, respectively. This differentiation was deliberate and intended to guide the specific focus areas for each act.[238] Furthermore, the inclusion of the term 'protection' in the title of the *Environment Act* was emblematic of its emphasis on sustainable development and the equitable use of natural resources. This nuanced approach to naming the acts reflects the multifaceted nature of environmental stewardship and regulation.

The *Water Act* and *Air Act* set up separate corporate bodies at the central and state levels, namely the Central Pollution Control Board (CPCB) and the State Pollution Control Board (SPCB), to execute the legislative objectives and attain the desired goals. In Union Territories and states where the State Board has not been established under the *Water Act*, the CPCB will act as the SPCB, or it can delegate the power to any person or body of persons specified by the central government.[239] The *Air Act* mandates the State Government to establish the SPCB.[240] The *Environment Act* does not establish anybody but empowers the Central Government to form any specialized authority to oversee the matters delegated.[241] The Central government is also authorized to entrust its powers under the act to anyone it deems fit.[242]

The *Water Act* and *Air Act* enumerate in detail the appointment, qualification, and removal of the Chairman and members of CPCB and SPCB. It is sufficient to note here that the Central Government and the State Government can appoint a maximum of 17 persons (including the Chairperson and the member secretary) to the respective boards. The most significant feature of

238 Supra note 41, p. 186.

239 *Section 4(4)* of the *Water Act*.

240 See *Section 5(1)* of *Air Act*, wherein, 'A Joint Pollution Control Board (JPCB) established by agreement between two or more contiguous state, as by the Central Govt. (in respect of one or more Union territory), and one or more State Govt. contiguous to such Union territory.'

241 *Section 3(3)* of Environment Act.

242 *Section 4*, id. See also, Bakshi, P. M. (1992). *The environment (protection) act, 1986* (pp. 26–27). Indian Law Institute.

this act is that 15 out of 17 persons should be experts in environmental protection and pollution control engineering. However, the appointment to the board depends on the government's discretion, and often, unqualified individuals are selected.[243]

Chapters III and IV of the *Water Act* and the *Air Act*, respectively, lay down the powers and functions of CPBC and SPBC. The CPBC is primarily responsible for the promotion of the cleanliness of rivers and streams (i.e., surface water),[244] improvement of air quality, and prevention, control, or abatement of air pollution in the country.[245] In addition to these, it should accomplish the following obligations: (a) advise the central government[246]; (b) coordinate the activities of the state board (SPBC), resolve disputes, provide technical assistance and guidance, and sponsor investigation and research concerning pollution problems; (c) lay down standards for river and stream water and quality of air; (d) organize a nationwide comprehensive training program about the preservation of water and air pollution[247]; and (e) establish laboratories to list the collected sample (i.e., polluting substance).[248]

A fleeting glance over the relevant sections reveals that the SPCB is the main 'regulating agency under these acts.' It is assigned the following numerous tasks: (a) to plan a comprehensive program for the prevention, control, or reduction of water and air pollution[249]; (b) to gather and share information about water and air pollution[250]; and (c) to give advice to the state government regarding any matter relating to the prevention, control, or abatement of pollution in water and air and regarding the location of industrial establishments.[251]

In addition, the SPCB discharges three important functions, that is, lay down and modify annual standards of water and air quality, periodically inspect the industrial and treatment plants, and revoke orders for discharge of pollutants into streams and atmosphere by considering the tolerance limits. The CPCB abides by the directives given by the Central Government, while the SPCB must follow the directions given by the Central Board and the State Government. In case of any inconsistency between the two directions, the matter rests with the Central Government.

Under the *Environment Act*, the Central Government is entrusted with the same functions as have been laid down for SPCB by the *Water Act* and *Air Act*. However, a shift has been made because the scope of the former is much

243 See Murthy, K. V. R. (1990). Pollution control: Need for strategic enforcement. *3 SCC (Journal)*, *77*, 78.
244 *Section 16(1)* of *Water Act*.
245 *Section 16(1)* of *Air Act*.
246 Ibid.
247 *Section 16(2)(h)* of *Water Act* and *Section 16(2)(f)* of *Air Act*.
248 *Section 17* of *Water Act*, *Section 17* of *Air Act*.
249 Ibid.
250 Ibid.
251 *Section 3(2)(iii)* of *Environment Act*.

wider. Some important features are: (a) establishing standards for environmental quality in its various aspects[252]; (b) restriction of areas where any industries, operations, processes, or classes of industries, operations, and processes may not be conducted or that may be conducted subject to certain restrictions and safeguards[253]; and (c) preparation of manuals and cards as guides relating to the prevention, control, and abatements of environmental pollution.[254]

The SPCB wields ample power to carry out its functions. Some of them are enumerated as: (a) to obtain information from the occupier or any person in charge of any industrial establishment about the discharge of pollutants in the water and atmosphere[255]; (b) to enter any place at a 'reasonable hour' to inspect whether any notice, order, or direction issued under the act has been complied with or not[256]; (c) to collect samples from any stream, well, sewage as trade effluent, or from any chimney, flue, dirt, or any other outlet for analysis in a manner prescribed by the act. Such scientific analysis or investigation results are admissible as evidence in the judicial process[257]; and (d) to take immediate measures in case of apprehension of any accident due to the discharge of polluting substances in the water or atmosphere.[258] In addition, the SPCB enjoys certain regulatory powers, such as prosecuting the polluter in a court of law, giving directions to the polluting industrial units for closure, or withdrawing its water supply, power, or other essential services.

Both these legislations (*Water* and *Air Acts*) impose a mandatory duty upon the person in charge of the premises to inform the SPCB when the emissions exceed the prescribed pollution limits. The criminal liability prescribed by these acts falls upon two types of persons, that is, natural/individual and corporate/fictitious persons. In some circumstances, the liabilities are concurrent, while, in others, the sole responsibility has been imposed upon the corporation. The circumstances wherein liability is imposed upon both the aforesaid categories of persons are enumerated as follows: (a) failing to observe the standards laid down by the state board (SPCB) in respect of the emission or discharge of pollutants[259]; (b) using a new outlet for the disposal of polluting substances by an established industry without the previous permission of the competent authority[260]; (c) obstructing any person acting under the direction or orders of the boards (i.e., CPCB and SPCB)[261];

252 *Section 3(2)(v)*, id.
253 *Section 3(2)(xiii)*, id.
254 Ibid.
255 *Section 20* of *Water Act* and *Section 25* of *Air Act.*
256 *Section 23* of *Water Act* and *Section 24* of *Air Act.*
257 *Section 21* of *Water Act* and *Section 26* of *Air Act.*
258 *Section 32* of *Water Act* and *Section 23* of *Air Act.*
259 *Section 25* of *Water Act* and *Section 22A* of *Air Act.*
260 *Section 42(1)(b)* of *Water Act*, *Section 38(b)* of *Air Act* and *Section 12(3)* of *Environment Act.*
261 Sections 20(2) and (3), 32(1) of Water Act.

and (d) obtaining consent under Sections *25* and *26* of the *Water Act* and Section 21 of the *Air Act* by making a false statement regarding the material particulars.

In addition to these, individual persons are also liable in the following circumstances: (a) in case he fails to provide information about the construction, installation, or operation of the establishment, disposal system, or pollution control equipment to the SPCB, Central Government, or any authorized officer, for the adequate performance of their duties[262]; (b) fails to intimate the occurrence of any accident or unforeseen act under Section 32 of the *Water Act* and Section 31 of the *Air Act*, and Section 9 of the *Environment Act*; (c) 'destroy, pull down, remove, injures or defenses any pillar, post or stake fixed in the ground or any notice or other matter put up, inscribe as placid, by or under the authority of the boards'[263] (i.e., CPCB & SPCB); and (d) 'destroy any works, or property belonging to the Board.'[264]

The three anti-pollution acts explicitly stipulate the provision concerning 'offenses by companies.'[265] Suppose a corporation is found guilty of an environmental crime. In that case, the person in charge of the company's business conduct and any directors, managers, secretaries, or other officers will also be held accountable and subject to punishment under the law.[266] As may be seen, vicarious liability has been introduced within the domain of environmental criminal law, perhaps to bring more coercive elements to the law: 'One must always keep in mind the broader perspective that the administration of criminal law is more a matter of substance than of force and should not be allowed to be defeated by pettifogging technicality.' The element of deterrence has also been introduced in the provisions. The deterrent aspect of punishment appears to be the guiding force behind the imposition of dual responsibility. A similar provision has also been made regarding 'Offences by Government Department,' wherein the board, department, or any officer who perpetrates such offense shall be held responsible.[267]

Austere modes of punishment have been stipulated by both the *Water* and *Air Acts*. The *Water Act* provides for imprisonment for a term ranging from three months to six years; in case the pollution continues even after conviction, the term may extend from one year to seven years. It also prescribes a maximum fine of 5,000 rupees. In cases where non-compliance with the directions of the state board (SPCB) continues, an additional fine may be imposed, extending to 1,000 rupees per day. The *Air Act* has enhanced the penalty in contravention of certain provisions; it prescribes imprisonment for one year

262 Section 42(1)(1) of *Water Act* and Section 38(a) of *Air Act*.

263 Section 42(1)(a) of *Water Act* and Section 38(1)(a) of *Air Act*.

264 Section 42(1)(c) of *Water Act* and Section 38(1)(c) of *Air Act*.

265 Provided that the offenses are committed by the company with the consent or connivance of or, is attributable to any neglect on the part of those officers of the company.

266 See Section 48 of *Water Act*, Section 40 of *Air Act*, and *Section 17* of *Environment Act*.

267 Sections 21 or *22*, or direction issued under Section 31A of *Air Act*.

and six months, which may extend to six years, and in addition, a fine of rupees 5,000, which may extend to 5,000 rupees for each day during the continuance of such failure. The maximum period of imprisonment prescribed by the act is seven years, while the maximum fine that may be imposed is rupees 10,000 under this act.

The *Environment Act* imposes stricter penalties for violating any provision, order, rule, or direction under this act. It may include a prison sentence of up to five years, a fine of up to one lakh rupees, or both. In the event of ongoing violations, there could be an additional fine of up to 5,000 rupees per day.

The intellectual community may question the effectiveness of current laws in penalizing large domestic and multinational corporations. The fines these laws impose are too low to have any real impact. These companies have significant financial resources that allow them to afford to pollute and pay the fines easily. Furthermore, the laws stipulate that the person in charge or officer responsible for the company's conduct can be held accountable for environmental offenses committed by the company. However, multinational corporations often hire local staff to oversee their operations in different countries. If these local staff members violate the laws, they bear the consequences, not the corporation or its foreign nationals. Therefore, this provision fails to achieve its intended purpose. The laws also do not hold multinationals accountable when they neglect to implement the same safety measures in our country as they are required to in their own countries. When it comes to addressing environmental offenses and holding guilty corporations accountable, there is a lack of emphasis on public involvement in these legislations. Although they allow concerned citizens to report environmental issues, there is a mandatory waiting period of 60 days before they can file a complaint with the board (SPCB) or the central government. This delay could allow environmental offenders to tamper with evidence and avoid responsibility. These legislations require the SPCB to file complaints for environmental crimes with specific magistrates. However, regular courts are often busy, resulting in delayed justice for these critical cases. Section 24 of the *Environment Act* specifies that offenders convicted under other acts with lesser punishments must receive the lesser penalty, which is a concerning setback for environmental protection.

The Indian Parliament enacted the *Biological Diversity Act*[268] in 2002 to protect and preserve the rich *in-situ* & *ex-situ* biological diversity of different parts of the country and combat the unauthorized commercial exploitation of the same in response to its international obligation. The act contemplates biodiversity as 'the variability among living organisms from all sources and the ecological complexes of which they are part and includes diversity within species or between species and of ecosystems,'[269] whereas biological resources

268 *Biological Diversity Act 2002* (18 of 2003).
269 Section 2(b).

mean plants, animals, and microorganisms or parts thereof, their generic materials, and by-products (excluding the value-added products) with actual and potential use or value but do not include human genetic material.[270] The latest version of this legislation has constituted different regulatory and quasi-adjudicatory bodies for achieving the objective of this legislation in the form of the National Biodiversity Authority and the State Biodiversity Board. The act also emphasizes biodiversity protection at the grassroots level by constituting the Bio-diversity Management Committee in the local bodies. The National Biodiversity Authority serves as the regulatory body responsible for granting permission to utilize biological resources for knowledge transfer, commercial use, and intellectual property applications.[271] The authority may also contest the granting of intellectual property by the outside authority on the biological resource obtained from India.[272] The State Bio-Diversity Board also, on the other hand, regulates the commercial exploitation of biological resources.[273] The Central Government has been given the power to develop national policies regarding the country's biodiversity.[274] It provides punishment for violations of Sections 3, 4, or 6, which may result in imprisonment for up to five years and a fine of up to ten lakh rupees.[275] Anyone who violates the orders of the Central and State Governments may be fined up to one lakh rupees. For subsequent offenses, the fine will be two lakhs.[276] In the context of a company, any individual who held a position of authority and responsibility for managing the company's affairs at the time of the offense will be held accountable and subject to appropriate legal consequences as per the relevant legislation.[277] While the *Biological Diversity Act* is not anti-pollution legislation, it directly or indirectly contributes to protecting biodiversity and the environment in the country.

Environmental pollution in India is a multifaceted issue, encompassing scientific, technological, economic, and societal challenges. Addressing this problem demands diligent attention and concerted efforts. In the case of *M.C. Mehta v. Union of India*,[278] the court recognized the intricacy of environmental pollution and stressed the necessity of unbiased scientific expertise to guide judicial decision-making. As a solution, the court proposed the establishment of independent centers, such as Ecological Science Research Groups, staffed with competent and public-spirited experts. These centers would function as knowledge hubs for the court and government, offering tailored scientific and

270 Sections 2(c).
271 Sections 3, 4, and 6.
272 Section 18(4).
273 Section 23 of the *Biological Diversity Act 2002*.
274 Section 36.
275 Sections 3, 4, 6, and 55.
276 Section 56.
277 *Section 57.*
278 *AIR 1987 SC 965.*

technological input as per their specific requirements. Earlier, the Supreme Court suggested that all High Courts in Indian provinces have a dedicated 'Green Bench' with a specialized focus on handling environmental issues exclusively.[279]

5.9.3 National Green Tribunal

The Supreme Court has underscored that prosecutions under the *Water Act*, *Air Act*, or *Environment Act* often face significant delays or inadequate attention in regular criminal courts due to heavy caseloads or insufficient focus on environmental concerns.[280] Moreover, industries frequently challenge the rulings of these courts in higher judicial instances, leading to protracted proceedings. Interim orders are commonly issued, restraining implementing authorities from enforcing their decisions and causing irreparable environmental harm. The court has proposed the establishment of specialized environmental courts exclusively dedicated to handling civil and criminal cases related to the environment. It has been recommended that these courts be staffed by individuals with legal or judicial expertise and a comprehensive understanding of environmental complexities. The judicial conclusion stressed the need for the Parliament of India to create laws establishing Environmental Tribunals. In 1995, during the 46th year of its Republic, the Parliament of India passed the *National Environment Tribunal Act* (referred to as the *Tribunal Act*). The object of the act reads as

> an Act to provide for strict liability for damages arising out of any accident occurring while holding any hazardous substance and for the establishment of a National Environment Tribunal for effective and expeditious disposal of cases arising from such accident, to give relief and damages to persons, property and the environment and for matter connected therewith as incidental thereto.

The preamble to this legislation underscores India's international commitment as a participant in the 1992 UNCED in Rio de Janeiro. This commitment entails the development of national laws addressing liability and compensation for victims of pollution and other environmental damages. The legislation led to the creation of the National Green Tribunal (NGT) in New Delhi and in other locations specified by the Central Government through a notification.[281] The Tribunal comprises Chairman, Vice-Chairperson, and

279 *Vellore Citizens Welfare Forum v. Union of India, AIR 1996 SC 2715.*
280 *Indian Council for Enviro-Legal Action and Others v. Union of India and Others, (1996) 3 SCC 212.*
281 Ibid., *Section 9(5).*

Judicial and Technical Members,[282] as specified by the Central Government in its notification. The Chairman and Vice-Chairman are individuals from the higher judiciary or Secretary of the government department who possess expertise in addressing legal, administrative, scientific, or technical aspects of the environment.[283]

This legislation underscores the necessity for technical members to possess experience or the ability to address administrative, scientific, or technical issues related to the environment.[284] Those overseeing the Tribunal should be environmental experts capable of handling complex problems and providing timely remedies. The Tribunal holds civil and criminal jurisdiction and serves as an investigating authority. Upon receiving an application, it may conduct an inquiry and, if deemed appropriate, may summarily reject an application or, after giving proper notice to the owner,[285] offer an opportunity for the involved parties to be heard.[286] It also has the authority to determine compensation for those affected by environmental pollution. The Tribunal is not strictly bound by the procedural aspects of the *Code of Civil Procedure 1908*, but it is required to uphold the principles of natural justice and other provisions of the act.[287] It has the authority to regulate its procedures and is granted all the powers of a Civil Court. Additionally, it restricts the jurisdiction of other Civil Courts from adjudicating disputes related to the environment.[288]

Non-compliance with an order issued by the NGT may lead to a penalty of up to three years in prison and a fine of up to one lakh rupees.[289] All proceedings before the Tribunal are considered judicial under Sections 193, 219, and 228 of the *Indian Penal Code, 1860*.[290] This act grants extensive powers and jurisdiction to the Tribunal. Its dual purpose is to investigate accidents resulting from hazardous industries and serve as an adjudicatory body for compensatory payments. Appeals against the Tribunal's decisions can be made to the Supreme Court.[291]

282 Ibid.
283 See Section 10.
284 Ibid.
285 *Section 2(o)* states:

> Owner means a person who owns, or has control over handing, any hazardous substance at the time of accident and include . . . (i) in the case, of a firm, any of its partners, (ii) in the case of an association, any of its members; and (iii) in the case of a company, any of its directors, managers, secretaries or other officers who is directly in charge of, and is responsible to, the company for the conduct of the business of the company.

286 See Section 5.
287 Ibid.
288 See Section 19.
289 See Section 25.
290 *Act 45 of 1860.*
291 See *Section 24.*

The NGT has significantly impacted environmental protection in India. The tribunal's composition of judicial and technical expert members allows for a multidimensional approach to environmental issues.[292] The diverse scientific expertise lends credibility to the NGT's decision-making process, promoting independence from organizational bias or corporate associations.[293] Judicial members highly value the expert members' contributions and acknowledge their substantial input in environmental matters.[294]

Despite its positive impact, the NGT faces accessibility challenges. The limited number of regional benches hinders access to justice for people in remote areas of India.[295] Currently, there are only five benches covering the entire country, making it difficult for stakeholders to register and follow cases far from their residences.[296] This limitation contradicts the act's aim of making the redressal process more accessible to victims of environmental damage.[297] Expanding its jurisdiction to include criminal law and providing more autonomy could boost its ability to prevent and mitigate environmental degradation.[298] Addressing resource constraints, both financial and human, is crucial to meeting the six-month timeframe for case disposal.[299] Compliance with NGT rulings and enhancing the capacity of regulatory bodies like pollution control boards are also essential for effectively implementing the tribunal's decisions.[300]

5.9.4 National Appellate Authority

The Parliament has also enacted the *National Environment Appellate Authority Act 1997*,[301] (hereinafter referred to as the *Appellate Act*), which provides

> for the establishment of a National Appellate Authority to hear appeals with respect to restriction of areas in which any industrial operation or process or class of industrial operation or process shall not be carried out or shall be carried out subject to certain safeguards under the *Environment (Protection) Act, 1986*, and for matters connected therewith or incidental thereto.

292 Gill, G. N. (2016). Environmental justice in India: The National Green Tribunal and expert members. *Transnational Environmental Law*, *5*(1), 175–205.
293 Ibid.
294 Ibid.
295 Muschött, K. (2022). *The National Green Tribunal of India* (MR4 Human Rights Clinique II, University College Stockholm).
296 Ibid.
297 Sharma, M. (2022). *Efficacy at the National Green Tribunal and its accessibility: An empirical study*. Lloyd Law College.
298 Muschött, K. (2022). *The National Green Tribunal of India* (MR4 Human Rights Clinique II, University College Stockholm).
299 Ibid.
300 Ibid.
301 Act 22 of 1997.

If any individual is adversely impacted by the approval granted for establishing an industry or a group of industries, they have the right to apply within 30 days of the approval.[302] The Appellate Authority is not bound by the *Civil Procedure Code 1908* but must adhere to the principles of natural justice and other provisions of the act.[303] Non-compliance with any order of the authority can lead to imprisonment for up to seven years, a fine of up to one lakh rupees, or both.[304] The proceedings before the court are considered judicial proceedings, as per Sections 193, 219, and 228 of the *Indian Penal Code 1860*. The act also stipulates that, following its enactment, the Civil Court or other authorities do not have the authority to consider appeals. The primary objective of the act is to ensure that proper impact assessments are conducted for upcoming industries and that they adhere to necessary anti-pollution measures. Furthermore, the *Public Liability Insurance Act 1991* mandates public liability insurance for facilities dealing with hazardous substances.[305] The primary objectives are to ensure compensation for the affected parties and to assist industries in meeting their obligations to settle substantial claims arising from major environmental disasters.

5.9.5 Section 135 in the Companies Act 2013

Protecting the natural environment is now seen as a key duty for business companies. Indian companies typically handle this and other social duties using four models: ethical, Statist, liberal, and stakeholder models.[306] The ethical model draws from religion and Gandhi's ideas,[307] while the Statist model reflects post-colonial Indian economic policies.[308] The (neo)liberal model prioritizes profits,[309] and the stakeholder model builds on Freeman's concept of stakeholder responsibility.[310] Studies show that companies do not stick to just one model but mix elements that best serve their interests.[311]

302 See Section 11.
303 See Section 12.
304 See Section 19.
305 Act 6 of 1991.
306 Kumar, R., Murphy, D. F., & Balsari, V. (2001). *Altered images: The 2001 state of corporate responsibility in India poll. Understanding and encouraging corporate responsibility in South Asia: Update one*. Tata Energy Research Institute.
307 Gupta, D., & Saxena, K. (2006). Corporate social responsibility in Indian service organisations: An empirical study. In *International conference on CSR agendas for Asia*. Kuala Lumpur, Malaysia, April 2006; Hart, J. G. (1994). The philosophy of Gandhi: A study of his basic ideas. *Philosophy East and West*, *44*(1), 149–168; Richards, G. (2005). *The philosophy of Gandhi: A study of his basic ideas*. Routledge.
308 Arora, B., & Puranik, R. (2004). A review of corporate social responsibility in India. *Development*, *47*(3), 93–100; Nilekani, N. (2008). *Imagining India: Ideas for the new century: [Exclusive excerpts]*. Allen Lane.
309 Friedman, M. (1970). A Friedman doctrine: The social responsibility of business is to increase its profits. *The New York Times Magazine*, *13*(1970), 32–33.
310 Freeman, R. E. (2010). *Strategic management: A stakeholder approach*. Cambridge University Press.
311 Mitra, R. (2012). "My country's future": A culture-centered interrogation of corporate social responsibility in India. *Journal of Business Ethics*, *106*, 131–147.

In 2011, India introduced the National Voluntary Guidelines for the Social, Environmental, and Economic Responsibilities of Business 2011 to boost companies' social responsibility through policy and financial support. Later, the country shifted gears by adding Section 135 to its *Companies Act 2013*, which put more constraints on businesses.[312]

The *Companies Act 2013*[313] aims to mainstream 'the practice of business involvement in CSR and make[ing] (businesses) socially, economically and environmentally responsible.'[314] It is one of the few laws worldwide that not only requires companies to perform social responsibilities but also specifies how much of their profits should fund these efforts.[315] Section 135 tightened regulations and put more focus on corporate stakeholders,[316] making certain companies spend on and report their CSR activities.[317] This shifted CSR in India from voluntary giving to a more structured approach aimed at creating economic value while tackling social issues.[318]

However, some worry that the 'growing intervention of state authorities in the field of CSR supports rather than corrects the rise of private governance, which involves profit-driven companies in the performance of political functions.'[319] Critics also say India's CSR laws are unclear and lack proper oversight.[320] While Section 135 clearly states how much profit should go to CSR,

312 Rahim, M. M., & Sayeed, M. A. (2024). Reaching an aim differently? Corporate social responsibility regulation in Australia and India. *Cardozo International and Comparative Law Review*, *7*(3), 821–865. https://rune.une.edu.au/web/handle/1959.11/61196

313 *The Indian Companies Act, 2013.*

314 Kumar, R., Murphy, D. F., & Balsari, V. (2001). *Altered images: The 2001 state of corporate responsibility in India poll. Understanding and encouraging corporate responsibility in South Asia: Update one.* Tata Energy Research Institute.

315 Gatti, L., Vishwanath, B., Seele, P., & Cottier, B. (2019). Are we moving beyond voluntary CSR? Exploring theoretical and managerial implications of mandatory CSR resulting from the new Indian Companies Act. *Journal of Business Ethics*, *160*, 961–972.

316 See p. 108, Nair, A. K., & Bhattacharyya, S. S. (2019). Mandatory corporate social responsibility in India and its effect on corporate financial performance: Perspectives from institutional theory and resource-based view. *Business Strategy & Development*, *2*(2), 106–116; Halkos, G., & Skouloudis, A. (2016). National CSR and institutional conditions: An exploratory study. *Journal of Cleaner Production*, *139*, 1150–1156.

317 Jumde, A., & Du Plessis, J. (2022). Legislated corporate social responsibility (CSR) in India: The law and practicalities of its compliance. *Statute Law Review*, *43*(2), 170–197.

318 Mitra, N. (2021). Impact of strategic management, corporate social responsibility on firm performance in the post mandate period: Evidence from India. *International Journal of Corporate Social Responsibility*, *6*(1), 1–15. Gatti et al., supra note 2, at p. 961.

319 See p. 542, from Krichewsky, D. (2017). CSR public policies in India's democracy: Ambiguities in the political regulation of corporate conduct. *Business and Politics*, *19*(3), 510–547.

320 Jumde, A., & Du Plessis, J. (2022). Legislated corporate social responsibility (CSR) in India: The law and practicalities of its compliance. *Statute Law Review*, *43*(2), 170–197.

it does not define CSR.[321] This gap allows companies to label some projects as CSR and dodge the law's requirements.[322]

In 2020, India's top 300 companies spent about two-thirds of the country's yearly CSR budget, nearly 10,000 crore rupees.[323] While the law seems to have improved CSR management, its impact is shallow.[324] It failed to truly motivate companies to respond to social and environmental needs. Many CSR programs aim to meet legal requirements and justify their operations rather than achieve social goals.[325] Some programs initially help with issues like female education, sanitation, and family planning, but many do not contribute to social and environmental causes.[326] Some programs even go against social values and environmental needs.[327] When companies are not truly committed to solving social issues through CSR, the problems caused by their programs can outweigh any benefits.

5.10 Conclusion

Domestic environmental laws are designed to regulate human impact on the environment, but they often fall short when it comes to addressing the actions of corporate polluters. This can be attributed to the lack of political will to enforce environmental laws and the issues of corruption. For instance, the oil spills in the Niger Delta region of Nigeria and the dumping of toxic waste in the Ivory Coast emphasize the need for stronger accountability and enforcement measures.

Corporate polluters often use complex legal structures to shield themselves from liability, which poses challenges for domestic regulatory frameworks to hold them accountable. Additionally, corporate polluters wield significant

321 Dharmapala, D., & Khanna, V. (2018). The impact of mandated corporate social responsibility: Evidence from India's Companies Act of 2013. *International Review of Law and Economics*, *56*, 92–104.

322 Ibid., p 4.

323 Srishti, & Singh, T. (2023). Why this is not CSR: A study of 5 major corporates. *Down to Earth*. www.downtoearth.org.in/blog/governance/why-this-is-not-csr-a-study-of-5-major-corporates-74587

324 Rahim, M. M., & Sayeed, M. A. (2024). Reaching an aim differently? Corporate social responsibility regulation in Australia and India. *Cardozo International and Comparative Law Review*, *7*(3), 821–865.

325 In 2016, only 27% of the companies who reported on CSR consulted intermediaries while preparing their CSR related policies; 16% of these companies included NGOs in their CSR policy framing exercise. See Naik, P., Parekh, A., Rustomji, S., D'Souza, M. F., & Ghosh, A. (2016). *Transforming India: The CSR opportunity*. Rockefeller Foundation. www.rockefellerfoundation.org/wp-content/uploads/Tranforming-India-The-CSR-Opportunity-August-2016.pdf

326 Jumde, A., & Du Plessis, J. (2022). Legislated corporate social responsibility (CSR) in India: The law and practicalities of its compliance. *Statute Law Review*, *43*(2), 170–197.

327 Ibid.

lobbying power, influencing the development of environmental regulations to their advantage. For example, the case of the Chevron oil company in Ecuador and the VW emissions scandal highlight the shortcomings of domestic regulatory frameworks in curbing corporate pollution.

To cope with the capacities of corporate polluters, the intensity of legal approaches within the regulatory framework for protecting the environment is increasing. However, enforcing complex environmental regulations, especially in developing countries, can be challenging due to insufficient funding and staff for regulatory agencies. To address these challenges, it is crucial to increase resources for regulators, such as funding and staffing, to combat environmental pollution by businesses effectively. Moreover, imposing higher penalties for non-compliance can encourage adherence to environmental regulations and deter corporate polluters from engaging in harmful activities. Lastly, enhancing transparency and accountability for corporate polluters can be achieved by increasing public access to information about corporate activities and mandating companies to disclose their environmental impact.

References

Ahmed, F., Ali, I., Kousar, S., & Ahmed, S. (2022). The environmental impact of industrialization and foreign direct investment: Empirical evidence from Asia-Pacific region. *Environmental Science and Pollution Research*, 1–15.

Airaksinen, J., & Albrecht, E. (2019). Arguments and their effects–a case study on drafting the legislation on the environmental impacts of peat extraction in Finland. *Journal of Cleaner Production*, *226*, 1004–1012.

American Lung Association. (2024). New York. Retrieved June 21, 2024, from www.lung.org/research/sota/city-rankings/msas/new-york-newark-ny-nj-ct-pa#ozone

Andrés Sáenz De Santa María, P. (2019). The European Union and the law of treaties: A fruitful relationship. *European Journal of International Law*, *30*(3), 721–751.

Arora, B., & Puranik, R. (2004). A review of corporate social responsibility in India. *Development*, *47*(3), 93–100.

Aruga, K., Islam, M. M., & Jannat, A. (2024). Assessing the CO_2 emissions and energy source consumption nexus in Japan. *Sustainability*, *16*(13), 5742.

Avenell, S. (2017). Transnational environmental activism and Japan's second modernity. *Asia-Pacific Journal-Japan Focus*, *15*(14).

Bakshi, P. M. (1992). *The Environment (Protection) Act, 1986* (pp. 26–27). Indian Law Institute.

Barrett, B. F., & Therivel, R. (2019). *Environmental policy and impact assessment in Japan*. Routledge.

Bates, G. M. (1992). *Environmental law in Australia*. LexisNexis Butterworths.

Becklump, P. (2019). *Federal and provincial jurisdiction to regulate environmental issues*. Economics, Resources and International Affairs Division. Retrieved March 15, from https://lop.parl.ca/sites/PublicWebsite/default/en_CA/ResearchPublications/201386E

Bichler, R. M. (2023). Harm and harmony – concepts of nature and environmental practice in Japan. *Histories*, *3*(2), 62–75.

Blackmore, E. (2023, October 4). The shocking river fire that fueled the creation of the EPA. *History*. Retrieved June 21, 2024, from www.history.com/news/epa-earth-day-cleveland-cuyahoga-river-fire-clean-water-act

Boissoneault, L. (2019, June 19). The Cuyahoga River caught fire at least a dozen times, but no one cared until 1969. *Smithsonian*. Retrieved June 21, 2024, from www.smithsonianmag.com/history/cuyahoga-river-caught-fire-least-dozen-times-no-one-cared-until-1969-180972444/

Botta, E., & Yamasaki, S. (2020). Policies, regulatory framework and enforcement for air quality management: The case of Japan. *OECD Environment Working Papers*, *156*, 0_1–60.

Brunswick, G. O. N. (2025). *About the clean air act*. Retrieved March 15, from www2.gnb.ca/content/gnb/en/departments/elg/environment/content/air_quality/clean_air/act.html

Bundesamt, U. (2024). *Laws of environmental liability, harm and criminal actions*. Retrieved June 21, 2024, from www.umweltbundesamt.de/en/environm-liability-a-environm-damage-law-envir#harmonisation-of-compensation-for-environmental-harm

Caradonna, J. L. (2014). Eco-warriors: The environmental movement and the growth of ecological wisdom, 1960s–1970s. In *Sustainability*. Oxford University Press.

Cioc, M. (1998). The impact of the coal age on the German environment: A review of the historical literature. *Environment and History*, *4*(1), 105–124.

Clean Energy Regulator. (2024). *Australian carbon credit unit scheme*. Retrieved June 21, 2024, from https://cer.gov.au/schemes/australian-carbon-credit-unit-scheme

Daniels, J. (2019, April 24). Los Angeles is still the smoggiest US city, report says. *CNBC*. Retrieved June 21, 2024, from www.cnbc.com/2019/04/24/los-angeles-is-still-the-smoggiest-us-city-report-says.html

Dharmapala, D., & Khanna, V. (2018). The impact of mandated corporate social responsibility: Evidence from India's companies act of 2013. *International Review of Law and Economics*, *56*, 92–104.

Dobson, S., Winter, J., & Boyd, B. (2019). *The greenhouse gas emissions coverage of carbon pricing instruments for Canadian provinces*. The School of Public Policy at the University of Calgary.

Douhaire, C. (2024). The climate decision of the German constitutional court and its implications on soil management. In *International yearbook of soil law and policy 2022* (p. 35). Springer.

Down to Earth. (2023). *Why this is not CSR: A study of 5 major corporates*. Retrieved June 21, 2024, from www.downtoearth.org.in/blog/governance/why-this-is-not-csr-a-study-of-5-major-corporates-74587

Ebisu, M., & Hagihara, K. (2019). Methods of environmental risk management for land contamination problems: Suggestions for Japan. *Building Resilient Regions*, 149–175.

Environmental Protection Authority (EPA). 2024). Climate change and NSW: Overview. *New South Wales Government*. Retrieved June 24, 2024, from www.epa.nsw.gov.au/your-environment/climate-change/climate-change-nsw-overview

Federal Ministry for the Environment, N. C., Nuclear Safety and Consumer Protection. (2025). *Federal nature conservation act*. Government of Germany. www.bmuv.de/en/law/federal-nature-conservation-act-bnatschg/

Freeman, R. E. (2010). *Strategic management: A stakeholder approach*. Cambridge University Press.

Friedman, M. (1970). A Friedman doctrine: The social responsibility of business is to increase its profits. *The New York Times Magazine*, *13*(1970), 32–33.

Fujikawa, K. (2012). The social structure of the environmental destruction caused by the Fukushima Nuclear Disaster. *Japanese Association for Environmental Sociology*, *18*, 45–59.

Fujikura, M. (2011). Japan's efforts against the illegal dumping of industrial waste. *Environmental Policy and Governance*, *21*(5), 325–337.

Fujioka, S. (2019). Overviews of waste management policies in Japan. *Building Resilient Regions*, 125–147.

Gallagher, T. (2022, November 18). Coca-Cola revealed as world's worst plastic polluter for fifth year in a row. *Euronews*. Retrieved June 21, 2024, from www.euronews.com/green/2022/11/18/coca-cola-revealed-as-worlds-worst-plastic-polluter-for-fifth-year-in-a-row

Gatti, L., Vishwanath, B., Seele, P., & Cottier, B. (2019). Are we moving beyond voluntary CSR? Exploring theoretical and managerial implications of mandatory CSR resulting from the new Indian Companies Act. *Journal of Business Ethics*, *160*, 961–972.

Gill, G. N. (2016). Environmental justice in India: The National Green Tribunal and expert members. *Transnational Environmental Law*, *5*(1), 175–205.

Godden, L., Peel, J., & McDonald, J. (2018). *Environmental law*. Oxford University Press.

Gupta, D., & Saxena, K. (2006, April). Corporate social responsibility in Indian service organisations: An empirical study. *International conference on CSR agendas for Asia*, Kuala Lumpur, Malaysia.

Halkos, G., & Skouloudis, A. (2016). National CSR and institutional conditions: An exploratory study. *Journal of Cleaner Production*, *139*, 1150–1156.

Hamilton, J. (2019, January 28). How California's worst oil spill turned beaches black and the nation green. *NPR*. Retrieved June 21, 2024, from www.npr.org/2019/01/28/688219307/how-californias-worst-oil-spill-turned-beaches-black-and-the-nation-green

Hart, J. G. (1994). The philosophy of Gandhi: A study of his basic ideas. *Philosophy East and West*, *44*(1), 149–168.

Hausotte, M., & Benisch, C. (2017). *Federal nature conservation and species protection legislation in Germany*. www.kerbtier.de/Pages/Themenseiten/enRechtslage.html

Hiwasaki, L. (2005). Toward sustainable management of national parks in Japan: Securing local community and stakeholder participation. *Environmental Management*, *35*, 753–764.

Hosoda, E. (2016). Waste policies and related legislation in Japan. In *The economics of waste management in East Asia* (pp. 3–37). Routledge.

Howell, B. (2023). The top 14 most polluting companies. *The Eco Expert*. Retrieved May 29, 2024, from www.theecoexperts.co.uk/blog/most-polluting-companies

Huttunen, R., Kuuva, P., Kinnunen, M., Lemström, B., & Hirvonen, P. (2022). *Carbon neutral Finland 2035–national climate and energy strategy*. Ministry of Economic Affairs and Employment of Finland.

IREES, I. F. R. E. A. E. S. (2016). *Process emissions in German industries and their relevance for Germany's national climate mitigation targets – an outlining of the problem and first options for action*. N. C. A. N. S. B. Federal Ministry for the Environment. www.bmuv.de/fileadmin/Daten_BMU/Download_PDF/Ressourceneffizienz/irees_prozessemissionen_en_bf.pdf

Ishimaki, M. (2024). Soil protection law in Japan. In *International yearbook of soil law and policy 2022* (p. 227). Springer.

Jumde, A., & Du Plessis, J. (2022). Legislated corporate social responsibility (CSR) in India: The law and practicalities of its compliance. *Statute law review*, *43*(2), 170–197.

Kaufman, N. (2019, June 6). What you need to know about a federal carbon tax in the United States. *Center on Global Energy Policy at Columbia University*. Retrieved June 21, 2024, from www.energypolicy.columbia.edu/publications/what-you-need-to-know-about-a-federal-carbon-tax-in-the-united-states/

Kawakatsu, T., Lee, S., & Rudolph, S. (2017). The Japanese Carbon Tax and the challenges to low-carbon policy cooperation in East Asia. In *Tax law and the environment:*

A multidisciplinary and worldwide perspective (pp. 85–103). IBFD (International Bureau of Fiscal Documentation).

Kennett, S. A. (1992). Federal environmental jurisdiction after Oldman. *McGill Law Journal*, *38*, 180.

Khoo, S.-M., & Rau, H. (2013). Movements, mobilities and the politics of hazardous waste. In *Environmental movements and waste infrastructure* (pp. 144–164). Routledge.

Kirikkaleli, D. (2023). Environmental taxes and environmental quality in Canada. *Environmental Science and Pollution Research*, *30*(55), 117862–117870.

Kobayashi, H. (2002). Japanese law for remediation of soil contamination. *Asia Pacific Journal of Environmental Law*, *7*, 25.

Krämer-Hoppe, R. (2021). The climate protection order of the federal constitutional court of Germany and the north-south divide. *German Law Journal*, *22*(8), 1393–1408.

Krichewsky, D. (2017). CSR public policies in India's democracy: Ambiguities in the political regulation of corporate conduct. *Business and Politics*, *19*(3), 510–547.

Kudo, Y., Noborio, K., Shimoozono, N., & Kurihara, R. (2014). The effective water management practice for mitigating greenhouse gas emissions and maintaining rice yield in central Japan. *Agriculture, Ecosystems & Environment*, *186*, 77–85.

Kumagai, H., & Kuba, T. (2016). Water purification by reducing the pollution burden. In *Basic studies in environmental knowledge, technology, evaluation, and strategy: Introduction to East Asia environmental studies* (pp. 105–121). Springer.

Kumar, R., Murphy, D. F., & Balsari, V. (2001). *Altered images: The 2001 state of corporate responsibility in India poll. Understanding and encouraging corporate responsibility in South Asia: Update one.* Tata Energy Research Institute.

Lachmayer, K. (2024). The constitutional context of climate change litigation. A comparative analysis of Germany and Austria. In I. Alogna, C. Billet, M. Fermeglia & A. Holzhausen (Eds.), *Climate change litigation in Europe. Regional, comparative and sectoral perspectives.* Larcier-Intersentia.

Leskinen, P., Belinskij, A., & Saarela, S. R. (2024). Integrating climate change into legislative drafting: An analysis of regulatory impact assessment obligations and practices in the EU and Finland. *Review of European, Comparative & International Environmental Law*, *33*(1), 45–56.

Margaritoff, M. (2021, October 2). The story of the New York City smog of 1966 that killed 200 people. *All That's Interesting.* Retrieved June 21, 2024, from https://allthatsinteresting.com/new-york-city-smog-1966

Márquez, D. I. (2015). Legal avenues for holding multinational corporations liable for environmental damages in a globalized world. *ARACÊ–Direitos Humanos em Revista*, *2*(3), 58–74.

Martines, F. (2014). Direct effect of international agreements of the European Union. *European Journal of International Law*, *25*(1), 129–147.

Mayanti, B., & Helo, P. (2023). Monetary and environmental damage cost assessment of source-separated biowaste collection: Implications of new waste regulation in Finland. *Waste Management & Research*, *41*(3), 664–675.

Mekonnen, G. B., & Tokai, A. (2020). A historical perspective of municipal solid waste management and recycling system in Japan: Learning for developing countries. *Journal of Sustainable Development*, *13*(3), 85.

Milder, S. (2022). Re-interpreting west Germany's ecological revolution: Environmental politics, grassroots activism, and democracy in the long 1970s. *European History Quarterly*, *52*(3), 332–351.

Mine, C. (2024). *St. Helen's smelting company v tipping.* Gauge Data Solutions Pvt. Ltd. Retrieved May 29, 2024, from www.casemine.com/judgement/uk/5a938b3d60d03e5f6b82ba20

Mitra, N. (2021). Impact of strategic management, corporate social responsibility on firm performance in the post-mandate period: Evidence from India. *International Journal of Corporate Social Responsibility*, *6*(1), 1–15.
Mitra, R. (2012). "My country's future": A culture-centered interrogation of corporate social responsibility in India. *Journal of Business Ethics*, *106*, 131–147.
Moshkal, M., Akhapov, Y., & Ogihara, A. (2024). Sustainable waste management in Japan: Challenges, achievements, and future prospects: A review. *Sustainability (2071–1050)*, *16*(17).
Muraki, H. (1999). Environmental laws of Japan: Selected environmental issues of the 1990s and the new millennium. *Asia Pacific Journal of Environmental Law*, *4*, 317.
Murthy, K. V. R. (1990). Pollution control: Need for strategic enforcement. *3 SCC (Journal)*, *77*, 78.
Muschött, K. (2022). *The national green tribunal of India (MR4 Human Rights Clinique II)*. University College Stockholm.
Naik, P., Parekh, A., Rustomji, S., D'Souza, M. F., & Ghosh, A. (2016). Transforming India: The CSR opportunity. *Rockefeller Foundation*. Retrieved June 21, 2024, from www.rockefellerfoundation.org/wp-content/uploads/Tranforming-India-The-CSR-Opportunity-August-2016.pdf
Nair, A. K., & Bhattacharyya, S. S. (2019). Mandatory corporate social responsibility in India and its effect on corporate financial performance: Perspectives from institutional theory and resource-based view. *Business Strategy & Development*, *2*(2), 106–116.
National Park Service. (n.d.). *The 1969 Cuyahoga River Fire*. U.S. Department of the Interior. Retrieved June 21, 2024, from www.nps.gov/articles/story-of-the-fire.htm
Nilekani, N. (2008). *Imagining India: Ideas for the new century: [Exclusive excerpts]*. Allen Lane.
Panagiotopoulou, V. C., Stavropoulos, P., & Chryssolouris, G. (2022). A critical review on the environmental impact of manufacturing: A holistic perspective. *The International Journal of Advanced Manufacturing Technology*, 1–23.
PreventionWeb. (2017). *Australia: Queensland climate adaptation strategy 2017–2030*. UNDRR. Retrieved June 24, 2024, from www.preventionweb.net/publication/australia-queensland-climate-adaptation-strategy-2017-2030
Rahim, M. M., & Sayeed, M. A. (2024). Reaching an aim differently? Corporate social responsibility regulation in Australia and India. *Cardozo International and Comparative Law Review*, *7*(3), 821–865. https://rune.une.edu.au/web/handle/1959.11/61196
Richards, G. (2005). *The philosophy of Gandhi: A study of his basic ideas*. Routledge.
Riley, T. (2017, July 10). Just 100 companies responsible for 71% of global emissions, study says. *The Guardian*. Retrieved from www.theguardian.com/sustainable-business/2017/jul/10/100-fossil-fuel-companies-investors-responsible-71-global-emissions-cdp-study-climate-change
Rung, N. (2022). *Europeanization of environmental policy in Germany: To what extent is the German environmental policy as illustrated in the case of the Rhineland Europeanized?* University of Twente.
Sahrakorpi, T. (2024). Working life, industrial loyalty, and environmental degradation in small-town Finland, 1950s–1980s. *The Historical Journal*, 1–24.
Seht, H. V., & Ott, H. E. (2000). *EU environmental principles: Implementation in Germany*. Wuppertal Institute for Climate, Environment and Energy.
Sharma, M. (2022). *Efficacy at the National Green Tribunal and its accessibility: An empirical study*. Lloyd Law College.
Similä, J. (2007). *Regulating industrial pollution: The case of Finland*. University of Helsinki.
Srishti, & Singh, T. (2023). Why this is not CSR: A study of 5 major corporates. *Down to Earth*. www.downtoearth.org.in/blog/governance/why-this-is-not-csr-a-study-of-5-major-corporates-74587

Sucharitkul, S. (1996). *Responsibility and liability for environmental damage under international law*. Digital Commons at Golden Gate University. https://digitalcommons.law.ggu.edu/cgi/viewcontent.cgi?article=1669&context=pubs;Responsibility

Teranishi, S. I. (2023). A brief history of environmental pollution in Japan. In *Environmental pollution and community rebuilding in Modern Japan* (pp. 1–16). Springer.

Thulin, L. (2019, April 22). How an oil spill inspired the first earth day. *Smithsonian*. www.smithsonianmag.com/history/how-oil-spill-50-years-ago-inspired-first-earth-day-180972007/

Tikkakoski, P., Aulake, M., & Paloniemi, R. (2024). Towards just transition: Tackling inequity and structural causes of vulnerability in key environment, health and climate related policies in Finland. *Environmental Science & Policy*, *156*, 103736.

Tsai, W.-T. (2016). Toxic volatile organic compounds (VOCs) in the atmospheric environment: Regulatory aspects and monitoring in Japan and Korea. *Environments*, *3*(3), 23.

Uekotter, F. (2017). *The greenest nation?: A new history of German environmentalism*. MIT Press.

Uhlig, U., Radigk, S., Uhlmann, W., Preuß, V., & Koch, T. (2026). Iron removal from the Spree River in the Bühlow pre-impoundment basin of the Spremberg reservoir. In *IMWA* (pp. 182–190). International Mine Water Association.

von Haaren, C., & Vollheyde, A.-L. (2019). Landscape planning in Germany: Not loved by all, but badly needed. *International Review for Spatial Planning and Sustainable Development*, *7*(4), 148–166.

Von Hirschhausen, C. (2018). German energy and climate policies: A historical overview. In *Energiewende "made in Germany" low carbon electricity sector reform in the European context* (pp. 17–44). Springer.

Wang, D., Dong, L., & Mei, J. (2023). An advanced review of climate change mitigation policies in Germany, France, and the Netherlands. *Environmental Research Letters*, *18*(10), 103001.

Watabe, A., Leaver, J., Ishida, H., & Shafiei, E. (2019). Impact of low emissions vehicles on reducing greenhouse gas emissions in Japan. *Energy Policy*, *130*, 227–242.

Weidner, H. (2002). Environmental policy and politics in Germany. In *Environmental politics and policy in industrialized countries* (pp. 149–201). MIT Press.

Winter, G. (2022). The intergenerational effect of fundamental rights: A contribution of the German federal constitutional court to climate protection. *Journal of Environmental Law*, *34*(1), 209–221.

Winter, J. (2020). Carbon pricing in a federal state: The case of Canada. *IFO DICE Report*, *18*(1), 13–19.

WorldData. (2024). *Biggest economies in 2022 by gross domestic product*. Retrieved May 29, from www.worlddata.info/largest-economies.php

World Population Review. (2024). *Carbon footprint by country*. https://worldpopulationreview.com/country-rankings/carbon-footprint-by-country

Wright, D. V. (2023). Canadian net-zero emissions accountability act: A bridge over the implementation gap? *University of New Brunswick Law Journal*, *74*, 59.

Yazdani, H. Q. (2021). No Carbon Left behind: Carbon pricing and the role of supplementary policies. *Texas Environmental Law Journal*, *51*, 357.

Životić, D., Jovanovski, G., Simić, V., Boev, I., Cvetkov, V., Makreski, P., Polomčić, D., & Ristić Vakanjac, V. (2024). Coal: Exploration, reserves, and utilization. *ChemTexts*, *10*(1), 1.

6 Sentencing Corporate Polluters

6.1 Introduction

Sentencing corporate polluters can be problematic in environmental jurisprudence.[1] There are several reasons behind this. This is mainly because corporations are economically and politically powerful and are considered economic development instruments. Many jurisdictions view corporate pollution as a form of 'unprovoked aggression,' yet they also consider economic priorities and 'necessities,' such as the pursuit of economic advantage, when deciding how to respond.[2] However, it is strongly believed that economic development at the cost of degrading the environment is unsustainable. Moreover, it attacks the human person and deprives individuals of their social, cultural, and economic gains. Such a view locates corporate environmental damages within the broader notion of harm, misuse of power, and gross injustice. From this perspective, this chapter discusses the moral and ethical bases upon which current law permits corporate exploitation of the environment. It also examines the nexus of different regulatory approaches for sentencing corporate polluters and critically assesses the development of this sentencing scholarship in environmental jurisprudence.

A country, regardless of its economy or political nature, can be rife with diverse political and legal issues that cause analysts and policymakers to overlook environmental hazards, pollution, and irresponsible polluters. However,

1 McMurry, R. I., & Ramsey, S. D. (1986). Environmental crime: The use of criminal sanctions in enforcing environmental laws. *Loyola of Los Angeles Law Review*, *19*, 1133; Lazarus, R. J. (1993). Assimilating environmental protection into legal rules and the problem with environmental crime. *Loyola of Los Angeles Law Review*, *27*, 867; Kagan, R. A., Gunningham, N., & Thornton, D. (2003). Explaining corporate environmental performance: How does regulation matter? *Law & Society Review*, *37*(1), 51–90.

2 Walters, R. (2012). Environmental crime in Scotland. In S. D. Fergusson (Ed.), *Criminal justice in Scotland* (pp. 164–184). Willan; Omrow, D. A. (2017). Abyssal ideology and the Amerindians of Guyana: An eco-crimes analysis of power, discourse, and cognitive injustice. *Journal of Human Rights and the Environment*, *8*(2), 229–249; Stoett, P. J., & Omrow, D. A. (2021). *Spheres of transnational ecoviolence*. Springer.

DOI: 10.4324/9781003279006-6

these hazards can lead to loss of lives, livelihoods, and lifestyles.[3] Usually, the environment becomes a concern when people are left in a situation with no escape from these hazards.[4] Analysts have found various factors contributing to environmental hazards, such as the interference of a country's political-legal system with emission control by polluting industries, the tendency of large corporations to justify pollution using science, and the use of compensatory mechanisms to obtain licenses for further pollution.[5] However, these analytical efforts are still insufficient as they do not quantify the extent of pollution caused by specific industries or corporations or provide solutions to address the issues.[6]

Conserving the environment in its natural state is impossible, making protecting it in its human-driven structure the only viable option.[7] Here, the environmental legal framework sets the standards for regulating the polluters but, at the same time, faces challenges in implementing the regulations, mainly where the industries offer social utility.[8] The framework is also confronted with the question of the pace of adaptability of rules to growing societal developments. Thus, it is necessary to address numerous issues, including people's engagement, their right to justice, the extent of pollution, and regulation policies.[9]

6.2 Challenges in Imposing Liability

Industrial production generally pollutes the natural environment; hence, the common perception is that all industrial corporations are detestable culprits responsible for environmental degradation and hazards.[10] However, this is partially misconceived.[11] Some corporations operate in a way that respects environmental obligations and use various mechanisms to ensure compliance with such obligations.[12] They do so by responding to different factors, including the pressures from workers, customers, and the people at large, accounting

3 Grant, D., Jorgenson, A., & Longhofer, W. (2020). *Super polluters: Tackling the world's largest sites of climate-disrupting emissions*. Columbia University Press.
4 Philippopoulos-Mihalopoulos, A. (2007). *Absent environments: Theorising environmental law and the city*. Routledge-Cavendish.
5 Grant, D., Jorgenson, A., & Longhofer, W. (2020). *Super polluters: Tackling the world's largest sites of climate-disrupting emissions* (p. 17). Columbia University Press.
6 Ibid.
7 Philippopoulos-Mihalopoulos, A. (2007). *Absent environments: Theorising environmental law and the city* (p. 76). Routledge-Cavendish.
8 Ibid., p. 84.
9 Ibid.
10 Louka, E. (2006). *International environmental law: Fairness, effectiveness, and world order* (p. 19). Cambridge University Press.
11 Ibid.
12 Ibid.

beforehand for the expenses incurred in discharging liabilities, and thinking twice about the business's goodwill among the clients.[13]

Attributing responsibility to extravagant polluters presents numerous challenges, ranging from a lack of awareness to society's tendency to treat their illegal activities as normal to overlooking them.[14] As a result, corporate carbon emitters generally remain behind the scenes when society regards the masses and the government authorities as liable for nature-driven disasters.[15] For example, the International Energy Agency (IEA)[16] emphasizes that industry-centric and industry-growing countries are the natural environment defaulters, disregarding the major contributions of the giant industrial polluters.[17] This hegemony in attributing responsibility is bound to render environmental crimes unremedied.[18]

The 'conventional approach' is one of the most commonly used methods of imposing liability.[19] It justifies the significant pollution caused by large industries by arguing that producing essential goods outweighs the environmental harm. However, this justification is flawed, especially when considering that the production rate of pollutants by certain industries, such as chemical companies in the United States, is relatively low. Furthermore, this approach fails to identify the main sources of pollution and lacks a strategy for reducing it. Critics argue that the conventional approach prioritizes market and technical forces over non-economic factors and overlooks the role of government policies in reducing pollution.[20] Additionally, this approach views grassroots environmental movements as unwarranted interference in regular industrial activities.

One of the most used methods of imposing liability is the 'conventional approach.' The thematic pillar of this approach is to justify the wanton pollution of giant industries based on the 'more social utility' argument, that is, the more extravagant the pollution, the more essential the production.[21] Such

13 Ibid.

14 Grant, D., Jorgenson, A., & Longhofer, W. (2020). *Super polluters: Tackling the world's largest sites of climate-disrupting emissions* (p. 4). Columbia University Press.

15 Ibid.

16 The International Energy Agency (IEA). (n.d.). *An autonomous intergovernmental organization established in 1974, primarily in response to the 1973 oil crisis. Its main objectives are to promote energy security among its member countries, provide reliable data and analysis on global energy markets, and support sustainable energy policies.* www.iea.org/

17 Grant, D., Jorgenson, A., & Longhofer, W. (2020). *Super polluters: Tackling the world's largest sites of climate-disrupting emissions* (p. 4). Columbia University Press.

18 Ibid., p. 5.

19 Hasnas, J. (2010). Where is Flex Cohen when we need him: Transcendental nonsense and the moral responsibility of corporations. *Journal of Law & Policy, 19*, 55; Petersen, T., Klauer, B., & Manstetten, R. (2009). The environment as a challenge for governmental responsibility – The case of the European Water Framework Directive. *Ecological Economics, 68*(7), 2058–2065.

20 Roman-Alcalá, A. M. (2013). Reconsidering sustainable development: Urbanization, political-economy, and deliberative democracy. *Berkeley Undergraduate Journal, 26*(1).

21 Grant, D., Jorgenson, A., & Longhofer, W. (2020). *Super polluters: Tackling the world's largest sites of climate-disrupting emissions* (p. 9). Columbia University Press.

justification is not tenable, particularly when the production rate of extravagant pollutant-emitters is much lower, as in the case of chemical industries in the United States.[22] Besides, such justification leads to its failure to identify the major causes of pollution and their reduction strategy.[23] The traditional approach is criticized for focusing too much on 'market and technical forces' at the expense of non-economic factors specific to the context.[24] Another criticism is that it prioritizes government policy as the primary driver for reducing pollution and views the efforts of *pro bono* pressure groups as unwarranted interference in regular industrial activities.[25]

Since the 'conventional approach' is problematic, the 'super polluters approach' is a suitable alternative for understanding the legal liabilities of corporate polluters.[26] The 'super polluters approach' consists of four aspects, namely, (a) 'disproportionalities' in identifying the causes of pollution, (b) the 'social conditions' that have causal connections with pollution, (c) the purported outcomes/consequences of 'efficiency,' and (d) 'the efficacy' of government policies and citizens' movements.[27] These aspects are counteractive *in toto* to those of the 'conventional approach.'[28] The 'disproportionality' aspect is used to calculate the totality of pollution in a sector, disregarding the proportion of production by a particular corporation.[29] The 'social conditions' aspect involves considering diverse factors in a society that have undeniable causal relations with pollution.[30] The 'efficiency' aspect advocates that technological efficiency would be a boomerang, that is, it would not predictably decrease pollution but rather increase the same.[31] The 'policy and movement' aspect rejects the seclusion of the government's policy in reducing pollution. Instead, it emphasizes the combination of policies and citizens' participation and movements as the efficient strategy for such reduction.[32]

22 Ibid.
23 Ibid., pp. 9–10.
24 Ibid., p. 10.
25 Ibid., p. 11.
26 Ibid., p. 18.
27 Ibid., p. 18.
28 Ibid., pp. 18–24.
29 Ibid., p. 19.
30 Ibid., p. 21.
31 Ibid., pp. 22–23; Stuart, D., & Woroosz, M. R. (2013). The myth of efficiency: Technology and ethics in industrial food production. *Journal of Agricultural and Environmental Ethics*, *26*, 231–256; David, P. A. (2001). *Tragedy of the public knowledge 'commons'? Global science, intellectual property and the digital technology boomerang* (Memorandum No. 2001-003). MERIT-Infonomics Research Memorandum series. Maastricht Economic Research Institute on Innovation and Technology and International Institute of Infonomics.
32 Grant, D., Jorgenson, A., & Longhofer, W. (2020). *Super polluters: Tackling the world's largest sites of climate-disrupting emissions* (p. 24). Columbia University Press.

Ideally, the foremost objective of the law regulating environmental issues, international, regional, or national, is to establish a regime where the environment is to be managed in a way that ensures the concept of 'natural resources as common resources' with no exclusive right of any particular user, citizens, corporations, or the State.[33] Since corporate polluters tend to gain maximum profit by extravagant exploitation of 'common resources' owned in abstract by the society at large, their exploitation is completely a violation of the environmental legal order.[34] However, terming elements of the environment as 'common pool resources' is more proper than terming them as 'common resources' as the former is accessible by all, not the latter (which can be brought under the management of the government or even the individual).[35] The practical benefit of this terminological shift is that polluters of 'common pool resources' are confronted by 'collective action' that ranges from determining the person(s) to be entrusted with management duty, allocating the benefits to them and the method of making good the person(s) who are not entrusted as such.[36] Once such determination is achieved, the next step is to bring the polluters to the mechanism of responsibility-attribution. In doing so, it is necessary to distinguish between polluters on a large scale and those on a small scale and burden them with reduction obligations proportionately.[37]

6.3 Understanding Sentencing

Sentencing is a complex and crucial process that involves determining the appropriate form of punishment following a conviction.[38] The sentencing task falls on the judiciary, which is responsible for interpreting laws within the legislative framework.[39] It involves weighing and balancing factors such as the offender's guilt, the seriousness of the offense, and any mitigating or aggravating circumstances in the particular case.[40]

Historically, sentencing was a cruel and barbaric expression of the king's disapproval of an individual's conduct, resulting in brutal punishments, including death penalties such as stoning, whipping, banishment, branding, stocks and pillory, poisoning, crucifixion, and beheading. However, as civilization

33 Louka, E. (2006). *International environmental law: Fairness, effectiveness, and world order* (p. 75). Cambridge University Press; Koul, D. (2014). Conservation through community: An attempt to untangle a tangled word. *Journal of Natural Resources and Development*, *4*, 25–26.

34 Louka, E. (2006). *International environmental law: Fairness, effectiveness, and world order* (pp. 75–76). Cambridge University Press.

35 Ibid., p. 76.

36 Ibid.

37 Ibid., p. 90.

38 Robinson, P. H. (1987). Sentencing system for the 21st century. *Texas Law Review*, *66*, 1; Tonry, M. (2006). Purposes and functions of sentencing. *Crime and Justice*, *34*(1), 1–53.

39 Hart, H. L. A. (2008). *Punishment and responsibility: Essays in the philosophy of law*. Oxford University Press.

40 Ashworth, A., & Kelly, R. (2021). *Sentencing and criminal justice*. Bloomsbury Publishing.

progressed, the humane aspect of punishment became more prominent. Philosophers like Bentham and Beccaria argued that punishment, being inherently evil, should be sufficient to deter crime, and no excessive punishment, including the death penalty, should be inflicted if a lesser penalty could achieve the same result.

Since then, many different thoughts and views on sentencing have emerged, and different countries have adopted their policies and laws.[41] This chapter aims to reconsider the goals and purposes of sentencing, the Benthamite notions reflected in the laws of India, the economic analysis of punishment, and finally, a discussion of the appropriate punishment for environmental offenses.

6.4 Aims of Sentencing

Nigel Walker has outlined the aims of sentencing as follows: (a) to protect offenders and suspected offenders against unofficial retaliation; (b) to reduce the frequency of behaviors prohibited by criminal law; (c) to cause the minimum suffering to offenders or others by the state; (d) to ensure the atonement of offenders through suffering for their offenses; and (e) to design a system for exact atonement for offenses, provided it does not impose excessive unofficial retaliation or inhumane suffering on the offender and does not increase the incidence of offenses, to show society's abhorrence of the crime.[42] So, when it comes to sentencing, it should be based on a rational approach that considers society's rejection of the behavior, efforts to prevent future problems, and a compassionate consideration for the offender. This leads us to the next aspect of theories that guide sentencing.

6.5 Theories of Sentencing

A multiplicity of goals lies behind the imposition of a criminal sentence: no single justice philosophy governs sentencing decisions.[43] Each jurisdiction employs its own sentencing philosophies, and each individual decision-maker views the purposes of sentencing differently.[44] In general, there are four

41 Lovegrove, A. (2012). *Judicial decision making, sentencing policy, and numerical guidance.* Springer Science & Business Media; Shane-DuBow, S. (1985). *Sentencing reform in the United States: History, content, and effect.* U.S. Department of Justice, National Institute of Justice.

42 Walker, N. (1980). *Punishment, danger, and stigma: The morality of criminal justice.* Rowman & Littlefield; Walker, N. (1997). Harms, probabilities, and precautions. *Oxford Journal of Legal Studies, 17*(4), 611–620.

43 Frase, R. S. (1997). Sentencing principles in theory and practice. *Crime and Justice, 22*, 363–433; Oleson, J. C. (2017). Sentencing theories, practices, and trends. In *The Palgrave handbook of Australian and New Zealand criminology, crime and justice* (pp. 363–377). Palgrave Macmillan.

44 Seigel, L. (2000). *Criminology* (7th ed., p. 556). Wadsworth.

theories or goals associated with the imposition of a sentence: (a) deterrence, (b) prevention, (c) retribution, and (d) reformation.[45]

6.5.1 Deterrence

Salmond views the deterrent aspect of punishment as the most significant.[46] To quote him: 'punishment is before all things deterrent and the chief end of the law of crime is to make the evildoer an example and a warning to all that are likeminded with him.'[47] In the same regard, Locke stated that every offense should result in what he termed 'a bad bargain for the offender.'[48] The deterrent theory of punishment suggests that the main goals of punishment go beyond simply stopping the offender from committing further crimes; it also acts as a warning to others who might have criminal inclinations. With punishment, there is no intent of retribution, but the expectation is to incite fear. Manu articulated that penalties serve the role of maintaining social order, protecting citizens, and ensuring that people remain active even in the absence of oversight. Punishment as a pillar of a rational state has, therefore, been a prudent thinking of able people throughout the ages.[49]

6.5.2 Prevention

The second essential object of punishment is prevention.[50] In other words, punishment must not only deter potential criminals from that code of behavior in the future, but it must also prevent the criminal from repeating the offense. Criminals are prevented from repeating their crimes by imprisonment, death, exile, forfeiture of office, etc. When a criminal is put behind bars, he is prevented from committing another crime. Patton writes that 'the preventive theory concentrates on the prisoner but seeks to prevent him from offending again. Death penalty and exile serve the same purpose of disabling the

45 Tonry, M. (2006). Purposes and functions of sentencing. *Crime and Justice*, *34*(1), 1–53; Bagaric, M. (1999). Sentencing: The road to nowhere. *Sydney Law Review*, *21*(4), 597–626; Ohlin, J. D. (2009). Towards a unique theory of international criminal sentencing. In G. Sluiter & S. Vasiliev (Eds.), *International criminal procedure: Towards a coherent body of law*. Cameron May.

46 Ohlin, J. D. (2009). Towards a unique theory of international criminal sentencing. In G. Sluiter & S. Vasiliev (Eds.), *International criminal procedure: Towards a coherent body of law*. Cameron May. Mishra, S. (2016). Theories of punishment: A philosophical aspect. *Imperial Journal of Interdisciplinary Research*, *2*(8), 74.

47 As cited in Mahajan, 1993, p. 136. See Mahajan, V. D. (1993). *Jurisprudence and legal theory* (5th ed.). Eastern Book Co.

48 Locke, J. (1690). *Second treatise of government*. Cambridge University Press.

49 Ibid.

50 Tasioulas, J. (2006). Punishment and repentance. *Philosophy*, *81*(2), 279–322; Slobogin, C. (2011). Prevention as the primary goal of sentencing: The modern case for indeterminate dispositions in criminal cases. *San Diego Law Review*, *48*, 1127.

offender.'[51] Justice Holmes restated this theory by asserting that no legislator can render certain actions illegal without demonstrating an intention to suppress those actions. One seems to draw and single out a universal aspect of punishment – its prevention.[52] The law aims to alter behavior by imposing pain for certain actions with the hope of achieving a particular motive, which is the motivation to not suffer such pain.[53] Their continuation of the action that is intended to bring pain results in pain, which is needed for the legislator's threats to remain credible.[54]

6.5.3 Retribution

In ancient times, punishment was primarily retributive. This theory posits that the offender ought to endure equal pain as he inflicted upon the victim in order to restore the social equilibrium disturbed by the criminal acts. In the views of a retributivist, society is entitled and obliged to defend itself against the injury inflicted upon it, and, as a consequence, society is obliged to impose a commensurate punishment that is proportional to the crime. Even with the formulation of the Code of Hammurabi,[55] which states an eye for an eye and a tooth for a tooth, it has been widely accepted that the offender has to suffer. The suffering is inflicted by the state in its corporate capacity.[56]

To rephrase what Kant, the German philosopher, stated: A judicial punishment must not serve merely as a means to achieve a particular good for the offender, society, or any other entity.[57] Instead, it should serve as the sole response to inflicting punishment for having committed a crime. The law of punishment, in the Kantian sense, is a categorical imperative. He offered the following example: Even if a community of citizens disbands with the agreement of every participant (for instance, the residents of an island who want to disperse into the wider world), they first have to execute the last remaining inmate for homicide within the prison walls so that all may receive whatever is rightfully theirs according to their actions.

51 Patton, D. E. (2010). Guns, crime control, and a systemic approach to federal sentencing. *Cardozo Law Review*, *32*, 1427.

52 Kelley, P. J. (1983). Critical analysis of Holmes's theory of torts. *Washington University Law Quarterly*, *61*(3), 681–744.

53 Hart, H. L. A. (2008). *Punishment and responsibility: Essays in the philosophy of law*. Oxford University Press; Schonsheck, J. (1994). *On criminalization: An essay in the philosophy of criminal law* (Vol. 19). Springer Science & Business Media.

54 Mahajan, V. D. (1993). *Jurisprudence and legal theory* (5th ed., p. 138). Eastern Book Co.

55 The Code of Hammurabi is one of the oldest deciphered writings of significant length in the world, dating back to around 1754 BC, created during the reign of Hammurabi, the sixth king of the First Babylonian Dynasty. It consists of 282 laws covering various aspects of daily life, including trade, family, labor, and property rights.

56 Ibid., p. 145.

57 Mahajan, V. D. (1993). *Jurisprudence and legal theory* (5th ed., p. 138). Eastern Book Co.

James Stephen emphasized that the purpose of punishment is to satisfy the desire for vengeance by making the criminal pay with his body. To quote him:

> [T]he criminal law serves to fulfill the passion of revenge in a similar way that marriage fulfills the sexual appetite. Punishment satisfies the feeling of pleasure that individuals experience when they know that the criminal has been brought to justice. This desire should be satisfied by imposing punishment to prevent the risk of private vengeance.[58]

6.5.4 Reformation

The reformative theory is currently the most popular and widely accepted theory for reforming offenders. It is based on the belief that nobody is born a criminal and that anyone who commits a crime is still a human being. They may have acted unlawfully under circumstances that might never occur again. The primary goal of punishment should be to foster moral reform so that the individual can reintegrate into society as a changed, law-abiding citizen. Supporters of this theory argue that with sympathetic, discreet, and caring treatment of offenders, it is possible to bring about a radical change in their characters. They claim that even a cruel, hardened prisoner can be transformed by kind words, while harsh punishments may make them stubborn and embittered toward life. As contended by Mahajan[59]:

> Man always kicks against pricks. Whipping will make him balk. The threat will result in resistance. Prison hell may create the spirit of defiance of God and man. Hanging a criminal merely implies that human beings have failed to reform the erring citizen.

Salmond has, however, observed:

> [T]he reformative element must not be overlooked, but neither must it be allowed to assume undue prominence. To what extent it may be permitted in particular circumstances to overrule the requirements of a strictly deterrent theory is a question of time, place and circumstances. In the case of youthful criminals, the chances of effective reformation are greater than that of adults, and the rightful importance of the reformative principle is, therefore, greater. In orderly and law-abiding communities' concessions may be made in the interests of reformation which in more turbulent society would be fatal to the public welfare.[60]

58 Ibid., p. 146.
59 Ibid., p. 138.
60 Salmond, J. W. (1893). *The first principles of jurisprudence*. Stevens & Haynes Law Publishers.

Another theory that may be briefly mentioned here is the *compensatory theory*. According to this theory, the purpose of punishment must be not only to prevent future crimes but also to pay off the victim. The argument is that the root cause of criminal behavior is greed, and if the offender is required to return the ill-gotten gains, the motivation for criminality will diminish.[61]

Each theory comes into play when a person is being sentenced. At times, a particular policy or goal gains prominence and takes priority in sentencing decisions for a period of time. Similarly, depending on the nature of the offense and the resulting harm intended, the legislature establishes its policy, focusing on one or more of these sentencing goals.

6.6 Sentencing Dispositions

6.6.1 Capital Punishment

Capital punishment, also known as the death penalty, refers to the state-sanctioned execution of an individual as a punishment for a crime.[62] It is typically reserved for the most serious offenses, often referred to as 'capital crimes' or 'capital offenses,' which can include murder, espionage, treason, and certain types of sexual offenses, depending on the jurisdiction.[63] From the beginning of civilization until the early 19th century, capital punishment was the norm, even for minor offenses. Feudal lords, chieftains, and religious leaders worldwide frequently imposed capital punishment.[64]

The movement against capital punishment began in England and Europe due to the influence of utilitarians such as Bentham[65] and Beccaria.[66] They argued that punishment, being inherently evil, should be only as severe as necessary to prevent crime and that excessive punishment, including capital punishment, should not be used when a lesser penalty could achieve the same result. In India, the death penalty continues to be prescribed for

61 Ibid., p. 147.

62 Powell, L. F. (1989). Capital punishment. *Harvard Law Review*, *102*(5), 1035–1046; McCafferty, J. A. (2017). *Capital punishment*. Routledge.

63 Marzilli, A. (2009). *Capital punishment*. Infobase Publishing; Goldberg, S. (1974). On capital punishment. *Ethics*, *85*(1), 67–74.

64 Ponnaian, M. (1992). *Criminology & Penology* (3rd ed., p. 212). Pioneer Books.

65 Jeremy Bentham (1748–1832) was a prominent English philosopher and social reformer, best known as one of the founders of utilitarianism, a moral philosophy advocating actions that maximize happiness and well-being for the greatest number of people. His ideas have had a significant impact on legal and political thought; Schofield, P. (2018). Bentham, Jeremy (1748–1832). In *The New Palgrave dictionary of economics*. Palgrave Macmillan. https://doi.org/10.1057/978-1-349-95189-5_566

66 Cesare Beccaria (1738–1794) was an Italian philosopher, criminologist, and legal theorist, widely regarded as a founding figure of modern criminology and a key advocate for criminal justice reform. His most influential work, *On Crimes and Punishments* (1764), laid the groundwork for contemporary ideas about law, punishment, and human rights.

the most serious offenses in the *Indian Penal Code 1860* and other special penal laws.

6.6.2 *Imprisonment*

Imprisonment is the most common form of sentencing for dealing with criminals. It serves as an effective way to remove criminals from society temporarily, acts as a general and individual deterrent, provides an opportunity for rehabilitation, and reinforces the social stigma associated with crime.[67] This form of punishment is employed for almost all types of crimes worldwide, from minor offenses to serious crimes. The length of imprisonment varies depending on the severity of the offense, ranging from three months to life imprisonment as the maximum penalty.

6.6.3 *Fines*

Imposing fines can be an effective form of punishment for offenses such as traffic violations, property damage, and environmental violations.[68] However, for more serious crimes like murder, rape, or kidnapping, whether fines can effectively serve as punishment is questionable. Additionally, one major drawback is that fines disproportionately impact the poor, as the wealthy can easily afford to pay significant fines, while the poor may struggle to pay even small amounts. Despite these limitations, fines are still considered necessary for addressing specific types of offenses.

6.7 Benthamite Notions of Offenses, Crimes, and Punishment

Jeremy Bentham's famous work, *An Introduction to Morals and Legislation*, elaborated on crime and punishment. His principle, based on utility, has formed the basis of laws, especially criminal law of many countries, India being one of them. According to him:

> [N]nature has placed humanity under the governance of two sovereign masters, pain and pleasure. It is for them alone to point out what we

67 Ibid., p. 132.

68 Siddique, A. (1993). *Criminology: Problems & perspectives* (p. 120). Eastern Book Co.; Indian Penal Code defines fines as follows:

> Fine is the most common punishment in every part of the world and it is a punishment the advantages of which are so great and obvious that we propose authorising the courts to inflict it in every case. . . . Imprisonment, transportation, banishment, solitude, and compelled labor are not equally disagreeable to all men. With fine, the case is different. In imposing a fine, it is necessary to regard the offender's financial circumstances as to the offence's character and magnitude. The mullet, which is ruinous to the laborer, is easily borne by a tradesman and is unfelt by a rich zamindar.

> ought to do and determine what we shall do. On the one hand, the standard of right and wrong; on the other, the chain of causes and effects are fastened to their throne.[69]

Bentham argued that most people aim to maximize their happiness, which he defined as the surplus of pleasures over pains.[70] He believed that all human actions stem from the hedonic calculus. According to him, acts of altruism, asceticism, love, duty, a desire for freedom, obedience to the law, and faith can all be reduced to individual pleasure and pain calculations.[71] He also believed that the considerations of pleasure and pain should be considered when designing sentences for offenses.[72] In his work, he suggested that the primary purpose of all laws is to increase the total happiness of the community by excluding anything that diminishes that happiness, in other words, to exclude harm.[73] However, Bentham accepted that punishment is fatal to the individual and also considered it malevolent. Hence, he reflected on punishment and concluded that it must only be inflicted if greater harm is not ensured. Because of that, he emphasized that there are instances where such punishment ought not to be administered, which are: (a) where it is aimless, that is, where there exists no mischief waiting to be averted, (b) where it must be futile, that is, where it cannot if it will prevent the mischief, (c) where it is too costly, that is, where the harm it would cause is greater than what is mitigated, and (d) where it is unnecessary, that is, where the harm may be prevented or cease of its own accord at a more economical rate.[74] He proposed four objectives for a legislator in an attempt to cut down on potential unlawful behavior: (a) suggests the most crucial task is to avoid any acts of offense whatsoever, (b) points out that if a misdeed has to be committed, may it be a less grievous one, (c) indicates the intention to commit malice needs to be reduced: to do as little of it as possible and still have the benefit desired, and (d) states whatever injury it aims to avert, do so in as inexpensive a manner as possible.[75]

69 Center for Economic Policy Analysis. (n.d.). *Jeremy Bentham (1748–1832)*. Retrieved November 28, 2024, from http://cepa.newschool.edu/het/profiles/bentham.htm

70 Varouxakis, G., & Philp, M. (2019). 7. "The first article to look to is power": Bentham, happiness and the capability approach. In *Happiness and utility: Essays presented to Frederick Rosen* (pp. 118–142). University College London.

71 University of Minnesota Duluth. (2025). www.d.umn.edu/cla/faculty/jhamlin/4111/2111-home/CD/TheoryClass/Bentham/Jeremy%20Bentham.htm

72 Bedau, H. (2004). Bentham's theory of punishment: origin and content. *Journal of Bentham Studies*, *7*, 1–15.

73 Veenhoven, R. (2010). Greater happiness for a greater number: Is that possible and desirable? *Journal of Happiness Studies*, *11*, 605–629.

74 Utilitarianism.com. (n.d.). *Jeremy Bentham: An introduction to the principles of morals and legislation*. Retrieved November 28, 2024, from http://www.utilitarianism.com/jeremy-bentham/index.html

75 Ibid.

When sentencing an offender, the goal is to nullify any 'pleasure' gained from the offense.[76] Since every individual is guided by pleasures and pains and weighs these before acting, it can be inferred that an offender must have considered their own pleasures and pains before committing an offense.[77] By imposing punishment, society aims to counteract the pleasures or 'happiness' gained from committing such acts.[78] Bentham argued that punishment is inherently negative and should not be administered when unnecessary or useless.[79] However, in cases where a person commits an offense, inflicting punishment becomes essential to outweigh the happiness derived from the act.[80] The punishment should ideally be slightly more severe than the pleasure gained from the offense. If the punishment matches the sum of pleasures gained, it may not serve as a sufficient deterrent.[81] Additionally, the more serious the offense, the greater the punishment should be in order to dissuade individuals from choosing to commit the offense.[82]

$$\text{Punishment} = \text{Pleasure derived from offense} + x$$

(x being the additional pain inflicted to outweigh the happiness)

The central idea of utilitarianism can be understood through its equation of pleasure and pain in the context of crime and punishment.[83] While early theorists believed that punishment and its severity were the only ways to rid society of evil, utilitarians introduced the concept of proportionate punishments.[84] This idea has been fundamental to the development of the country's penal laws.[85]

6.8 Economic Analysis of Crime and Punishment

In recent years, the economic analysis of crime and punishment has become common in legal theory and practice. Gary Becker's seminal work, *Crime and Punishment: An Economic Approach* (1968), laid the foundation for applying

76 Hanafy, H. (2021). Bentham: Punishment and the utilitarian use of persons as means. *Journal of Bentham Studies, 19*(1), 1–23.
77 Koh, T. Y. (2024). The judgement of pleasure in Bentham's political thought. *Revue d'études benthamiennes, 25.*
78 The Judgement of Pleasure in Bentham's Political Thought.
79 Bedau, H. (2004). Bentham's theory of punishment: origin and content. *Journal of Bentham Studies, 7,* 1–15.
80 Sverdlik, S. (2019). Bentham on temptation and deterrence. *Utilitas, 31*(3), 246–261.
81 Ibid.
82 Ibid.
83 McHugh, J. T. (2008). Utilitarianism, punishment, and ideal proportionality in penal law: Punishment as an intrinsic evil. *Journal of Bentham Studies, 10,* 1–16.
84 Hanafy, H. (2021). Bentham: Punishment and the utilitarian use of persons as means. *Journal of Bentham Studies, 19*(1), 1–23.
85 Landau, N. (2005). Summary conviction and the development of the penal law. *Law and History Review, 23*(1), 173–189.

economic principles to crime. Becker argued that individuals make rational choices based on the costs and benefits of committing crimes, which has influenced both legal theory and policy.[86] In support of this analysis, the ***rational choice theory*** posits that individuals weigh the potential benefits of criminal activity against the risks of apprehension and punishment. This framework has been widely adopted in criminology and legal studies, emphasizing the importance of deterrence in shaping laws and penalties. The economic analysis of crime often incorporates the deterrence theory, which suggests that the certainty and severity of punishment can deter criminal behavior.[87] This concept has been extensively studied and applied in legal contexts to evaluate the effectiveness of various punitive measures.

Many legal scholars and policymakers now utilize CBA to assess the impacts of laws and regulations related to crime and punishment.[88] This approach helps in understanding the economic implications of legal decisions and the allocation of resources in the criminal justice system. Take, for example, the case of shoplifting. The benefit to the shoplifter is the utility of the items taken, while the cost involves the possibility of arrest and the associated fine and imprisonment. In a single act of shoplifting, the thief considers the value of the item they want to take. The shoplifter's choice problem may be represented as follows:

$$\frac{\text{Max } B(x) - C(x)}{x}$$

where x is the item's value, $B(x)$ is the benefit that the item offers the shoplifter, and $C(x)$ is the expected cost the shoplifter faces.

The criminal justice system must decide on the amount and type of penalties to be imposed on the shoplifter.[89] Let us assume the fine is denoted as F

86 Becker, G. S. (1968). Crime and punishment: An economic approach. *Journal of Political Economy*, *76*(2), 169–217; Loughran, T. A., Paternoster, R., Chalfin, A., & Wilson, T. (2016). Can rational choice be considered a general theory of crime? Evidence from individual-level panel data. *Criminology*, *54*(1), 86–112; Becker, G. S. (1976). *The economic approach to human behavior* (Vol. 803). University of Chicago Press.

87 Cameron, S. (1988). The economics of crime deterrence: A survey of theory and evidence. *Kyklos*, *41*(2).

88 Cohen, M. A. (2016). *The "cost of crime" and benefit-cost analysis of criminal justice policy: Understanding and improving upon the state-of-the-art.* SSRN 2832944; Draper, A. (2009). Punishment, proportionality, and the economic analysis of crime. *Journal of Bentham Studies*, *11*, 1–32; Friehe, T., & Miceli, T. J. (2017). On punishment severity and crime rates. *American Law and Economics Review*, *19*(2), 464–485; Roman, J. (2013). Cost-benefit analysis of criminal justice reforms. *NIJ Journal*, *272*, 31–38; Roman, J., & Farrell, G. (2002). Cost-benefit analysis for crime prevention: Opportunity costs, routine savings and crime externalities. *Crime Prevention Studies*, *14*, 53–92.

89 Cook-Cox, A., Loftin, C. M., & May, D. C. (2025). Item values and prior offenses: An examination of key elements in shoplifting charging decisions in a rural jurisdiction. *American Journal of Criminal Justice*; Robinson, P. H., & Darley, J. M. (2007). Intuitions of justice: Implications for criminal law and justice policy. *Southern California Law Review*, *81*, 1.

rupees, without considering the value of the stolen item. Criminal activities are often not directly observable. Not all criminals are caught, so the fine is imposed only with a certain probability. This probability is determined by the resources allocated to crime detection. Let e represent the level of enforcement, and $\pi(e)$ represent the likelihood of apprehension, with e being the expenditures on crime detection and enforcement by the police. The shoplifter's problem can now be written as follows:

$$\frac{\max B(x) - \pi(e)F}{x}$$

The amount of crime that the individual chooses the value of the items shoplifted is the x that maximizes this expression. The state has to determine or set e and F. The criminal, through his choice of x, harms other people. Let this harm be denoted by $H(x)$, and $c(e)$ denote the cost of enforcement. Since the state wishes to minimize the net costs of the criminal activity, the objective function may be represented as follows:

$$\frac{\text{Min } H(x) - \pi(e)F(x) + c(e)}{F(e)}$$

The state determines the level of enforcement and the fine, knowing that these choices impact the incidence of shoplifting. We first notice in the second equation that the expected cost of the crime to the criminal, denoted as $F(e)$, does not depend on the size of the crime, x. This means that the criminal will select the level of x that maximizes their net benefits or choose not to commit the crime at all. If the benefit function increases as x grows, in cases where the crime is purely driven by economic reasons, only the most valuable items would be stolen. Since the shoplifter faces the same punishment regardless of the item's value, it is logical for them to steal the most valuable item. This suggests that an effective deterrent should impose a marginal cost on the criminal. If the cost is not related to the size of the crime, the criminal might engage in the largest feasible crime.

Punishment must fit the crime because the criminal should face higher costs for more severe crimes.[90] Accordingly, the equation may be restructured to make the fine facing the criminal proportional to the magnitude of the crime:

$$\frac{\text{Max } B(x) - \pi(e)Fx}{x}$$

90 Friehe, T., & Miceli, T. J. (2017). On punishment severity and crime rates. *American Law and Economics Review*, *19*(2), 464–485.

The level of crime chosen will be that which equates marginal benefit to marginal cost:

$$MB(x^*) = \pi(e)F$$

In general, higher levels of enforcement and larger fines should lead to larger costs for the criminal, resulting in reduced criminal activity.[91] This economic analysis can be effective in determining the appropriate fines for environmental offenders.[92] As previously discussed, fines are among the most important and effective forms of punishment for such offenses. However, determining the specific amount of these fines requires careful consideration. The economic model suggests calculating the monetary benefits reaped by the offender or offenders (particularly in cases involving corporations), which entails examining the profits and/or income generated through the activities causing pollution. This analysis imposes a fair number of fines that would disrupt the overall benefits obtained, providing an incentive for refraining from such activities in the future.

6.9 Sentencing in Environmental Offenses/Crimes

The lawmaker and the judge both face difficulty when it comes to sentencing environmental offenses.[93] On the one hand, the legislature struggles to apply standard sentencing norms in relation to environmental offenses, and on the other hand, the judiciary tends not to view the matter as an 'offense' and consequently does not impose the appropriate sentence meant to provide maximum utility. This is particularly so given three aspects.

First of all, environmental offenses do not fall under any of the conventional types of crimes. It is an offense peculiar to itself where the notion of traditional

91 Bar-Ilan, A., & Sacerdote, B. (2004). The response of criminals and noncriminals to fines. *The Journal of Law and Economics*, *47*(1), 1–17.

92 Baumann, F., Bienenstock, S., Friehe, T., & Ropaul, M. (2023). Fines as enforcers' rewards or as a transfer to society at large? Evidence on deterrence and enforcement implications. *Public Choice*, *196*(3), 229–255; Blondiau, T., Billiet, C. M., & Rousseau, S. (2015). Comparison of criminal and administrative penalties for environmental offenses. *European Journal of Law and Economics*, *39*, 11–35; Segerson, K., & Tietenberg, T. (2018). The structure of penalties in environmental enforcement: An economic analysis. In *Economics and liability for environmental problems* (pp. 333–354). Routledge.

93 Environmental offenses refer to violations of laws and regulations designed to protect the environment. These offenses can occur at various levels, including local, national, and international, and they typically involve actions that harm natural resources, ecosystems, or public health. Environmental offenses can be categorized into several types: pollution, wildlife crimes, deforestation and land use violations, violation of environmental regulations, climate change offenses, and resource exploitation.

crimes *actus non facit reum, nisi mens sit rea*, does not apply.[94] The offense of murder can easily be constructed on the basis of the harm wrought, which is the death of the victim, and the mental culpability of the offender. In the case of environmental offenses, there is no so-called guilt principle. What does exist, however, are merely expressions of careless and inattentive behavior, also known as negligent conduct, which, as far as classification goes, are deemed to be strict liability offenses.

Second, the peculiar, elusive problem that is aware of some harm but does not perceive what harm occurs brings us to discussion. To put it in slightly different words, while an industrial activity may have some effect on a person's health and safety, there could very well be irreversible environmental degradation for some future generations because of an act committed at present. The injury is, therefore, not perceivable instantaneously or invisibly.

Third, the commission of environmental offenses is very difficult to associate with a concrete individual or a group.[95] Although there are individual polluters who could be identified as causing pollution of the environment, the great majority consists of corporations and large industrial houses which, in the course of their doing business, somehow disregard the breathing space and safety standards. In fact, such deviant behavior is accepted as standard operating procedures by the business environment. Corporations can be held liable – much has been done in this direction – but the reality remains that constructing effective legal mechanisms for enforcing criminal liability on such offenders is rendered almost impossible.[96] In all likelihood, the extant formulas of punishment that can be administered will have to be fined, losing almost all of the important objectives of punishment as a deterrent mechanism in a Benthamite legal framework.

For this reason, the prosecution of environmental offenses remains a challenge.[97] Still, the development of better methods is possible within the boundaries of traditional sentencing frameworks and objectives. The considered aims of ecological crimes, as stated, should be within reasoning or logic of

94 '*Actus non facit reum, nisi mens sit rea*' is a Latin legal maxim that translates to 'an act does not make a person guilty unless there is a guilty mind.' This principle is foundational in criminal law and encapsulates the dual requirement for establishing criminal liability: both a wrongful act (actus reus) and a guilty mind (*mens rea*).

95 White, R., & Heckenberg, D. (2014). *Green criminology: An introduction to the study of environmental harm*. Routledge; Papathanasiou, K. (2017). Environmental criminal law: A vital part of the regulatory framework. In *Environmental law and economics* (pp. 513–526). Springer.

96 White, R. (2009). Researching transnational environmental harm: Toward an eco-global criminology. *International Journal of Comparative and Applied Criminal Justice*, *33*(2), 229–248; Brisman, A. (2007). Crime-environment relationships and environmental justice. *Seattle Journal for Social Justice*, *6*, 727–761.

97 Westerhuis, D. S. (2013). A harm analysis of environmental crime. In R. Walters, D. S. Westerhuis & T. Wyatt (Eds.), *Emerging issues in green criminology: Exploring power, justice and harm* (pp. 197–217). Springer; Adshead, J. (2013). Doing justice to the environment. *The Journal of Criminal Law*, *77*(3), 215–230.

deterrence, denunciation, prevention, and reformation. A consideration of punishments also reveals that fines, which Attiyah views as the basis of compensatory theory, have a predominating position, although it is important to note that this should not be the sole approach to punishment.

In light of the above, it is equally justifiable to make use of the sentencing framework proposed in the UK in relation to ecological crimes.[98] This group first proposed some aggravating and extenuating circumstances relating to pollution for a given region and then suggested appropriate sentencing frameworks to be applied to the same after determining recourse to the said elements. Any of the listed considerations below may lead toward the escalation of culpability of a defendant, be it an individual or a company, thus substantially worsening any of the five offenses: (a) the offense was found to be a breach of law willfully or recklessly, as opposed to from carelessness; (b) the defendant in question acted out of financial self-interest, whether for profit or cost saving, for example by failing to implement requisite putative measures or dole out payment for the requisite license; (c) the defendant has disregarded advice/caution/warning from relevant bodies of authority; (d) the defendant has disregarded relevant concerns raised by employees or other stakeholders; (e) the defendant is said to have had knowledge of the particular risks pertinent, that is, if he has willingly disposed of 'special' waste; and (f) the defendant's attitude toward the environmental authorities am espoused indifference or hostility.

The following factors regarding the actual or likely magnitude of the damage may further increase the seriousness of the offense: (a) the pollutant was, or had the potential to be, harmful, widespread, or could have enduring impacts; (b) human and animal health, as well as plant life, was impacted, particularly if a protected species was involved or if a designated nature reserve was impacted; (c) there was an extensive cleanup and restoration of the site, or rehabilitation of the animals, and (d) other legal activities were suspended or severely disturbed.

If the defendant has prior beliefs for repeat offenses or has previously defaulted on serving the sentence, such evidence should be regarded as a reason for increasing the sentence, but not so far as to be considered excessive concerning the circumstances of the case.

6.9.1 Factors for Mitigating Sentences

The following factors can be used to justify an adjustment to any offense deemed less serious: (a) the fact that the individual defendant played a relatively minor role in the crime or bore lesser responsibility than others; (b) the fact that the defendant truly, and for good reason, did not possess the

98 The Sentencing Advisory Panel. (2000). *Environmental offences: The Sentencing Advisory Panel's advice to the Court of Appeal, United Kingdom.*

requisite knowledge or understanding of the rules pertinent to the action he was undertaking; and (c) the fact that the charge was the result of an error in judgment.[99]

The court should consider some other individual personal mitigating circumstances which include (a) the defendant's early reporting of the crime and their full cooperation with law enforcement, (b) the defendant's exemplary record regarding environmental practices, (c) the fact that the defendant took immediate rectifying action, and (d) foretasted admission of guilt pled in due course.[100]

6.9.2 *The Choice of Sentence*

In most cases, a penalty works best for breaches of these laws because (a) there is usually no violence nor direct harm, and (b) it appears that the breach is usually committed through a lack of adequate planning on the part of the defendant at the time.[101]

6.9.3 *The Level of Fine*

Generally, neither persons nor organizations should be allowed to benefit financially from acts of misconduct.[102] The punishment should fully take into account any profits gleaned by the offender due to their inaction, making it financially irrational not to prevent an offense. In contrast, any voluntary actions taken by the defendant may persuade the court to reduce the fine, which otherwise would have been imposed.[103]

The amount of the fine in question should be proportional to how much the defendant's conduct deviated from the relevant statutory environmental

99 Meixner Jr., J. B. (2021). Modern sentencing mitigation. *Northwestern University Law Review*, *116*, 1395–1410; Roberts, J. V. (2011b). Punishing, more or less: Exploring aggravation and mitigation at sentencing. In J. V. Roberts (Ed.), *Mitigation and aggravation at sentencing* (pp. 1–14). Cambridge University Press.

100 Kristl, K. T. (2006). Making a good idea even better: Rethinking the limits on supplemental environmental projects. *Vermont Law Review*, *31*, 217.

101 Roberts, J. V. (2011a). *Mitigation and aggravation at sentencing*. Cambridge University Press; Skinnider, E. (2011). *Victims of environmental crime: Mapping the issues: International centre for criminal law reform and criminal justice policy*. In. Nobles, M. R. (2019). Environmental crime and contemporary criminology: Making a difference. *American Journal of Criminal Justice*, *44*, 656–669.

102 Karpoff, J. M., Lott, J., John R., & Wehrly, E. W. (2005). The reputational penalties for environmental violations: Empirical evidence. *The Journal of Law and Economics*, *48*(2), 653–675.

103 Epstein, R. A. (1979). Nuisance law: Corrective justice and its utilitarian constraints. *The Journal of Legal Studies*, *8*(1), 49–102.

standard that should have been observed.[104] The evaluation of the seriousness of the case should take into consideration the level of blameworthiness of the defendant in causing or creating the risk of relevant ecological damage.[105] This must be set off against the level of actual or risky damage that the defendant has caused or that has occurred. Fines should be great when the defendant's blameworthiness is significant, even if the degree of environmental damage is less than what could reasonably have been expected. Such a situation might occur where, through initial action by authorities, extensive damage has been avoided due to prompt action or some favorable fortuitous element such as weather conditions.[106] On the other hand, in a situation where the damages are far greater than what could reasonably be expected, the sentence should, in consideration of the environmental impacts, focus more on the offender's responsibility.[107]

The judgment must integrate the financial capabilities of an individual or the business in question.[108] Concerning a large company, the penalty should be sufficiently severe so that it has some real value economically. When added to the negative publicity resulting from prosecution, this must be enough to exert pressure on management and shareholders to lax regulatory compliance and overhaul company policy.[109] In this regard, it should be noted that where a large company has occasioned pollution on a substantial scale, it is only the company itself (and not individual directors) who will have sufficient financial resources to incur an amount of fine commensurate with the damage caused.[110]

With respect to smaller companies, the courts need to be more considerate, as imposing a harsher punitive fine would have disastrous effects. A harsh economic backlash could force the company into complete closure, which would leave employees unemployed and impact the economy of the region. On the other hand, this would severely limit the ability of the organization to improve compliance with the law intended to enhance procedure. Non-profit organizations that do not have shareholders should also be considered. The court may

104 Karpoff, J. M., Lott, J., John R., & Wehrly, E. W. (2005). The reputational penalties for environmental violations: Empirical evidence. *The Journal of Law and Economics*, *48*(2), 653–675.

105 O'Hear, M. M. (2004). Sentencing the green-collar offender: Punishment, culpability, and environmental crime. *Journal of Criminal Law & Criminology*, *95*, 133.

106 Kluin, M., Ansems, L., & Brands, J. (2025). On bad intentions and harmful consequences: Understanding public perceptions of environmental crime seriousness. *Crime, Law and Social Change*, *83*(1), 3.

107 Arguedas, C. (2013). Pollution standards, technology investment and fines for non-compliance. *Journal of Regulatory Economics*, *44*, 156–176.

108 Atkinson, N. (2023). Profiting from pollution. *Yale Journal on Regulation*.

109 Preble, K. A., & Early, B. R. (2024). Enforcing economic sanctions by tarnishing corporate reputations. *Business and Politics*, *26*(1), 102–123.

110 Dang, T. V., Wang, Y., & Wang, Z. (2022). The role of financial constraints in firm investment under pollution abatement regulation. *Journal of Corporate Finance*, *76*, 102252.

choose to reduce the set punitive fine or extend the duration of the payment of the fine, resulting in potentially broader allocations of ratable spending. Seizing such assets might be an appropriate measure when vehicles, plants, or equipment are utilized in the commission of an environmental crime such violations.

6.9.4 Determining the Company's Ability to Pay

Given the myriad of companies with varying types and sizes, it would be very difficult to set one universal measure of financial punishment for every organization.[111] Nevertheless, it could be possible to set the fine on a percentage basis of the following: (a) turnover – the value of sales made by the company in the last three years; (b) profitability – the value of net profit before tax and dividends over the last three years; and (c) liquidity – the current value of short-term assets compared to short-term liabilities.[112]

6.9.5 Community Sentences

When dealing with more serious cases involving a single offender, the court should consider whether it would be better to impose a community sentence instead of a fine.[113] A community service order, which includes a requirement to make amends to the community, may be the most suitable type of community sentence. However, this order can only be given if the offense could lead to a prison sentence.[114]

6.9.6 Custodial Sentences

The court can impose a prison sentence in cases where the defendant is an individual.[115] For environmental offenses committed by individuals, only the most serious cases warrant a prison sentence. To justify a prison sentence, the case must involve significant harm or a high risk of harm, along with a high level of responsibility on the part of the offender.[116] Therefore, a prison

111 Pollak, P. (2011). *Fine chemicals: The industry and the business*. John Wiley & Sons.

112 Behn, R. D. (2003). Why measure performance? Different purposes require different measures. *Public Administration Review*, *63*(5), 586–606.

113 Chui, W. H. (2013). Community sentences. In *Understanding criminal justice in Hong Kong* (pp. 212–234). Willan; Solomon, E., & Silvestri, A. (2008). *Community sentences digest*. Centre for Crime and Justice Studies.

114 Bottoms, A., Gelsthorpe, L., & Rex, S. (2013). *Community penalties*. Routledge.

115 Frase, R. S. (1997). Sentencing principles in theory and practice. *Crime and Justice*, *22*, 363–433; Ulmer, J. T., & Johnson, B. (2004). Sentencing in context: A multilevel analysis. *Criminology*, *42*(1), 137–178.

116 Kluin, M., Ansems, L., & Brands, J. (2025). On bad intentions and harmful consequences: Understanding public perceptions of environmental crime seriousness. *Crime, Law and Social Change*, *83*(1), 3.

sentence should be taken into consideration when (a) there was an intentional or a willful disregard of breaching the law and the defendant acted for some financial reason, whether through profit or cost saving; (b) human health has been compromised or placed in danger; and (c) the pollutant was either harmful, widespread, or pervasive or likely to spread or have a prolonged impact.[117]

6.9.7 Compensation

Compensation as a sentencing option involves requiring offenders to provide financial restitution to victims or affected parties as part of their sentence.[118] This is commonly used in criminal justice systems to address the harm caused by the offender's actions and to promote restorative justice.[119] The main objective of compensation as a punishment is to repay both the economic and non-economic damages.[120]

Compensation is typically regulated by a combination of statutory laws, common law principles, and international treaties.[121] Different jurisdictions have specific laws that define the rights of affected parties and the responsibilities of polluters or other responsible parties.[122] Overall, the court tends to issue a compensation order when a clear victim is present, such as a landowner who has faced costs to clean up their property or restore a watercourse contaminated by the defendant's actions. Typically, they first determine the amount of the fine before addressing the issue of compensation.[123]

6.9.8 Costs

A court typically allocates costs in favor of the prosecuting agency. These costs should encompass expenses related to the investigation, file preparation, and presentation; however, they must not surpass the actual and reasonable expenses incurred by the prosecutor. The awarded costs should generally align with the level of the imposed fine. The court should first determine the amount of the fine, then consider compensation, and finally evaluate the costs.

117 Alonso, A. I., & South, N. (2024). Incorporating a one health approach into the study of environmental crimes and harms: Towards a "one health green criminology". *The British Journal of Criminology*, *10*, 1–16.

118 Billiet, C. M., & Rousseau, S. (2014). How real is the threat of imprisonment for environmental crime? *European Journal of Law and Economics*, *37*, 183–198.

119 Fletcher, G. P. (1980). Punishment and compensation. *Creighton Law Review*, *14*, 691–700.

120 Narveson, J. (1992). Moving from punishment to compensation. *Canadian Journal of Law & Jurisprudence*, *5*(1), 57–68.

121 Pfennigstorf, W. (1979). Environment, damages, and compensation. *American Bar Foundation Research Journal*, *4*(2), 347–448.

122 White, R. (2017). Reparative justice, environmental crime, and penalties for the powerful. *Crime, Law and Social Change*, *67*, 117–132.

123 Campbell, T. (1984). Compensation as punishment. *UNSW Law Journal*, *7*, 338–350.

In cases where the total amount exceeds the defendant's financial capacity, the costs should be reduced instead of the fine. Compensation should take priority over both the fine and the costs.

6.9.9 *Disqualification*

In suitable circumstances, the court may choose to exercise its authority to issue an order disqualifying the defendant from serving as a company director for a designated period.

6.10 Enforcement of Sentencing in Environmental Cases

6.10.1 *Civil Remedies*

6.10.1.1 *Strict Civil Liability*

The polluters are liable to pay damages for environmental damage concerning waste disposal,[124] and this liability is strict in the same sense as was developed in *Rylands Case.*[125] The basis for imposing strict liability nationally[126] is found in international law.[127] As per EU law, the term 'polluters' here has a broader connotation to include everyone concerned with waste disposal, such as importers; this widening is criticized for being undue and unjustifiable.[128]

In cases where environmental actions are based on claims that rely on scientific or technical issues, experts in these fields are often called upon as witnesses.[129] When such actions are purely civil and rely on facts, the parties bear the burden of proof to prove them on a 'preponderance of evidence' or balance of probabilities.[130] In cases where the actions are challenges to government policies,[131] the standard is the *Wednesbury unreasonableness* test,[132] which requires the claimant to prove 'illegality, irrationality, procedural impropriety, or disproportionality'[133] entrenched in those policies.[134]

124 Philippopoulos-Mihalopoulos, A. (2007). *Absent environments: Theorising environmental law and the city* (p. 201). Routledge-Cavendish.
125 *Rylands v Fletcher* [1868] UKHL 1.
126 Gilpin, A. (2000). *Dictionary of environmental law* (p. 236). Edward Elgar Publishing.
127 *Civil Liability Convention*, 1975.
128 Philippopoulos-Mihalopoulos, A. (2007). *Absent environments: Theorising environmental law and the city* (p. 201). Routledge-Cavendish.
129 Gilpin, A. (2000). *Dictionary of environmental law* (p. 340). Edward Elgar Publishing.
130 Ibid.
131 Ibid.
132 *Associated Provincial Picture Houses Ltd. v Wednesbury Corporation [1948] 1 KB 223.*
133 *Council of Civil Service Unions v Minister for the Civil Service [1984] UKHL 9.*
134 Gilpin, A. (2000). *Dictionary of environmental law* (p. 340). Edward Elgar Publishing.

6.10.1.2 Representative Enforcement

Civil suits are generally filed by the very person aggrieved since they involve an issue of *locus standi*. However, in certain situations, such suits may be filed by an individual on behalf of some or many others when they all share a common 'environmental grievance.'[135] Such an action may be termed 'class action' or representative enforcement, which is conducive to lifting procedural tardiness and obliging many by a single decision.[136] An individual is also permitted to institute a suit against the polluters for his or her personal grievance, irrespective of whether the damage is limited to him or her or common to others.[137]

6.10.1.3 Compensation

Compensation may be claimed by filing suits against polluters in case they violate their duty to ensure the availability of information on how many environment-damaging substances are in their possession, as is evident in the U.S. system. Separate judicial forums are ideally there to enforce the law[138] and grant such reliefs as are within the jurisdictions of ordinary civil courts.[139]

Monetary compensation is provided for any environmental damage caused to common or individual property, movable and immovable.[140] Direct compensation by the polluters purports to fill the inadequacy of funds to be managed to repay the victims.[141]

6.10.1.4 Civil Administrative Remedies

Administrative remedies are mostly used in offenses/crimes related to water, sound, and air pollution. Water polluters are obligated to follow the rules relating to maintaining water quality,[142] and in case of violation, they can be brought to the clutches of the law.[143] The oil-carriage system is a source of environmental pollution,[144] the oil-carrying vessels are permitted to navigate only after a license is obtained and the licensing requirements are fulfilled,[145] and they may face license termination in case of a subsequent violation of those requirements.[146]

135 Ibid., p. 339.
136 Ibid.
137 Ibid.
138 *Land and Environment Court Act*, 1979 (NSW, Australia).
139 Gilpin, A. (2000). *Dictionary of environmental law* (p. 173). Edward Elgar Publishing.
140 Ibid.
141 Ibid., p. 236.
142 *Federal Water Pollution Control Act 1956* (US).
143 Gilpin, A. (2000). *Dictionary of environmental law* (p. 122). Edward Elgar Publishing.
144 Ibid., p. 236.
145 *Oil Pollution Act 1990* (US).
146 Ibid.

Rules relating to bringing polluters' activities within compulsory insurance schemes are another vital aspect of administrative mechanisms, which allow victims of environmental detriment to be readily compensated.[147] The extent of compensation is calculated to include costs for pre-damage (preventive) and post-damage (corrective) treatment and costs for the safe disposal of damaging substances.[148]

6.10.1.5 *Remedies for 'Injurious Affection'*

Development projects that benefit the public often emit various pollutants, including 'noise, vibration, smell, smoke, fumes, artificial lighting,' which devalue the estates surrounding such projects; this is known as 'injurious affection.'[149] This affection may be remedied by awarding compensation, which may often be inadequate.[150] Nevertheless, that inadequacy should be disregarded, and affection should be tolerated, at least in an emergency.[151]

6.10.1.6 *International Law on Civil Liability for Environmental Damages/Offenses*

States are duty-bound to establish domestic statutory mechanisms that would provide liability to make good the environmental damage, territorial and extra-territorial, resulting from development initiatives[152] such as pollution caused by using 'space object[s]'[153] or the 'transboundary movement and disposal of hazardous wastes.'[154] Concerning extraterritorial damage caused by pollutant activities carried out within a state's territory, the 'state sovereignty' argument cannot be sustained in international law to justify such damage.[155] States must also have more international legal frameworks for safeguarding against such damage.[156]

147 Gilpin, A. (2000). *Dictionary of environmental law* (p. 237). Edward Elgar Publishing.
148 Ibid., pp. 236–237.
149 Ibid., p. 151.
150 Ibid.
151 Ibid.
152 United Nations Conference on Environment and Development. (1992). *Rio Declaration on environment and development* (Principle 13). United Nations.
153 United Nations. (1972). *Convention on international liability for damage caused by space objects.* United Nations Office for Outer Space Affairs. www.unoosa.org/oosa/en/ourwork/spacelaw/treaties.html
154 United Nations Environment Programme. (1989). *Basel convention on the control of trans-boundary movements of hazardous wastes and their disposal.* United Nations. www.basel.int/TheConvention/Overview
155 *Trail Smelter Arbitration (United States v. Canada)*, 3 U.N. Rep. Int'l Arb. Awards 1905 (1941).
156 United Nations Conference on Environment and Development. (1992). *Rio Declaration on environment and development* (Principle 22). United Nations.

The Iraq-Kuwait War of 1990 led the international community to adopt various measures, including establishing the United Nations Compensation Commission through UNSC Resolution 687 to distribute funds as compensation for environmental claims.[157] There were negotiations in the 1990s in the European Community (EC) to set up a regional framework to bring industrial polluters within a mechanism where they could be obliged to pay compensation for civil wrongs.[158] These negotiations saw daylight when the EC formulated the Directive on Environmental Liability concerning the Prevention and Remedying of Environmental Damage (Environmental Liability Directive or ELD) in 2004.[159] The directives obliged the EC Members to adopt administrative mechanisms where 'operators' would be required to prevent environmental damage ('preventive principle') or compensate the same ('polluters pay principle').[160] Such a mechanism may be flexible or less so, depending on what the concerned member thinks is appropriate, considering the case's circumstances.[161] The directives may have extensive applications by defining the term 'operator' widely, including farmers. The operators are subjected, under the Directives, to two types of liability for their pollution: (a) strict liability, in the sense of *Rylands* case,[162] in case of environmental damage caused by certain prescribed acts in Annex III, and (b) negligence-based liability, in the sense of the *Donoghue* case,[163] in the case of acts other than prescribed ones.[164] However, the Directives are criticized, *inter alia*, for treating farmers as 'operators' that may hinder them from fully carrying out their agrarian activities.[165] It is submitted that the directives have created the scope to benefit the farmers and to receive agreement-based best compensation from industrial polluters where the latter's performed undertakings cause obstacles to the former's essential activities.[166]

In the 1990s when Nauru, a state in the Pacific Region that had been naturally bestowed with large amounts of phosphate in its mines, improved its GDP by allowing some countries, including Britain, Australia, and New Zealand, to excavate phosphate which subsequently got depleted as a result of massive exploitation, these countries made a deal to pay damages to Nauru in

157 Gilpin, A. (2000). *Dictionary of environmental law* (p. 329). Edward Elgar Publishing.
158 Jack, B. (2016). *Agriculture and EU environmental law* (p. 193). Routledge.
159 Rudall, J. (2020). *Compensation for environmental damage under international law* (p. 77). Routledge.
160 European Parliament and Council Directive 2004/35/EC of 21 April 2004 on environmental liability with regard to the prevention and remedying of environmental damage, OJ L 143, 30.4.2004, pp. 56–75 (Art. 8).
161 Jack, B. (2016). *Agriculture and EU environmental law* (p. 193). Routledge.
162 *Rylands v Fletcher* [1868] UKHL 1.
163 *Donoghue v Stevenson* [1932] UKHL 100.
164 Rudall, J. (2020). *Compensation for environmental damage under international law* (p. 77). Routledge.
165 Jack, B. (2016). *Agriculture and EU environmental law* (p. 110). Routledge.
166 Ibid., pp. 110–112.

upcoming 20 years.[167] Although Nauru primarily used the damages to rejuvenate its economy by initiating different government projects, including a relocation project, it soon realized that the damages were inadequate. It instituted legal action in the International Court of Justice (ICJ), impleading Australia and compelling it to make a further deal for paying more compensation.[168] The most viable system, as prevalent in the EU and U.S. frameworks, to determine whether an amount of compensation is adequate is based on a three-part test: (a) calculation of environmental damage, immediate and recurrent, by conducting data analysis from a particular project; (b) ascertaining the feasibility of the amount proposed; and (c) comparison of damage to the amount, taking into account the inflation rate.[169]

6.10.2 Criminal Remedies

Environmental laws often include penalties for non-compliance.[170] These penalties usually involve imprisonment, fines, and other punitive measures.[171] For instance, a U.S. Federal Court recently awarded $507.5 million in compensation for oil spills that caused significant environmental damage to over 30,000 individuals, including fishermen, residents, and landowners in Alaska.[172] This amount was considered punitive and served as a form of punishment, representing a criminal remedy for the environmental damage caused.[173]

In NSW, Australia, the environmental law encompasses a range of offenses, such as willful or negligent environmental damage. Companies found guilty of such offenses may face penalties of up to $1,000,000, while individuals may be fined up to $250,000 and sentenced to seven years in jail.[174] This law also addresses minor environmental offenses and grants the courts the authority to issue orders preventing repeat offenses by polluters.[175]

Environmental laws in China impose penalties for environmental violations, such as improper waste disposal and actions that endanger wildlife.[176] Recently, a Shanghai court sentenced Mr. William Ping Chen, a U.S. citizen, to ten years[177] in prison for 'smuggling prohibited waste' into China.[178] Criminal remedies are

167 Gilpin, A. (2000). *Dictionary of environmental law* (p. 226). Edward Elgar Publishing.
168 Ibid.
169 Rudall, J. (2020). *Compensation for environmental damage under international law* (pp. 79–80). Routledge.
170 Gilpin, A. (2000). *Dictionary of environmental law* (p. 123). Edward Elgar Publishing.
171 Ibid.
172 *In re Exxon Valdez* [2006] 472 F.3d 600.
173 Gilpin, A. (2000). *Dictionary of environmental law* (p. 123). Edward Elgar Publishing.
174 Ibid.
175 Ibid.
176 Criminal Law of the People's Republic of China 1997 *Article 4.*
177 *William Ping Chen v People's Republic of China* [1997] Shanghai No.1 Intermediate People's Court CLI.C.66811.
178 Gilpin, A. (2000). *Dictionary of environmental law* (p. 37). Edward Elgar Publishing.

considered very effective in mitigating damage because they can be used by government authorities as alternatives to mere fiscal actions, particularly when such actions are insufficient to safeguard against law violations.[179]

Following the concerns from several European countries on criminal enforcement of environmental damage, a regional legal framework[180] was adopted in 1998, which persuaded, in principle, the Members to introduce penal remedies in domestic laws. Still, it did not specify any punishment and left the matter to the wisdom of the respective legislatures of the Members.[181]

6.10.3 *Administrative Remedies*

Administrative authorities are granted powers under environmental law to issue licenses for initiating, modifying, or revoking licenses, inspecting industrial projects, and investigating violations of environmental rules.[182] For example, in the United States, a water project needs to obtain a permit by demonstrating that it meets the standards outlined in the law.[183] Therefore, individuals affected by pollution caused by legal breaches may seek administrative remedies.

6.10.3.1 *'Product Charges' as Administrative Mechanism*

Development projects with the potential to cause environmental harm may be required to pay 'product charges.' These charges serve two purposes: to reduce the harm caused and to encourage polluters to minimize their impact.[184] The amount of these charges may vary depending on the raw materials used in the production process.[185] One important aspect of this approach is that when Belgium introduced 'product charges' in 1993, it faced criticism for making it difficult to simultaneously achieve environmental goals and facilitate the movement of goods across EU countries.[186] According to the Rio Declaration, states are expected to implement a system that imposes costs on product inputs, taking into account the ability of polluters to bear these costs, the interests of the general public, and the maintenance of multilateral trade and financing.[187]

179 Ibid., p. 123.
180 Convention on the Protection of the Environment through Criminal Law 1998.
181 Rudall, J. (2020). *Compensation for environmental damage under international law* (p. 79). Routledge.
182 Gilpin, A. (2000). *Dictionary of environmental law* (p. 3). Edward Elgar Publishing.
183 *Clean Water Act 1977* (US).
184 Gilpin, A. (2000). *Dictionary of environmental law* (p. 251). Edward Elgar Publishing.
185 Ibid.
186 Ibid.
187 United Nations Conference on Environment and Development. (1992). *Rio Declaration on environment and development* (Principle 16). United Nations.

6.10.3.2 Fiscal Impositions vis-à-vis 'Command-and-Control' Actions

Fiscal sanctions, including imposing high taxes on polluters, are an emerging concept for controlling pollution[188] as these are likely to outweigh the financial benefits and profits gained at the cost of environmental rule violations. However, the state machinery still favors traditional 'command-and-control' actions[189] as these are easier to implement.

6.10.3.3 Public Hearings as Administrative Mechanism

Public hearings with the concerned authorities are often arranged so that people may actively consult with the authorities so that governmental policies having implications for the environment do not violate the rights of the public at large or individually.[190] These hearings may be mandated by statutes or by an anticipated threat to the violation of environmental rights.[191] The governments also hold these hearings to comply with their obligations under IEL.[192]

6.10.3.4 Cost-Benefit Analysis as a Prior Requirement for Development Initiatives

Any development project may be initiated only if it can be shown that the benefits from such a project would be more than the costs involved,[193] as is evident in U.S. law.[194] This requirement is known as 'benefit-cost analysis' in the U.S. legal system and 'CBA' in the UK legal system.[195] Although this requirement originated regarding water source management, it has been widely used in other areas, including pollution control.[196] Thus, this requirement can be used as an administrative tool both before initiating a project and after that, in the former as a prerequisite for permission to initiate and in the latter for withdrawal of permission.[197]

6.10.3.5 Accessibility to Information as an Administrative Mechanism

Ensuring the availability of information is an effective administrative mechanism whereby polluters are required to make information relating to their

188 Gilpin, A. (2000). *Dictionary of environmental law* (p. 87). Edward Elgar Publishing.
189 Ibid.
190 Ibid., p. 189.
191 Ibid.
192 United Nations Conference on Environment and Development. (1992). *Rio Declaration on environment and development* (Principle 10). United Nations.
193 Gilpin, A. (2000). *Dictionary of environmental law* (p. 20). Edward Elgar Publishing.
194 *Hood Control Act 1936* (US).
195 Gilpin, A. (2000). *Dictionary of environmental law* (p. 20). Edward Elgar Publishing.
196 Ibid.
197 Ibid., pp. 20–21.

pollution open and accessible to the concerned governmental authorities or the public at large.[198] The objective of this mechanism is to make people aware of the extent to which polluters are complying with environmental laws and standards.[199] Besides this merit, the mechanism has some demerits, such as it may affect the image of a particular company and reduce its business, and it may be abused by administrative authorities, who may use it as a threatening device to industrialists in general; authorities may show 'public interest' as a justification for obtaining information.[200]

An aggrieved person 'having sufficient interest' may subject polluters' breach of this obligation to judicial review, where the activities of the concerned authorities may be challenged on the grounds of malfeasance, misfeasance, or nonfeasance.[201] The courts conducting the review may scrutinize the propriety of those activities from a 'substantive or procedural' point of view or even invalidate any impugned regulatory system if it is untenable in the *Wednesbury* sense.[202] For example, the Russian Federation was held liable for environmental damage in a privately run project due to its inability to regulate the project in accordance with environmental standards.[203]

6.10.3.6 Selling License of Pollution

Another standard that is followed as an administrative system is that the law sets the ceiling of pollution for a particular polluter, who may sell his/her license to other polluters in case the ceiling has yet to be reached.[204] This has a significant impact on small-scale industrialists in reducing the higher costs involved in compliance, as is evident in the U.S. system,[205] and thus is seen as praiseworthy for motivating them to reduce pollution.[206]

Clerical or procedural errors, unwanted and unfair competition among officials, and faulty implementation processes often hampered the administration and regulatory systems. These challenges pose serious challenges in administrative enforcement that need to be addressed and improved.[207]

198 Louka, E. (2006). *International environmental law: Fairness, effectiveness, and world order* (p. 131). Cambridge University Press.
199 Louka, E. (2006). *International environmental law: Fairness, effectiveness, and world order*. Cambridge University Press.
200 Ibid.
201 Fitzmaurice, M. (2009). *Contemporary issues in international environmental law* (p. 174). Edward Elgar Publishing.
202 Ibid., p. 190.
203 *Fadeyeva v Russian Federation* (2005) 45 EHRR 10, para 90.
204 Louka, E. (2006). *International environmental law: Fairness, effectiveness, and world order* (p. 90). Cambridge University Press.
205 Ibid.
206 Ibid., pp. 90, 102.
207 Ibid., p. 63.

As part of the improvement initiative, the system should include diverse decentralized and independent mechanisms so that the failure of one mechanism due to corruption or non-compliance with due process does not lead to the failure of another.[208] This can be ensured if a multi-layered regulatory system is established where the functions of each authority are within the clutches of checks and balances by another.[209] Here, the argument for more social utility is to be outweighed by the regulation of more compliance.[210] This compels policymakers to permit only such equipment to ensure a maximum production rate and limit pollutants to a minimum level.[211] This is the crux of the debate among two groups: the pro-environment group and the anti-environmental group. While the former's understanding is that the discharge of unregulated pollutants has considerable harmful effects on the environment generally and climate specifically, and thus they must be brought within an efficient regulatory framework, the latter's emphasis is on maximum utilization of natural resources to achieve a high level of industrial outcomes. Thus, any action restraining such utilization on the plea of so-called environmental justice is unfruitful.[212] This debate leads to a dilemma where the government needs administrative actions.

6.10.4 Preventive Remedies

The title itself signifies the objective of this principle. It rests on the basic understanding of the well-known maxim 'prevention is better than cure.' It is impossible to completely prevent environmental pollution; if any industry contaminates a river through waste or emits pollutants into the air, restoring the previous condition is unfeasible. Therefore, pollution should be controlled at the primary level.[213] Before establishing any industry, if it is possible to assess the harm it may inflict on the environment, restrictions should be imposed upon its operation, or insistence should be placed upon the use of more sophisticated and eco-friendly technology.

The concept of 'EIA' is part of the above principle. It involves assessing the adverse effects of hazardous industries on the environment. It is also necessary to test the impact of industrial chemicals (waste) on the health of surrounding inhabitants. The other dimension of this principle is to keep pollution under

208 Ibid., p. 64.

209 Ibid.

210 Grant, D., Jorgenson, A., & Longhofer, W. (2020). *Super Polluters: Tackling the world's largest sites of climate-disrupting emissions* (p. 3). Columbia University Press.

211 Ibid., p. 7.

212 Ibid., p. 8.

213 van Zeben, J., & Rowell, A. (2020). *A guide to EU environmental law*. University of California Press.

control.[214] It has been stated that an utterly pollution-free environment is not possible, so it is essential to fix the level of pollution that would be sustainable for the environment.

The long-standing proverb 'prevention is better than cure' is also recognized in IEL. In this case, taking preventive measures to limit damage beforehand is more suitable than providing costs afterward to ameliorate the harm already caused.[215] Such measures extend to a wide range of activities, including formulating an effective control plan for industrial undertakings likely to cause environmental harm, educating people in general and policymakers in particular about the value of maintaining environmental resources in *status quo*, allowing the pro-environment NGOs to carry out their activities in this area, obliging the industrial producers to initiate their projects and to make international trade in an environment-friendly manner and enacting appropriate laws for furthering these measures.[216]

One of the primary objectives of the UN Watercourse Convention[217] (to be called hereinafter 'UNWC') is to oblige the member states to take measures that can limit, minimize, and prevent environmental damage from the territorial polluters' undertakings likely to occur in another member state.[218] Thus, the UNWC urges its members to limit the pollutants 'at their sources' to prevent extraterritorial damage.[219] Certain IEL emphasize adopting preventive and curative measures if the national economic and technical resources permit.[220]

6.10.5 Precautionary Remedies

Environmental damage involved in industrial projects must be calculated using various scientific, economic, and technical assessment methods. Scientific

214 *Air (Prevention and Control of Pollution) Act 1981* provides provision to that effect, viz. Section 16 (1)(h) 'lay down standards for the quality of air'; Section 22,

> No person operating any industrial plant in any pollution control area shall discharge as course as permit to be discharged the commission of any air pollution control area shall discharge as course as permit to be discharged the commission of any pollutant in excess of the standards laid down by the State Board under clause (g) of sub-section (1) of Section 17.

Section 17 of the *Environment (Protection) Act 1986*, is more comprehensive in comparison to the *Air Act*, in that, 'No person carrying on any industry operation or process shall discharge as emit or permit to be discharged or emit or permit to be discharged or emitted any environmental pollutant in excess of such standards as may be prescribed.'

215 United Nations Environment Programme. (1982). *Nairobi Declaration* (Principle 9).

216 Ibid.

217 *Convention on the Law of the Non-navigational Uses of International Watercourses*, 1997.

218 Louka, E. (2006). *International environmental law: Fairness, effectiveness, and world order* (p. 224). Cambridge University Press.

219 Ibid.

220 United Nations Environment Programme. (1995). *Washington declaration on protection of the marine environment from land-based activities.*

assessments may often fail to determine the exact risks with certainty, and prospective polluters tend to use this uncertainty to avoid liability arising from industry-caused environmental harm.[221]

This area of the precautionary principle debars the polluters from utilizing 'scientific uncertainty' as a tool.[222] It originated in the 1970s due to Germany's emphasis on adopting an environment-conservation approach, which was a diametric shift from the traditional liability-imposing approach.[223] Following this, various binding international law instruments and soft law documents began to recognize the principle.[224]

This principle is part of the protective measures in environmental law that focuses on taking action even in the absence of adequate scientific evidence if there is reasonable apprehension about environmental risk. While the precautionary principle seems to overlap with the preventive principle on the surface, the fundamental difference between the two is their underlying scientific rationale. The precautionary principle suggests that caution must be taken, even in cases where there is no scientific evidence backing a claim, especially when that claim could lead to the release of harmful pollutants that must be managed.[225] In essence, the precautionary principle obliges the state to take action to control potential damage regardless of concrete evidence to show that such discharge poses actual damage.[226] In India, this concept marks the following: (a) environmental measures – by the State Government and the statutory authority – must anticipate, prevent, and attack the causes of environmental degradation, and (b) concerns abound with a high probability of suffering severe and irreversible damage, a lack of knowledge should not serve to delay action to mitigate environmental harm.[227] Ultimately, however, the foundational principle is to mitigate the violation of the environment, conserve it as a resource, and promote less ecologically destructive activities.[228]

221 Philippopoulos-Mihalopoulos, A. (2007). *Absent environments: Theorising environmental law and the city* (p. 130). Routledge-Cavendish.

222 Ibid.

223 Ibid., p. 131.

224 Gilpin, A. (2000). *Dictionary of environmental law* (p. 250). Edward Elgar Publishing.

225 Supra note 23.

226 The White Paper, *This common inheritance: Britain's environmental strategy*, adopts a qualified version of this principle where it states:

> [W]hen there are significant risk of damage to the environment, the Government will be prepared to take precautionary action to limit the use of potentially dangerous pollutants, even where scientific knowledge is not conclusive, if the balance of likely costs and benefits justified it.

Purdue, M. (1991). Integrated pollution control in the Environmental Protection Act 1990: A coming age of environmental law? *Modern Law Review*, *54*, 534–535.

227 *Vellore Citizen's Welfare Forum* v. *Union of India*, AIR 1996 SC 2715 at p. 2721 (per Kuldip Singh J.).

228 *A.P. Pollution Control Board v. M.V. Nayudu*, AIR 1999 SC 812, at p. 820 (per M. Jagannadha Rao J.).

The fundamental goal is not just to safeguard society's health, property, and economic interests but also to preserve the environment for its own sake.[229] This was reaffirmed in the Rio Conference of 1992 in its Principle 15.[230]

As regards the depletion of the ozone layers, the Vienna Convention[231] reminded the members about the precautionary principle that they recognize domestically and globally.[232] Similarly, the Montreal Protocol to the Convention[233] echoed the same voice with a special emphasis on using 'developments in scientific knowledge.'[234] It applauded various states' adoption of the principle domestically and globally.[235] Subsequently, some regional declarations[236] and conventions[237] also embodied the principle. The most notable development was the inclusion of the precautionary principle into the CBD[238] and UNFCCC.[239] Although the UNFCCC explains the principle elaborately, being a 'framework convention' is a non-binding instrument. The Rio Declaration,[240] to ensure mass application of the principle,[241] explained the 'precautionary principle' in the following well-articulated words:

> [W]here there are threats of serious or irreversible damage to the environment, lack of full scientific certainty should not be used as a reason for postponing cost-effective measures to prevent environmental degradation.[242]

This wording is criticized by some jurists for being ambiguous, arguing that the polluters may make considerable promises to adopt measures to limit environmental damage without being able to implement the same.[243] This argument is rebutted in the way that the adoption of 'cost-effective measures,' as required by the precautionary principle, turns out to be an ambiguous

229 Ibid.

230 Principle 15: To protect the environment, the precautionary approach shall be widely applied by states according to this capability. Where there are threats of serious or irreversible damage, lack of full scientific certainty shall be used as a reason for postponing cost-effective measures to prevent environmental degradation.

231 Vienna Convention for the Protection of the Ozone Layer 1985.

232 Ibid., preamble para. 5.

233 Montreal Protocol on Substances that Deplete the Ozone Layer 1987.

234 Ibid., preamble para. 6.

235 Ibid., preamble para. 8.

236 Bergen Ministerial Declaration on Sustainable Development in the ECE Region 1990, para. 7.

237 Convention on the Protection of the Marine Environment of the Baltic Sea Area (Helsinki Convention) 1992, art. 3.2.

238 Convention on Biological Diversity (Biodiversity Convention) 1992, preamble para. 9.

239 United Nations Framework Convention on Climate Change (UNFCCC) 1992, art. 3.3.

240 Rio Declaration on Environment and Development 1992.

241 Gilpin, A. (2000). *Dictionary of environmental law* (p. 249). Edward Elgar Publishing.

242 United Nations Conference on Environment and Development. (1992). *Rio Declaration on environment and development* (Principle 15). United Nations.

243 Gilpin, A. (2000). *Dictionary of environmental law* (p. 249). Edward Elgar Publishing.

explanation of scientific certainty regarding the anticipated environmental hazards.[244]

While the preventive measures are taken by the government where an industrial undertaking is calculated to produce such 'high risks' that they are likely to outweigh the costs to remedy the ecological damage, the precautionary measures are taken where they are capable of controlling the polluting substances likely to create environmental dangers, although uncertain scientifically, and the remedial costs are conductive enough.[245] Thus, the consultation process between governmental authorities and industrialists is to be carried out based on collected data, with the objective of avoiding irreparable ecological loss and calculating the outcomes expected from the cost-effective measures.[246]

Application for Precautionary Principle

The principle is primarily applied when the threat of environmental damage is so high that exact quantification with 'scientific certainty' is not required, nor is the causation of damage by the act proven; rather, it solemnly requires immediate action to limit the damage even before initiating the project.[247] Therefore, the operational sphere of the principle is the situation of 'scientific uncertainty' plus 'high risk.'[248] However, there should not be a misunderstanding that the principle does not require any calculation; in fact, there is a need to show a 'projection' reached through collecting and analyzing information that creates a strong presumption in favor of the existing high risk.[249]

The traditional role of environmental law in treating a particular act as legal or illegal has been to determine the line between the environment's inner element, conservation, and the outer element, other considerations such as policy or financial matters.[250] The bar is demarcated with the great help of science.[251] Therefore, the precautionary principle requires polluters to make every effort to attain scientific certainty, and in case of failure, they are obliged to adopt cost-effective measures.[252] They try to achieve this certainty through a two-step process consisting of 'perception and comprehension' of threats to environmental damage. Then, they imagine the existing situation as a hypothetical future so that they can stop certain undertakings if its (hypothetical) future is

244 Ibid.
245 United Kingdom. (1992). *British white paper on the environment.*
246 *Australian Intergovernmental Agreement on the Environment*, 1992.
247 Philippopoulos-Mihalopoulos, A. (2007). *Absent environments: Theorising environmental law and the city* (p. 131). Routledge-Cavendish.
248 Ibid.
249 Ibid.
250 Ibid.
251 Ibid.
252 Ibid., p. 132.

terrible for the environment.[253] The precautionary principle ceases to operate whenever a scientific certainty is reached through data analysis.[254]

The principle of 'risk assessment,' regarded generally as a requirement for obtaining a permit, obliges the polluters to show the existing calculated risk that the polluters may make. The preventive principle imposes a duty upon them to limit the risk, and the precautionary principle attributes the obligation to take cost-effective remedial measures that will be able to make good pre-project and post-project damage.[255] However, the statutory requirement to comply with these three principles may translate into a three-tier burden that purports to assess risk to the fullest possibility and capacity.[256] The distinction between prevention and precaution is somewhat blurred in IEL. Some jurists argue that this differentiation is not strictly maintained in environmental law documents, which contain both principles without making a clear distinction. Instead, the emphasis is on following both principles to address pollution.[257]

Due to the lack of scientific certainty, the precautionary principle creates a high presumption of damage as a reason not to initiate a dangerous project. It also acts as a normative measure in a regulatory framework where scientific certainty is achieved.[258] Thus, precaution is a recurrent measure as long as the knowledge falls short of identifying the exactness of damage.[259]

6.10.6 Proximity Remedies

Industrial projects built in urban areas or even in rural populated areas can produce two-fold environmental threats: one arising from pollution as part of industrial activities and another from the nearness of individuals residing near those projects.[260] The polluters are held responsible here based on the principle of proximity, that is, due to the proximity of people, the polluters cannot escape liability for any environmental hazards.[261] The process of determining proximity vis-à-vis remoteness of people is based on the tortious principle of the *foreseeability* test,[262] namely, whether the polluters could have foreseen, hypothetically, the ecological damage.[263]

Environmental laws oblige the governmental authorities to respect the reaction of the people within the proximate region of industrial sites to the

253 Ibid.
254 Ibid., p. 133.
255 Ibid., p. 131.
256 Ibid.
257 Ibid.
258 Ibid., p. 133.
259 Ibid., p. 134.
260 Ibid., p. 137.
261 Ibid.
262 Ibid., p. 163.
263 *Donoghue v Stevenson* [1932] UKHL 100.

anticipated damage and to reshape the policy of dealing with polluters both administratively and judicially.[264] The authorities often must balance the political manifesto and regional people's interests.[265] It is argued that rapid urbanization often disregards the principle of proximity, as the segregation of industrial sites from the vicinity of population centers is not always possible, mainly when there is enough space to relocate.[266] However, this argument suffers from a dilemma: many urbanization plans act differently to effectuate segregation or, at least, establish sites with sufficient safety precautions, considering the principle of proximity.[267] The differentiated urbanization plans emphasize legal mechanisms with less regard to 'economic considerations.'[268]

Modern environmental regulatory systems have shifted from the traditional method of solely ensuring compliance with legal rules to setting up fully fledged policies where consultation with industrial polluters and the local population is, *inter alia*, considered a significant element.[269] Thus, a compelling 'environmental impact statement' requires prospective polluters to show, among other things, the nature of the locality (residential or industrial) and its people (living within close or remote distance of the proposed projects).[270]

Almost all industrial undertakings involve various tools, including fire, corrosive substances, and moving machines, which are inherently dangerous and capable of damaging life, property, and ecological elements.[271] Environmental laws invariably oblige the promoters of these undertakings to submit an approximately quantitative assessment of risks likely to occur.[272] One of the areas of assessment is for the promoters to show justification for electing a particular place for undertaking and to substantiate the capability of proposed safety measures to minimize the explosion-driven damage likely to affect the people living in proximity, the academic people attending educational institutions in the vicinity and the patients and attendants in medical centers in the neighborhood.[273] This locality assessment aims to inform license-granting authorities about a project's impacts on the societal setup, such as changes in livelihoods, cultures, behavioral patterns, and social relationships engendered in the locality.[274] This assessment is known as 'social impact assessment (SIA).' In this way, the authorities become well-equipped with sufficient information

264 Philippopoulos-Mihalopoulos, A. (2007). *Absent environments: Theorising environmental law and the city* (p. 204). Routledge-Cavendish.
265 Ibid.
266 Ibid., p. 205.
267 Ibid.
268 Ibid.
269 Gilpin, A. (2000). *Dictionary of environmental law* (p. 103). Edward Elgar Publishing.
270 Ibid., p. 104.
271 Ibid., p. 139.
272 Ibid.
273 Ibid.
274 Ibid.

to determine the propriety of the safety protocols vis-à-vis social unrest (forced migration and change of livelihoods).[275]

Besides the economic impacts, some other aspects must be considered while complying with laws recognizing the proximity principle. These aspects include the availability of easement rights (air, water, and light), structures as parts of history and heritage,[276] existing industrial projects in proximity,[277] and accessibility to essential services.[278]

The development projects proposed to situate in the vicinity of an ecologically 'protected area' are to be stopped by the government of the concerned country.[279] International law obliges the states to ensure, by policy and legislation, the imperishability of protected 'wetlands'[280] from the interference of polluters.[281] The device to be adopted in this regard by the states is 'wise use,'[282] interpreted as 'sustainable use' of natural resources[283] to fulfill the requirements of existing generations without undermining those of successive generations.[284] Thus, states are heavily burdened not to permit any industrial undertaking likely to endanger the essential features of an enlisted wetland,[285] whatever the polluters' advance plea of economic or social utility.[286]

There is a scholarly altercation as to the appropriate method to determine the causation-based environmental damage.[287] This results from two parallel standards for proving causation in civil (tortious) wrongs, including environmental ones.[288] The common law countries follow the 'proximate causation standard'[289] as developed in the UK based on the *foreseeable consequence* test,[290] replacing the earlier *direct consequence* test.[291] On the other hand, civil law countries apply the

275 Ibid.
276 Ibid., p. 33.
277 Ibid., p. 82.
278 Ibid., pp. 82–83.
279 Philippopoulos-Mihalopoulos, A. (2007). *Absent environments: Theorising environmental law and the city* (p. 43). Routledge-Cavendish.
280 Ramsar Convention on Wetlands of International Importance Especially as Waterfowl Habitat 1971, art. 3.1.
281 Ibid., art. 3.2.
282 Ibid., art. 2.6, art. 3.1, art. 6.2(d), and art. 6.3.
283 Gillespie, A. (2007). *Protected areas and international environmental law* (p. 43). Martinus Nijhoff Publishers.
284 Report of the World Commission on Environment and Development: Our Common Future 1987, para. 27.
285 Ramsar Convention on Wetlands of International Importance Especially as Waterfowl Habitat 1971, art. 3.2.
286 Gillespie, A. (2007). *Protected areas and international environmental law* (p. 43). Martinus Nijhoff Publishers.
287 Ibid., p. 49.
288 Ibid.
289 Ibid.
290 *Overseas Tankship (UK) Ltd v Morts Dock and Engineering Co Ltd (The Wagon Mound) (No. 1)* [1961] AC 38.
291 *In Re Polemis and Furness, Withy & Co Ltd* [1921] 3 KB 560.

'direct causation standard.'[292] The essential distinction between 'proximate' and 'direct' is that in the former, the causal link between act/omission and damage is broken by the occurrence of a *novus actus interveniens*[293] (literally: 'an act intervening'),[294] but in the latter, the link remains unbroken.[295] The suitable approach is to apply both standards according to the requirements of the facts of the cases; for instance, while the proximate causation may be applied in case of mismanagement of ammunition left by the enemy state through deliberate detonation, the direct causation may be applicable in case of forceful migration of refugees as a result of war-driven ecological hazards.[296]

6.10.7 Subsidiary Remedies

The concept of 'subsidiary,' found in commercial law, is also applied in environmental law to control pollution.[297] It asserts that '[T]he primary responsibility and decision-making competence should rest with the lowest possible level of authority of the political hierarchy.'[298] A continent's ecology comprises the environmental conditions of all its countries. The two are strongly related; the former entirely depends upon the latter. If any part of a country's environment is polluted or degraded, it affects the continent's ecology. This concept of transboundary pollution is an integral part of the subsidiary principle.[299]

6.10.8 Polluter Pays Remedies

Polluter Pays Remedies is a commonly found in international treaties as well as local jurisprudence.[300] This principle has two highlighted aspects:

292 Gillespie, A. (2007). *Protected areas and international environmental law* (p. 49). Martinus Nijhoff Publishers.

293 Ibid.

294 *Carslogie Steamship Co Ltd v Royal Norwegian Government* [1952] AC 292.

295 Gillespie, A. (2007). *Protected areas and international environmental law* (p. 49). Martinus Nijhoff Publishers.

296 Ibid.

297 Craig, P. (2012). Subsidiarity: A political and legal analysis. *JCMS: Journal of Common Market Studies*, *50*, 72–87.

298 Sands, P. (1990). European Community environmental law, the European Court of Justice, and common-interest groups. *Modern Law Review*, *53*, 685; see also the following point:

> The debate on the Maastricht Treaty brought to the forefront the issue of subsidiary. Subsidiary is the principle which states that if something can be carried out more effectively at a level in the hierarchy lower than community level, then that is where it should be affected. It is the principle of the lowest common denominates.

Supra note 29.

299 Lenaerts, K. (2017). The principle of subsidiarity and the environment in the European Union: Keeping the balance of federalism. In *European environmental law* (pp. 129–178). Routledge.

300 Ambec, S., & Ehlers, L. (2016). Regulation via the polluter-pays principle. *The Economic Journal*, *126*(593), 884–906.

on the one hand, it is employed as a compensatory mechanism, and on the other, it is a preventive mechanism.[301] The polluter should be held liable for the destruction brought about to the environment on the compensatory side, and there may be severe financial penalties for the polluters on the preventive side. This principle comprises four different perspectives: (a) there is a possibility of requiring criminal liability for the polluter; (b) an obligation to indemnify is imposed upon the polluter; (c) an eco-tax or carbon tax can be levied upon him; and (d) there may be law of the state that creates a duty to the polluter to assist in the protection of the environment.[302]

It should be noted that in the United States, the principle was incorporated by the Comprehensive Environmental Response Compensation and Liability Act of 1980. This was adopted by the European Communities Council as a possible means to protect the Environment.[303] This principle was also stressed in The Rio Declaration regarding its application in domestic legislation.[304] The principle has been invoked in different judgments by the Supreme Court of India as well as other High courts.[305] The court has defined this principle as '[t]he absolute liability for harm to the environment extends not only to

301 Schwartz, P. (2010). The polluter-pays principle. In *Research handbook on international environmental law*. Edward Elgar Publishing.

302 Barthakur, A. (2021). Polluter pays principle as the key element to environmental law. *International Journal of Scientific and Research Publications*, *11*(3), 274–277.

303 The principle goes thus:

> The Council stresses that in the interest of more efficient environmental protection in the context of effectively integrating environment and economic policy and meeting the fundamental objective of sustainable development, in particular which comply with the 'polluter pays principle,' it is necessary to back up current, direct environmental regulations, based on command and control approach, with economic and fiscal instruments aimed at influencing the reason and behavior of producers and consumers, to discharge wasteful and polluting process and product and to promote technologies and productive processes which are consistent with resource conservation.

304 Principle 13 declares:

> States shall develop national law regarding liability and compensation for the victims of pollution and other environmental damage. States shall also cooperate in an expeditions and more determined manner to develop further international law regarding liability and compensation for adverse effects of environmental damage caused by activities within this jurisdiction or control to area beyond their jurisdiction.

Principle 16 adds:

> National authorities should endeavour to promote the internalization of environmental costs and the use of economic instruments, taking into account the approach that the polluter should, in principle, bear the cost of pollution, with due regard to the public interest and without disturbing international trade and investment.

305 See *Vellore Citizen Welfare Forum* v. *Union of India* AIR 1996 AIR SC 2715 (per Kuldip Singh J.); see also *Indian Council for Enviro-Legal Action v. Union of India*, AIR 1996 SC 1069; *M.C. Mehta v. Kamal Nath* (1997) SCC 388; *M.C. Mehta v. Union of India* (Taj Mahal Case), (1997) 2 SCC 353; *M.C. Mehta v. Union of India* (1997) 2 SCC 411.

compensate the victim of pollution but also the cost of restoring the environmental degradation.'[306]

Since the advent of the decolonization process in the second half of the 20th century, many independent countries have witnessed proliferating industrial development.[307] This led the global community to reshape environmental rules, *inter alia*, by proposing using economic tools to control pollution.[308] As a result, non-binding soft laws[309] started to recognize the polluter pays principle. The principle applies to obliging polluters to pay monetary compensation for the utilization of natural resources and for harm caused by their polluting activities.[310] This payment can be made to the extent of environmental harm (subsequent payment) or when obtaining a license from the authorities (previous payment).[311] The purpose of the principle is to outweigh the benefits obtained from pollution.[312]

States enact environmental laws to conserve the health of the people at large and environmental resources from polluting activities without interfering with polluters' business benefits.[313] As a result, the laws require the polluters to make damage-limiting costs as an internal aspect of the products and thereby sell eco-friendly products at higher costs.[314] This is known as the 'internalization of costs,' and the process employed here is the 'CBA.'[315] In this way, lawmakers burden administrative authorities with a duty to regulate polluting activities, relying on the wisdom of the polluters.[316] Here, the authorities utilize the polluter pays principle as a regulatory system.[317]

Scholars have criticized the principle in several ways. They argue that it may be difficult to calculate the monetary value of environmental harm in certain situations, especially when the damage is unquantifiable, such as in the case of infant harm.[318] They also claim that the principle effectively gives polluters

306 Ibid.
307 Gilpin, A. (2000). *Dictionary of environmental law* (p. 242). Edward Elgar Publishing.
308 Ibid.
309 Declaration on Environmental Policy 1974, para. 6.
310 Gilpin, A. (2000). *Dictionary of environmental law* (p. 246). Edward Elgar Publishing.
311 Ibid.
312 Ibid.
313 Driesen, D. M. (2003). *The economic dynamics of environmental law* (p. 15). MIT Press.
314 Ibid.
315 Ibid.
316 Ibid.
317 Ibid.
318 Hanley, N. (2002). The economic value of environmental damage. In M. Bowman & A. Boyle (Eds.), *Environmental damage in international and comparative law: Problems of definition and valuation*. Oxford University Press; Tekie, H., & Lindblad, M. (2013). Methodologies for monetary valuation of environmental impacts-State of the art. *CPM the Swedish Life Cycle Center, Gothenburg*, 22–25.

free rein to engage in polluting activities however they please, as long as they are willing to pay for the damages afterward.[319] Additionally, they argue that monetary compensation often fails to fully restore the affected individuals, and distributing compensation may not ensure that it's allocated according to the needs of the affected people.[320] Polluters may use these criticisms to their advantage. Furthermore, the complexity of attributing liability to a specific project in an area with multiple industrial projects may allow polluters to evade responsibility.[321] In light of these criticisms, some suggest that prohibiting polluting activities may be a more suitable alternative to compensation.[322]

The more recent spectrum of the principle is that polluters' monetary payments are to be used not to compensate for the damage already occurring but to limit pollution by making the payment an input material in the production process.[323] The effect is that the polluters, without being entitled to governmental bounty or fiscal rebate, must pass on the costs to consumers through increased prices.[324] This may also be a point of criticism, but this 'internalization' process is a matter of preference, contemporary because it renders the products eco-friendly.[325]

Nevertheless, this principle has already received strong recognition in the international environmental regulation frameworks. It was first recognized systematically in the Rio Declaration.[326] This recognition led to the principle's subsequent reaffirmation in various national, regional, and other international instruments.[327] The Rio Declaration encourages states to comply with the principle and

> promote the internalization of environmental costs and the use of economic instruments, taking into account the approach that the polluter should, in principle, bear the cost of pollution, with due regard to the public interest and without distorting international trade and investment.[328]

319 Konisky, D. M., & Woods, N. D. (2012). Environmental free riding in state water pollution enforcement. *State Politics & Policy Quarterly, 12*(3), 227–251; Luppi, B., Parisi, F., & Rajagopalan, S. (2009). *Environmental protection for developing countries: The polluter-does-not-pay principle.*
320 Gilpin, A. (2000). *Dictionary of environmental law* (p. 246). Edward Elgar Publishing.
321 Ibid., p. 247.
322 Ibid., pp. 246–247.
323 Ibid., p. 247.
324 Ibid.
325 Ibid.
326 United Nations. (1992). *Rio Declaration on environment and development.* United Nations.
327 Gilpin, A. (2000). *Dictionary of environmental law* (p. 247). Edward Elgar Publishing.
328 United Nations Conference on Environment and Development. (1992). *Rio Declaration on environment and development* (Principle 15). United Nations.

Regionally, the Sofia Convention[329] recognized the principle[330] and the EC's regulatory framework on the environment strongly advocates for the same.[331] ELD,[332] recognizing the polluter pays principle,[333] emphasizes using additional compensatory mechanisms if the preliminary damages are inadequate to ensure restorative justice for the affected people.[334] The Directive attributes liability to polluters for harms resulting from intentional acts or failure to take due care.[335] The Directive requires the EU countries to adopt these rules in their domestic laws.[336]

Domestic environmental law is not violative of the principle on the ground that it specified an area called for vulnerable people, depriving them of economic rights if it provides for rules to consider the 'sources of pollution' at the time of framing the project design.[337] Moreover, this principle is widely practiced in domestic agricultural legal frameworks. In general, agricultural law has two aspects in terms of compliance of polluters with their duties.[338] One is reactive; that is, they should refrain from damaging the environment, and in case of failure, they are to pay monetary compensation.[339] Another aspect is being proactive. Agricultural producers and farmers often develop a system that benefits farming and biodiversity.[340] In this proactive aspect, the farmers' affirmative activities are necessary to encourage the state authorities and not to disregard those activities on the plea of increasing production with less concern for biodiversity matters.[341]

Domestic environmental laws may include two mechanisms for guiding authorities. The first is a 'health-based' mechanism, which requires authorities to ensure that minimizing environmental harm adequately protects people's health and environmental balance. The second is a 'technology-based' mechanism, which obligates authorities to require polluters to minimize harm using advanced technological equipment.[342] However, administrative authorities must not demand that polluters limit pollution to an unreasonably expensive extent. Instead, the responsibility to protect the environment should be

329 *Convention on cooperation for the protection and sustainable use of the Danube River* (Sofia Convention), 1994, art. 2(4).
330 Gilpin, A. (2000). *Dictionary of environmental law* (p. 73). Edward Elgar Publishing.
331 Jack, B. (2016). *Agriculture and EU environmental law* (p. 120). Routledge.
332 *Directive 2004/35/CE on environmental liability with regard to the prevention and remedying of environmental damage* (Environmental Liability Directive or ELD), 2004.
333 Ibid., preamble, para. 2.
334 Ibid., art. 8.
335 Ibid., art. 7.
336 Ibid., art. 3.
337 Case C-258/00 *Commission v France* [2002] ECR I-05959.
338 Jack, B. (2016). *Agriculture and EU environmental law* (p. 246). Routledge.
339 Ibid.
340 Ibid.
341 Ibid.
342 Driesen, D. M. (2003). *The economic dynamics of environmental law* (pp. 15–16). MIT Press.

allocated among polluters on an equitable basis, according to their needs and capacity.[343]

6.11 Sentencing Corporations for Committing Environmental Crimes/Offenses

Based on the guidelines provided, the most effective punishment for environmental offenses would be to impose heavy fines on corporations for violations.[344] The fines should be based on the corporation's capacity to pay, with higher fines imposed on those with greater financial means. Additionally, it is important to consider the possibility of restoring the damaged environment. If there is a chance to repair the damage, polluters should be required to do so, including covering the costs of treating affected people and resettling their habitat.[345] In cases where the damage is permanent, alternative environmental resources may need to be created.[346] Keith notes:

> Some examples of the court's creative use of fines are: requiring a convicted company to pay $100,000 to promote the conservation of fish habitat; ordering a company to pay $30,000 to develop a local toxic waste program; or directing a corporation to pay their fine to a local school board for environmental education. There is little doubt that fines will continue to be used by the courts in sentencing environmental offenders.[347]

In respect of corporations, the disclosure and non-indemnification of directors may represent other sentencing patterns. Regarding the former, the court may compel a company to publicly disclose its environmental records. A poor record, in itself, could undermine the company's goodwill and impose a sanction on its business operations. Adds Keith:

> In the well-known case of *R. v. Bata Industries Ltd.*, the court ordered the company to publish on the front of their newsletter for international distribution the facts leading to their conviction, the name of the directors involved, and the details of the penalties and terms of probation. The use of publication . . . is especially effective when the company's reputation is vital to its success in the marketplace.[348]

343 Ibid., p. 16.

344 Karpoff, J. M., Lott, J., John R., & Wehrly, E. W. (2005). The reputational penalties for environmental violations: Empirical evidence. *The Journal of Law and Economics*, *48*(2), 653–675.

345 Ibid.; Mazzotta, M. J., Opaluch, J. J., & Grigalunas, T. A. (1994). Natural resource damage assessment: the role of resource restoration. *Natural Resources Journal*, 153–178.

346 Mazzotta, M. J., Opaluch, J. J., & Grigalunas, T. A. (1994). Natural resource damage assessment: The role of resource restoration. *Natural Resources Journal*, 153–178.

347 Keith, N. A. *Creative environmental sentencing: Making the punishment fit the crime.* Retrieved November 28, 2024, from http://www.esemag.com/1196/sentence.html

348 Ibid.

The second aspect focuses on ensuring that fines imposed on company directors or employees are not reimbursed by the company, as this serves as a strong deterrent. A key case addressing this issue is *R. v. Bata Industries Ltd.*, where Bata Industries was convicted under the OWRA for allowing industrial waste to contaminate the ground. Two of its directors were also found guilty under the same act for failing to exercise reasonable care to prevent the discharge and were each fined $12,000. Additionally, the court imposed a probation condition that prohibited the company from reimbursing the directors for the fines. On appeal, the Ontario General Division Court reduced the fines to $6,000, deeming this amount sufficient to deter the directors personally and to send a broader message to other corporate leaders about the consequences of ignoring environmental laws. However, the court upheld the condition that the company could not indemnify the directors. Bata appealed the indemnification prohibition, and the Court of Appeal found that the condition was not appropriate under the *Provincial Offences Act*, which allows probation orders to include measures aimed at preventing future offenses or aiding in the rehabilitation of the defendant. The Court decided that the prohibition against indemnification did not align with these objectives and was not intended to deter Bata or other corporations from environmental violations but rather focused on penalizing the directors directly.[349]

Imprisonment should remain a punishment option for individual offenders.[350] The effectiveness of imprisonment as a deterrent, for prevention, and/ or for rehabilitation cannot be denied.[351] As stated by Judge McPherson:

> An actual period of prison custody is likely to have a real deterrent effect on others minded to commit like offences over and beyond that in other cases. If offenders consider that they might succeed in escaping with nothing more than a financial penalty, it may be that they would take the risk of doing so for the profit that appears to be recoverable for acts like this.[352]

It is clear that '[m]ajor environmental offences, particularly when there is a high degree of criminality involved because of the repetitive nature of the conduct, will call for the imposition of custodial sentences.'[353]

349 Keith, N. A. *Creative environmental sentencing: Making the punishment fit the crime.* Retrieved December 30, 2005, from http://www.esemag.com/1196/sentence.html

350 Drago, F., Galbiati, R., & Vertova, P. (2009). The deterrent effects of prison: Evidence from a natural experiment. *Journal of Political Economy, 117*(2), 257–280.

351 Duwe, G. (2017). *The use and impact of correctional programming for inmates on pre-and post-release outcomes* (Vol. 48). US Department of Justice.

352 Irwin, J. M. (2005). *Environmental offences, sentencing principles and evidentiary issues.* Paper presented at the Australian Environmental Law Enforcement Conference, October 28.

353 Ibid.

Another sentencing pattern that may successfully be adopted is community service. This may be applied to both persons and corporations. Community Service involves the spirit of social service for human welfare. Instead of penalizing the offenders for any violation, the court may order the construction, management, maintenance, or setting up of institutions beneficial to the neighborhood or community. Environmental projects may be undertaken as an alternative to sentencing for improving air or water quality in association with the government, where necessary. The concept of reformation may thereby be achieved, for both the offender and the environment.

Sentencing is a crucial process that aims to reduce and prevent specific criminal behaviors in individuals. Therefore, the legislature and judiciary should establish appropriate limits and methods for sentencing. As mentioned, no single theory or principle of sentencing can be considered as the most important. It should be a combination of all these theories and principles to ensure environmental safety, minimize damage or harm, and enable individuals to continue their work or industrial processes easily. This approach can contribute to the success of sustainable development, benefiting the environment and its inhabitants.

6.12 Conclusion

The term 'sustainable development' was first used in 1987 by the World Commission on Environment and Development (Brundtland Commission). The Report described the term in the following manner:

> Humanity can make development sustainable – to ensure that it meets the needs of the present without compromising the ability of future generations to meet their own needs. The concept of sustainable development does imply limits – not absolute limits but limitations imposed by the present state of technology and social organization on environmental resources and by the ability of the biosphere to absorb the effect of human activities. But technology and social organization can be managed and improved to create a new era of economic growth.[354]

The cardinal features of this report were that, on the one hand, there is a need for industrial and technological growth, which is opposed to environmental preservation. At the same time, the other should be organized in such a way that the biosphere can tolerate such activity. Precisely, it mandated in favor of a balanced approach and recommended the adoption of eco-friendly technology. The principles previously discussed were evolved to meet this end.

354 World Commission on Environment and Development. (1987). *Our common future.* Oxford University Press.

As mentioned, some principles are 'preventive' while others are different. The preventive approach was needed to curtail pollution at the grassroots level because it is irretrievable and long-lasting if any harm is committed to the environment. On the contrary, having a pollution-free, clean society is impossible. So, the aim was to keep the pollution under control. The principle, like 'polluter pays,' served this purpose. This principle incorporated two aspects: (a) the offender should be held liable to make good the harm he committed and (b) to deter potential offenders. The deterrent form of punishment is predominant in the punishment of environmental offenses, but unfortunately, the quantification of punishment and imposition of criminal liability are also significant in this context. Scientific implementation of criminal responsibility and severe punishments are required for adequate deterrence. The incapacitation of the offender may also be strongly recommended. Incapacitation implies the closure of the polluting industry and, further, the winding up of the corporation which has failed to follow the legal provisions. Imposing proportionate liability based on the economic condition of the corporation (i.e., the larger the corporation, the larger the penalty that should be imposed) or the imposition of absolute liability upon the polluter industry will be the appropriate steps to fight the problem.

The European Court of Human Rights (ECtHR) interpreted the term 'right to life'[355] in a broader sense so that it includes the right not to suffer environmental damage, directly or indirectly, from polluters or state authorities due to their administrative and regulatory negligence.[356] The ECtHR held the Turkish government liable for the death of 39 individuals from an explosion that happened in a project near a slum, on the ground that the concerned government authorities failed to fulfill the obligation to find out the risk involved in the project to the neighbors, before permitting the development work.[357] The Court extended the liability to violating the 'right to life' enshrined in the Convention.[358] This decision sheds light on some important aspects. First, whether the government fulfilled its obligation or not is a question of fact that has to be determined by looking into the legal basis for the government's particular act, the extent of the inquiry procedure before the act, and the implications of the action in terms of the effect on the concerned stakeholder(s).[359] Second, when a project poses a threat of environmental damage, the government's responsibility will fluctuate according to the extent of the mitigation strategy.[360] Finally, there must be a checks-and-balances sys-

355 Protocol 1 to the European Convention on Human Rights (ECHR) 1950, art. 2.

356 Philippopoulos-Mihalopoulos, A. (2007). *Absent environments: Theorising environmental law and the city* (pp. 201–203). Routledge-Cavendish.

357 *Öneryıldız v Turkey* (2005) 41 EHRR 20.

358 Ibid.

359 Philippopoulos-Mihalopoulos, A. (2007). *Absent environments: Theorising environmental law and the city* (p. 201). Routledge-Cavendish.

360 Ibid., p. 203.

tem among the organs of the State, particularly, the legislatures and executive organs of governments, if negligent or outrageous, must be respectful to the judgments of courts and shall not dilute the functional independence of these organs.[361]

References

Adshead, J. (2013). Doing justice to the environment. *The Journal of Criminal Law, 77*(3), 215–230.

Alonso, A. I., & South, N. (2024). Incorporating a one health approach into the study of environmental crimes and harms: Towards a "one health green criminology". *The British Journal of Criminology, 10*, 1–16.

Ambec, S., & Ehlers, L. (2016). Regulation via the polluter-pays principle. *The Economic Journal, 126*(593), 884–906.

Arguedas, C. (2013). Pollution standards, technology investment and fines for non-compliance. *Journal of Regulatory Economics, 44*, 156–176.

Ashworth, A., & Kelly, R. (2021). *Sentencing and criminal justice.* Bloomsbury Publishing.

Atkinson, N. (2023). Profiting from pollution. *Yale Journal on Regulation Bulletin.* Retrieved from https://www.yalejreg.com/bulletin/profiting-from-pollution/

Bagaric, M. (1999). Sentencing: The road to nowhere. *Sydney Law Review, 21*(4), 597–626.

Bar-Ilan, A., & Sacerdote, B. (2004). The response of criminals and noncriminals to fines. *The Journal of Law and Economics, 47*(1), 1–17.

Barthakur, A. (2021). Polluter pays principle as the key element to environmental law. *International Journal of Scientific and Research Publications, 11*(3), 274–277.

Baumann, F., Bienenstock, S., Friehe, T., & Ropaul, M. (2023). Fines as enforcers' rewards or as a transfer to society at large? Evidence on deterrence and enforcement implications. *Public Choice, 196*(3), 229–255.

Becker, G. S. (1968). Crime and punishment: An economic approach. *Journal of Political Economy, 76*(2), 169–217.

Becker, G. S. (1976). *The economic approach to human behavior* (Vol. 803). University of Chicago Press.

Bedau, H. (2004). Bentham's theory of punishment: Origin and content. *Journal of Bentham Studies, 7*, 1–15.

Behn, R. D. (2003). Why measure performance? Different purposes require different measures. *Public Administration Review, 63*(5), 586–606.

Billiet, C. M., & Rousseau, S. (2014). How real is the threat of imprisonment for environmental crime? *European Journal of Law and Economics, 37*, 183–198.

Blondiau, T., Billiet, C. M., & Rousseau, S. (2015). Comparison of criminal and administrative penalties for environmental offenses. *European Journal of Law and Economics, 39*, 11–35.

Bottoms, A., Gelsthorpe, L., & Rex, S. (2013). *Community penalties.* Routledge.

Brisman, A. (2007). Crime-environment relationships and environmental justice. *Seattle Journal for Social Justice, 6*, 727.

Cameron, S. (1988). The economics of crime deterrence: A survey of theory and evidence. *Kyklos, 41*(2).

Campbell, T. (1984). Compensation as punishment. *UNSW Law Journal, 7*, 338.

361 Ibid.

Chui, W. H. (2013). Community sentences. In *Understanding criminal justice in Hong Kong* (pp. 212–234). Willan.

Cohen, M. A. (2016). *The "cost of crime" and benefit-cost analysis of criminal justice policy: Understanding and improving upon the state-of-the-art.* https://ssrn.com/abstract=2832944 or http://dx.doi.org/10.2139/ssrn.2832944

Cook-Cox, A., Loftin, C. M., & May, D. C. (2025). Item values and prior offenses: An examination of key elements in shoplifting charging decisions in a rural jurisdiction. *American Journal of Criminal Justice.* Advance online publication. https://doi.org/10.1007/s12103-025-09800-3[1]

Craig, P. (2012). Subsidiarity: A political and legal analysis. *JCMS: Journal of Common Market Studies, 50,* 72–87.

Dang, T. V., Wang, Y., & Wang, Z. (2022). The role of financial constraints in firm investment under pollution abatement regulation. *Journal of Corporate Finance, 76,* 102252.

David, P. A. (2001). *Tragedy of the public knowledge "commons"? Global science, intellectual property and the digital technology boomerang (Memorandum No. 2001–003).* MERIT-Infonomics Research Memorandum series. Maastricht Economic Research Institute on Innovation and Technology and International Institute of Infonomics.

Drago, F., Galbiati, R., & Vertova, P. (2009). The deterrent effects of prison: Evidence from a natural experiment. *Journal of Political Economy, 117*(2), 257–280.

Draper, A. (2009). Punishment, proportionality, and the economic analysis of crime. *Journal of Bentham Studies, 11,* 1–32.

Driesen, D. M. (2003). *The economic dynamics of environmental law.* MIT Press.

Duwe, G. (2017). *The use and impact of correctional programming for inmates on pre- and post-release outcomes* (Vol. 48). US Department of Justice.

Epstein, R. A. (1979). Nuisance law: Corrective justice and its utilitarian constraints. *The Journal of Legal Studies, 8*(1), 49–102.

Fitzmaurice, M. (2009). *Contemporary issues in international environmental law.* Edward Elgar Publishing.

Fletcher, G. P. (1980). Punishment and compensation. *Creighton Law Review, 14,* 691.

Frase, R. S. (1997). Sentencing principles in theory and practice. *Crime and Justice, 22,* 363–433.

Friehe, T., & Miceli, T. J. (2017). On punishment severity and crime rates. *American Law and Economics Review, 19*(2), 464–485.

Gillespie, A. (2007). *Protected areas and international environmental law.* Martinus Nijhoff Publishers Leiden.

Gilpin, A. (2000). *Dictionary of environmental law.* Edward Elgar Publishing.

Goldberg, S. (1974). On capital punishment. *Ethics, 85*(1), 67–74.

Grant, D., Jorgenson, A., & Longhofer, W. (2020). *Super Polluters: Tackling the world's largest sites of climate-disrupting emissions.* Columbia University Press.

Hanafy, H. (2021). Bentham: Punishment and the utilitarian use of persons as means. *Journal of Bentham Studies, 19*(1), 1–23.

Hanley, N. (2002). The economic value of environmental damage. In M. Bowman & A. Boyle (Eds.), *Environmental damage in international and comparative law: Problems of definition and valuation.* Oxford University Press.

Hart, H. L. A. (2008). *Punishment and responsibility: Essays in the philosophy of law.* Oxford University Press.

Hasnas, J. (2010). Where is Flex Cohen when we need him: Transcendental nonsense and the moral responsibility of corporations. *Journal of Law & Policy, 19,* 55.

Jack, B. (2016). *Agriculture and EU environmental law.* Routledge.

Kagan, R. A., Gunningham, N., & Thornton, D. (2003). Explaining corporate environmental performance: How does regulation matter? *Law & Society Review*, *37*(1), 51–90.
Karpoff, J. M., Lott, J., John, R., & Wehrly, E. W. (2005). The reputational penalties for environmental violations: Empirical evidence. *The Journal of Law and Economics*, *48*(2), 653–675.
Keith, N. A. *Creative environmental sentencing: Making the punishment fit the crime*. Retrieved November 28, 2024, from www.esemag.com/1196/sentence.html
Kelley, P. J. (1983). Critical analysis of Holmes's theory of torts. *Washington University Law Quarterly*, *61*(3), 681–744.
Kluin, M., Ansems, L., & Brands, J. (2025). On bad intentions and harmful consequences: Understanding public perceptions of environmental crime seriousness. *Crime, Law and Social Change*, *83*(1), 3.
Koh, T. Y. (2024). The judgement of pleasure in Bentham's political thought. *Revue d'études benthamiennes*, *25*.
Konisky, D. M., & Woods, N. D. (2012). Environmental free riding in state water pollution enforcement. *State Politics & Policy Quarterly*, *12*(3), 227–251.
Koul, D. (2014). Conservation through community: An attempt to untangle a tangled word. *JNRD-Journal of Natural Resources and Development*, *4*, 25–26.
Kristl, K. T. (2006). Making a good idea even better: Rethinking the limits on supplemental environmental projects. *Vermont Law Review*, *31*, 217.
Landau, N. (2005). Summary conviction and the development of the penal law. *Law and History Review*, *23*(1), 173–189.
Lazarus, R. J. (1993). Assimilating environmental protection into legal rules and the problem with environmental crime. *Loyola of Los Angeles Law Review*, *27*, 867.
Lenaerts, K. (2017). The principle of subsidiarity and the environment in the European Union: Keeping the balance of federalism. In *European environmental law* (pp. 129–178). Routledge.
Loughran, T. A., Paternoster, R., Chalfin, A., & Wilson, T. (2016). Can rational choice be considered a general theory of crime? Evidence from individual-level panel data. *Criminology*, *54*(1), 86–112.
Louka, E. (2006). *International environmental law: Fairness, effectiveness, and world order*. Cambridge University Press.
Lovegrove, A. (2012). *Judicial decision making, sentencing policy, and numerical guidance*. Springer Science & Business Media.
Luppi, B., Parisi, F., & Rajagopalan, S. (2009). *Environmental protection for developing countries: The polluter-does-not-pay principle* (Paper No. 09-08). Minnesota Legal Studies Research. Available at SSRN: https://ssrn.com/abstract=1339063
Marzilli, A. (2009). *Capital punishment*. Infobase Publishing.
Mazzotta, M. J., Opaluch, J. J., & Grigalunas, T. A. (1994). Natural resource damage assessment: The role of resource restoration. *Natural Resources Journal*, 153–178.
McCafferty, J. A. (2017). *Capital Punishment*. Routledge.
McHugh, J. T. (2008). Utilitarianism, punishment, and ideal proportionality in penal law: Punishment as an intrinsic evil. *Journal of Bentham Studies*, *10*, 1–16.
McMurry, R. I., & Ramsey, S. D. (1986). Environmental crime: The use of criminal sanctions in enforcing environmental laws. *Loyola of Los Angeles Law Review*, *19*, 1133.
Meixner Jr., J. B. (2021). Modern sentencing mitigation. *Northwestern University Law Review*, *116*, 1395.
Mishra, S. (2016). Theories of punishment; A philosophical aspect. *Imperial Journal of Interdisciplinary Research*, *2*(8), 74.
Narveson, J. (1992). Moving from punishment to compensation. *Canadian Journal of Law & Jurisprudence*, *5*(1), 57–68.

Nobles, M. R. (2019). Environmental crime and contemporary criminology: Making a difference. *American Journal of Criminal Justice, 44*, 656–669.
O'Hear, M. M. (2004). Sentencing the green-collar offender: Punishment, culpability, and environmental crime. *Journal of Criminal Law & Criminology, 95*, 133.
Ohlin, J. D. (2009). Towards a unique theory of international criminal sentencing. In G. Sluiter & S. Vasiliev (Eds.), *International criminal procedure: Towards a coherent body of law*. Cameron May.
Oleson, J. C. (2017). Sentencing theories, practices, and trends. In *The Palgrave handbook of Australian and New Zealand criminology, crime and justice* (pp. 363–377). Palgrave Macmillan.
Omrow, D. A. (2017). *Abyssal ideology and the Amerindians of Guyana: An eco-crimes analysis of power, discourse and cognitive injustice* [PhD dissertation, York University, Toronto, Ontario].
Papathanasiou, K. (2017). Environmental criminal law: A vital part of the regulatory framework. In *Environmental law and economics* (pp. 513–526). Springer.
Patton, D. E. (2010). Guns, crime control, and a systemic approach to federal sentencing. *Cardozo Law Review, 32*, 1427.
Petersen, T., Klauer, B., & Manstetten, R. (2009). The environment as a challenge for governmental responsibility – The case of the European Water Framework Directive. *Ecological Economics, 68*(7), 2058–2065.
Pfennigstorf, W. (1979). Environment, damages, and compensation. *American Bar Foundation Research Journal, 4*(2), 347–448.
Philippopoulos-Mihalopoulos, A. (2007). *Absent environments: Theorising environmental law and the city*. Routledge-Cavendish.
Pollak, P. (2011). *Fine chemicals: The industry and the business*. John Wiley & Sons.
Powell, L. F. (1989). Capital punishment. *Harvard Law Review, 102*(5), 1035–1046.
Preble, K. A., & Early, B. R. (2024). Enforcing economic sanctions by tarnishing corporate reputations. *Business and Politics, 26*(1), 102–123.
Roberts, J. V. (2011a). *Mitigation and aggravation at sentencing*. Cambridge University Press.
Roberts, J. V. (2011b). Punishing, more or less: Exploring aggravation and mitigation at sentencing. In J. V. Roberts (Ed.), *Mitigation and aggravation at sentencing* (pp. 1–14). Cambridge University Press.
Robinson, P. H. (1987). Sentencing system for the 21st century. *Texas Law Review, 66*, 1.
Robinson, P. H., & Darley, J. M. (2007). Intuitions of justice: Implications for criminal law and justice policy. *Southern California Law Review, 81*, 1.
Roman, J. (2013). Cost-benefit analysis of criminal justice reforms. *NIJ Journal, 272*, 31–38.
Roman, J., & Farrell, G. (2002). Cost-benefit analysis for crime prevention: Opportunity costs, routine savings and crime externalities. *Crime Prevention Studies, 14*, 53–92.
Roman-Alcalá, A. M. (2013). Reconsidering sustainable development: Urbanization, political-economy, and deliberative democracy. *Berkeley Undergraduate Journal, 26*(1).
Rudall, J. (2020). *Compensation for environmental damage under international law*. Routledge.
Salmond, J. W. (1893). *The first principles of jurisprudence*. Stevens & Haynes Law Publishers.
Schofield, P. (2018). Bentham, Jeremy (1748–1832). In *The New Palgrave dictionary of economics*. Palgrave Macmillan. https://doi.org/10.1057/978-1-349-95189-5_566
Schonsheck, J. (1994). *On criminalization: An essay in the philosophy of criminal law* (Vol. 19). Springer Science & Business Media.
Schwartz, P. (2010). The polluter-pays principle. In *Research handbook on international environmental law*. Edward Elgar Publishing.

Segerson, K., & Tietenberg, T. (2018). The structure of penalties in environmental enforcement: An economic analysis. In *Economics and liability for environmental problems* (pp. 333–354). Routledge.
Shane-DuBow, S. (1985). *Sentencing reform in the United States: History, content, and effect.* US Department of Justice, National Institute of Justice, Office of Justice Programs.
Siddique, A. (1993). *Criminology: Problems & perspectives.* Eastern Book Co.
Skinnider, E. (2011). *Victims of environmental crime: Mapping the issues: International centre for criminal law reform and criminal justice policy.* https://globalinitiative.net/wp-content/uploads/2017/12/ICCLR-Victims-of-Environmental-Crime.pdf
Slobogin, C. (2011). Prevention as the primary goal of sentencing: The modern case for indeterminate dispositions in criminal cases. *San Diego Law Review*, *48*, 1127.
Solomon, E., & Silvestri, A. (2008). *Community sentences digest.* Centre for Crime and Justice Studies.
Stoett, P. J., & Omrow, D. A. (2021). *Spheres of transnational ecoviolence.* Springer.
Stuart, D., & Woroosz, M. R. (2013). The myth of efficiency: Technology and ethics in industrial food production. *Journal of Agricultural and Environmental Ethics*, *26*, 231–256.
Sverdlik, S. (2019). Bentham on temptation and deterrence. *Utilitas*, *31*(3), 246–261.
Tasioulas, J. (2006). Punishment and repentance. *Philosophy*, *81*(2), 279–322.
Tekie, H., & Lindblad, M. (2013). Methodologies for monetary valuation of environmental impacts-State of the art. *CPM the Swedish Life Cycle Center, Gothenburg*, 22–25.
Tonry, M. (2006). Purposes and functions of sentencing. *Crime and Justice*, *34*(1), 1–53.
Ulmer, J. T., & Johnson, B. (2004). Sentencing in context: A multilevel analysis. *Criminology*, *42*(1), 137–178.
University of Minnesota Duluth (2025). www.d.umn.edu/cla/faculty/jhamlin/4111/2111-home/CD/TheoryClass/Bentham/Jeremy%20Bentham.htm
van Zeben, J., & Rowell, A. (2020). *A guide to EU environmental law.* University of California Press.
Varouxakis, G., & Philp, M. (2019). 7. "The first article to look to is power": Bentham, happiness and the capability approach. In *Happiness and utility: Essays presented to Frederick Rosen* (pp. 118–142). University College London.
Veenhoven, R. (2010). Greater happiness for a greater number: Is that possible and desirable? *Journal of Happiness Studies*, *11*, 605–629.
Walker, N. (1980). *Punishment, danger and stigma: The morality of criminal justice.* Rowman & Littlefield.
Walker, N. (1997). Harms, probabilities and precautions. *Oxford Journal of Legal Studies*, *17*(4), 611–620.
Walters, R. (2012). Environmental crime in Scotland. In *Criminal justice in Scotland* (pp. 164–184). Willan.
Westerhuis, D. S. (2013). A harm analysis of environmental crime. In *Emerging issues in green criminology: Exploring power, justice and harm* (pp. 197–217). Springer.
White, R. (2009). Researching transnational environmental harm: Toward an eco-global criminology. *International Journal of Comparative and Applied Criminal Justice*, *33*(2), 229–248.
White, R. (2017). Reparative justice, environmental crime, and penalties for the powerful. *Crime, Law and Social Change*, *67*, 117–132.
White, R., & Heckenberg, D. (2014). *Green criminology: An introduction to the study of environmental harm.* Routledge.

7 Concluding Remarks

> 'By destroying nature, environment, man is committing matricide, having in a way killed Mother Earth. Technological excellence, growth of industries, economical gains have led to depletion of natural resources irreversibly. Indifference to the grave consequences, lack of concern and foresight have contributed in large measures to the alarming position.'
>
> – Justice Arijit Pasayat[1]

Since the dawn of humanity, people have depended on the environment in order to survive and progress. Resources have always provided an environment that is warm and beneficial to support humans and physically, mentally, and spiritually nurture them. With the advance of civilization, there has been a clear change from protecting the environment to utilizing it for increasing materialistic wants and needs. This change brings severe consequences to the ecological state and life on Earth.

Environmental pollution and degradation mark a vicious challenge that the world provides attention to. Countries, IOs, businesses, and many social groups have come together to provide plans to tackle this disaster with the aim of protecting both life and future generations. They know that the issues stem from excessive chemical usage, nuclear testing, rapid urbanization, industrialization, unscientific use of natural resources, increased chemical use, and nuclear testing. These factors have led to the accumulation of GHGs and carbon dioxide in the atmosphere, depletion of the ozone layer, desertification, deforestation, rising sea levels, and changes in seasonal cycles. Industrial pollution, however, has never decreased; rather, it is rising at an alarming rate. In this circumstance, environmental jurisprudence has a crucial role in protecting natural resources; it offers regulatory options at international and national levels for facilitating business operations without exploiting natural resources.

1 See *K. M. Chinnappa and T. N. Godavarman Thirumalpad* v. *Union of India and Ors.* AIR 2003 SC 724.

DOI: 10.4324/9781003279006-7

Corporate criminal liability is a vital topic in environmental jurisprudence. Over the last couple of years, corporate criminal liability has attracted increased attention, primarily due to the catastrophic environmental disasters caused by reckless corporations and the broader public's growing awareness of the need to protect the environment. Undoubtedly, this has contributed to the creation of a sophisticated legal framework to hold corporations liable for their irresponsible business activities at the level of public law, which sanctions against the irresponsible behavior of business activities to their environment.

The concept of corporations committing crimes against the environment is based on the principle that a corporation, being a legal person, is capable of bearing the responsibility of the actions of its employees and agents that commit harm to the environment. This concept of corporate liability derives from the more developed notion of corporate personhood, which argues that corporations as entities are given certain rights and obligations like a human being. This is of great importance, especially when one considers the magnitude of the damage and pollution and environment-related activities by businesses and industries. By imposing criminal liability on corporations for their actions, this jurisprudence aims to deter corporations from engaging in environmentally harmful activities and foster a culture of corporate social responsibility.

The idea of viewing corporations as offenders for committing crimes against the environment has developed with the creation of laws or the enhancement of already existing ones. For example, the principle of strict liability has been incorporated in environmental crimes, which entail that a corporation could be prosecuted for causing environmental damage whether it was intentional or not. This shows that corporations are required to take all necessary steps to avert causing environmental damage and, at the same time, they must be held responsible for any damage that occurs, even if it was not intended.

The framework for corporate criminal liability exists, albeit imperfectly, in both national and international systems. At the domestic scope, different countries have adopted policies and laws that subject corporations to criminal liability for environmental crimes. Such laws often impose various forms of punishment such as fines, imprisonment, and remedial action. In addition to such domestic legislation, there are also international treaties and agreements dealing with corporate criminal liability for environmental offenses. Perhaps, the most important is the UNTOC which has appendices requiring member states to provide for the criminal liability of corporations for environmental offenses. Likewise, the Basel Convention on the Control of Transboundary Movements of Hazardous Wastes and Their Disposal imposes criminal responsibility on corporations for illegal waste trafficking. The basis for corporate criminal liability in environmental jurisprudence is also reinforced by judicial decisions and principles of law developed by courts in different jurisdictions. For instance, courts have used the doctrine of vicarious liability to impose responsibility on corporations for the acts of their employees or agents that result in environmental damage. Furthermore, there have been cases where the courts have acknowledged the notion of corporate due diligence, which posits that a corporation must take all reasonable measures to avoid committing environmental crimes.

A broad range of corporate criminal liability can arise from environmental crimes. These criminal liabilities are typically divided into three categories of crimes: pollution crimes, natural resource crimes, and wildlife crimes. Pollution crimes include putting harmful pollutants into the air, water, or land and can include illegal dumping, emission violations, and water pollution. Natural resource crimes include the illegal extraction or realization of natural resources such as logging, illegal mining, or illegal fishing. Wildlife crimes include the destruction or unlawful trade of protected species and the destruction of their natural habitats. All three categories of environmental crimes can result in considerable damage to the environment, hence why corporate liability is required so that corporations can be made answerable for their deeds. The punishments for such crimes are, in most cases, extremely harsh, resulting in hefty fines, imprisonment, or paying for corrective measures to be taken. That said, not all crimes will result in a corporate criminal charge. The majority of these crimes must fulfill certain prerequisites at various stages of the proceedings to finalize the charge, such as establishing a duty of care, breaching that duty, and causing environmental damage. Moreover, companies might be able to use the due diligence defense, which demonstrates that the corporation took all appropriate measures necessary to avert the environmental crime from happening.

Establishing corporate criminal liability for environmental crimes can be a complex task and, at times, quite challenging. One of the key issues complicating such efforts is demonstrating that the actions of corporations are causally linked to the resulting environmental damage. This is especially problematic in large-scale environmental destruction case scenarios, where pinpointing the harm-causing actions of the corporation is not straightforward. Also lacking in clarity is establishing the degree of negligence or the level of negligence ascribed to the corporation for its environmental crime, thereby creating another hurdle in claiming corporate criminal liability. Some laws specify that the corporation has some level of knowledge that some or all of their actions will result in environmental damage, which is also difficult to prove, especially for enormous corporations with expansive organizational frameworks and multi-tiered income decision systems. Another challenge adding to the already burdened issues surrounding corporate criminal liability for environmental offenses is the jurisdictional ambiguity. As most corporations operate globally, it becomes nearly impossible to single out which jurisdiction is able to put the corporation on trial for the alleged crimes. This could cause conflicts of double jeopardy, where a corporation is charged concurrently in more than one jurisdiction for the same crime, or to gaps where a corporation can evade responsibility simply by maintaining operations in areas with weak or no laws concerning the environment.

Government agencies play an important role in promoting and enforcing corporate social responsibility with respect to the environment and ensuring that corporations do not commit environmental crimes. Supervisory agencies have the authority to oversee the industry's observance of the environmental laws and regulations and enforce compliance action when it is required. A clear responsibility of supervisory bodies is to carry out inspection and investigative activities in regard to corporate compliance with environmental requirements. This can be through examining corporate documents, visiting the sites, and taking samples to examine if there is any damage to the environment. Where regulatory non-compliance is uncovered, the agency is empowered to impose sanctions, bring charges, and require corrective action. Apart from their enforcement powers, supervisory authorities also promote corporate environmental accountability by creating policies, strategies, and documents that outline the responsibilities of businesses in relation to the environment. By adequately engaging with other industry partners, supervisory authorities can play a crucial role in ensuring that corporations understand their environmental responsibility and the necessary steps to prevent environmental damage.

Many best practice measures can be implemented at the corporate level to reduce environmental deficiencies and minimize exposure to corporate criminal liability. One of the most important actions that a corporation can perform is to design an EMS and put it into practice. An EMS means an organization approaches the environmental management of its activities in a responsible manner. It ensures compliance with all legislation that is relevant to the organization's operations. Another key proactive step includes the creation of a corporate environmental policy. This policy should clearly express the corporation's attention to the environmental effects of its activities and be communicated to all personnel and relevant parties. Also, there should be a consistent policy supported by an appropriate structural hierarchy that has specific responsibilities assigned for environmental management and compliance. Apart from an EMS and environmental policy, corporations also need to promote and invest in awareness and training programs for their employees. This training should address the specific environmental risks associated with the corporation's operations. The outcome should ensure that every employee understands his or her responsibilities as well as the risks of failing to comply with the responsibility. Lastly, corporations must improve these practices by actively conducting reviews aimed at achieving better effectiveness in meeting environmental and management best practices and standards. This may include performing periodic audits and assessments as well as consulting with outside specialists for advice on new environmental issues and trends.

The future of corporate criminal liability in environmental jurisprudence will likely be determined by the ongoing progress of both national and international laws on the environment, the greater activity of regulatory bodies in supervising the fulfillment of corporate environmental responsibilities, and the sensitivity toward the value of the environment. It appears that the scope of criminalized environmental misconduct by corporations will expand, growing in monetary and social consequences as well. Additionally, there will probably be more focus on the so-called direct enforcement of corporate environmental responsibility so that regulatory bodies actively supervise and enforce compliance with the applicable environmental law. There appears to be a growing determinism that as the corporations become more concerned with environmental responsibilities, there will be more emphasis on the adoption of architectural safeguards standards intended to avert environmental infractions preemptively. These developments will aid in environmental preservation and, financially, help decrease the consequences of corporate environmental crime through the mitigation of reputation and cost.

In the context of environmental jurisprudence, corporate criminal liability is one of the mechanisms employed to ensure that a corporation is held accountable for environmental offenses. Through this jurisprudence, it attempts to develop the culture of corporate social responsibility and, at the same time, prevent corporations from performing actions that are detrimental to the environment by making them answerable to the consequences of their deeds. However, studying corporate criminal liability's intricacies in the context of environmental jurisprudence requires understanding the legal foundations within the framework of general law that govern this branch of law. In this book, we examined the theory of corporate criminality related to environmental degradation, the rationale of corporate criminal responsibility in environmental law, and the ecological crimes that may incur corporate criminal liability.

Corporate criminal liability regarding environmental law is an emerging area of law, and in that regard, it has a number of issues and difficulties in its actual enforcement. This book highlighted problems in defining corporate criminal liability for environmental crimes, including the enforcement by other arms of government in corporate social responsibility. Lastly, preventive measures, as well as policy and strategies to avert environmental crimes by corporations, were advanced alongside the evolution of corporate liability in environmental law jurisprudence.

Clearly, there are difficulties with assigning corporate criminal liability for environmental crimes; however, corporations need to understand their responsibility toward the environment and make efforts to comply with laws and guidelines. By adopting the recommended preventive approaches and policies, the corporations stand to reduce the risk of corporate liability and enhance environmental protection for coming generations.

> The environment is where we all meet; where we all have a mutual interest; it is the one thing all of us share.
>
> – Lady Bird Johnson

The Earth does not belong to us: we belong to the Earth.

– Marlee Matlin

The greatest threat to our planet is the belief that someone else will save it.

– Robert Swan

We do not inherit the Earth from our ancestors; we borrow it from our children.

– Native American Proverb

Index

Kolibri 360 GmbH
Ferdinand-Jühlke-Straße 7
99095 Erfurt, Deutschland
produktsicherheit@kolibri360.de